FIQH AL ZAKAH
(VOLUME II)

A COMPARATIVE STUDY OF *ZAKAH*, REGULATIONS AND PHILOSOPHY IN THE LIGHT OF QUR'AN AND *SUNNAH*

DR. YUSUF AL QARADAWI

Dar Ul Thaqafah

Dar Ul Thaqafah

2023 CE – 1444 H

Translation of the Qur'ān

It should be perfectly clear that the Qur'ān is only authentic in its original language, Arabic. Since perfect translation of the Qur'ān is impossible, we have used the translation of the meaning of the Qur'ān throughout the book, as the result is only a crude meaning of the Arabic text.

Qur'ānic verses appear in speech marks proceeded by a reference to the Surah and verse number. Sayings (*Hadith*) of Prophet Muhammad ﷺ appear in inverted commas along with reference to the Hadith Book and its Reporter.

ﷺ – صلى الله عليه وسلم (Peace be upon him)

ﷻ – سبحانه وتعالى (Glory to Him, the Exalted)

FIQH AL ZAKAH
(VOLUME II)

A COMPARATIVE STUDY OF *ZAKAH*, REGULATIONS AND PHILOSOPHY IN THE LIGHT OF QUR'AN AND *SUNNAH*

DR. YUSUF AL QARADAWI

TRANSLATED BY:

DR. MONZER KAHF

TABLE OF CONTENTS

Page

FIQH AL ZAKAH (VOLUME II)

PART FOUR : *ZAKAH* DISTRIBUTION

PROLOGUE 3

CHAPTER ONE :   THE POOR AND THE NEEDY 5

CHAPTER TWO: *ZAKAH* WORKERS 23

CHAPTER THREE: THOSE WHOSE HEARTS ARE BEING
                                    RECONCILED 33

CHAPTER FOUR: LIBERATING SLAVES 43

CHAPTER FIVE: PERSONS UNDER DEBT 49

CHAPTER SIX: FOR THE SAKE OF GOD 57

CHAPTER SEVEN: THE WAYFARER 75

CHAPTER EIGHT: ISSUES RELATED TO THE DESERVING
                                    CATEGORIES 83

CHAPTER NINE: CATEGORIES TO WHOM *ZAKAH* MUST
                                    NOT BE PAID 87

Page

PART FIVE :   METHODS OF *ZAKAH* FULFILLMENT

CHAPTER ONE: THE ROLE OF THE STATE 113

CHAPTER TWO: THE PLACE OF INTENTION IN *ZAKAH* 135

CHAPTER THREE: PAYMENT VALUE 139

CHAPTER FOUR: TRANSPORTING *ZAKAH* 145

CHAPTER FIVE: PRE-PAYMENT AND DELAYED PAYMENT
                                    OF *ZAKAH* 151

CHAPTER SIX: QUESTIONS ABOUT *ZAKAH* FULFILLMENT 159

**PART SIX :   OBJECTIVES OF *ZAKAH* AND ITS EFFECTS
                        ON THE INDIVIDUAL AND SOCIETY**

INTRODUCTION 167

CHAPTER ONE: OBJECTIVES OF *ZAKAH* AND ITS EFFECTS
                                    ON THE INDIVIDUAL LIFE 169

CHAPTER TWO: OBJECTIVES OF *ZAKAH* AND ITS
                                    EFFECTS ON SOCIETY 181

PART SEVEN: *ZAKAH* OF FAST-BREAKING [*ZAKAH* OF *AL FITR*]

CHAPTER ONE: MEANING, RULINGS, AND PHILOSOPHY
                                    OF FAST-BREAKING *ZAKAH* 197

CHAPTER TWO: ON WHOM IS IT OBLIGATED? 201

CHAPTER THREE: AMOUNT AND KIND OF *ZAKAH* OF *AL FITR* 207

CHAPTER FOUR: TIME OF PAYMENT 215

CHAPTER FIVE: RECIPIENTS OF *ZAKAH* OF *AL FITR* 219

Page

PART EIGHT :   DUES AND TAXES OTHER THAN *ZAKAH*

CHAPTER ONE: THE OPINION THAT THERE ARE NO OTHER
                      FINANCIAL DUES BESIDE *ZAKAH* 225

CHAPTER TWO: THE VIEW THAT OTHER DUES BESIDES
                      ZAKAH MAY BE IMPOSED 229

CHAPTER THREE: DISCUSSION AND ANALYSIS 241

PART NINE :   *ZAKAH* AND TAXES

PROLOGUE 249

CHAPTER ONE: THE ESSENCE OF EACH *ZAKAH* AND TAXES 251

CHAPTER TWO: THEORETICAL FOUNDATION FOR LEVYING
                      TAXES AND *ZAKAH* 257

CHAPTER THREE: ASSETS SUBJECT TO *ZAKAH* AND TO TAXES 265

CHAPTER FOUR: PRINCIPLES OF LEVYING TAXES AND *ZAKAH* .. 273

CHAPTER FIVE: PROPORTIONALITY AND PROGRESSIVENESS
                      OF TAXES AND *ZAKAH* 283

CHAPTER SIX: ENFORCEMENT OF TAXES AND *ZAKAH* 287

CHAPTER SEVEN: IS IT PERMISSIBLE TO LEVY TAXES BESIDE
                      ZAKAH? 297

CHAPTER EIGHT: CAN TAXES SUBSTITUTE FOR *ZAKAH*? 315

EPILOGUE 321

INDEX 327

INDEX OF NAME 331

REFERENCES 351

FIQH AL ZAKAH

PART FOUR

ZAKAH DISTRIBUTION

1. Poor and needy

2. Workers in zakah administration

3. Those whose hearts are being reconciled

4. Freeing slaves

5. Those under labilities

6. In the way of God

7. Wayfarers

8. Issues about deserving categories

9. Categories to whom *zakah* cannot be Given

PROLOGUE

Like prayer, *zakah* in the Qur'an is an aggregate principle without much detail. Qur'an does not give rates, *nisab*, kinds of wealth that are *zakatable*, or the conditions for *zakatability*. Sunnah, verbal and practical, provides the details of *zakah*. the second source of *Shari'ah* after the Qur'an, Sunnah is essential for any explanation of *zakah*. God says, "And We have sent down unto thee the message that thou mayeth explain clearly to people what is sent for them, and that they may give thought."[1] Abu Daud reports that a man told the Companion 'Imran bin Husain, "O Aba Nujaid, you tell us sayings that we do not find in the Qur'an" 'Imran was upset and told the man, "Dido you find 'On each forty *dirhams*, one *dirham* is obligated', 'on each so and so Goat, one Goat is obligated,"and 'on each so and so camels so much is obligated? Did you find all that in the Qur'an?" The man answered, "No." Then 'Imran asked, "Where do you get these from? You took them from us and we got them from the Prophet (p)," and he mentioned other similar matters.[2]

Qur'an defines *zakah* distribution

Although *zakah* is discussed in the Qur'an as an inclusive concept, the areas where it can be spent are specifically mentioned in the Qur'an; they are not left to rulers or opinionators to decide according to their whims. At the time of the Messenger (p), some greedy individuals attempted to take some proceeds of *zakah*, but when the Prophet did not give them attention, they criticized and censured the Prophet so much that God sent verses deploring their greed and uncovering their hypocrisy. Those same verses go on to name the categories that deserve *zakah*: "And among them are men who slander thee in the matter of the distribution of *sadaqat*. If they are given part thereof, they are pleased, but if not, behold, they are indignant. If only they had been content with what God and His Apostle gave them, and had said, 'sufficient unto us is God, God and His Apostle will soon give us of His bounty, to God do we turn our hopes.' That would have been the wise course. The *sadaqat* are for the poor and the needy, and those employed to administer the funds, for those whose hearts have been recently reconciled to Truth, for those in bondage and in debt,. in the cause of God, and for the wayfarer. Thus is it ordained by God, and God is full of knowledge and wisdom."[3]

Abu Daud reports from Ziad bin al Harith al Sada'i, "I came to the Messenger of God (p) and gave him my pledge." The narrator recounts a long story and then continues, "A man came to the Prophet and said, 'Give me some of the proceeds of the *sadaqah*.' The Messenger of God (p) said, 'God does not leave the distribution of the *sadaqah* to a Prophet or anyone else. He Himself ordains the distribution to eight categories. If you are in any of these categories, I will give you what you deserve.'"[4]

The significance of distribution details in the Qur'an

Economists and socioldgists note that in taxation systems, the determination of the usage of proceeds is more important than the collection of funds, because governments usually have sufficient means to collect taxes efficiently and justly. It is in the usage of these funds that misconduct appears more often. It is essential that the proceeds of *zakah* be distributed and not kept in the treasury of the state, as was done before Islam by emperors and kings with the levies they imposed on their subjects. History tells that in most cases, taxes were imposed on the weak and poor to be spent luxuriously by kings and lords.

With the emergence of Islam, *zakah* was imposed as a relief to the poor and weak classes, but it was necessary to specify the deserving categories with words of God Himself.

Footnotes to Prologue

1. *Sura al Nahl*, 16:44.

2. Al Mundhiri, *Mukhtasar Sunan Abu Daud*, Vol. 2, p. 174.

3. *Sura al Tawbah*, 9:58-60.

4. In the chain of this saying is 'Abd al Rahman bin Ziad bin An'am al Ifriqi. More than one scholar criticizes him. See al Mundhiri, *op cit.*, Vol. 2, p. 230.

CHAPTER ONE

THE POOR AND THE NEEDY

The poor and the needy are the first two categories of *zakah* deservants mentioned in *sura al Tawbah*, which illustrates that the first target of *zakah* is to eliminate poverty and destitution from society. This purpose of *zakah*, being the most important, is mentioned alone in some sayings, such as the saying narrated by Mu'adh, when the Prophet sent him to Yemen: "Inform them that God has prescribed on them a *sadaqah*, taken from the rich among them and rendered to the poor among them."

Definitions of the poor and needy

Abu Yusuf, the disciple of Abu Hanifah, and Ibn al Qasim, the disciple of Malik, believe the poor and the needy are one category.[1] The majority of scholars disagree. In fact, the poor and the needy are two subsets of one category. Jurists and commentators on the Qur'an differ as to the specific meaning of "the poor" and "the needy", especially when the two words are mentioned together. Many scholars argue that these two words are inter-related, so that if one of them is mentioned, it includes both, but when they are mentioned together in one statement, they carry slightly different meanings. In the verse "The *sadaqat* are only for . . . ." the two words appear together.

Al Tabari selects the view that the word "poor" means the person who is in need, but is also modest enough not to beg,[2] while the needy is the person who is in need but humbles himself in begging. He argues that the word "need" has this connotation, as in the verse, "They were in humiliation and misery [need]."[3] The correct saying, "A needy person is not one who is satisfied with one or two dates but . . . the person who is modest," is not a linguistic explanation of the word "needy" but rather an assertion by the Prophet of the value of modesty. This is like his style in the saying, "The strong is not one who conquers others in wrestling, but one who controls himself when he is angered."[4] Commenting on the saying about the needy, al Khattabi rightly argues that "the needy is a person who goes around begging, since the Prophet brought the attention of his audience to the fact that beggars' needs may be satisfied by what he or she receives, while a person who is in need but does not beg may be forgotten, so his or her need passes unsatisfied."[5]

Jurists also do not agree as to whose state is worse, the poor or the needy. Shafi'ites and Hanbalities believe the status of the poor is worse, while Malikites and Hanafites believe the needy is in more dire circumstances. Both provide semantic arguments in support of their views. All of them, however, determine that differences in the meaning of "poor" and "needy" are not solvable and irrelevant to the analysis of *zakah*.

Hanafites define the poor as a person who has properties and/or income not sufficient to satisfy his or her essential needs. His or her property is either below *nisab* or used up for basic needs like shelter and clothing. The needy is a person who owns nothing. Accordingly, a deservant of *zakah* in this category, whether poor or needy, may be:

1. A deprived individual who owns nothing.
2. A person who owns shelter, furniture, clothing, but not in sufficient quantity to satisfy basic needs.
3. A persons who owns less than *nisab* of money.
4. A person who owns less than *nisab* of other than money, such as camels, provided the value of his or her property is less than two hundred *dirhams*.[7]

According to the other three major schools of jurisprudence, the poor and the needy are not defined with regard to *nisab*, but to satisfaction of essential needs. A poor person is one whose wealth and income are far from satisfying his or her essential needs, while a needy person is one whose wealth and income fall not much short of the satisfaction of essential needs. According to this criteria, a person who deserves *zakah* as a poor or needy may be:
1. A person who has no property or income at all.
2. A person whose wealth and income satisfy a little bit of his/her essential needs.
3. A person whose wealth and income satisfy more than half of essential needs but still fall short of fulfillment of those needs.

As for satisfaction of needs, Malikites and Hanbalites consider a one year period for such satisfaction, while Shafi'ites look to the expected life of the person. Shams al Din al Ramli argues that by taking the rest of the expected life of the poor or needy person, one may not expand the category of *zakah* deservants to include the rich, because a person who owns some property that yields a return sufficient to satisfy essential needs cannot be categorized as poor or needy.[8] A poor or needy person may own an adequate residence in which he or she lives,[9] yet his or her income may not be sufficient for the satisfaction of essential needs; the same may be said of adequate clothing, women's jewelry, books, and tools for craftsmen. Moreover, property not under the control of the owner which the owner cannot use to reduce the level of poverty is not counted, such as property in another country, or under legal obstacles that prevent the owner from using the property.[10]

Contrasting the poor and needy with the rich

It may be necessary to look at the definition of richness as given by jurists, since by such contrast one may determine exactly the boundary of the poor and needy category. *Zakah* must not be given to the rich. The Prophet said ". . . to be taken from the rich and rendered to the poor," and "The *sadaqah* is not lawful to the rich."[11] Giving the rich *zakah* means some poor person is not being given *zakah*, and this violates the objective of *zakah*, as stated by Ibn Qudamah.[12] By knowing who the rich are, we can as define by way of elimination the poor and needy.

Here again jurists do not have one unanimous decision. According to Suffian Al Thory and Ibn al Mubarak, and Ishaq Ibn Rahawah,[13] richness that excludes a person from a *zakah* recipient[14] is fifty *dirhams*, one-fourth the *nisab* of money. Ibn Mas'ud narrates, "The Messenger of God (p) said 'A person who asks while he has what makes him rich, whatever he gets appears on the Day of Judgement as cuts on his face.' The Prophet was asked, 'What is richness?' He answered, 'Fifty *dirhams* or its equivalent in gold.'" Ahmad is reported to share this definition only if the property is in money terms, but critics of *hadith* grade this saying from Ibn Mas'ud weak.[15]

Even if it were correct, the saying does not determine the eligibility for receiving *zakah*; all it indicates is the prohibition of begging or asking for charity, if a person owns fifty *dirhams*. Some scholars argue that fifty *dirhams* were substantial enough for the satisfaction of essential needs at the time of the Prophet and others interpret the sayings as addressed to specific individuals for whom fifty *dirhams* were sufficient. Supporting the first interpretation, al Khattabi says "There is nothing in the saying to indicate that a person who owns fifty *dirhams* is not eligible for *zakah*. The saying showed it is hateful to beg for alms, since begging may only be allowed at times of urgency and this does not apply to one who has fifty *dirhams*."[17]

Hanafites describe the rich person as one who owns *nisab* of any *zakatable* item, be it camels, money, or any other commodity, or one who owns non-*zakatable* items in excess of essential needs by the amount of two hundred *dirhams*. Their argument is based on a point that a person who owns *nisab* is *zakatable*, and a *zakatable* person is considered rich because *zakah* is taken from the rich. Anyone who owns *nisab* cannot be described as poor. They also present a saying, "He who begs while having what makes him rich is asking people in excess." The Prophet was asked, "What makes him rich?" and replied, "Two hundred *dirhams*." This saying, however, is weak. Additionally, it does not concern eligibility for *zakah*, but the prevention of begging.[18]

Hanafites add that a person who owns non-*zakatable* items in excess of a person's needs must be described as rich, if the value of the surplus is two hundred *dirhams* or more, on the grounds that non-*zakatable* items that are used for the satisfaction of essential needs like food, shelter, and clothing are not considered in defining richness, even if their total value is high. Al Hasan al Basri is reported to have said, "They [the Companions] used to give *zakah* to the person who owns ten thousand *dirhams* worth of mares, personal arms, slaves for service, and residence." Items like these satisfy essential needs.[19] In *al Fatawa*, a person who owns houses and stores whose rent is not sufficient for his or her needs, is given *zakah*. According to Muhammad, this person is poor and eligible to receive *zakah*, while Abu Yusuf disagrees. As for a person who has two hundred *dirhams* worth of food, it is argued that if this quantity is sufficient for only a month, the person is eligible for *zakah*, while if it is barely sufficient for a year, some say the person is not eligible and others argue he or she is eligible, on the basis that the Prophet (p) used to save for his wives food sufficient for a year. Winter garments, not needed in the summer, are not counted in defining richness. According to *al Tatar Khaniyah*, from *al Sughra*, a person who owns a residence larger than his needs, so that he only uses part of it, is also eligible for *zakah*. According to Muhammad, a person who owns land and buildings, whose total return is less than the person's needs, is eligible for *zakah*, while such an individual is not eligible according to Abu Hanifah and Abu Yusuf. Ibn 'Abidin gives the example of the woman who owns jewelry that she uses, in an amount which is more than *nisab*, and argues that she must not be *zakatable*, if jewelry is included as essential needs. He quotes from *al Tatar Khaniyah* that such a woman is *zakatable* according to al Hasan bin 'Ali, and comments that the answer depends on whether jewelry is counted among essential needs or not.[20]

Lastly, Malik, Ahmad, and al Shafi'i define richness as satisfaction of essential needs, regardless of property and income. A person whose essential needs are satisfied is rich and is eligible for *zakah*. A person whose essential needs are not fully satisfied, whether he/she owns *nisab* or more of money or other items, is eligible. Al Khattabi quotes Malik and al Shafi'i that "there is no specific, objective definition of richness. It depends on circumstances, needs, and available means of satisfying them. Al Shafi'i says 'Judging by money alone is not fair, because a person may be considered rich, yet his or her wealth and earnings are below what is needed for his personal and family expenses."[21]

This last definition of richness seems to be supported by the texts and spirit of *Shari'ah* as well as the linguistic use of the word "rich":

A. The Prophet is reported to have told Qubaysah bin al Mukhariq, who asked for help in a financial responsibility that he took upon himself for the reconciliation of two parties, "Asking [for financial help] is not permissible, except for one of three people: a person who is impoverished is allowed to ask until he or she obtains sufficient sustenance . . . . "[22] thus determining the criteria as sufficient sustenance.

B.   Being in need is being poor; being rich is the opposite. Thus anyone who is in need is poor and anyone who can sustain himself or herself is not poor. God says, "O ye people, it is ye who are poor [have need] of God." An ancient poet exclaims, "and I am poor of her good doing" meaning in need of it.

Two points arise from this approach. Firstly, he who has means that satisfy his needs, whether *zakatable* or non-*zakatable* assets, or income and earnings, is not eligible to receive *zakah*. Family needs are included. Consequently, waged or salaried individuals are not eligible as long as their periodical earnings are sufficient to satisfy their essential needs, even though they may not own any *nisab* as a stock of wealth. Secondly, that person who owns *nisab* of one or more *zakatable* items may be considered poor and eligible for *zakah* if the property he or she owns is not sufficient to fulfill his/her needs. Accordingly, a person who owns trade inventory that is worth one thousand *dinars* or more, but whose income is below the amount needed to satisfy his/her needs--because of a slack in the market, or a big family--is eligible to receive *zakah*. The same applies to other *zakatable* items. Thus, being a recipient of *zakah* does not prevent a person from being subject to *zakah* at the same time, since the level of richness that makes *zakah* obligatory is defined by owning *nisab*, along with other known conditions, while richness that prevents receiving *zakah* is defined by the satisfaction of essential needs.[23] Ahmad says a person who owns real estate or a farm, whose income is ten thousand or more, is eligible for *zakah* if that income does not satisfy his or her essential needs.[24]

The poor who are capable of earning

A person who chooses to be idle and to live at the expense of society through charity and financial help despite being strong enough and capable of working and earning, is not eligible for *zakah* according to Shafi'ite and Hanbalite scholars, who say *zakah* must not be expended under the title of poor and needy to a rich person or a person capable of working at a job whose income is adequate to for personal and family need.[25] In my opinion, this view is supported by the texts and principles of *Shari'ah*, to the extent that some Hanafites, who permit giving *zakah* to the poor person capable to earning, say it is not good for such a person to take *zakah*; i.e. if paying him is permissible, it is not lawful on his part to receive *zakah*. The majority of Hanafites maintain that receiving *zakah* is not prohibited here, but undesirable.[26] Some Malikites support the Shafi'ites and Hanbalites in their view.[27]

In principle, Islam obligates working on each capable man. The state is supposed to provide jobs and economic opportunities for people to work and earn their sufficiency. The Prophet says, "No person could eat food better than that earned by his own hands work"[28]. It is not permitted for a person who finds a job within his ability that would give him sufficient income to refuse it and live on charity or begging. In one of his sayings, the Messenger of Islam (p) frankly states, "The *sadaqah* is not lawful to a rich person or a capable and not handicapped person."[29] Al Tabari reports from Zuhayr al 'Amiri that he met 'Abd Allah bin 'Amr bin al 'As and asked him to whom *zakah* belongs. 'Abd Allah replied, "It is for the lame, blind, and every handicapped or disabled person." Zuhayr asked, "Is there not a right to administrators of *zakah* and fighters for the sake of God?" 'Abd Allah said, "Fighters and administrators are permitted by God in as much as their work deserves," and continued, "The *sadaqah* is not lawful to the rich or the strong person who is not handicapped."[30] This last sentence of 'Abd Allah is reported as attributed to the Prophet by 'Abd Allah himself and several other Companions.[31]

Physical power and ability alone is not sufficient, because what matters is earning sufficient income. Al Nawawi says, "If a capable person cannot find employment, *zakah* is lawful for him, because he is unable to earn."[32] In another saying the Prophet adds this explanation. 'Ubaid Allah bin 'Adi bin al Khiyar narrates that two men told him they went to the Prophet and asked for some *zakah*. The Prophet looked at them thoroughly and found them strong and said, "If you wish, I will give you, but the rich and the strong who earn have no share in it [*zakah*]."[33] The Prophet gave them the choice because he did not know the truth of their circumstances. They appeared to be strong and capable, but they may have not been able to find jobs that would give them income for at least sufficient subsistence. This saying is used by scholars to derive that officers of *zakah* are required to advise the potential *zakah* recipient whose real circumstances are not evident, that *zakah* is not lawful for the rich or the strong who can earn sufficient income.[34]

It is noted that sufficiency of earning is what matters and not only having an income, since absolute inability is not a condition for receiving *zakah*.[35] According to al Nawawi, what matters is an occupation that suits the person physically and socially and that provides sufficient income. On the other hand, the prohibition of *zakah* remains applicable to a person who is able but insists on remaining idle, in spite of the availability of suitable jobs.

In summary, a capable person must satisfy the following conditions in order to be prevented from receiving *zakah*:
1. He finds a job.
2. The job is lawful in *Shari'ah*.
3. The requirements of the job are within the person's ability.
4. The job is suitable for the person, his social status, and physical and spiritual ability.
5. The job earns him income sufficient for personal and family needs.

This implies that every capable person is required to find employment that gives him an income sufficient to satisfy his needs. Society at large and the state specifically are required to help such a person find a job. The person who is incapable of earning-- because of a disability such as age, sickness, or handicap--or because of lack of job opportunities-- and all whose incomes are not sufficient to satisfy their needs are eligible to receive *zakah*. This is the justice and mercy of Islam. One must compare it with injust and unmerciful principles of materialist thinkers who say "No food for the person who does not earn."

Individuals totally devoted to worship are not eligible

One of the admirable rulings recorded by Muslim jurists is that persons who are able to earn but spend all their time worshiping, praying, fasting, etc., without having an income or resources of their own, are not eligible to receive *zakah*, because the reward of worship is confined to the worshiper,[36] and because he or she is ordained in the Qur'an to work and walk through the tracts of the earth in search of sustenance. Islam does not recognize asceticism or monasticism. Working to earn sufficiency in sustenance is a high-ranking form of worship, provided it is performed with a good intention and commitment to the boundaries of God.

Full-time students are eligible

Devoting one's time fully to acquiring a useful branch of knowledge does not remove a person from eligibility for *zakah*. Such a person may be given *zakah* in order to help him or her achieve that purpose, including the cost of necessary books, regardless of whether the branch of knowledge sought is earthly or religious. Seeking knowledge is a social obligation that some-members of the society must undertake. The benefit of this knowledge extends to the whole society, and *zakah* is due to two kinds of persons--those in need of relief and those needed by the Muslim society.

Some jurists add the condition that a student, if able to earn, must be outstanding in order to be eligible for *zakah*.[37] They have a point. This is usually practiced by governments today when they offer scholarships.

The modest poor who can hardly be recognized have preference

It must be underlined that the people who deserve *zakah* most are not beggars, especially since many of them take begging as a profession, but rather those whose modesty prevents them from asking for help. The Prophet (p) emphasizes that "A needy person is one who is modest.. Read if you like they beg not importunately from all and sundry.[38] The verse describes the poor migrants in Madinah who were serving the faith and did not have sufficient resources to satisfy their essential needs, but did not ask people or beg for help, out of modesty.[39] Such people deserve the help of *zakah* more, as the Messenger of God guides us. In another version of the same saying, the Prophet says "The needy person is not one who goes around begging people, who can be satisfied by a bite or two or a date or two. The [true] needy person is one who finds not sufficiency but is not remembered by others, so that they give him, nor does he stand begging people."[40] This brings our attention to many individuals and families who have financial difficulties but rarely let them be known by others. Al Hasan al Basri was asked whether a person who owns a house and servant can take *zakah*. His answer was a affirmative, if the person is in need.[41] Muhammad bin al Hasan gives a similar answer when asked about a person who owns land and buildings whose income does not fulfill all his needs, as reported by Ibn Abidin.[42]

Moreover, the opinion of Ahmad about similar cases was mentioned earlier.[43] Similar things are reported from Shafi'ites and Malikites.[45] *Zakah* does not aim only to improve the state of the totally deprived and financially broken, but also of those who do not find full satisfaction of their essential needs.

How much are the poor and needy given?

The different views of jurists on this issue can be grouped into two major trends. The first is to give as much as is sufficient to satisfy the essential needs commonly known in society, without determining any specific amount, and the second is to give a specific amount in whose determination jurists differ.

The first trend seems to be more consistent with the texts and objectives of *zakah*. Two major opinions can be pointed out in this trend, namely, to give what satisfies essential needs for the lifetime, or only for one year.

The first opinion: satisfying lifetime needs

This opinion aims at giving the poor what is sufficient to remove them from the poverty level forever, in such a way that they would not need *zakah* in the future. In *al Majmu'*, al Nawawi says:

Our Iraqi colleagues, along with many from Khurasan [northeast of what is today Iran] believe that the poor and the needy must be given in such a way that they are permanently removed from poverty into sufficiency. This is the very opinion of al Shafi'i. They provide as supportive evidence the saying from Qubaysah bin al Mukhariq al Hilali that the Messenger of God said "Begging [or asking] is not permissible, except for one of three cases, It is lawful for a person who carries a financial charge [in reconciliation of] disputing people, to ask until he obtains sufficiency of sustenance; a person who is struck by a disaster that wipes his health out is permitted to ask until he reaches sufficiency of sustenance, and a person struck by poverty to the extent that three wise clansmen confirm that he is really hit by poverty is permitted to ask until he obtains sufficiency of sustenance. O Qubaysah, any asking beyond these three cases is evil on the part of the person who asks." Reported by Muslim in his correct collection.

Our colleagues argue that asking is permitted by the Messenger of God until sufficiency is reached. This means the purpose of the distribution of *zakah* is to make the poor and needy reach their sufficiency as stated above. A craftsman would be given an amount sufficient to buy tools and equipment that allow him to work and gain his sustenance. This certainly differs according to time, country, and ability of individuals. Some of our colleagues give examples that a person who sells vegetables may be given five or ten *dirhams*, while a person whose profession is selling jewels would be granted ten thousand *dirhams*, if he cannot reach sufficiency with less than that amount. People of other professions would be given according to the requirement of their profession. Farmers would be given farming land or portions thereof that would be sufficient to gain them sufficiency of sustenance. As for those who have no craft or ability, they must be given sustenance sufficient for the rest of their lives, regardless of one year limitations.[46]

Shams al Din al Ramli, the commentator on *al Minhaj* of al Nawawi, says about this saying, "The poor and needy who are not earners should be given what suffices then for the average life expectancy in their area, because the aim of *zakah* is to insure that the poor is under no more pressure of need. If he/she lives longer, *zakah* should continue on a yearly basis. It is not necessary to give the poor and needy money to suffice for the rest of their lives; they may be given capital investment whose returns would be sufficient for their maintenance, provided that ownership of the property transfers to the poor and can be bequeathed to their heirs." Al Ramli continues,

The officer of *zakah*, but not the payer when he distributes *zakah* directly, has the right to force the recipient to buy, for example, real estate, and to prevent him or her from disposing of it. If the return of such capital investment becomes less than sufficient, additional distribution must be made to the same recipient. Al Mawardi says "a person who has, for example, ninety but needs a hundred to be able to earn sufficient return, should be given the difference, even though the ninety, if spent on living expenses, may be sufficient for many years."This applies only to individuals who cannot earn by work or profession. As for professionals and workers, they should be given the capital necessary for their productive work, that would provide them with sufficient income. If a person knows more than one profession, the least amount of capital needed would be given, and if that profession does not produce sufficient income, an added capital investment such as real estate should be granted."[47]

This is what al Shafi'i mentions in *al Umm*, and later became the view of the bulk of his disciples. Ahmad is reported to have expressed a similar view, and is followed by some Hanbalites.[48] Al Khattabi comments on the saying from Qubaisah, "The upper limit of giving in *zakah* is the provision of sufficiency of sustenance. This differs from one person to another, and there is no definite amount that applies to all people in all their different circumstances."[49]

This view is also consistent with what is reported from 'Umar. 'Umar declares, "When you give, make [the recipient] rich."[50] In his actual practice, he gave such amounts that made the poor rich. A person came to him complaining of poverty. 'Umar gave that person three camels just to help him out of need, camels being the most valuable assets for Arabs then, and went on to advise his *zakah* officers to "repeat the distribution of the *sadaqah* on people, even if you give them a hundred camels." In another incident, he declared his policy to be "Indeed, I shall repeat the distribution of *sadaqah* to the poor, even if one of them has one hundred camels."[51] 'Ata' says, "I would have loved to see a *zakah* payer give what is due on him to one Muslim family in such a way that makes them really relieved."[52]

It is obvious that, according to this opinion, the Muslim state can establish factories and businesses, making them all owned by the poor and needy, whose returns and income would be sufficient to maintain the recipients, and prevent them from disposing of these properties.

The second opinion: giving one year's sustenance

This is the view of the Malikites, most of the Hanbalites, and most other jurists. They argue that the poor and needy must be given their sufficiency for one full year, no more and no less, on the grounds that the Prophet used to keep for his family food needed for one year,[53] and that *zakah* is collected on a yearly basis, so its distribution must be on a yearly basis too.[54]

Sufficiency for one year cannot be determined by any given amount, since it depends on circumstances, needs, and size of family.[55]

Enrichment of the concept of sufficiency

In order to fully understand the concept of sufficiency or satisfaction of essential needs as used in Islamic jurisprudence, we must mention several points. First, essential needs include, in addition to food, clothes, and shelter, the fulfillment of other essential human drives, especially the sexual drive. Islam, on one hand, does not allow celibacy, and on the other hand forbids wanton sexual practices. Islam ordains marriage for everyone who can afford it, as the Prophet says "He who has the means and ability must get married, because this helps one lower one's gaze and guard one's modesty."[56] Consequently, *Shari'ah* is expected to help those who want to be married but do not have the necessary financial means. Scholars argue that marriage expenses are included in the level of sufficiency for those who have no spouses and need to get married.[57] Some scholars go as far as assuming that, for a man who is not satisfied with one wife, the cost of marrying a second wife is also part of his level of sufficiency.[58]

'Umar bin 'Abd al 'Aziz, who is usually called the fifth of the Wise Successors, ordered people to search for the needy, those who are under burden of debt, and those who are seeking marriage, in order to help them from the treasury of the Muslim state.[59] This view is originally based on the saying from Abu Hurairah that a man came to the Prophet (p) and said, "I have married a woman from the *Ansar*." The Prophet said, "How much mahr did you give her?" The man answered, "Four *uqiyyah* [160 *dirhams*]." The Prophet exclaimed, "Four *uqiyyah*?" As if you are cutting silver from the side of this mountain! We do not have what we can give you [to help] but we may send you on a mission where you may gain something."[60] This saying indicates that the Prophet was wont to give funds from the treasury for such a purpose, but did not have enough at the moment, so he tried other means for help.

By the same token, seeking knowledge is a basic value in Islam. Knowledge is the door that opens to faith and the guide for practicing righteousness. Faith by imitation is not accepted, nor is worship with ignorance. God says clearly "Are they equal, those who know and those who do not know?"[61] and "The blind and the seeing are not alike, nor are the depths of darkness and the light."[62] And the Messenger (p) says, "Seeking knowledge is an obligation on each Muslim."[63] Knowledge which is urged to be taught is not confined to knowledge of religion: it includes every branch of knowledge that is useful to Muslims in their earthly life, such as knowledge of the human body, the economy, construction, technology, and military science. All these are societal requirements that must be undertaken by some individuals according to confirmed opinions of great scholars.

It is no surprise that jurists of Islam declare that knowledge seekers who devote all their time to study and research are deservants of *zakah*, while those who devote all their time to worshiping God are not included, because worshiping according to Islamic standards, does not require devoting all one's time, while seeking excellence in a branch of knowledge requires all one's time. A worshiper benefits him-or herself only, while a learned person benefits other people too.[64] Jurists go even further to decide that a poor person who seeks knowledge may take *zakah* to pay for books necessary for his or her study.[65] Furthermore, some Hanafites permit transporting the proceeds of *zakah* from one country to another for poor individuals who seek knowledge, while transporting *zakah* is generally not allowed.[66]

Discussion and analysis

In comparing these two views, one must note that they are not exclusive. Each of them may be the best when applied in the proper arena.

The poor and the needy may be classified into two subcategories. First are the poor and needy who can work and earn sustenance, such as craftsman and those who know any kind of business that needs capital or equipment for its practice. It is obligated to give them what they need in order to enable them to earn their sustenance for the rest of their lives, so that they are no longer on the list of *zakah* recipients. Second, there are those who are incapable of earning because of a physical handicap, like the elderly, or social handicap, like widows who are raising children. They may be given sufficiency for one year, provided that it is repeated every year. It may even be advisable to give them monthly payments instead of yearly payments.

It is interesting to note that after I made this distinction of the sub-categories of the poor and needy, I discovered that I was preceded by some Hanbalite scholars. The commentator on *Ghayat al Muntaha*, after mentioning the opinion of Ahmad on the case of a person who owns real estate which yields returns that are not sufficient for the person's living, writes, "Such a person has the right to be given his sufficiency from *zakah*, such as an amount needed to buy equipment, or needed capital, if the person is a businessman. On the other hand, other kinds of the poor and needy should be given what suffices them for one year, since *zakah* is repeated every year."[67]

The trend that suggests giving a definite amount

Abu Hanifah and his disciples argue that no more than two hundred *dirhams* per person can be given to any poor or needy individual. Others decide a maximum of fifty *dirhams* can be given; yet others argue that food for one day is to be given. Ibn Hazm rejects these opinions because "payment of *zakah* may be very large or very small, without any limitation, since both Qur'an and Sunnah do not obligate any limit."[68]

The opinion of al Ghazali

In his *al Ihya'* al Ghazali selects giving what is sufficient for one full year and argues that this has its origin in the fact that the Messenger (p) used to keep food sufficient for one year for his own family.[69] Moreover, one year is a reasonable span of time for estimating the needs of the person. Al Ghazali adds:

There are different opinions as to how much should be given. Some scholars say as little as sustenance for one day and night, arguing that this is indicated by the saying reported from Sahl bin al Hanzaliyah that the Prophet (p) prevented begging for the rich, whereupon he was asked what was richness, and answered "Dinner and supper.[70] Others argue that payment must be up to the limit of richness, as determined by *nisab*, since God obligates *zakah* on the rich only. These scholars add that the poor may take from *zakah* an amount equal to *nisab* for each person in the family. Yet other jurists determine richness at fifty *dirhams* or its equivalent in gold, on the grounds of the saying reported from Ibn Mas'ud that the Messenger

(p) said, "He who begs while he has what makes him rich will appear on the Day of Judgement with cuts on his face." The Prophet was asked, "What is richness?" He answered, "Fifty *dirhams* or its equivalent in gold."[71] It is argued that the chain is not strong enough. Some others also say the Limit is only forty *dirhams*, as quoted by 'Ata'.

At the other extreme, we find jurists going on the high side. Some say the poor person should be given what is needed to buy a farm that would enrich him for the rest of his life, or business capital for the same, in accordance with 'Umar's statement, "When you give, you must enrich." Some people go as far as saying that a person who is impoverished must be given to the extent that brings him back to his previous standard of living, be it ten thousand *dirhams*, unless it is uncustomary. When Abu Talhah was so occupied with working in his orchard that he missed prayer, he decided to give the orchard away as charity, but the Prophet said, "Give it to your kindred, that is better for you , . . ." Abu Talhah then granted it to Hasan and Abu Qatadah. An orchard for two men is a whole lot of enrichment . . . .

The claim that one day's food is enough in *zakah* distribution looks unacceptable. The supportive saying refers only to the matter of begging and not to *zakah* distribution. If one has to choose between this opinion and that which provides for the price of a farm, the latter is more sensible, although it is inclined toward extravagance. I believe that the most rational is to be moderate in giving one year's sufficiency of sustenance, since giving more is extravagant, while giving less is too restrictive.[72]

Interestingly, al Ghazali makes this argument in a book devoted generally to the manners of modesty and Sufism.

Abu 'Ubaid prefers giving more

After mentioning the story of Abu Talhah's giving of the orchard to Hasan and Abu Qatadah, Abu 'Ubaid asks how much the value of such an orchard would be, especially if it is added that Abu Talhah tried to hide his charity out of fear that somebody might think of his action as showing off on his part, because it was big. Abu 'Ubaid adds "although this charity was only voluntary, what applies to it applies to the obligation of *zakah*, since if it were forbidden to take big amounts from the proceeds of *zakah*, it would be more forbidden to take big amounts from voluntary charity, and if it is lawful to take that much in charity, it should be as lawful to take that much in the form of obligatory *zakah*."[73] Abu 'Ubaid goes on to mention the statements of 'Umar, 'Ata', and others, referred to earlier in this chapter, then says, "All narrations and evidence indicate that what is given to the poor and needy has no limit. Rather, it is preferred that more be given, as long as the distributors make their decisions without bias or personal preferences. A rich man who sees that a righteous family is in need of a residence and buys that residence for them, paying a big amount in order to provide that family with a decent home out of his *zakah*, would not only be performing his *zakah*, but also doing the best that would please God. The same applies to a rich man who liberates a slave who is under oppression, although he may have to pay a big lump sum."[74]

The aim is providing an adequate level of living

The preceding discussion shows that the objective of *zakah* distribution is to realize an adequate and suitable standard of living and to help Muslims stay above the poverty level. The minimum of such standards is the provision of reasonable food, clothing, and shelter, as stated by Ibn Hazm, al Nawawi, and many others.

Al Nawawi says, "According to the view of our colleagues in the Shafi'i school, the consideration is for food, clothes, shelter and other needs, at a standard that is suitable but not extravagant for the poor person and all members of his family."[75]

Using contemporary terms, the other needs must include education, health care, and other social necessities that can only be determined by time and locale; no absolute definition can be applied to all cases.

Zakah provides regular help

It is essential to observe that the preceding discussion leads to the view of *zakah* as regular and continuous relief to the poor, whether newly impoverished or disabled and handicapped, whereby people who need to be removed from poverty are given what satisfies their needs, while people who cannot earn are given regular relief at certain intervals. Let us look at an incident from the time of 'Umar, which provides insight into the distribution of *zakah*. 'Umar was napping at midday in the shade of a tree. A bedouin woman came and looked around, then approached him. She said, "I am a needy woman and I have children, 'Umar, the Prince of the Believers, sent Muhammad bin Maslamah to distribute *zakah* in our area, but he did not give us any. Would you please talk to him on our behalf?" 'Umar told his servant Yarfa' "Bring me Muhammad bin Maslamah." The woman, not knowing to whom she was talking, said, "It would be more helpful if you went with me to Muhammad bin Maslamah." 'Umar said,. "He will come, God willing." Then Yarfa' came with Muhammad to 'Umar, and said, "Peace be upon you, O Prince of Believers . . . ." The woman felt embarassed upon discovering she had been addressing the Caliph. 'Umar said, "By God, I have always selected the best of you as officers. What will we answer God when He asks about this lady?" The eyes of Muhammad were filled with tears, and 'Umar continued, "God sent to us His Prophet, and we believed and followed him as he was doing what God ordained him to do. He distributed the *sadaqah* to its deservants among needy people until God took his soul; then God gave us Abu Bakr as a ruler, who followed the tradition of the Messenger until he died. Then God made me ruler, and I did my best to select the best of you as my officers. When you go next time to her area, give her the *sadaqah* of last year and the year before. I don't even know whether I want to send you any more." Then 'Umar asked for a camel to give her along with some flour and oil, and addressed the woman, "Take these and meet us in Khaibar, for we are heading there." When the woman met him in Khaibar, he gave her two more camels, saying, "This might sustain you until Muhammad bin Maslamah reaches you. I have ordered him to give you your right from last year and the year before it."[76]

This story is rich in lessons on the purpose and manners of *zakah* distribution. It tells how deep is the feeling of responsibility a Muslim leader has toward his people. It also illustrates how well citizens were educated about their rights and how freely they could approach the state and its officers to pursue their rights. It also shows that *zakah* is the basic pillar of solidarity in Muslim society, in addition to being a regular and continuous relief for the person who is in need. Lastly, this story indicated that 'Umar's policy was to give enriching amounts and that he felt in so doing he was following the tradition of the Messenger and Abu Bakr.

Footnotes

1.   *Hashiyat al Dusuqi,* Vol. 1, p. 492, and *Sharh al Azhar*, Vol.1, p. 509.

2.   *Tafsir al Tabari,* Vol. 14, pp. 308-309.

3.   *Sura al Baqarah*, 2:61.

4.   The saying is agreed upon as narrated by Abu Hurayrah. See *Bulugh al Maram*, p. 302. See also *al Mughni*, Vol. 6, p. 457.

5.   Ma'alim al Sunnan, Vol. 2, p. 232.

6.   The orientalist Joseph Schacht stoops to cheap slurs in the *Encyclopedia of Islam* when he discusses the difference between the poor and the needy. He writes, "The difference usually stated between the poor and the needy is merely arbitrary. Any how, Muslim scholars are accustomed to interpret definitions in such a way that they themselves are included in one of these two categories." See the *Encyclopedia of Islam*, Arabic translation Vol. 10, p. 360.
    This foolish accusation comes from one who lacks the scrupulousness of a learned person. Scholars like al Sarakhsi, Ibn al 'Arabi, al Nawawi, Ibn Qudamah, Ibn Hazm, and other jurists who discuss these definitions obviously had no ambition to receive *zakah* payments. All these scholars were rich and known donors to charity, in addition to their renowned modesty of living. This is plain to all who study their biographies. As for Schacht's claim that the difference in definitions is always arbitrary, this can only be a result of his ignorance of the Arabic language, since it is known to scholars of Arabic that if two terms are linked by an additive article in the same context, there must be a difference between them, although we know that the semantic difference in definition is immaterial here because both poor and needy persons are included in the recipients of *zakah*.

7.   *Majm' al Anhur*, printed with *Durr al Muntaqa*, pp. 220 and 223.

8.   *Nihayat al Muhtaj*, Vol. 6, pp. 151-153.

9.   Shafi'ite jurists do not agree on the case of a person who is accustomed to live in rented residences and has at the same time the value of a residence, whether this person should be treated as poor or not. Al Ramli, in *Nihayat al Muhtaj*, considers such a person poor, while others do not. See *Hashiyat al Shabiramalsi on Nihayat al Muhtaj*, Vol. 6, p. 150.

10. *Ibid*, pp. 150-151.

11. Reported by Abu Daud and al Tirmidhi; the latter grades it good.

12. *Al Mughni*, Vol. 2, p. 523.

13. *Ma'alim al Sunnan*, Vol. 2, p. 226.

14. One may add a second level of richness, that is richness that makes begging prohibited. This level of richness is below richness that makes taking *zakah* prohibited, because begging is not allowed except in dire necessity.

15. Reported by Abu Daud, al Nasa'i, Ibn Majah, and al Tirmidhi. The latter grades it good, while others grade it weak. See *Mukhtasar al Sunan*, by al Mundhiri, Vol. 2, pp. 226-227.

16. *Al Insaf*, a book of Hanbalite jurisprudence, Vol. 2, pp, 221-222 .

17. *Ma'alim al Sunan*, Vol. 2, p. 226.

18. *Radd al Muhtar*, Vol.2, pp. 88-89, and *Majma' al Anhur*, p. 223.

19. *Bada'i al Sana'i,* by al Kasani, Vol.2, p. 48.

20. *Radd al Muhtar, op cit.*

21. *Ma'alim al Sunan*, Vol. 2, p. 227.

22. Reported by Muslim, Abu Daud, and al Nasa'i. See *Mukhtasar al Sunan*, Vol.2, saying no. 1575.

23. *Sharh Ghayat al Muntaha*, Vol. 2, p. 135.

24. *Al Mughni*, Vol. 2, p. 664.

25. *Al Majmu'*, Vol. 6, p. 228.

26. *Majma' al Anhur*, p. 220.

27. The author of *Hashiyat al Dusuqi*, Vol. 1, p. 1494, attributes it to Yahya bin 'Umar.

28. Reported by al Bukhari and others. See *al Targhib wa al Tarhib* of *al Mundhiri*, Vol. 2, beginning of chapter on sale contracts.

29. Reported by the five. Al Tirmidhi grades it good.

30. *Commentary on al Tabari,* edited by Mahmud Shakir, Vol. 14, p. 231.

31. Extended to the Prophet by Abu Hurairah, Jablah bin Junadah, Jabir, Talhah, 'Abd al Rahman bin Abu Bakr, and Ibn 'Umar. See *Nasb al Rayah*, Vol. 2, pp. 399-401, and *Musannaf Ibn Abi Shaibah*, Vol. 3, pp. 207-209.

32.   *Al Majmu'*, Vol. 6, p. 191.

33.   Reported by Ahmad, Abu Daud, and al Nasa'i. Ahmad comments, "What a good saying it is?" Al Nawawi says, "This saying is correct." See *al Majmu'*, Vol. 6, p. 189. Abu Daud and al Mundhiri make no comment. See *Mukhtasar al Sunan*, Vol. 2, p. 233.

34.   *Nayl al Awtar*, Vol. 4, p. 170.

35.   *Al Majmu'*, Vol. 6, p. 190.

36.   *Al Rawdah*, of al Nawawi, Vol. 2, p. 309, and *al Majmu'* , Vol. 6, P. 191.

37.   *Ibid, Sharh Ghayat al Muntaha*, Vol. 2, p. 137, and *Hashiyat al Rawd al Murbi'*, Vol. 1, p. 400.

38.   *Sura al Baqarah*, 2:273.

39.   *Commentary on Ibn Kathir*, Vol. 1, p. 324.

40.   The saying, in its two versions, is agreed upon.

41.   *Al Amwal*, p. 556.

42.   *Radd at Muhtar*, Vol. 2, p. 88.

43.   *Al Mughni*, Vol. 2, p. 525.

44.   *Al Majmu'*, Vol. 6, p. 192.

45.   *Sharh al Khirshi' bi Hashiyat al 'Adawi Ala Khalil*, Vol. 2, p. 215, and *Hashiyat al Dusuqi*, Vol. 1, p. 494.

46.   *Al Majmu'*, Vol. 6, pp. 193-195.

47.   *Nihayat al Muhtaj* with *Sharh al Minhaj* of al Ramli, Vol. 6, p. 159.

48.   *Al Insaf*, Vol. 3, p. 238.

49.   *Ma'alim al Sunan*, Vol. 2, p. 239.

50.   *Al Amwal*, p. 565.

51.   *Ibid*.

52.   *Ibid*, p. 566.

53.   Agreed upon.

54. Some Malikites agree on giving the sufficiency for more than one year if *zakah* is not distributed every year. See *Hashiyat al Dusuqi,* Vol. 1, p. 494.

55. *Sharh al Khirshi,* Vol. 2, p. 219. It is sated in *Hashiyat al Dusuqi,* Vol. 1, p. 494, that "it is lawful to give the poor once every year what is needed for their expenses, including clothing , but if there are plenty of funds, the value of a servant and the dowry of a wife may be added."

56. Reported in al Bukhari's chapter on fasting.

57. *Hashiyat al Rawd al Murbi',* Vol. 1, p. 400, and the footnote on p. 147, Vol. 2, of *Matalib Uli al Nuha.*

58. *Sharh Kitab al nil wa Shifa' al Alil,* in Abadi Jurisprudence, Vol. 2, p. 135.

59. *Al Bidayah wa al Nihayah,* by Ibn Kathir, Vol. 9, p. 200.

60. *Nail al Awtar,* Vol. 6, p. 316. One *uqiyyah* equals forty *dirhams,* while one sheep is estimated at five to ten *dirhams.* Thus such an amount is rather too much for the person who asked for help here.

61. *Sura al Zumar,* 39:9.

62. *Sura al Fatir,* 35:19-20.

63. Reported by Ibn 'Abd al Barr in the chapter on knowledge from Anas; al Suyuti marks it correct.

64. *Al Majmu',* Vol. 6, p. 190.

65. *Al Insaf,* Vol. 3, pp. 165 and 218.

66. *Radd al Muhtar,* Vol. 2, p. 94.

67. *Matalib Uli al Nuha,* Vol. 2, p. 136.

68. *Al Muhalla,* Vol. 6, p. 156.

69. Reported by al Bukhari and Muslim.

70. Reported by Abu Daud and Ibn Habban.

71. Al 'Iraqi comments, "This saying is reported by the four." Al Tirmidhi grades it good, while al Nas'i and al Khattabi grade it weak.

72. Al Ghazali, *Ihya' Ulum al Din,* Vol. 1, p. 201.

73. *Al Amwal,* p. 561.

74. *Ibid,* p. 567.

75. *Al Majmu',* Vol. 6, p. 191, and *al Rawdah,* Vol. 2, p. 311.

76. *Al Amwal,* p. 599.

CHAPTER TWO

ZAKAH WORKERS:
MANAGERIAL AND FINANCIAL APPARATUS

Workers in the collection and distribution of zakah are the third category of *zakah* recipients. They are made recipients in order to avoid any possible attempt on their part to impose additional duties on *zakah* payers for their own benefit. This emphasizes the autonomy of the *zakah* institution. The very mention of this category in the Qur'an immediately after the poor and the needy, who are the major targets of *zakah*, is itself a claer indication that *zakah* collection and distribution are functions of an organization of paid employees. It is part of the social structure of the Islamic state and not an individual practice or an activity of a certain religious body.[1]

The state is required to collect and distribute *zakah*

Jurists say that the Islamic state is required to appoint collectors and distributors of *zakah*. The Prophet (p) and his successors used to assign officers to these duties. For example, Abu Hurairah is reported by al Bukhari and Muslim to say that the Messenger of God (p) assigned 'Umar bin al Khattab to *sadaqah*. It is also reported by al Bukhari and Muslim from Sahl bin Sa'd that the Prophet (p) appointed Ibn al Lutbyyah to the *sadaqah*. There are many other sayings that refer to such appointments. It is to be expected that there will always be people who have wealth but do not know how much they are required to pay, and people who know what to pay, but have a tendency to be miserly; officers are thus needed for both information and collection.[2] The state must send officers at the time of harvest to farmers, and must establish *zakah* payment months so that other payers know when collection officers are expected.[3]

Duties of workers in the *zakah* organization

1. Collection Department   2.   Distribution Department

Jobs in the *zakah* organization include collecting, keeping records, gathering information, and distribution. This can be classified into two major functions directly related to *zakah*: the collection function and the distribution function.

23

The collection function is similar to that of taxation officers. It certainly includes gathering statistics of *zakah* payers and their *zakatable* items, the actual collection of *zakah*, in money or in kind, and keeping payments in suitable storage facilities. One can divide this function into several sections:

A. *Rikaz* and minerals.
B. Grains and fruits.
C. Livestock.
D. Money and business assets.

As for the distribution of *zakah*, many of its activities are similar to the activities of social insurance or welfare departments in modern state. Workers in this section must be trained to exert their best efforts to seek out deservants, discover the degree of their need, and assure that the distributed *zakah* reaches them quickly. Al Nawawi says "The state and its *zakah* distribution officers should keep records of deservants, their number, and their individual needs, so that their due *zakah* can reach them quickly, especially since some collected items may be perishable."[4]

This function may be divided into several sections:

A. The incapable poor and needy, which include the elderly, orphans, widows raising children, handicapped, and retarded persons.

B. The needy who can earn.

C. Those burdened by liabilities.

D. Refugees, street people, and persons seeking asylum.

E. Funds used to help the message of Islam be known in non-Muslim countries and to help liberate Muslim lands, etc.

The distribution of total proceeds of *zakah* among the different categories of recipients is subject to the discretion of the state and its *shura* council [parliament], taking the local, national, and global interests of Muslims as one people into consideration.

Additional notes on the deservability of *zakah*

Departments charged with the distribution of *zakah* must do their utmost to be sure that recipients truly deserve *zakah*, and that all deservants are given fairly. A few notes and regulations deduced by jurists from the available sayings are of help in this regard:

A. Poor and needy deservants must not have wealth or income sufficient for their complete sustenance. Incapability is not a condition, since an earner may not find a job, and a person who earns less than what he or she needs deserves help to satisfy his or her needs.

B. Work is to be sufficient and suitable for the person. For example, a scholar or professor is not obligated to work as a manual laborer. *Zakah* is lawful for such persons until they find a suitable job.

C. A person who can earn but is a full-time student (i.e. if he or she were to take an earning job, they must quit seeking education) is eligible for *zakah*. This person can benefit Muslims by his or her knowledge. A person who is not expected to achieve in a branch of knowledge and can work and earn is not eligible for *zakah*, even if he or she resides at school.

D. A person who owns real estate whose income is below the person's needs is counted poor. He or she should be given from *zakah* the amount needed to supplement the person's income. A student or teacher is not required to sell his or her books as long as they are needed for his/her performance.

E. If a person, known to be wealthy, claims to be in need, the claim should not be accepted without evidence.

F. A person known as poor needs no evidence of his/her poverty.

G. If a person whose general conditions would normally preclude having income (such as an old or disabled person) claims to be in need, his/her claim is accepted without evidence. But if the claimant is young and strong, he may be asked to testify under oath, according to a minority of Shafi'ites. Most Shafi'ites do not require such swearing, since Ahmad, Abu Daud, and al Nasa'i report that two men asked the Prophet (p) to give them *sadaqah*. The Prophet, after looking them over thoroughly, found them strong and said "If you like, I will give you, but there is no share in this [*zakah*] for the rich or the strong who can earn." It is the duty of the distributor to remind and teach recipients about *zakah*.

H. If a poor person claims that he or she has a family, evidence is required.

I. The same is true for a person who claims to be overburdened by debt. Evidence can be testimony of two honest people, or that the need of the person be publicly known. It is not meant to take the form of court procedures.[5]

Some sayings mention ". . . a person so struck by poverty that three wise persons from his clan say he is impoverished." Al Khattabi comments, "This applies to the person who is known to have been affluent, and suddenly something happens to his wealth, especially if poverty is not visible in the person's lifestyle. If doubt arises, his poverty must be confirmed by people who know him well enough to give their opinions. The description of these three people of reason is mentioned to establish that they are not likely to be fooled. This is not a form of legal testimony. If a group of the person's neighbors know that he is in need, that is sufficient evidence to justify giving him/her *zakah*."[6]

Eligibility conditions for *zakah* workers

1. Being Muslim is required, since working in *zakah* is a form of public control [*wilayah*] of Muslims. In all positions of public control, being Muslim is a requirement. Certain jobs not directly related to the collection and distribution of *zakah* are exempt from this condition, such as guards and drivers. Ahmad is reported to permit non-Muslims in *zakah* jobs because the term "workers of *zakah*" is general and not limited to Muslims; additionally, what is paid to workers is only compensation for their work.[7] However, although this is a gracious position of Ahmad, it is still preferred that 'those who implement this critical obligation of Islam be Muslims. Ibn Qudamah says, "because these jobs require honesty and entail some control over Muslims, the condition of being Muslim must be fulfilled, especially since it is unreasonable that people who do not believe in *zakah* be entrusted to implement it. Moreover, disbelievers are described in the Qur'an as not trustworthy and 'Umar said, 'Do not take them as confidantes, since God labels them traitors." 'Umar condemned the appointment of a Christian as registrar by Abu Musa. *Zakah* as a pillar of Islam, is more important than registration."[8]

2. The candidate must be sane and past the age of puberty, i.e. addressed by *Shari'ah* ordinances.

3. Trustworthiness is a requirement, since the *zakah* officer will be handling public funds. He or she must be righteous and honest so as not to oppress the rich or neglect the rights of the poor.

4. General and complete knowledge of *zakah* rulings and regulations is a must for officers who are in charge of the overall organization of *zakah*. An ignorant person cannot perform well and would make many errors that would make him or her a liability for the *zakah* institution.[9] As for workers whose jobs are strictly limited, they are only required to know their jobs.

5. Efficiency and performance is required. Officers of *zakah* must be efficient in their work and capable of achieving the targets of *zakah*. God says, "Truly the best of people for thee to employ is he who is strong and trustworthy."[10] Speaking for Yusuf, (p) God says, "Set me over the storehouses of the land; I am indeed trustworthy and knowledgeable."[11]

6. The candidate must not be one of the descendents of the Prophet Muhammad's family, according to most scholars. His family includes all descendents of Hashem [The Prophet' s great grandfather] because al Fadl bin al 'Abbas and al Muttalib bin Rabiah [cousins of the Prophet Muhammad] asked the Prophet to employ them on *sadaqat*. One of them said, "O Messenger of God, we come to you seeking jobs in administrating *sadaqat*, so we can earn some of them like other people, and perform [the service] that is due on us like others." The Prophet said, "Indeed, the *sadaqah* is not to be given to Muhammad or the family of Muhammad. It is the impurities [left after cleansing the wealth] of people." Reported by Ahmad and Muslim. In another version reported by the same, the Prophet says, "Indeed the *sadaqah* is not lawful to Muhammad or to the

family or Muhammad."[12] This saying discourages the family of the Prophet from taking *zakah*. Since *zakah* is public property, the Prophet did not want his family to have any inclination to take from it.

Al Nasir believes it is permissible for descendents of Hashem to be employed in the *zakah* organization and receive compensation. This is also expressed by al Shafi'i and Ahmad. Abu Ya'la says, "It is permissible to appoint to the collection and distribution of *zakah* a person otherwise forbidden to receive *zakah*, such as descendents of Hashem and slaves, because what they receive is not *zakah* but merely the price of their labor. Certainly, the amount given depends on the amount of labor provided."[13] Al Kharaqi says, "The *sadaqah* must not be paid to descendents of Hashem, disbelievers, or slaves, unless they are employees of the *zakah* agency. Then they may be paid the worth of their labor." This means these scholars interpret the saying mentioned above as a discouragement and not a prohibition.

Those who understand the saying as prohibition argue that payment of *zakah* to descendents of tho Prophet is prohibited, but their appointment to the *zakah* agency is not prohibited, as long as they either work for free or receive compensation from other funds.[14]

7. Must the sex of the appointee be male? Some jurists add this condition on the grounds that these jobs entail control over public funds and in jobs of public control, women should not be appointed. They have no evidence to support their view except the saying of the Prophet (p) "A people who give control of their affairs to a woman shall not succeed."[15] But this saying applies only to positions that entail public control whose decisions have national consequences. Jobs of *zakah* cannot be included in the realm of this saying.

Some jurists argue that it is not reported that a woman was ever appointed *zakah* officer. This is not, in my opinion, sufficient reason, because of circumstantial economic and social surroundings of women in those ages. Additionally, not doing something at some time is not evidence that it is prohibited. Others also argue that the literal meaning of the verse "and the workers in it" does not include females, because the word used for workers is the masculine plural.[16] If this argument were correct, women would also not be given *zakah* if they are poor, because the Arabic word used in the Qur'an for the poor is in the masculine plural. This is totally contradictory to *ijma*, since grammatically, women are included in the Arabic masculine plural, unless otherwise is implied by the context.

The truth is there is no base to the claim that women must not be appointed in *zakah* administration positions, as long as Islamic standards of conduct-modesty, avoidance of unnecessary competition and mixing with men--are observed. In fact, although these general rules make men more suited to jobs that require daily contact with *zakah* payers, there are certain jobs in the *zakah* organization in which women can do better than men, such as contacting widows and handicapped women and assessing their needs.

8.   Some jurists add the condition that appointees of the *zakah* agency must be free, i.e. slaves cannot be employed by this agency. This is denied by other jurists because of a report by al Bukari and Ahmad that the Messenger of God said "Listen and obey, even if an Ethiopian slave whose head is like a raisin is appointed over you," especially since the job itself can be performed regardless of the free or slave status of the employee.[17]

Amount of worker compensation

Workers of the *zakah* agency are paid salaries equal to the market value of their labor. Al Shafi'i is reported to have suggested that total compensation for workers must not exceed one-eighth of the total proceeds of *zakah*, based on his opinion that total proceeds must be divided equally among the eight recipient categories. The majority does not accept such limitation. One may suggest that the Shafi'ite opinion has the merit of restricting the cost of collection.

A worker in the *zakah* organization need not be poor in order to receive compensation for his or her labor. Abu Daud reports that the Prophet (p) says "The *sadaqah* is not lawful to any rich person, except these five: A fighter for the sake of God, a worker on *zakah*, a person under the burden of liabilities, a person who buys a *zakah* item from a recipient, and a person given a gift by a needy person who received this gift as *zakah*."[18]

The Prophet was very strict in protecting the public funds of *zakah*, and allowed no non-deservant to take any of them under any label. 'Adi bin 'Umairah reports, "I heard the Messenger of God saying, "Whoever is employed on any collection job, and hides from us even a needle or more, it is embezzling, and he will carry what he embezzled on the Day of Judgement."[19] A black man from the *Ansar*--I can almost see him now--stood and said, "O Messenger of God, accept my resignation of the job [you gave me]." The Prophet inquired 'Why?' and the man answered, "I heard you saying (such and such)." The prophet continued, "And I say now, whoever we employ in a job must bring forward all that he collects, the little and the big. What we give him after that, he should take, and what we do not give him he should leave alone." Reported by Abu Daud and others. In another saying Abu Rafi' says, he was passing by al Baqi' [a cemetary] with the Prophet (p). The Prophet said, "Woe to you, woe to you!" Abu Rafi says, "I was stunned and retreated to the back, afraid that he meant me." The Prophet said, "What is the matter? Come on." I asked, "Did I do anything wrong?" and he said, "Why do you ask that?" I answered, "You said woe to me." The Prophet said, "No, [not to you] to the person [in the grave]. I sent him to collect *zakah* from the land of (so and so) and he embezzled a *namirah* [a special garment made of wool]. He is clothed in one like it from the Fire." Reported by al Nas'i and Ibn Khuzaimah in his correct collection. From 'Ubadah bin al Samit, it is reported that the Messenger of God (p) commissioned him on the *sadaqah*, and told him "O Abu al Walid, Fear God. You must not appear on the Day of Judgement carrying a camel that shouts or a cow that moos or a sheep that bleats [out of embezzlement]." 'Ubadah said, "O Messenger of God, could that happen?" He replied, "Yes, by the name of He is Whose Hand is my soul." "Ubadah said, "By the name of He Who in truth sent you, I do not accept to be appointed by you on any job at all." Reported by al Tabarani in his *al Mu'jam al Kabir* via a correct chain. 'Ubadah, a great and renowned Companion, responded as he did because he wanted to be on the safe side.

Gifts to officers are unlawful

In as much as officers are required to declare everything they collect and put in the *zakah* fund, they are forbidden to accept gifts from *zakah* payers. Any such gift is considered a bribe, because it may influence the estimation of *zakah* due, at the expense of deservants.

Abu Hamid al Sa'idi says the Prophet (p) appointed a man from the tribe of al Azd named Ibn al Lutbyyah on *sadaqah* collection. When he came back, the collector said, "This is yours, and this was given to me as a gift." The Messenger of God (p) stood [addressing the gathering] and praised and thanked God, then said, "I employed a man from you at a job that God gives me control over. Then he comes and says 'This is yours and this is a gift that was given to me.' Why does he not sit in his father and mother's house and wait for his gift to be brought to him, if he sincerely thinks [that it is an innocent gift on their part]?! By God, nothing any of you takes without true right, but when you face God an the Day of Judgement will be carried by you. Let me not recognize any of you coming before God carrying a camel that is shouting or a cow that is mooing or a sheep that is bleating." Then he raised his two hands so high that the whiteness of his underarms was seen, and said, "O my Lord, did I inform them?" Reported by al Bukhari, Muslim, and Abu Daud.[20]

Kindness to the rich

The Prophet (p) advised his *zakah* collectors to be kind, courteous, and moderate, and selected them from the best of his Companions. It was mentioned that the Messenger of God advised estimators, "Be easy in estimation, since orchards may have trees assigned to the poor, needy, family, and passers-by."

It is advisable that collectors pray for *zakah* payers, since God tells His Messenger, "Out of their wealth take a *sadaqah* so thou might purify and sanctify them by it, and pray on their behalf. Verily thy prayers are a source of security for them." 'Abd Allah bin Abu Awfa narrates that his father came to the Messenger of God (p) and gave him the *zakah* due on his wealth. The Prophet said, "My Lord, have mercy on the family of Abu Awfa."[21]

Can other public officers be paid from zakah?

Ibn Rushd mentions that some jurists approve of this on the grounds that the benefit of these public officers' work extends to all Muslims.[22] In *al Nil* and its commentary in *Abadi fiqh*, it is stated that *zakah* may be given to workers in the *zakah* organization as well as other public officers, such as judges and governors. These people may be given as much as their labor is worth, even if they are rich, because they are occupied by public service from pursuing their own interests.[23] The majority of scholars argue that such officers must be paid from other resources of the stats.

Footnotes

1. See the chapter on the relation of the state to *zakah*, in the next part.

2. *Al Majmu'*, Vol. 6, p. 167.

3. *Ibid*, p. 170.

4. *Al Rawdah*, Vol. 2, p. 337.

5. *Al Majmu'*, Vol. 6, p. 189 plus.

6. *Ma'alim al Sunan*, Vol. 2, p. 238.

7. *Al Mughni*, Vol. 2, p. 654.

8. *Ibid*, Vol. 6, p. 460.

9. *Al Majmu'*, Vol. 6, p. 167, and *Sharh Ghayat al Muntaha*, Vol. 2, p. 137.

10. *Sura al Qasas*, 28:26.

11. *Sura Yusuf*, 12:55.

12. *Nail al Awtar*, Vol. 4, p. 175.

13. *Al Ahkam al Sultanyyah*, by Abu Ya'la, p. 99, and *al Majmu'*, Vol. 6, p. 168.

14. *Nail al Awtar*, Vol. 4, p. 175.

15. Reported by al Bukhari, via al Hasan al Basri from Abu Bakrah.

16. *Sharh Ghayat al Muntaha*, Vol. 2, p. 137.

17. *Ibid*, p. 138.

18. In *al Majmu*, al Nawawi says "this saying is good or correct, reported by Abu Daud via two chains. One of them is via 'Ata' from Abu Sa'id from the Prophet, and the other from 'Ata' from the Prophet as *mursal*. Its two chains are good." In *Mukhtasar al Sunan*, al Mundhiri says "it is also reported from the Prophet by Ibn Majah." Abu 'Amr al Nahwi adds, "it is linked up to the Prophet by a group, through Zaid bin Aslam."

19. In reference to *sura Al 'Imran*, 3:161, "If any person embezzles [anything] he shall, on the Day of Resurrection, restore what he embezzled."

20. *Al Targhib wa al Tarhib*, by al Mundhiri, Vol. 1, p. 277.

21. Reported by Ahmad, al Bukhari and Muslim.

22. *Bidayat al Mujtahid*, Vol. 1, p. 267.

23. *Al Nil* and its commentary, Vol. 2, p. 134.

CHAPTER THREE

THOSE WHOSE HEARTS ARE BEING RECONCILED

Those whose hearts are being reconciled include persons who have recently been brought to Islam, or who need to strengthen their commitment to this faith, and individuals whose evil can be forestalled or who can benefit and defend Muslims.

Indications of the inclusion of this group

The very presence of this category as recipients of *zakah* emphasizes the fact that *zakah* is not personal charity or merely a worship left to individual practice. Distribution to this category is not, by nature, a job that individual acting independently can undertake. It is a political decision made by the decision-making body of the state. Only the state can determine the need at a given time for reconciling hearts and the qualifications of deservants under this title.

Subdivisions of this category

A. One group in this category is that of individuals who are close to becoming Muslims, or whose clans may become Muslim, like Safwan bin Ummayyah who was granted safety by the Prophet the day Makkah was conquered. The Prophet gave him so many camels loaded with goods after the battle of Hunain that he said, "This is the giving of one who fears not poverty." Muslim and al Tirmidhi report from Sa'id bin al Musayyib from Safwan his statement, "By God, when the Prophet gave me, he was the person I hated most. He continued to give me until he became my most beloved person."[1] Safwan became a committed Muslim. Ahmad reports, via a correct chain, from Anas that "Never was the Messenger of God (p) asked to give anything for accepting Islam but he gave it. A man once came and asked to be given something for accepting Islam. The Messenger ordered him to be given enough sheep to fill the distance [between two hills] from the sheep collected as *sadaqah*. The man went back to his clan saying, 'O my folks, accept Islam, for Muhammad gives like one who fears not poverty."[2]

B. The second group includes those who may do harm to Muslims, to whom giving *zakah* stops them from hurting Muslims. Ibn 'Abbas narrates that certain people came to the Prophet who, if they are given *sadaqat,* praise Islam and declare it a good religion, but if not, malign Islam.[3]

C. The third group consists of individuals who have just embraced Islam, to whom giving helps them be steadfast. When al Zuhri was asked, who comprise those whose hearts are being reconciled? he said, "Whoever embraces Islam from among the Jews and Christians." He was then asked, "Even if they were rich?" "Even if they were rich," he answered.[4] Al Hasan answered a similar question by saying, "They are individuals who embrace Islam."[5] It is understandable that persons who embrace Islam may have to make several sacrifices and may be persecuted, ostracized, or even threatened financially by the communities in which they live. Such a person is undoubtedly in need of support and encouragement.

D. Also in this category are prominent Muslims whose social status is respected by disbelievers who have status in their own communities, such that giving these Muslims encourages their non-Muslim counterparts to consider embracing Islam. It is said that Abu Bakr's giving to Adi bin Hatim and al Zibriqan bin Badr, who were obviously committed Muslims, is of this nature.[6]

E. Muslim leaders whose faith is shaky can be given *zakah* in this category. Such individuals may have great influence on Muslims, and giving them generously could strengthen their faith and commitment. An example is the Makkans who were given generously by the Prophet after the battle of Hunain.[7]

F. Muslims giving on the borders of a Muslim country who are expected to defend Muslim land against any attack from enemies.

G. Muslims whose influence is needed in the *zakah* collecting process to persuade would be rebels to pay their *zakah.* By using such influence, the government avoids having to fight those who reject paying *zakah.*[8]

Al Shafi'i says those whose hearts are being reconciled include newcomers into Islam, and that disbelievers must not be given *sadaqah.* He argues that the gift of the Prophet (p) to some disbelievers after the battle of Hunain was not from *zakah,* but either from fay' or the Prophet's personal property. Al Shafi'i adds, "God makes it mandatory that the *zakah* of Muslims be rendered to Muslims and not to disbelievers.[9] The Prophet told Mu'adh *zakah* was '. . . to be taken from the rich among them and rendered to the poor among them.'"

Al Razi in his commentary quotes al Wahidi as saying, "God does not make Muslims in need of reconciling the hearts of unbelievers. The head of state may find it beneficial to Muslims to reconcile the hearts of some individuals. This is only permissible if those individuals are Muslims, since it is not allowed to extend *zakah* to unbelievers. Unbelievers whose hearts must be reconciled can be given from fay' and not *sadaqat*." Al Razi comments, "The statement of al Wahidi may give the impression that the Prophet gave unbelievers *zakah*, but such a thing never happened. However, the verse of *zakah* distribution nowhere specifies that the hearts being reconciled are those of unbelievers, since the term 'those whose hearts are being reconciled' may include Muslims as well as non-Muslims."[10]

By the same token, since the term used in the Qur'an includes Muslims and non-Muslims, there is no reason for restricting it to Muslims. Unbelievers may be reconciled from *zakah*. Qatadah says "Those whose hearts were reconciled were often pagan bedouins whom the Prophet (p) used to reconcile through giving *zakah* in order to bring them to faith.[11] In the saying from Anas quoted earlier about the man to whom the Prophet gave sheep from *zakah* and who returned and said to his clan, "Accept Islam; Muhammad gives like one who fears not poverty," it appears he was not Muslim before being given. Granting unbelievers *zakah* in order to bring them to Islam, is, according to al Qurtubi, "a form of *jihad*." "Unbelievers are three kinds: those who understand reason and dialogue, those who do not and must be conquered, and those who can be reconciled by generosity and benevolence. The Muslim state should deal appropriately with each group."[12]

Does giving for reconciliation end with the Messenger's death?

Ahmad and his disciples believe the ruling on heart reconciliation is permanent, which is the opinion of al Zuhri and Abu Ja'far al Baqir.[13] It is also taken up by the Ja'fari and Zaidi schools.[14] Yunus says "I asked al Zuhri about this matter, and he said he knew of no change in this ruling," Abu Ja'far al Nahhas comments, "Accordingly, the ruling on heart reconciliation is firm. Whenever there is a need for reconciling a person's heart, he [or she] may be given *zakah*."

Al Qurtubi quotes al Qadi 'Abd al Wahhab--a Malikite--as saying, "If such persons are needed sometimes by the state, they may be given *zakah*." Likewise, al Qadi Ibn al Arabi remarks, "The way I see it, if Islam becomes strong, this group of recipients becomes null, but if they are needed, they may be given their share, the same way the Messenger of God (p) used to give them. It is correctly reported that "Islam started atypical and unique and will again become as atypical and unique as it started."[15] It is mentioned in *al Nil* and its commentary--Abadi--that "this category is dropped as long as the state is strong and in no need of reconciling people, but reconciling is permitted when need arises, to avoid harm to Muslims or bring them benefit."[16] Al Nawawi quotes al Hasan as saying, "Today there must be no reconciliation of hearts from *zakah*."[17] al Sha'bi says,"Those whose hearts are to be reconciled were a group at the time of the Prophet (p) which, when Abu Bakr took charge, came to an end."[17] Al Nawawi quotes al Shafi'i as saying, "If unbelievers are reconciled, they must only be paid fay' and not *zakah,* since the latter must not be given to non-Muslims." As for reconciling Muslim's hearts, al Shafi'i is reported to disallow giving them after the state of Islam becomes strong; the second view says it is permissible to give them the same way they were given by the Prophet.[18]

As for Malikites, they also have two opinions, one allowing and one disallowing giving this group *zakah.*[19] Hanafites believe there must be no giving for reconciliation after the death of the Prophet, (p). This, according to al Kasani, is the correct and authentic view, because the Companions were unanimous on that count. Both Abu Bakr and 'Umar did not give anything from *zakah* funds to reconciling hearts, and none of the Companions disapproved of this. It is reported that upon the death of the Messenger of God, individuals who were given *zakah* for reconciling their hearts asked Abu Bakr to document this in writing. Abu Bakr did so, and they went and showed it to 'Umar, whereupon 'Umar grabbed the document and tore it up, saying, "Indeed, the Messenger of God (p) used to give you in order to reconcile you to Islam, but today God has strengthened this religion. If you remain steadfast in Islam, [it is well and good] but if you do not, there is nothing between us but the sword." They left him and ran to Abu Bakr, complaining, "Is the *Khalifah* you or 'Umar?" Abu Bakr replied "He is if he so wishes, " and approved of 'Umar's action. Al Kasani adds "this was known to the bulk of the Companions, and none disapproved. This becomes a unanimous *ijma'.* Furthermore, the Prophet used to give these people in order to reconcile them to Islam. The Muslim state was then weak and its people were few, While the disbelievers were more numerous and stronger. But thanks be to God, the Muslim state today is strong. Its people are more in number and in strength, and it is well established on earth, while the unbelievers are humiliated. It is a rule in *Shari'ah* that whenever a ruling can be rationally attributed to a specific reason, if the reason is nulled, the ruling is dropped."[20]

In brief, the opinion of al Kasani can be summarized in two main points: One, the ruling is nulled by the *ijma'* of the Companions, and two, the ruling of reconciliation is caused by a rational reason, and it is dropped if its cause does not exist.[21]

Refuting claims of annulment

In fact, the two points of al Kasani are incorrect. The ruling is not annulled, and the need to reconcile hearts has not ceased. The action of 'Umar does not indicate annulment of this category, since those whose hearts were reconciled in a certain era may not be needed in another era. At each time, the determination of the need to reconcile hearts and the specification of individuals to be included is decided by the executive authority according to what benefits Islam and Muslims.

Scholars of *usul* affirm that the dependency of a ruling on a defined element is an indication that the element is the cause of the ruling. The spending of *zakah* in the case on hand depends on the need for reconciliation of hearts. This indicated that reconciliation is the reason for payment. Consequently, whenever the need for reconciliation exists, payment is permissible, and vice versa. At a given time, the process of reconciling certain persons may be finished, and the step taken by 'Umar would then be taken, the same way that *zakah* workers would not be paid if at one point there were no workers of *zakah*. That does not mean this category is eliminated from future consideration. 'Umar did not annul payment to 'individuals whose hearts are being reconciled' nor was there an *ijma'* on such annulment. He simply judged that there were no deservant in that category at that point in time.[22] The statement of al Hasan and al Sha'bi that "today there are no individuals who are being reconciled, " is understood similarly as a fact of the age they lived in.

Annulment of a ruling enacted by God can only be made by God through revelation to His Messenger, and therefore can only take place during the time of the Message. Annulment is dictated only when two authentic texts of Qur'an or Sunnah totally contradict each other and we know that one of them came after the other chronologically. The question on hand has only one, affirmative text, which determines this category as a recipient of zakah. There is no text which contradicts this Qur'anic verse. How can annulment be attributed to a verse in the Qur'an without a text from the revelation? Al Shatibi writes, "Rulings of *Shari'ah*, after they are confirmed, cannot be claimed null except by confirmed, authentic evidence, since the ruling were initially obligated by completely authentic evidence. This is why scholars unanimously agree that a correct but single-chain saying cannot annul Qur'an or sayings narrated by a group, because the single-chain narration, though authentic and correct, is not absolutely confirmed like narration by groups."[23] Needless to say, the sayings and doings of a Companion cannot annul Qur'anic-texts, especially since the action of the Companion on hand does not even signify annulment. Ibn Hazm, even before al Shatibi, says, "It is not permissible to any Muslim who believes in God and the Last Day to claim that anything in Qur'an or Sunnah is annulled without affirmative evidence, because God says, "We sent not an apostle but to be obeyed In accordance with the will of God"[24] and "Follow, O people, the revelation given unto you from your Lord."[25] Everything sent by God as Qur'an or as Sunnah must be followed, and anyone who claims that something is annulled implies that it must not be followed and is not required, which is obviously disobedience to God, unless authentic and confirmed proof supports the annulment. Accepting anything to the contrary of the above rule leads to wiping out the whole of *Shari'ah*, since what would then be the difference between a claim of annulment and a rejection of a verse or saying? This kind of behavior represents total apostation from Islam. We cannot allow an ordinance made by God or His Apostle to be waived, except by equally undeniable and authentic evidence."[26]

In conclusion, payment for reconciliation of hearts is part of *zakah* distribution, determined by a clear verse in *sura al Tawbah*, and not annulled or idled by anything. Abu 'Ubaid remarks, "This verse is a clear text. We know of no annulment of it in the Book or in Sunnah. Whenever there are individuals who can be brought closer to Islam by being given generously and it is not to the benefit of Muslims to let them be driven away or to fight them, the Islamic state may decide to give them *zakah* in reconciliation of their hearts. This action is supported by three facts: the texts of Qur'an and Sunnah, promotion of the best interests of Muslims, and the hope that such individuals may be guided to the path of Islam once they have the opportunity to study it."[27] In *al Mughni*, Ibn Qudamah, supporting the view of Ahmad that this category of recipients is permanent, says:

On our side is the Book of God and the tradition of His Messenger. God mentions reconciliation of hearts among the categories of *zakah* spending, and the Prophet used to give generously for reconciliation, as stated in famous reports. He continued to do this until he died. It is unacceptable to abandon the Book of God and the tradition of His Messenger except by authentic annulment from God or His Messenger, and annulment is not confirmed by mere possibility. Moreover, such annulment can only take place during the life of the Prophet (p), because the texts required for annulment ceased to be revealed upon his death. A text in Qur'an can only be annulled by another text in the Qur'an itself; there is no such text. By what virtue is one asked to abandon Qur'an and Sunnah and revert to mere human opinions, or statements of a Companion? Scholars do not consider the statement of a Companion strong enough to stand in opposition to analogy, so how could such an opinion stand against the Qur'an and Sunnah?! Al Zuhri too says "I know of nothing that annuls the category of those whose hearts are being reconciled."[28] Lastly, 'Umar's action does not contradict Qur'an or Sunnah, since when Muslims do not need those individuals who were paid in the past, they may choose to cease such payment, and if the need arises in the future to pay the same individuals or others, that can be done. In reality, this principle applies to all categories. A category may not exist at a certain time, but that does not mean it is eliminated because it may exist at some later time.[29]

The need to reconcile hearts does not cease

The claim that there is no more need for heart reconciliation after the spread of Islam and the establishment of its state is rejected for the following reasons:

1. Some Malikites assert that the reason for giving a person whose heart is being reconciled is not that person's benefit to Muslims, but rather, bringing that person closer to Islam and breaking the barriers that may be hindering him from opening his mind to Islam. In other words, the purpose of the payment is to save the payee from the fire of Hell.[30] Thus, this payment is a form of calling for Islam [*da'wah*] that may be effective with some people. It is the obligation of Muslims to help others seek the guidance of God and lead them out of the darkness of ignorance and the agony of disbelief that leads to Hellfire. A person may convert to Islam for material gains, but once he or she starts understanding this religion, he or she may embrace it whole-heartedly. Abu Ya'la reports from Anas that "A man came to the Messenger of God (p) embracing Islam for some earthly gain, not accepting Islam except for that purpose, but by nightfall Islam became more beloved to him than the whole earth and what is on it." And in another version, "A man asked the Prophet (p) for some earthly material gain for which he would embrace Islam . . . " and so on.[31]

The above applies when the person whose heart is being reconciled is an unbeliever, but not all who are given under this title are unbelievers. Some may have embraced Islam very sincerely, but are oppressed and persecuted by their communities. Giving them is a required relief; it encourages them on the path of truth and supports them while their faith is still tender.

2. The claim that there is no longer need for heart reconciliation is based on the erroneous assumption that reconciliation is only done when the Muslim state is weak. This is an unnecessary restriction and an unrealistic assumption. In contemporary

politics, we observe that strong states, like the United States, provide help to poor states in order to reconcile these small and weak states to the objectives of the government of the United States. Al Tabari says in this regard that "God makes *zakah* fulfill two objectives, namely satisfying the needs of Muslims and strengthening the cause of Islam. The cause of Islam covers rich and poor alike, since what is given for this purpose is not aimed at erasing destitution, but at strengthening commitment to Islam. Fighters for the sake of God are given *zakah* regardless of whether they are rich or poor. Payments to those whose hearts are being reconciled are made regardless of their wealth, because giving them is supporting the call of Islam. The Prophet (p) gave *zakah* for reconciliation of hearts after God had opened for him most of Arabia and after the Islamic state was well-established. There is no support in Sunnah for those who claim that after the strengthening of Islam and its state there is no need for reconciling hearts."[32]

3. Lastly, times have changed and Muslims are no longer masters of the land. Actually, Islam has returned to being a stranger; the Muslim nation suffers under pressure and aggression from many other states. Muslims are weak and can only complain to God. If weakness is a reason for distribution towards reconciling hearts, it exists today.

Who has the right to pay for heart reconciliation?

Decisions regarding reconciling hearts are the duty of the Islamic state. The Prophet (p) and his Successors affirmed this responsibility as part of the state's executive affairs. If the state does not fulfill its responsibility in collecting and distributing *zakah*, Muslim organizations can make decisions about distributing to individuals whose hearts are being reconciled.[34] If the government does not undertake this duty, nor are there organizations that distribute *zakah*, can a Muslim individual who distributes his own *zakah* use part of it for reconciling an unbeliever's heart? In my opinion, a Muslim individual must not make decisions concerning heart reconciliation, except in the very rare case where no other destination of *zakah* is available. Such a case may apply to Muslims living in non-Muslim countries, although it is preferable even under such circumstances to dispose of *zakah* for the spread of Islam or to send it to the poor and needy in Muslim countries.

How can the share of heart reconciliation be spent today?

If we agree that reconciliation of hearts by payment from *zakah* is permissible, to whom should this share be given today? In order to answer this question, we must remember that the purpose of this share is to bring hearts closer to Islam, affirm their commitment to its cause, support the weak, and prevent harm that could be inflicted on Muslims or on their religion. These objectives could be achieved by giving aid to non-Muslim countries, persons, organizations, and tribes, to bring them closer to the cause of Islam. It could also be extended to support research, and utilize mass media that teaches the religion of Islam and defends its cause against attackers. Many people enter into the fold of this religion every year who do not find encouragement or support from their governments and communities or even from the governments of Muslim countries. The share of heart reconciliation can be expended to such people, an idea consistent with the opinions of al Zuhri and al Hasan. Christian missionaries spend millions every year for the spread of their religion, although theirs does not have an institution like *zakah* devoted to this purpose. It is true that Islam spreads on its own merit because of its inner persuasive power, but it is equally true that most of those who embrace Islam in non-Muslim countries do not receive even nominal support or compensation for the sacrifices they make when they embrace Islam. There are many Islamic organizations that attempt to fill this gap but are desperate for financial support, especially in areas like Africa and many poor countries.

Payment for heart reconciliation from sources other than *zakah*

It is always possible that the Muslim state appropriate some of its funds derived from sources other than *zakah*, for the purpose of heart reconciliation, if the other categories of *zakah* recipients can hardly be satisfied with the total proceeds of *zakah*. This is consistent with the opinion of al Shafi'i that payments for heart reconciliation to unbelievers must be made from sources other than *zakah*.

Footnotes

1. *Commentary of Ibn Kathir*, Vol. 2, p. 325.

2. *Nayl al Awtar*, Vol. 4, p. 166.

3. *Commentary of al Tabari*, Vol. 14, p. 313.

4. *Ibid*, p. 314, and *al Musannaf*, Vol. 3, p. 223.

5. *Al Musannaf, ibid*, and *al Iklil*, by al Suyuti, p. 119.

6. *Commentary al Manar*, Vol. 10, pp. 574-577.

7. *Commentary al Qurtubi*, Vol. 8, pp. 179-181.

8. *Al Majmu'*, Vol. 6, pp. 196-198, and *Ghayat al Muntaha* and its commentary, Vol. 2, p. 141 plus.

9. *Al Umm*, Vol. 2, p. 61.

10. *Commentary al Razi*, Vol. 16, p. 111.

11. *Commentary al Tabari*, Vol. 14, p. 314.

12. *Commentary al Qurtubi*, Vol. 8, p. 179.

13. *Commentary al Tabari*, Vol. 14, p. 314-316, and *al Mughni*, Vol. 2, p. 666.

14. *Al Bahr*, Vol. 2, p. 179, and *Sharh al Azhar*, Vol. 1, p. 513, and *Fiqh al Imam Ja'far*, Vol. 2, p. 90.

15. *Al Qurtubi*, op. cit.

16. *Al Nil,* Vol. 2, pp. 134, 136.

17. *Al Tabari*, Vol. 14, p. 315.

18. *Al Majmu'*, Vol. 6, pp. 197-198.

19. *Al Qurtubi, op cit.* Al Khatabi in *Ma'alim al Sunan*, Vol. 2, p. 231, says "their share is fixed and must be paid to them." Ibn Qudamah says the same in *al Mughni*, Vol. 2, p. 666.

20. *Al Bada'i*, Vol. 2, p. 45.

21. *Radd'al al Muhtar*, Vol. 2, p. 82, quoting from *al Bahr*.

22. This disproves the claim of some contemporary writers that it is permissible to neutralize or contradict texts if it is to Muslims' common benefit, which they base on 'Umar's action regarding those whose hearts were being reconciled. Such a claim is made by Subhi al Mahmasani, among others, in his *Falsafat al Tashri'*, p. 178, where he claims that 'Umar dared to oppose the text about reconciliation, because such opposition was spurred by the public interest of Muslims." Similarly, Mahmud al Lababidi makes the claim that "the nation, as represented by its consultative authority, can freeze or oppose certain texts for the common benefit." See his article, "*al Sultahal Tashri'yyah fi al Islam*" ["Legislative Authority in Islam] in the review *Risalat al Islam* issued by Daral Taqrib Bayn al Madhahib, Cairo. The latter uses this action of 'Umar as an example. Scholars from al Azhar replied to al Lababidi in several articles, such as the article "*Bahth 'ala Bahth*" ["analysis of an Article"] by the late Muhammad Muhammad al Madani.

23. *Al Muwafaqat*, Vol. 3, p. 64.

24. *Sura al Nisa'*, 4:64.

25. *Sura al A'raf,* 7:3.

26. *Al Ihkam fi Usul al Ahkam*, part 20, chapter titled "How to Recognize Annulled Texts," p. 458, Vol. 1, al Imam print.

27. *Al Amwal*, p. 607.

28. Hanafites differ on determining factors that annul the ruling of heart reconciliation, which is confirmed by a text in the Qur'an. Some of them claim the annulling factor is *ijma'*, attempting to make *ijma'* out of 'Umar's position. This is farfetched, as explained above. Some try to find documentation on which such *ijma'* is based. Here they also diverge into two groups. Ibn Nujaim in *al Bahr* presents the verse in *sura al Kahf,* "Say: The truth is from your Lord; let he who will believe and let he who will reject

it," which was quoted by 'Umar in arguing with his opponents. Ibn 'Abidin says, "*Ijma* cannot be the annulling factor, because annulment cannot be made after the death of the Prophet." Others claim the annulling factor is the Prophet's instructions to Mu'adh when he sent Mu'adh to Yemen. See *Radd al Muhtar*, Vol. 2, p. 83.

The fact is that all these attempts are fruitless. The verse from *sura al Kahf* is Makkan. It cannot annul a Madinan verse, which was revealed a long time after. Additionally, there is no contradiction between the two verses. The saying from Mu'adh is not an annulling factor; it mentions only the poor as recipients because the poor are the most important category. If this saying annuls one category, it must eliminate all the rest of them--why should it only eliminate the category of heart reconciliation? 'Ala' al Din bin 'Abd al Aziz, a Hanafite, says "The best way out is to assume that the Prophet's action was appropriate to his time, because strengthening the call of Islam could be served by payment to reconciling hearts. After his death, the same objective could be achieved without such payments." But Hanafites do not generally agree with the explanation of 'Ala' al Din, which is clear from the efforts of Ibn al Humam to negate 'Ala's opinion. See *Commentary al Alusi*, Vol. 3, p. 327.

29. *Al Mughni*, Vol. 2, p. 666.

30. *Hashiyat al Sawi* on *Bulghat al Salik*, Vol. 1, p. 232.

31. The author of *Majma' al Zawa'id* says it is "reported by Abu Ya'la; the men of its chain are among the men of the correct collections." Vol. 3, p. 104.

32. *Commentary al Tabari*, ed. Shakir, Vol. 14, p. 316.

33. Hanafites themselves say that if one attributes a ruling to certain reasons, and those reasons cease to exist, that is not sufficient proof to negate the ruling, since a ruling does not require the continuous presence of its reason, as in the case of slavery. Thus there is always need for proof to indicate that such a ruling is waived, even when its reason does not exist anymore. But they go on to argue that we need not specify the reason whenever *ijma'* exists. See *Radd al Muhtar*, Vol. 2, pp. 82-83.

34. In *Sharh al Azhar*, Vol. 1, p. 513, it is said that reconciling hearts is allowed if done by the state for the benefit of Muslims, but is not permissible to anyone else. Some Zaidis allow individual *zakah* payers to give toward heart reconciliation.

CHAPTER FOUR

LIBERATING SLAVES

Why the switch from "to" to "in"?

The verse listing categories of *zakah* recipients [9:60] counts eight categories, but mentions four of them using the preposition "to"--to the poor, to the needy, to the workers, to those whose hearts are being reconciled--and uses the preposition "in" with the other four categories--in freeing slaves, in (aid of) those under debt, in the way of God, in (aid of) the wayfarer. The Qur'an is perfect; not even a change of preposition is done in vain, so why is "to" [the Arabic "li"] used first and "in" [the Arabic "fi"] used later?

Al Zamakhshari says the use of the preposition "in" for the last four categories indicates they are more deservant of *zakah* than the first four, since "in" indicates a place inside which things are put, meaning that these last four categories are containers in which *sadaqat* should be put.[1] In al Intisar, Ibn al Munayyir comments on al Zamakhshari's note, "The other, more important, difference is that *zakah* is given to the first four categories in such a manner that they become its owners while *zakah* is not necessarily given to persons in the last four categories, but spent for their benefit. In other words, *zakah* is given to the master of the slave to gain the slave's freedom; it is also given for the sake of God, to the creditor of those under debt, or to help the wayfarer reach home."[2] Al Razi notes, similarly to Ibn al Munayyir, that "to" indicates ownership, while "in" cannotes the purpose of the spending. In summary, *zakah* is given to the first four categories, while it is given for, and not necessarily to the last four categories.[3] The same is stated in al Khazin's commentary.[4]

Rashid Rida,[5] followed by the late Mahmud Shaltut,[6] divides categories that deserve *zakah* into two kinds: individuals and interests. Individuals include the first four plus those under debt and the wayfarer, while interests include freeing, slaves and the sake of God. The author of *al Manar* uses the additive conjunction "and" before the word "those under debt" and "wayfarer," relating these two categories to the first four, since the preposition "in" is used immediately before "liberating slaves" and "sake of God." This non-sequential addition does not show proper respect for the eloquence of the Qur'an. It is better to take the additions in sequence, grouping the last four categories together, because they are preceded by the preposition "in" which is the choice of al Zamakhshari, Ibn al Munayyir, al Razi, and others. Ibn Qudamah supports the view of al Razi and his colleagues, saying Four categories receive *zakah* such that it becomes their property forever and they do not need to return it. The other four categories do not take *zakah* but to spend it for a pre-determined purpose, and if they do not spend it for that purpose, it can be taken back from them. The last four categories take *zakah* in order to use it toward fulfilling some objectives, while the first four categories are themselves objectives of *zakah*. For example, the purpose of *zakah* is fulfilled by giving the poor, thus making the poor rich. On the other hand, if a person in one of the last four categories ware given an amount of *zakah* for a purpose which can be achieved by spending a lesser amount, the reminder must be returned, except in the case of the fighter for the sake of God,"[7] (This lost exception does not apply to military equipment such as weapons and horses, which must be returned to the *zakah* fund.) This distinction made by Ibn Qudamah is undoubtedly correct. He could have supported it by quoting the change of preposition used in the Qur'an with the listed categories, as noted by the commentator of Ghayat al Muntaha.[8]

The meaning of "in liberating slaves"

Spending *zakah* in liberating slaves may take two forms:

1. This *zakah* can be used to help a contracted slave pay his master. A contracted slave (*al 'abd al mukatab*) is a slave who has an agreement with his master that upon paying the master an agreed upon amount, the slave gains freedom. God orders Muslims to contract slaves who desire liberating contracts. God also ordains Muslims to help slaves provide the contractual ransom to their masters. God says, "and if any of your slaves ask for a deed in writing [to enable them to earn their freedom for a certain sum] give them such a deed if ye know any good in them; yea, give them something yourselves out of the wealth which God has given you."[9] In other words, God also orders the masters to help slaves pay their contractual sum. In addition to this, God assigns a share of *zakah* for liberating slaves. Abu Hanifah, al Shafi'i, their disciples, and al Laith bin Sa'd, consider the verse of *zakah* a specific reference to contracted slaves. They present as evidence a report that Ibn 'Abbas interprets the verse " . . . and in liberating slaves," to mean contracted slaves. This is said to be supported by the last sentence of the above mentioned verse.[10]

2. The second way of liberating is to buy the slave with the proceeds of *zakah* and liberate him or her. This can be done by the state, a *zakah* payer, or a group of *zakah* payers together. This is the opinion of Malik, Ahmad, and Ibn Ishaq. Ibn al 'Arabi argues that this is apparent from the words of the Qur'an, because the word used translates as "necks" which, whenever used in reference to slaves in the Qur'an, means liberating them. If God meant the specific sub-category of contracted slaves, He would have mentioned it by its name. According to Ibn Al 'Arabi, the contracted slave may be given *zakah* as a person under debt and not under the title of liberating slaves, except by over-generalizing the term.[11]

Actually, the verse includes both meanings, However, it is said that Ibrahim al Nakha'i and Sa'id bin Jubair, both Followers, do not like purchasing slaves with *zakah* and then liberating them, since such an action benefits the liberator because of the concept known in Islamic jurisprudence as *al wala'* [mutual support] between the liberator and the liberated slave. *Wala'* between them means that if the liberated slave has no other heirs, his liberator may inherit his estate upon his death. Malik argues that since *zakah* is due for God's sake, the liberator must not gain any personal benefit. Thus, the person who liberates slaves from the proceeds of his own *zakah* should not be granted the *wala'* of the freed slave. This *wala'* belongs to all Muslims as represented by their state.[12]

Abu 'Ubaid reports that Ibn 'Abbas finds no error in a person liberating slaves with his own *zakah* and comments that Ibn Abbas is much more of an authority than al Nakha'i and Ibn Jubair, and his opinion is much preferred, especially since al Hasan, a Follower, and the majority of scholars agree with Ibn 'Abbas.[13] Abu 'Ubaid adds that even if the liberator may inherit ex-slave's estate as a result of *al wala* between them, he may also have to pay, for example, the ransom for a killing the liberated slave may commit, in application of the same principle of al wala.[14]

It should be realized that the difference in opinion applies only to the case where the individual *zakah* payer liberates slaves out of his or her *zakah*, but if the Islamic state takes that action, Muslims agree that the state can use any combination of the two forms of slave liberation mentioned above. Some scholars even prefer that the state use the two forms together, as suggested by al Zuhri when he wrote to 'Umar bin 'Abd al Aziz that "the share of liberating slaves is divided into two parts, half for Muslim contracted slaves and the other half for buying Muslim slaves and liberating them."[15] Of course, there is no reason for the restriction of dividing this share in half.

Islam preceeded other cultures in eliminating slavery

It should be noted that Islam was the first system to start a gradual mass elimination of slavery, by using several means together. Islam first dried up the sources of slavery by prohibiting the kidnapping and selling of free persons, legal slavery of debtors and criminals, or the enslaving of prisoners of wars waged for aggression or economic benefit. Only one source of slavery, morally-lawful war aimed at preventing aggression and oppression, was left intact.[16] Even in such a war, the Islamic state need not enslave prisoners of war. This is only an option left open in order to provide for treatment comparable to that which Muslim prisoners receive from the unbelievers. Qur'anic texts regarding prisoners of lawful wars do not even mention slavery as an option. The Qur'an says, "When ye have thoroughly subdued them, bind a bond firmly on them; thereafter is the time for either generosity or ransom."[17]

At the same time, Islam prescribes continuous means for liberating slaves. Islam urges freeing slaves, and makes it one expression of submission to God, as well as a compensation performed by persons seeking forgiveness for sins or errors, such as breaking fast in Ramadan or breaking an oath. Islam requires freeing slaves as compensation for beating him without right. Masters are ordered in the Qur'an to contract their slaves for freedom against an agreed upon sum, and the Muslim society is called upon to help contracted slaves financially and provide them with jobs so they earn the amount needed for their freedom. God says "And if any of your slaves ask for a deed in writing [to enable them to earn their freedom for a certain sum] give them such a deed if ye know any good in them; ye give them something yourselves out of the wealth which God has given you."[18] In addition, God makes liberation of slaves one of the eight objectives of *zakah*. The amount of *zakah* assigned for freeing slaves may be on one-eighth, or more or less, of this huge, continuous source of funds in the Muslim society.[19] This category may sometimes take most or all of the proceeds of *zakah*, if other groups of *zakah* recipients are satisfied, as happened in the time of 'Umar bin 'Abd al 'Aziz. Yahya bin Sa'id says, "'Umar bin 'Abd al Aziz sent me as an officer on the *zakah* of Africa. I collected it and searched for poor people to give it to, but found none. We searched for deservants to give *zakah* to, but found that 'Umar bin 'Abd al 'Aziz had made all people satisfied. Then I bought slaves and freed them with *zakah*."[20] If Muslims had the chance to fully implement their religion under a just and wise state for an extended period of time, slavery would have been wiped out from their lands long before it actually was.

Freeing Muslim prisoners of war with *zakah*

The share of *zakah* proceeds used to gain the freedom of Muslim slaves can include Muslim prisoners of war who have fallen in the hands of enemies of the Islamic state, according to Ahmad, on the grounds that both cases gain the freedom of Muslims.[21] Ibn al 'Arabi, a Malikite, says that scholars differ on whether this is permissible. Asbagh says it is not allowed, while Ibn Habib believes it is allowed. The latter argues that if *zakah* is otherwise going to be used to gains the freedom of a Muslim slave owned by another Muslim in a Muslim society, freeing Muslims from an oppressive unbelieving enemy, obviously takes priority.[22] There are many ongoing wars in the world today in which Muslims fall prisoner in the hands of non-Muslims; gaining their freedom becomes one of the objectives of *zakah*.

Helping peoples under colonialism with *zakah*

In the *commentary al Manar*, the late Rashid Rida says "liberating has its modern equivalent in liberating people from the humiliation and oppression of colonial power, which is mass liberation as compared to freeing individual slaves."[23] Shaikh Mahmud Shaltut emphasizes, ". . . I think we have today a form of slavery that is more dangerous to humanity. It is the enslavement of peoples ideas, wealth, and authority, depriving them of their freedom in their own land. The enslavement of an individual ends with the death of the person, but today entire nations and peoples are enslaved, generation after generation, in a continuous form of overwhelming oppression under ruthless power. This form of enslavement deserves extermination and deserves more efforts to liberate people from it, not only by using the proceeds of *zakah* and charity, but also by sacrificing all our wealth and ourselves. This must open our eyes to the tremendous responsibility of rich Muslims to help peoples of the Muslim nation."[23]

Although Rida and Shaltut correctly describe the unbearable oppression inflicted on colonized nations by aggressive powers, I do not agree on expanding the meaning of freeing slaves to such and extent, because words should not be so loosely applied. As for helping the oppressed peoples, we have great opportunity under the title of *zakah* spent "for the sake of God," in addition to all the resources of Muslim states and people that must contribute toward the liberation of Muslims and Muslim lands.

Footnotes

1. *Commentary al Kashshaf,* Vol. 2, pp. 45-46.

2. *Al Intisaf min al Kashshaf,* printed on the margins of the above commentary.

3. *Al Tafsir al Kabir*, by al Razi, Vol. 16, p. 112.

4. Quoted by al Jamal in his notes on the *Commentary al Jalalain*, Vol. 2, p. 292.

5. *Commentary al Manar*, Vol. 10, pp. 586-590.

6. *Al Islam, 'Aqidah wa Shari'ah*, pp. 111-113.

7. *Al Mughni,* Vol. 2, p. 760.

8. *Matalib Uli al Nuha,* Vol. 2, p. 151.

9. *Sura al Nur,* 24:33.

10. *Al Tafsir al Kabir*, Vol. 16, p. 112, see also *al Hidayah* and *Fath al Qadir*, Vol. 2, p. 17.

11. *Ahkam al Quran*, Vol. 2, p. 955.

12. *Al Amwal*, pp. 608-609.

13. *Ibid.*

14. *Ibid.*

15. *Ibid.*

16. 'Ali 'Abd al Wahid Wafi, *Huquq al Insan fi al Islam*, pp. 139-161, Awqaf Ministry print, Cairo.

17. *Sura al Qital,* 47:4.

18. *Sura al Nur,* 24:33.

19. This is in addition to raising the level of spiritual, moral, and material dignity of slaves, to the extent of making them like brothers to their masters. They should eat from the same food, wear the same quality clothes, and not be forced to work more than their capacity, in addition to the prohibition of injuring and beating them, or even using the word "slave" in addressing them.

20. Biography of 'Umar bin 'Abd al 'Aziz, by Ibn 'Abd al Hakam, p. 59.

21. *Al Rawd al Murbi'*, Vol. 1, p. 402.

22. *Ahkam al Qur'an*, Vol. 2, p. 956.

23. *Commentary al Manar*, Vol. 10, p. 598.

24. *Al Islam, Aqidah wa Shari'ah*, p. 446.

CHAPTAR FIVE

PERSONS UNDER DEBT

The sixth category of *zakah* deservants is persons under debt. According to the Hanafite school, this group includes all who do not own *nisab* above what is needed to pay their debts.[1] On the other hand, Malik, al Shafi'i, and Aamad distinguish between two kinds of debtors, those whose debts are for personal use and those whose debts are caused by their social and political responsibilities. This distinction implies differences in the ruling of those two categories, and each shall be discussed alone.

Those under debt for personal reasons

This subcategory is limited to individuals who are under debts used for personal reasons and do not have assets and income sufficient to rid them of their debt in addition to satisfying their essential needs. Debts may have been borrowed for consumer expenditures, including marriage, medical bills, building a house for personal residence, etc., and debt resulting from accrued liability toward others. Al Tabari reports from Abu Ja'far from Qatadah that the state must pay from the treasury debts of those who borrowed without extravagance, yet do not have enough funds to repay their creditors.[2]

Also in this group are those hit by natural disasters or accidents that destroy their assets and force them to borrow in order to continue fulfilling basic needs. Mujahid is reported to have said, "Three kinds are included in this sub-category: a person whose wealth is destroyed by flood, a person whose wealth is destroyed by fire, and a person with many dependents and no means, who borrows to support his family."[3] In the saying from Qubaisah bin al Mukharib, reported by Ahmad and Muslim, the Prophet (p) allowed a person hit by a catastrophe that wipes out his wealth, to ask the state for the *zakah* which is his right, until he procures sufficiency of sustenance.

Zakah is thus an insurance against the financial effects of catastrophes and accidents, an insurance which preceded all known forms of insurance by several hundred years. This insurance is of higher quality and comprehensiveness than modern forms of insurance in the West. Western insurance compensates only subscribers, with contractual amounts proportionate to the premium paid, which allows the wealthy to insure for higher sums, while the Islamic insurance of *zakah* compensates those affected by disaster, without requiring them to contribute premiums, and the amount of compensation is determined by the need of the affected persons, and not by their ability to pay premiums.

Conditions for giving *zakah* to this subcategory

Four conditions must be met before aid is given to those under personal debts:

1. The debtor must be in need of financial aid. Persons who own wealth sufficient to cover their debts may not be given from *zakah*.[4] Individuals who do not own sufficient wealth but can pay their debts from their earning may still be eligible for *zakah* on the grounds that repaying the loans from their income would take time. This condition does not imply that the debtor must be totally destitute. Scholars explicitly state that shelter, clothing, furniture, utensils, servants, and transportation if needed are not considered wealth from which loans must be paid. If the amount of debt is more than available wealth of the debtor, *zakah* may be given to pay the difference.

2. The debt must have stemmed from Islamically lawful activity, such as borrowing to support the family. Loans used for prohibited practices, such as consumption of alcoholic beverages, or extravagance in lawful items cannot be paid with *zakah*. Extravagance in lawful items is prohibited by the verse "O children of Adam, wear your beautiful apparel at every time and place of prayer; eat and drink, but waste no by excess, for God loves not the extravagant."[5] This condition is based on the principle that giving *zakah* to pay a debt caused by prohibited spending is like helping sinners and encouraging others to indulge in sin. If the debtor repents, he or she may be given *zakah*, since repentance washes out what preceded it. Some jurists add the condition that a period of time sufficient to confirm the sincerity of repentance must lapse before the repentant debtor can be given *zakah* to pay due debts caused by unlawful activity.

3. The debt must be due immediately. If the debt is deferred, scholars differ on whether the debtor may be given *zakah*. Some disapprove of this and others approve if the debt is due within one year. On the other hand, some scholars argue that debtors of deferred loans may be given *zakah* regardless of the due date of their loans, on the grounds that they are included in the general definition of individuals under debt.[6] I think any choice between these three opinions can only be made after knowing the total proceeds of *zakah* and the requirements of other categories of deservants. Then, depending on the residual, one can expand the coverage of deferred debts or restrict it.

4. The debt must be due to other humans. Obligations to God, such as due *zakah* and compensation for breaking certain conditions in *Shari'ah* [kaffarat] are excluded.[7] Malikites do not require this condition, while Hanafites include *zakah* itself among debts to God that can be paid from *zakah*.

How much can be given those under debt for personal reasons?

A person under debt is given an amount sufficient to rid him or her of debts. Since the *zakah* payment in this case is exclusively for the payment of debts, if any or all of the debts are fulfilled by other means (such as by volunteers) or discounted by the creditors, the portion of *zakah* not used for the satisfaction of debts must be returned to the *zakah* institution.

Digression: The noble position of Islam toward debtors

It is worthwhile to digress briefly and look at Islam's stance on debtors and borrowing:

A. Islam teaches Muslims moderation and economy in living and encourages them to avoid borrowing.

B. If circumstances force Muslims to borrow, they must do so after careful planning and with full intention of paying back the loan. The Prophet says, "As for the person who takes funds from others with the intention of returning them, God helps him fulfill his due, but as for the person who takes funds with the intention of consuming and destroying them, God will destroy him."[9]

C. If the debtor is unable to pay all or some of his debts in spite of evidence that shows his good intention, the state saves him from the burden and humiliation of debt. It is said that "debts are a source of depression in the night and humiliation in the day." The Prophet used to supplicate God, "O my Lord, I seek refuge in You from the burden of debt and from defeat by the enemy, and from giving enemies [the opportunity to] gloat."[10]

Debts are not only a source of anxiety and insecurity for the borrower, but they also affected the borrower's behavior and morality. The Prophet (p) often asked God for protection from being under debt. He was asked why he associated seeking refuge from debts with seeking protection from punishment in the grave, from the temptation of worldly life, and from the temptation of the false messiah. He answered,"Indeed, when a man is burdened by debt, if he speaks he lies and if he promises he breaks his promises."[11] The Prophet used several means to discourage his Companions from borrowing, even declining to pray at the funeral of a person who died leaving unfulfilled debts. Knowing how disgraced a person would be if the Prophet refused to pray at his funeral, one can realize the extensive effect of such discouragement.

When the Islamic state prospered, and the resources of its treasuries became manifold, the Prophet started paying the debts of Muslims from the state. Abu Hurairah narrates that the Messenger of God was often brought the coffin of a man who died in debt. The Prophet would ask, "Did he leave anything to pay his debts?" If the answer was yes, the Prophet would pray for the body, and if the answer was no, he would say, "Pray for your friend." Then, when God opened lands and their treasures for him, he said, "I am more responsible for believers than their own selves. He who dies leaving debts due on him, I take responsibility for their payment."[12] The Prophet (p) encouraged Muslims to help people under debt, in brotherhood, in obedience to God, and in aspiration of reward from God. Abu Sa'id al Khudri says, "A man at the time of the Messenger of God (p) suffered financial loss because of fruits he bought; his debts accumulated until he went bankrupt. The Messenger of God (p) said, "Give him charity . . ." people gave him charity, but that was not sufficient to pay all the man's debts. The Messenger of God (p) said to the man's creditors, "Take the present funds, and you have nothing more."[13]

The last and most important means of helping debtors is the share God prescribes for them in *zakah* funds. By this means, Islam frees debtors from the obligation and humiliation of their loans. The world has never known another system which includes in its very constitution the rights of debtors to financial aid. By paying these debts, *zakah* achieves two objectives: relieving those burdened by debts and providing guarantees to creditors, which helps all members of the community feel secure about extending loans to each other. In this way, Islam relieves those under debts without forcing them to liquidate essential assets needed for their living. 'Umar bin 'Abd al Aziz wrote his province governors to "pay the debts of those under debts." Some of his governors wrote back, "There are people who own shelters, servants, mares, and furniture, yet are under debt." 'Umar answered, "A Muslim needs a home to reside in, a servant to help in housekeeping, a mare to ride in war, and furniture in his house. Yes, pay the debts of such people."[14] This system of justice and mercy that came from God fourteen centuries ago is incomparable to man-made systems and modern bankruptcy laws. In the Roman canon, if a debtor is unable to pay his debts, he must be enslaved if free and imprisoned or killed if already a slave.[15] In pre-Islamic Arabia, debtors who could not pay their debts were sold to the benefit of the creditor.[16] God says, "If the debtor is in difficulty, grant him time till it is easy for him to repay. But if ye remit the debt by way of charity, that is best for you, if ye only knew."[17]

Those under debts for social purposes

This category includes benevolent persons of stature who undertake activities for the public interest, such as reconciliation of disputes among groups and individuals, often by paying compensation and ransom from their own assets. They may also undertake projects of public benefit, such as building orphanages, mosques, hospitals for the poor, or schools for children, which may put them in debt. Persons of this kind are helped to pay their debts with *zakah*.[18] According to some Shafi'ites, such individuals should be paid what satisfies their debts, even if they are rich.[19] Qubaisah bin al Mukhariq al Hilali says, "I accepted a financial responsibility [to reconcile two disputing groups] and I went to the Messenger of God (P) to ask for help. He said, "Stay here until [the proceeds of] *zakah* come, so we can give you from it." The Prophet Continued, "O Qubaisah, asking is not permissible except for three persons: One who accepts financial responsibility [for reconciling people] may lawfully ask until that financial charge is satisfied. Then he must not seek any more help. One who is struck by disaster that wipes out his wealth may lawfully ask until he reaches a satisfactory level of sustenance, and one hit by poverty such that three wise clansmen confirm that he is struck by poverty may ask until he procures sufficiency of sustenance. O Qubaisah, any asking beyond that is evil. It is eaten by the person who accepts it as evil."[20]

This saying indicates that a person who accepts financial responsibility in the process of reconciling differences among other people can ask for *zakah* to help discharge that responsibility, even if that person were rich, because the condition of sufficiency of sustenance does not apply.[21]

Paying the debts of deceased persons from *zakah*

Al Nawawi says there are two opposing views among Shafi'ites about this. Some believe it is not permissible to pay the debts of deceased persons from *zakah*. This view is consistent with the opinion of al Nakha'i, Abu Hanifah, and Ahmad. The other opinion is to allow this action, on the basis of the general implication of the pertinent verse. This is also the view of Abu Thawr.[22] It is reported that Ahmad argues that *zakah* payment for the debts of the deceased cannot be made because such payment must be made to the debtor himself and the debtor in this case is dead.[23] Al Khirashi, in his commentary on the text of Khalil, says "It makes no difference whether the debtor is dead or alive. The sate must pay the debts from *zakah*. Some jurists even argue that debts of deceased persons have priority over those of living persons, since the latter may be able to pay in the future."[24] Al Qurtubi remarks,[25] "Scholars of our school as well as other schools think the debts of deceased persons may be paid from *zakah*, since as a debtor, he is included in the term "those under debt"; especially since the Prophet (p) said, "I am more responsible for every believer than his own self; he who leaves wealth, it is for his family, but he who leaves behind debts or dependents, they are my responsibility."[26] This is also the view of the Ja'fari school.[27]

In my opinion, the texts and spirit of Shari'ah do not prevent the payment of a deceased person's debts from *zakah*. This is supported by the fact that God, in the verse about *zakah* deservants, distinguishes between two kinds of categories. The first are deservants to whom *zakah* is paid such that they became owners of what they receive while *zakah* is not necessarily paid to the second group, but on their behalf. Those under debts are of the second kind, so it must be permissible to pay the debts of deceased persons from *zakah*. This is the opinion approved by Ibn Taimiyah.[28] It is supported by the above saying.

Giving loans from *zakah*

I think there is a sound analogy between borrowers and those under debt. This analogy allows giving loans from *zakah*, which is consistent with the broad objectives of *zakah*. Persons who need loans can be given *zakah* under the title of those under debt. In this way, *zakah* can contribute practically to the elimination of interest. This is the view which the late Abu Zahrah, Khallaf and Hasan express in their study of *zakah*.[29] They argue that if fair debts can be paid from *zakah*, why not, even by priority, give interest-free loans from *zakah*? Muhammad Hameedullah of Hyderabad expresses a similar opinion in his study entitled Banking Without Interest.[30] He supports his opinion by stating that individuals under debt are of two kinds: those who cannot pay back already-used debts, and those who need loans which they can pay back in the future.[31] Thus Hameedullah considers persons who need loans as persons under debt, but one may argue that persons who need loans are obviously not under debt before they receive the loan. Consequently the argument of Abu Zahrah and his colleagues is stronger.

Footnotes

1. *AL Bahr al Ra'iq*, Vol. 2, p. 260, and *Radd al Muhtar*, Vol. 2, p. 63.

2. *Commentary of al Tabari*, Vol. 14, p. 338.

3. *Ibid*, and *Musannaf Ibn Abi Shaibah*, Vol. 3, p. 207.

4. In another opinion attributed to al Shafi'i, persons under debts may be given even if they are rich. See *al Majmu'*, Vol. 6, p. 207, and *Nihayat al Muhtaj*, Vol. 6, p. 155.

5. *Sura al A'raf*, 7:31.

6. For this condition, see *al Majmu'*, Vol. 6, pp. 207-209, *Nihayat al Muhtaj*, Vol. 6, pp. 154-155, and *Hashiyat al Khirashi on Khalil*, Vol. 2, p 218.

7. *Hashiyat al Sawi*, Vol. 1, p. 233.

8. *Al Majmu'*, Vol. 6, p. 209.

9. Reported by al Bukhari, Ahmad, and Ibn Majah from Abu Hurairah. See *Kanz al 'Ummal*, Vol. 6, p. 114.

10. In *Bulugh al Maram*, p. 313, al Hafiz says, "reported by al Nasa'i and graded good by al Hakim as from 'Abd Allah bin 'Umar, extended to the Prophet.

11. Reported in al Bukhari's chapter on borrowing, section on seeking protection from debt.

12. Agreed upon, See *Bulugh al Maram*, p. 180, and *Kanz al 'Ummal*, Vol. 6, pp. 118-122.

13. *Bulugh al Maram*, p. 117, section on bankruptcy and restrictions.

14. *Al Amwal*, p. 556.

15. As mentioned in *Ruh al Din al Islami*, p. 328.

16. *Commentary al Qurtubi*, Vol. 3, p. 271.

17. *Sura al Baqarah*, 2:80.

18. *Al Rawd al Murbi'*, Vol. 1, p. 402.

19. Some Shafi'ites believe a person who borrows for ransoming a prisoner of war, building a structure for public benefit, or serving guests, can be given *zakah* if he is rich, in the sense of owning real estate and not money. See *al Rawdah*, Vol. 2, p. 319. Al Ramli comments, "Even if those whose wealth is money are also included, that could not be unreasonable, in recognition of their benevolince." See *Nihayat al Muhtaj*, Vol. 6, p. 155.

20. Reported by Ahmad, Muslim, al Nasa'i and Abu Daud,. See *Nail al Awtar*, Vol. 4, p. 168.

21. *Commentary al Qurtubi*, Vol. 8, p.184.

22. *Al Majmu'*, Vol. 6, p. 211.

23. *Al Mughni*, Vol. 2, p. 667.

24. *Hashiyat al Khirashi,* and the notes of al 'Adawi on it, Vol. 2, p. 218.

25. *Commentary al Qurtubi*, Vol. 8, p. 185.

26. Agreed upon.

27. *Fiqh al Imam Ja'far*, Vol. 2, pp. 91-92.

28. *Fatawa Ibn Taimiyah*, Vol. 1, p, 299.

29. *Halqat al Dirasat al Ijtima'iyah*, p. 254.

30. Published by Maktabat al Manar, Kuwait, in its series towards a sound Islamic economy, no. 2.

31. *Ibid*, pp. 8-9.

CHAPTER SIX

FOR THE SAKE OF GOD

The seventh category of *zakah* distribution is expressed in the Qur'an as "*fi sabil Allah*" [in the way of God]. To whom is this share of *zakah* paid? The linguistic meaning of the term is quite obvious. "*Sabil*" means way, and "*sabil Allah*" is the way that leads to pleasing God. Ibn al Athir says ". . . 'sabil Allah' is general enough to cover every action or deed sincerely intended for the sake of God, including fulfilling religious obligations and voluntary worships and deeds. When the term '*fi sabil Allah*' is not modified, it usually means *jihad* [fighting for the sake of God], so the term often appears to be restricted to the meaning of jihad." This analysis of the term '*fi sabil Allah*' by Ibn al Athir shows two important points:

1. The term originally means every action intended solely to serve the cause of God, including all good deeds, individual and collective.

2. Unmodified, the term is commonly understood to mean fighting for the sake of God, since frequent usage almost restricts the meaning to fighting for the sake of God.

These two meanings of the term tell a whole story of differences among jurists on this seventh category of *zakah* distribution. Obviously, all agree that fighting for the sake of God is included in this category; their differences center on whether this category may also cover other good deeds intended to please God. The following discussion describes the opinions of jurists on this matter.

The Hanafite view

According to Abu Yusuf, the category of *fi sabil Allah* includes fighters who do not have sufficient funds for rides and expenses in such a way that impedes them from fighting. *Sadaqah* is lawful to them even if they are able to earn income, since working would deter them from fighting. Muhammad understands the term to include those who want to perform pilgrimage but cannot do so for lack of money. He presents as evidence a report that a man who devoted his camel in the way of God (*fi sabil Allah*) was ordered by the Messenger of God (p) to carry pilgrims on it. Additionally, pilgrimage is for the sake of God, as it is an obedience to his ordinances.

Some Hanafites argue that this category includes full-time students. The author of *al Fatawa al Zahiriyyah* mentions only this category in his interpretation of the term *fi sabil Allah*. Others reject this interpretation on the grounds that when the verse was revealed, the concept of full-time students did not exist. Others reply that studying full time can mean acquiring knowledge of *Shari'ah*, as practiced full-time by those Companions who accompanied the Prophet (p) to receive knowledge from him in Madinah, known as the people of *al Suffah* [the name of the place in front of the Prophet's mosque in Madinah where these people used to live in tents]. In *al Bada'i'*, al Kasani says all those who do deeds of obedience to God and promote good actions can be helped as *fi sabil Allah*, following the original linguistic meaning of the term. Ibn Nujaim in *al Bahr* comments, "It is obvious that the condition of poverty is necessary in all cases,"[2] but Rashid Rida argues that such a restriction eliminates the whole category of in the way of God as a separate group of recipients, since the first category covers all poor persons.[3,4]

In conclusion, jurists of the Hanafite school agree on the necessity of poverty as a condition in all their interpretations of "for the sake of God" but it is argued that their interpretations are merely semantic exercises, in view of this condition, since it means that all persons in this category can be given as poor, except those who can earn. The Hanafites thus add nothing, because the poor and needy get their share of *zakah* regardless of whether they can be qualified as in the way of God or not. The question remains, why does God make "in the way of God" a category of its own?

It must be noted that all Hanafites agree that *zakah* must become the owned property of its necessarily human recipients--it cannot be spent to build mosques, parks, dams, irrigation projects, roads, and highways or for pilgrimage or even *jihad*, because all these do not fulfill the condition that recipients become owners of *zakah*.[5]

The Malikite view

In *Ahkam al Qur'an*, Ibn al 'Arabi quotes Malik's remark, "The ways of God are manifold, but I know of no disagreement that what is meant by *fi sabil Allah* here is fighting, as distinct from other ways of God," Muhammad bin 'Abd al Hakam's says "From *sadaqah,* the value of food, arms, and other tools of war [of the fighters] can be paid. This includes preventing enemies from invading Muslim lands, since all these are actions related to fighting for the sake of God. The Prophet (p) gave one hundred camels from *sadaqah* in reconciliation after the attack against Sahl bin Abi Khathamah. He did so in order to prevent a major violent disturbance."[6]

The author of *Sharh al Dardir* on *Matn Khalil* writes, "*Zakah* can be given to fighters and border guards, and to buy war machinery, such as weapons and horses. Fighters may take *zakah* even if they are rich, since they are given because they are fighting for the sake of God and not because of poverty. Spies can also be given *zakah*, even if they are unbelievers."[7]

The Malikite view can be summarized as follows:

1. They agree that "in the way of God" is restricted to fighting and guarding Muslim land.

2. They approve of giving fighters and border guards even if rich. The Malikite view seems closer to the apparent meaning of the Qur'anic text, which distinguishes between "the sake of God" as a category and the poor as another category. It is also closer to Sunnah, because the Prophet says, "The *sadaqah* is not lawful to any rich person except in five cases. . . ," and he mentions the fighter for the sake of God. Ibn al 'Arabi disregards the condition of poverty, saying this is an addition to the text, and according to the Hanafites themselves, an addition to a text is modification or annulment of the original text, which can only be done by another text from the Qur'an.[8]

3. The majority of the Malikites allow general spending for military purposes, such as buying arms and horses, and building barracks and military ships.

In fact is that the Malikite opinion is more in harmony with Qur'anic expression, which uses the preposition "in" instead of "to" when introducing this category. Qur'anic expression apparently indicates that spending must be in the interest of fighting, not necessarily to the fighters.

The Shaifi'ite view

Along with al Nawawi in *al Minhaj* and Ibn Hajar al Haithami in his commentary on the same, Shafi'ites believe "in the way of God" includes voluntary fighters who do not receive salaries from the government. To use Ibn Hajar's words, "volunteer fighters fight without salaries when motivated, and otherwise they work in businesses and crafts." He adds, "*Sabil Allah* linguistically means the way that leads to Him. It is often used to mean fighting for His cause, which may mean martyrdom that leads to pleasing God. Then the term was applied to those who fight without compensation, since they sacrifice more than salaried soldiers and deserve to be given what helps them undertake this duty, even if they are rich."[9]

Al Shafi'i in *al Umm* says, "Neighbors of the area where *zakah* is collected who fight can be given the share for the sake of God whether they are poor or rich. People other than fighters must not be given this share unless they defend or guard the fighters. *Zakah* may be given to those who prevent disbelievers from attacking them."[10] His condition that only neighbors can be given is based on his principle that *zakah* must not be transferred from one area to another. In *al Rawdah*, al Nawawi says, "Fighters can be given their expenses and clothing for the period from the time they leave to fight until the time they come back, even if they stay at border points for a long period. Two opinions exist about paying all his expenses or only increments caused by traveling to war. The fighter may also be given money to buy a mare, weapons, and other tools of war. What he buys becomes his permanently. However, it is permissible to lease the ride and weapons from someone else and supply them to the fighters; this depends on the availability of funds. Fighters who do not know how to fight riding should not be given the value of a mare." Al Nawavi adds, "In some commentaries on *al Miftah,* it is stated that the fighter may be given his expenses as well as the expenses of his family during all the period he is absent. Most scholars do not mention the expenses of the family, but it sounds reasonable. The state may give the fighter's ride and arms to him permanently, rent or lease them for the fighters, or buy and keep them in trust [*waqf*] which after the end of the war would be returned to the state to be used by other fighters.[11]

Shafi'ites discuss whether regular salaried soldiers can be given this *zakah* if the state's resources are insufficient to pay its enlisted army, and there is need to defend Muslims against outside aggression. According to al Nawawi, the correct answer is negative, since financing those payments is obligated on the rich in addition to *zakah.*[12] The question remains, what if rich Muslims do not have sufficient surplus wealth to pay the regular army? Ibn Hajar feels it is permissible to pay them *zakah.*[13]

It is remarkable that Shafi'ites agree with Malikites on restricting this category to fighting and fighters, giving even rich fighters, and spending on the necessities of the fighters, such as weaponry and equipment. They differ only in that Shafi'ites require that fighters be unsalaried volunteers in order to deserve such payment and restrict this share to one-eighth of the total proceeds of *zakah.* This is based on the opinion of al Shafi'i that the eight categories of deservants must have equal shares, which will be discussed in the next chapter.

The Hanbalite view

Like Shafi'ites, Hanbalites restrict the term *fi sabil Allah* to volunteer fighters who receive no regular salaries, or who receive less than what is sufficient for them, even if they are rich. Border guards are included with fighters. It is stated in *Ghayat al Muntaha* and its commentary that the state may buy horses with *zakah* and give them to the fighters, even if the fighter is a *zakah* payer. It is permissible to buy warships, as well as all other equipment, as decided by the state. On the other hand, an individual *zakah* payer has no authority to buy a horse and devote it to fighting for the sake of God, because individual *zakah* payers are required to pay *zakah* and this is not payment.[13]

There are two reports from Ahmad concerning pilgrimage. The first is that pilgrimage is included in this category. A poor person may be given *zakah* to perform obligatory pilgrimage, based on a saying from Umm Ma'qil al Asdiyyah. Her husband had devoted a camel for the sake of God, and she planned to make *'Umrah* [visiting the Grand Mosque in Makkah for a ritual other than pilgrimage]. When she asked to use the camel, her husband refused. She mentioned this to the Prophet. The Prophet (p) ordered him to let her use the camel, saying, "Pilgrimage and *'Umrah* are for the sake of God."[15] This is reported from Ibn Abbas and Ibn 'Umar. It is also the opinion of Ishaq. The second report from Ahmad is that pilgrimage must not be paid for with *zakah.* This is consistent with the opinion of the majority. In *al Mughni,* Ibn Qudamah states "this is better, because the term 'for the sake of God,' when not qualified, applies only to *jihad* (fighting for God's cause) . Most use of the term *'fi sabil Allah'* in the Qur'an is intended to mean *jihad,* so the verse about *zakah* must be understood likewise. The fact is that *zakah* can be expended on two kinds of people: those who need *zakah,* such as the poor and needy or debtors, and those who are needed by Muslims, such as fighters, people whose hearts are being reconciled, and people under debts because of mediation between disputing groups. Pilgrimage of the poor fits in neither group. It is not in the public interests of Muslims, nor do the poor need it, because poor persons are not obligated to perform pilgrimage. God makes having sufficient financial means a condition for the obligation of pilgrimage. Preferably, such help must not be given to the poor from *zakah,* but saved to be used for the public benefit of Muslims.[16]

The saying from Umm Ma'qil is disputed because of weakness in its chain of narrators. Granted it were correct, some Shafi'ites reply that pilgrimage is for the sake of God, no doubt, but nevertheless the term *fi sabil Allah* in the verse on *zakah* distribution means only fighting, because the Prophet's saying, *"Sadaqah is not lawful to the rich, except one of five cases . . . ,"* mentions the fighter for the sake of God. Moreover, the use of the saying from Umm Ma'qil is irrelevant, since the camel was devoted for God's sake but not necessarily to fighting for God's sake. "For God's sake" here may include carrying persons to pilgrimage or giving rides to those who need rides without granting them ownership of the camel, while *zakah* requires transfer of ownership.[17]

Points of agreement of the four schools

The four schools agree on three points:

1. *Jihad* (fighting for God's sake) is definitely included in the category *"fi sabil Allah."*

2. It is lawful to give the fighters *zakah.* Spending *zakah* on equipment and arms is not agreed upon.

3. It is not permissible to spend *zakah* on public interests or general good deeds such as irrigation canals, dams, mosques, schools, roads, and highways, etc. These must be paid for from other state funds, such as *fai'* and *kharaj.* Hanafites do not allow this on the grounds that the recipients must own what is paid them, while others do not allow it on the grounds that such spending is not included in the eight categories. As for al Kasani's above-quoted statement, it is restricted by his condition that *zakah* must be made owned by the recipient.

Abu Hanifah alone requires that the fighters be poor in order to be given *zakah,* and Ahmad alone allows payment to pilgrims and visitors of the Sacred Mosque in Makkah. Shafi'ites and Hanbalites share the condition that fighters be volunteers, while all but the Hanafites agree on spending *zakah* on equipment, arms, and other necessities of *jihad.*

Those who expand the meaning of "for the sake of God"

Some scholars, early and contemporary, tend to expand the meaning of the term "for the sake of God," to include good deeds in general, in accordance with the original indication of the term. Al Razi in his commentary on the Qur'an remarks that the apparent meaning of the term *fi sabil Allah* is not restricted to fighters. He adds, "For this reason, al Qaffal's explanation of the verse mentions that some jurists allow spending *sadaqat* on all kinds of good deeds, including supplying coffins for the deceased and building fortifications and mosques, since 'in the way of God' covers all these."[18] But al Razi does not name these jurists, and makes no comment on his quote from al Qaffal.

Ibn Qudamah attributes this opinion to Anas bin Malik and al Hasan al Basri, who say "*Zakah* given on bridges and highways is acceptable."[19] He concludes that this statement allows expending *zakah* on building and repairing bridges and roads, but Abu 'Ubaid's elucidation of the context of this statement gives it a different meaning. He explains that Muslim merchants used to pass through the *'ushr* officers' booth on bridges and highways to pay dues on merchandise brought in the country (25% percent of the value of the merchandise). Abu 'Ubaid reports that some Followers, including Ibrahim and al Sha'bi say it is permissible to count what is paid to those tax officers as obligated *zakah*. This is explicitly attributed to al Hasan, who, Abu 'Ubaid argues, agrees with Anas, Ibrahim, al Shaibah, and Muhammad bin 'Ali.[20] A similar story is reported by Ibn Abi Shaibah from Anas and al Hasan, under the title of "counting what is paid to *'ushr* officers as *zakah*."[21] Ibn Qudamah's understanding of the statement by Anas and al Hasan is thus incorrect, since "given on bridges" means paid at bridges and not spent on bridge construction and repair.

The Ja'fari view

The book *al Mukhtasar al Nafi'* explains that "in the way of God" includes everything that benefits Muslims or brings them closer to God, such as pilgrimage, fighting, and building irrigation systems. Some Ja'farites say it only relates to *jihld*.[22] The author of *Jawahir al Kalam fi Sharh Shara'i' al Islam*, a Ja'fari encyclopedia of jurisprudence, states that public interests such as irrigation, mosques, pilgrimage, and all good deeds are included under "in the way of God". He adds, "This is the view of the majority of later scholars, supported by the implication of the term itself, since '*sabil*' is way, and the way of God includes everything that pleases God, whether fighting for His cause or other things."[23]

The Zaidi view

It is mentioned in *al Rawd al Nadir*, a book of Zaidi jurisprudence, that *zakah* must not be spent on buying coffins for the deceased or building mosques. Zaidis who allow this argue that such good deeds are included in 'the way of God', and although the term is often used for fighting, especially in the early eras of Islam, this popular usage must not restrict the original meaning of the term. All that brings a person closer to God must be included, except when the term is restricted by qualifiers. The author of *al Bahr* agrees that the term is clearly general, except when restricted by specific evidence.[24]

The author of *Sharh al Azhar* partially agrees, saying it is permissible to spend the residue of this share on the public interest of Muslims, as stated by al Hadi. Abu Talib emphasizes, "This can be done only after satisfying the needs of the poor." Some commentators on *Sharh al Azhar* purpose that not only this share's residue be spent for the general interest of Muslims, but also what is left from the other seven categories.[25]

The opinion of Siddiq Hasan Khan

In *al Rawdah al Nadiyyah*, Siddiq Hasan Khan, a follower of *ahl al hadith* with an independent mind, says, "*Sabil Allah* means the way to Him. No doubt the greatest way to God is fighting for His sake, but there is no proof that this share of *zakah* is restricted to this meaning alone. It is permissible to spend on any way to God. Since this is the linguistic meaning of the term, we must stick to it, unless we have evidence to the contrary." He continues, "among the ways to God is supporting scholars who achieve public and religious interests for the sake of God, whether they are rich or poor. This is especially important, because scholars are the heirs of the prophets and the torchbearers of religion. Through them this religion of Islam is preserved."[26]

Contemporary opinions

In his commentary on the Qur'an, the late Jamal al Din al Qasimi quotes without comment al Razi's statement that the apparent meaning of the term is not restricted to fighters, the statement attributed by al Qaffal to some jurists, and a statement from *al Taj*, that every way intended for God which is good in itself is included under "for the sake of God."[27]

Rashid Rida, in *al Manar*, says: The truth is that the sake of God includes all public interests of Muslims necessary for the establishment of religion and state, not including individual interests. Thus pilgrimage is not included because it is an individual obligation required from those who can afford it, but the general establishment of the pillar of pilgrimage is included. Spending *zakah* on building highways for pilgrimage and providing pilgrims with water and health services are included if there are no better uses in the way of God."[28] He continues, "The sake of God covers all legitimate public interests by which religion and state are maintained. No doubt fighting and buying weapons and spending on soldiers top this list. Fighting that is meant here is that which is done in order to make God's word supreme on earth. A similar view is reported from Muhammad bin 'Abd al Hakam, who includes in this share of *zakah* building military and charitable hospitals, roads and armies, non-commercial railroads, military airports, fortifications, and military ships. Also included are expenses of training and travelling for speakers, writers, and the like who go to the lands of unbelievers to inform them about Islam and spread the word of God. God says 'let there be among you a group that calls for good . . . .'[29,30]

Mahmud Shaltut interprets *fi sabil Allah* "to mean also the public interests that are not individually owned, but owned by God for the benefit of his creatures. The first of these is military preparation through which Muslims can prevent aggression and preserve the integrity of their society. This includes funding research and building roads, hospitals, and military equipment, in addition to sending Muslims to unveil the beauty of Islam to unbelievers. It also includes supporting those who preserve and memorize the Qur'an, for through them God keeps this glorious Book intact until the Day of Judgement."[31] Shaltut responded to a question about building mosques, "If the mosque to be built is the only one in the village or if the existing mosque is not sufficient for all the people of the village, it is permissible in *Shari'ah* to spend *zakah* for building and repairing mosques. Building the mosque in this case is included under 'for the sake of God' in the verse on *zakah* distribution. It is necessary, however, to mention that this issue is disputed among scholars, but what I feel comfortable with and give my religious opinion about is what is cited above, if the mosque cannot be done without."[32]

Sheikh Hasanain Makhluf answered affirmatively a question on the payment of *zakah* to charitable Islamic organizations, based on al Qaffal's and other scholars' interpretation of *fi sabil Allah*.[33]

Analysis and weighing

Those who expand the meaning of "in the way of God" depend on the original linguistic meaning of the term, while those who restrict the meaning to fighting for God's cause (who are the majority of scholars from the four schools of jurisprudence) depend on two points: that *zakah* must be made owned by the recipient,[34] and that public interest projects are not one of the eight categories. The verse is exclusive because it begins, "The *sadaqat* are only for . . ." as is the saying, "Indeed, God gives His ruling on *zakah*, and divides it into eight parts. . . ." This is presented as argument by Ibn Qudamah in al Mughni.[35]

As for the first point, the preposition used with the category of the sake of God is "in" [*fi*], which dose not imply ownership. Based on this distinction, scholars say it is permissible to buy and free slaves or pay debts of the deceased from *zakah*, although *zakah* paid in these cases is not owned by the recipients. Moreover, the requirement of making *zakah* owned by the recipients is fulfilled when *zakah* is paid to the government's *zakah* agency. Once received by the state, it can be spent at the state's discretion.

As for the second point, the restriction of the expenditure of *zakah* proceeds to the eight categories cannot convince those who expand the meaning of 'for the sake of God', because they always argue that things like building mosques are included in the share of *fi sabil Allah*. It is necessary to determine whether this category is restricted to fighting and defending Muslim or covers other public interests too. To do this, we must survey the use of this term in the Qur'an.

The term 'sabil Allah' in Qur'an

The term '*sabil Allah*' appears in the Qur'an more than sixty times,[36] in either of two ways: more frequently preceded by the preposition "in" [*fi*] as in the verse on *zakah* distribution, and twenty-three times preceded by the preposition "from" [*'an*]. In those twenty-three places the term is preceded by one of two verbs that mean to prevent or mislead, such as "Those who reject faith and keep off (people) from the way of God have verily strayed far, far away from the path," "The unbelievers spend their wealth to hinder (people) from the path of God . . ." and "But there are among people those who purchase idle tales, without knowledge (or meaning) to mislead (people) from the Path of God." When the term *sabil Allah* is preceded by. "in", as in the verses "Spend in the way of God," and those who migrate in the way of God," "fighting in the way of God," "those who fight in the way of God," they kill and they are killed," and "and do not say about those killed in the way of God 'they are dead,'" how should the term be interpreted?

The word *sabil* is "way" and "*sabil Allah*" is the path that seeks the nearness and pleasure of God. God sent prophets to guide His creatures to Him, and ordained the last of His messengers to "call for the way of thy Lord with wisdom and kind preaching," and ordered His Messenger to "Say: This is my Way; I do invite unto God on evidence clear as sight itself--I and whoever follows me ." Opposition to the way of God is the way of the *taghut* or evil transgression, which is called for by Satan and his followers, and which ends at the Fire and earns the wrath of God. Comparing these two ways, God says, "Those who believe fight in the cause of God, and those who reject faith fight in the cause of evil." Those who call to the way of God are few, those who prevent people from it many: "They spend their wealth in order to prevent (people) from the way of God," "and there are people who buy vain talk in order to divert from the way of God," "and if you obey most of those who are on earth, they would divert you from the way of God. The responsibilities and demands of the way of' God are sizable, and worldly desires of people usually stand against it. The Qur'an warns against pursuing these desires: "and do not follow your whims, because that indeed shall take you astray from the way of God." If enemies of God expend money and effort to prevent people from the way of God, it is the duty of the supporters of God's cause to sacrifice effort and wealth in the way of God. This is why Islam devotes part of obligatory *zakah* to this cause, in addition to the general encouragement of believers to spend for the sake of God.

The term "*sabil Allah*" associated with spending

The term "*sabil Allah*," when associated in the Qur'an with spending, is used in two ways:

1. The general meaning, derived from the original linguistic one, covers all virtues and good deeds, as in the verses, "The parable of those who spend their substance in the way of God is that of a grain of corn: it groweth seven ears, and each ear hath a hundred grains. God giveth manifold increase to whom He pleases," "Those who spend their substance in the cause of God, and follow not up their gifts with reminders of their generosity or with injury, their reward is with their Lord. On them shall be no fear, nor shall they grieve." No one can claim that "*sabil Allah*" is restricted to fighting for God's cause in these verses. Condescension and insult to the recipient mentioned in the verse can only be done toward the poor and needy. "*Sabil Allah*" has a broad meaning in the

verse, "and those who hoard in treasures gold and silver, and spend it not in the way of God, promise them severe punishment," as stated by Ibn Hajar, and is not restricted to fighting. Otherwise, giving wealth to the poor, needy, and wayfarer would be a form of hoarding.[37] Some contemporary writers claim that "*sabil Allah*," when associated with spending, is restricted to fighting,[38] but such a claim is unsupported by evidence.

2. The second meaning restricts *"sabil Allah"* to supporting the religion of God, fighting its enemies, and raising high the word of God on earth. The context within which the term is used determines whether it refers to the broad or restricted meaning. When the term is used in association with the idea of fighting for God's sake, it must also mean spending for His cause, as in, "And spend of your substance in the way of God and make not your own hands contribute to your destruction,"[39] "Spending" here refers to rasing high the word of God by fighting the enemies of Islam, because fighting in the way of God is mentioned in the verse before it. Other examples are the verses, "And what cause have ye why ye should not spend in the way of God? for to God belongs the heritage of the heavens and the earth. Not equal among you are those who spent (freely) and fought before the victory (with those who did so later); those are higher in rank than those who spent (freely) and fought afterward, but to all God has promised a goodly (reward),"[40] and "against them make ready your strength to the utmost of your power, including steeds of war to strike terror into (the hearts of) the enemies of God and your enemies and others besides , whom ye may not know. Whatever ye shall spend in the cause of God shall be repaid unto you and ye shall not be treated unjustly."[41]

It is obvious that."in the way of God" refers to fighting the enemies of God, as elucidated by the correct saying, "He who fights to make the word of God supreme is fighting for the sake of God".[42] This specific meaning is what is usually called *jihad*, but it must be noted that support of the cause of God includes more than fighting, especially when the term used is "make *jihad* in the way of God."

Which meaning applies to the *zakah* distribution verse?

In my opinion, the general meaning is not suitable to this verse, since the verse lists specific deservants of *zakah*, as confirmed by the saying of the Prophet (p), "Indeed, God does not accept the ruling of a prophet, or anybody else on [the distribution of] *sadaqat* so he Himself gave His ruling, and divided it into eight parts." Moreover, the general meaning of "*sabil Allah*" includes in fact the other seven categories. Why then does God ennumerate the other seven? The glorious words of God are void of useless repetition or redundancy. There must be a distinct meaning for the category of "in the way of God." Therefore, Muslim jurists and Qur'an commentators have for centuries understood this term to means *jihad* (fighting for His cause), as well as supporting fighting. Scholars state, Whenever the term "*sabil Allah*" is left unrestricted, it means fighting for God's sake." Ibn al Athir says, "The term became specific to *jihad* as a result of frequent use." This understanding is supported by a report of al Tabarani that one day, some Companions were with the Messenger of God and saw a strong young man. They said, "We hope this youth and strength are used in the way of God,"[43] meaning in *jihad*.

Several correct sayings from the Prophet and his Companions indicate that the immediate meaning of the term "*sabil Allah*" is *jihad*. Among these are the correct report that 'Umar said, "I gave a mare in the way of God," meaning for *jihad*; the saying reported by al Bukhari and Muslim that "A departure in the morning or a return in the evening in the way of God is better than the world and what is in it," the saying reported by al Bukhari that "He who gives a mare in the way of God out of faith in Him and belief in His promise, will have the eating, drinking, excretion, and urination of the mare add [weight] to his scale [of good deed] on the Day of Judgement;" the saying reported by al Nasa'i and al Tirmidhi that, "He who spends an amount in the way of God, it is recorded for him seven hundred-fold," and the saying reported by al Bukhari, "He whose feet are dirtied in the way of God will never be touched by the Fire."[44] No one understands "*sabil Allah*" in those quotations to mean anything but *jihad*.

Above all, the interpretation of "*sabil Allah*" to mean fighting is supported by the saying that *zakah* is not lawful to the rich except in five cases, among them being the fighter in the way of God. Accordingly, I do not expand the meaning of the term "*fi sabil Allah*" so as to include all good deeds. On the other hand, I do not restrict it to military fighting alone. *Jihad* for the sake of God includes supporting His cause by writing, and speaking as much as by fighting. *Jihad* may be educational, journalistic, social, economic, or political *jihad* as much as military *jihad*. We must remember that in all kinds of *jihad*, the essential condition is that the action helps make God's word supreme on earth.

Al Tabari says, "*Fi sabil Allah*" means spending to support the religion of God, its way of life, its law which is God's gift to humanity, and to fight its enemies, the disbelievers." The first part of al Tabari's statement is obviously indicative that all actions aimed at establishing this religion are "*fi sabil Allah*", but fighting disbelievers mentioned in the last part is only one way of supporting Islam, since sometimes religion can be supported by cultural means instead.

The majority of scholars in the four schools of jurisprudence restrict this share to financing fighters and defenders of Islam. Today we must add fighters of opposing ideologies, since cultural colonialism is worse than military colonialism. This expanded meaning of *jihad* is supported by the fact that *jihad* is not restricted to military action. When the Prophet (p) was asked which *jihad* is better, it is authentically reported that he answered, "A word of truth in the presence of an oppressive ruler."[45] Muslim reports from Ibn Mas'ud in his correct collection that the Messenger of God (p) said, "There is no prophet sent by God to any nation before me but had from among his people close companions and friends who pursued his tradition and followed his orders. After them, generations came who say what they do not do, and do what they are not ordered to do. He who makes *jihad* against them with his hands is a believer; he who makes *jihad* against them with his tongue is a believer, and he who makes *jihad* against them in his heart is a believer. Not a single grain of faith exists beyond that." The Prophet (p) also says, "Make *jihad* against those who associate partners with God, with your wealth, your selves, and your tongues."[46]

Furthermore, writing, lecturing, and organizing work in the way of God are included in *jihad* by analogy, even if they are not mentioned specifically by the Prophet (p) since such efforts are necessary to support and defend Islam, to resist aggression against its ideology, society, and state, and to make God's word supreme on earth. We noted earlier in this book that Ibn Rushd says, "Those who allow payment to *zakah* workers even if they are rich also allow payment to judges and persons who work for Muslims' public interest."[47] We also noted that some Hanafite jurists include in the category of wayfarers every person detached from his or her wealth and unable to make use of it, even if such a person is in his or her hometown. By the same token, all activities that fulfill the same purpose of fighting for the sake of God must be treated like *jihad*. Analogy can be applied in *zakah*; every school of jurisprudence applies analogy in *zakah* one way or another, and this is an appropriate analogy.

I believe the term "in the way of God" (*fi sabil Allah*) includes fighting and activities that achieve the same goal as fighting, which is consistent with the opinion of the majority of jurists. It must also be noted that certain activities may be included as "in the way of God" in certain periods in certain countries, which may not be included in other lands or times. Establishing an Islamic school, for example, though beneficial to Muslims, is not included in *jihad*. Yet in a country whose educational institutions are dominated by secularists, communists, or missionaries, one of the best means of *jihad* is establishing an Islamic school to protect Muslim children from such destructive and demoralizing preaching. Likewise, an Islamic library may sometimes be only a good and beneficial project, but may at other times in other places be a *jihad*. The same thing may be stated about an Islamic hospital that protects Muslim patients from being exploited by missionary hospitals, and other cultural projects that perform similar tasks.

Activities included under "for the sake of God" today

The wars in which the Companions and Followers battled were fought solely to help people quit the worship of human creatures for the worship of God, the creator, to eradicate oppression and establish the justice of Islam. Some people think this kind of war does not happen anymore and that contemporary wars in Muslim countries are merely nationalistic, having nothing to do with religion, so *zakah* must not be given to Muslims who fight such wars.

Such thinking is grossly erroneous, because, first of all, Islamic *jihad* is not restricted to the wars in which the Companions fought . It is true that the wars fought by the Companions and Followers are unique in the history of humanity, in regard to the goals of the Muslim fighters, their manners, and their moral behavior during and after the wars. No doubt the wars of the Companions are the most ideal wars in Muslim history, but history has witnessed many other wars in which Muslims defended their values, sacred places, and communities, which are no less sacred than the wars of the Companions and Followers, and which defended Muslim lands against Mogul and Crusader aggressors. If the fighting of the Companions and Followers were for the cause of Islam, the fighting of leaders like Nur al Din, Salah al Din, and Qutuz were in defense of the home of Islam. *Jihad* is obligatory in order to protect Muslim land as much as it is obligatory to protect the Islamic faith. Fighting in defense of Muslim land is legitimate Islamically, if it is not based simply on love of a country. A Muslim may leave the homeland of his ancestors and go live where Islam is fully implemented, as the Prophet and his Companions did by migrating from Makkah to Madinah for the sake of God.

The most honorable form of *jihad* nowadays is fighting for the liberation of Muslim land from the domination of the unbelievers, regardless of their religion or ideology. The communist, and the capitalist, the Westerner and the Easterner, Christian, Jew, pagan, or unbeliever, all are aggressors when they attack and occupy Muslim land. Fighting in defense of the home of Islam is obligatory until the enemy is driven away and Muslims are liberated.

Today, Muslim land is occupied in Palestine, Kashmir, Eritria, Ethiopia, Chad, Western Somalia, Cyprus, Samarkand, Bukhara, Tashkund, Ozbekstan, Albania, and several other communist occupied countries. Declaring a sacred war to save these Muslim lands is an Islamic requirement, and fighting for such purposes in those occupied territories is in the way of God, for which *zakah* must be spent.

Not all fighting by Muslims is in the way of God

Some people believe every military action taken by Muslims is in the way of God, regardless of its objectives. An essential distinction must be made between fighting for the sake of God and nationalistic or class wars. Fighting for the sake of God is motivated purely by Islamic vision and directed toward making the word of God supreme, or defending the homeland of Islam and Muslims. Any war devoid of this spiritual content is an earthly war, whether waged by Muslims or unbelievers. Wars detached from the above goals and directions cannot be financed by *zakah*. Let us suppose that a group of Albanian or Central Asian communists of Muslim origin decided to fight the Soviet communists in order to liberate their homeland and establish a nationalistic, independent communist state. Is such a war *jihad* in the way of God, and can *zakah* be spent on such a war? My answer is an emphatic no, because a central Asian communist, though of Muslim origins, is no better than a Russian communist, since national and racial differences are disregarded in Islam. A war for liberation form a group of oppressors for the benefit of another group of oppressors is not an Islamic war. Only fighting for establishing the religion of God on earth is sacred in Islam, and only this kind of war deserves the sacrifice of human souls and material wealth. Fighting for the liberation of Muslims and Muslim land from colonialism and other forms of oppression are acceptable as means to establishing Islam on earth, but fighting for the sake of liberating the soil and mud in order to establish other ideologies is not recognized as *jihad*, and cannot be financed by *zakah*. Abu Muhammad 'Abd al Ghani al Hafiz reports, via his own chain, from 'Abd al Rahman bin Abi Na'm, "I was sitting with 'Abd Allah bin 'Umar, when a woman came and said, "O Abu 'Abd al Rahman, my husband, in his last will, says his wealth should be spent in the way of God." Ibn 'Umar said, "Let it be spent as he wished, in the way of God." 'Abd al Rahman said, "You did not answer her question." 'Abd Allah said, "What do you want me to tell her? Should I tell her to give the money to these troops that destroy land and cut off roads?" I said,

"What would you tell her then?" 'Abd Allah replied, "I would tell her to give it to righteous people, to pilgrims to the sacred House of God. They are the comers to al Rahman, they are the comers to al Rahman; they are the comers to al Rahman."[48] Ibn 'Umar hesitated to describe the war of his time as in the way of God, although the troops then had only one banner, one slogan, and one direction, that of Islam. What would Ibn 'Umar say about armies of our time, that do not even mention the name of God or the word Islam, armies whose men do not pray or worship God and whose generals are sunk in drinking and immorality? What would he say about armies whose ideologies are based on secularism, which has no place for God, His Messenger, or His sacred Book?

The group reports from Abu Musa , "The Messenger of God (p) was asked about a man who fights out of bravery, a man who fights out of patriotism, and a man who fights out of pride, to be seen [by men]-- which of these is for the sake of God. The Prophet answered, "He who fights for the word of God to be supreme is for the sake of God."[57] This saying provides the criteria to distinguish between *jihad* and non-Islamic war, between the way of God and the way of aggression. The way of God aims at making the religion of God supreme.[49]

Re-establishment of the Islamic state is *jihad*

The best way to spend the share of "in the way of God" today is, as the reformist Rashid Rida suggests, to establish an association of Islamic activists to collect *zakah* and spend it to re-establish the Islamic state. He suggests that "*Jihad* for establishing the Islamic state is even more important than *jihad* to protect it, and that one of the ways to re-establish the Islamic state is to promote the call for Islam and defend its ideology, when defending it by the sword is not needed.[50]

The most important form of jihad today is serious, purposive organized work to re-build the Islamic society and state and to implement the Islamic way of life in the political, cultural, and economic areas. This is certainly the most deserving area of *zakah*.

Armies are normally financed by the state's regular resources. This was the case in the early Islamic state, which financed its army from *fai'* and *kharaj*. It is also the case today that the government's general budget provides for its army. Financing a regular army requires huge resources that by far exceed the proceeds of *zakah*. If modern armies were to depend on *zakah*, they would take perhaps all of its proceeds and still need more.

Therefore, I believe that cultural, educational, and informational *jihad* in the way of God should be given priority today, as long as such jihad is a purely Islamic effort that aims at re-establishing the Islamic state. Examples of activities that desperately need finance from *zakah* in order to serve the cause of making the word of God supreme are building centers for the call to Islam [*da'wah*] which provide correct and pure Islamic information to men and women throughout the world, and establishing Islamic centers even in Muslim countries, to provide Islamic education and training, and protect the faith of Muslim youth from deviation, agnosticism, and behavioral corruption. Such centers are crucial, for they prepare Muslim youth to support Islam and resist the aggression of its enemies. Another example is the establishment of a purely Islamic newspaper, which would provide guidance to Muslim men and woman in their daily lives and lead Islamic political and social awareness. Issuance of Islamic books is yet another area where *jihad* in way of God can be practiced, for it is crucial to reveal the treasures of this religion as a better way of life. Yet another example of *jihad* is to provide full-time workers in the way of God. These and similar activities deserve the share of *zakah* for the sake of God.

Footnotes

1.   *Al Nihayah*, by Ibn Athir, Vol. 2, p. 156.

2.   *Al Ikhtiyar li Ta'lil al Mukhtar*, Vol. 1, p. 119, *al Bahr al Ra'iq*, Vol. 2, p. 260, and *Radd al Muhtar*, Vol. 2, pp. 83-84.

3.   *Tafsir al Manar*, Vol. 1, p. 580, second edition.

4.   Hanafite scholars raise this objection and do not give a satisfactory answer. The author' of *al Bahr* quotes from *al Nihayah*, "Take detached isolated fighters and pilgrims: If they have no wealth in their homes, they are poor, and if they do, they are wayfarers. Then they are but a special category of poor, that is, detached and isolated poor." See *al Bahr*, Vol. 2, p. 260, and *Radd al Muhtar*, Vol. 2, p. 84, Nevertheless, a special kind of poor is poor anyway. Al Alusi, in his commentary, Vol. 3, p. 328, says, "The correct view is that mentioned by al Jassas in *al Ahkam*: He who is rich in his home does not deserve *zakah*, but if such a person joins the fighting in the way of God, he needs weapons, transportation, and maintenance, things not needed when he is home. Such a person may be given *zakah*, in spite of his wealth."

5.   *Radd al Muhtar*, Vol. 2, p. 85.

6.   *Ahkam al Qur'an*, Vol. 2, p. 957.

7.   *Al Sharh al Saghir*, with *Hashiyat al Sawi*, pp. 233-234.

8.   *Ahkam al Qur'an*, op. cit.

9.   *Tuhfat al Muhtaj*, with *Sharh al Minhaj*, Vol. 3, p. 96.

10.   *Al Umm*, Vol. 2, p. 60.

11.   *Al Rawdah*, Vol. 2, pp. 326-327.

12.   *Ibid*, p. 321.

13.   *Tuhfat al Muhtaj*, Vol. 3, p. 96.

14.   *Matalib Uli al Nuha*, Vol. 2, pp. 147-148.

15.   Reported by Ahmad and the four. The saying is weak because there is an unknown person and a criticized person in its chain. Additionally, the saying is disturbed. Abu Daud reports the same trough another chain, which includes Muhammad bin Ishaq, who is also criticized. See *Nail al Awtar*, Vol. 4, p. 181.

16.   *Al Mughni,* Vol. 6, pp. 470-471.

17.   *Tuhfat al Muhtaj, op. cit.*

18.   *Tafsir al Razi,* Vol. 16, p. 113.

19.   *Al Mughni,* Vol. 2, p. 167.

20.   *Al Amwal*, pp. 573-575.

21.   *Al Musannaf,* Vol. 3, p. 166. The text of this narration is "Whatever is taken from you on bridges is *zakah* that satisfies the obligation of *zakah.*"

22.   *Al Mukhtasar al Nafi'*, p. 59, Dar al Kitab, al 'Arabi print.

23.   *Jawahir al Kalam*, Vol. 2, p. 79, *Shara'i al Islam* by al Hilli, Vol. 1, p. 87, Dar maktabat al Hayat print, and *Fiqh al Imam Ja'far*, Vol. 2, p. 92.

24.   *Al Rawd al Nadir*, Vol. 2, p. 428, and *al Bahr*, Vol. 2, p. 182.

25.   *Sharh al Azhar* and its commentary, pp. 515-516.

26.   *Al Rawdah al Nadiyah*, Vol. 1, pp. 206-207.

27.   *Mahasin al Ta'wil,* Vol. 7, p. 3181.

28.   *Tafsir al Manar*, Vol. 10, p. 585.

29.   *Sura al 'Imran*, 3:104.

30.   *Ibid*, p. 587.

31.   *Al Islam, 'Aqidah wa Shari'ah*, pp. 197-98.

32.   Mahmud Shaltut, *al Fatawa*, p. 219.

33.   Hasanain Makhluf, *Fatawa Shar'iyah*, Vol. 2.

34.   *Fath al Qadir*, Vol. 2, p. 20.

35.   *Al Mughni*, Vol. 2, p. 167.

36.   See *al Mu'jam al Mufahras li Alfaz al Qur'an al Karim.*

37. *Fath al Bari*, Vol. 3, p. 172.

38. *Al Nizam al Iqtisadi fi al Islam*, by al Nabhani, published by Hizb al Tahrir, p. 208.

39. *Sura al Baqarah*, 2:195.

40. *Sura al Hadid*, 57:10.

41. *Sura al Anfal*, 8:60.

42. Agreed upon. It is narrated by Abu Musa al Ash'ari.

43. In *al Targhib*, al Mundhiri says, "reported by al Tabarani. The people of the chain are the same as the people of the correct collection," Vol. 3, p. 4.

44. Al Mundhiri in *al Targhib* lists all these sayings, Vol. 2, chapter on jihad.

45. Reported by Ahmad, al Nasa'i, al Baihaqi in *al Shu'ab*, and al Diya al Maqdisi from Tariq bin Shihab, Al Mundhiri says it is reported by al Nasa'i and its chain is correct. See al Munawi, *al Taisir*, Vol. 1, p, 182.

46. Reported by Ahmad, Abu Daud, al Nasa'i, Ibn Habban, and al Hakim, from Anas. Al Hakim says it is correct. This is approved by others. See *al Taisir*, Vol. 1, p. 485.

47. *Bidayat al Mujtahid*, Vol. 1, p. 267.

48. *Tafsir al Qurtubi*, Vol. 8, p. 185. It seems that this story is the source of the report from Ibn 'Umar that he said, "Pilgrimage is "in the way of God" as one understands from the context in *al Qurtubi*. It must be noted that the words of Ibn 'Umar indicate that "the way of God" when not restricted means *jihad*, and he gives it another interpretation only because of the corruption of the troops.

49. This is mentioned in *al Muntaqa* . See *Nail al Awtar*, Vol. 7, pp. 226-227.

50. *Ibid.*

51. *Tafsir al Manar*, Vol. 10, p. 598.

CHAPTER SEVEN

THE WAYFARER

Who is the wayfarer?

According to the majority of scholars, the wayfarer [*ibn al Sabil*] is the traveler on the way from one locale to another. Literally, the term means "son of the road".

This form of expression ("son of such-and-such") is common in Arabic.[1]

Al Tabari reports from Mujahid, "The wayfarer has a right to *zakah* even if rich, as long as he or she is cut off from his or her wealth. Ibn Zaid says, 'The wayfarer is the traveler, rich or poor, who has lost his means of expenditure or depleted them while on the road. Helping this person is obligatory.'"[2]

Care for the wayfarer in the Qur'an

The Glorious Qur'an mentions the wayfarer eight times, in the context of encouraging kindness toward him or her. In Makkan suras , God says, "and give the kindred his right, and the needy and the wayfarer, and do not be wasteful."[3] Then give the kindred their right, and the needy, and the wayfarer: that is best for those who desire the sake of God."[4] In Madinan suras, God designates for the wayfarer a share of wealth spent in the way of God. God says, "They ask thee, what should they spend. Say: What you spend of good wealth, spend it for God, and parents, and kindred, and orphans, and the destitute, and the wayfarer."[5] God ordains good doing to the wayfarer in the verse "And worship God, and do not associate anything in partnership with him, and be kind to parents and close relatives, and orphans, and the destitutes, and close neighbors, and far neighbors, and close companions, and the wayfarer, and he whom your right hand possesses."[6] God also gives the wayfarer a share of the fifth taken from war booty: "and realize, that which you acquire as booty of anything , one fifth of it is for God, and the Messenger, and close relatives, and orphans, and the needy, and the wayfarer."[7] Also God provides a share of the *fai'* to the wayfarer, saying "that which God gives as *fai'* from the people of the villages, it is for God, and the Messenger, and close relatives, and orphans, and the destitute and the wayfarer so that it may not circulate between the rich among you."[8] Lastly, God gives a share of *zakah* to the wayfarer in the verse we are studying. Moreover, helping the wayfarer is among the deeds of righteousness in the verse"... And gives funds -- in spite of loving them -- to close relatives, orphans, the destitute, the wayfarer, the beggar, and in liberating slaves, and establishes prayer and gives *zakah*."[9]

Reason for the attention given the wayfarer

The reason for the attention given the wayfarer in the Qur'an is that Islam encourages travelling for several reasons.

A. Travelling for work and opportunity. God says, "and, walk in its [earth's] tracks and eat out of His sustenance."[10] "And others travel on the earth seeking from the bounties of God and others fight in the way of God."[11] The Prophet (p) said, "Travel so that you become rich."[12].

B. Travelling to seek knowledge and meditate on the signs of God in the world, and on His animal and human communities. God says, "Say: Walk on the earth and see how He started the creation."[13] "Many were the ways of life that have passed away before you. Travel through the earth and see what was the end of those who rejected Truth."[14] and "Do they not travel through the land, so that their hearts (and minds) may thus learn wisdom and their ears may thus learn to hear?"[15] The Messenger (p) says, "He who takes a path seeking knowledge, God will make easy for him a way to the Garden."[16] and "He who goes out in pursuit of knowledge is in the way of God until he returns."[17]

Early Muslim scholars provide ideal examples in their ardent travelling in pursuit of knowledge, which is recorded with admiration by contemporary scholars.

C. Travel for *jihad* in the way of God. This includes defending Muslim land, calling to Islam, liberating the oppressed and punishing those who break pledges with Muslims. God says, "Go ye forth, (whether equiped) lightly or heavily, and strive and struggle with your wealth and your persons in the way of God: that is best for you, if ye but knew"[18] and "If there had been immediate gain (in sight) and the journey easy, they would, without doubt , have followed thee but the distance was long (and weighed) on them."[19] God promises, "Nor could they spend anything (for the cause) small or great, nor cut across a valley, but their deed is inscribed to their credit, that God may requite their deed with their best possible reward."[20] The Prophet (p) says, "A single departure in the morning or a return in the evening in the way of God is better than the world and what is in it."[21]

D. Travel to perform pilgrimage to the sacred House of God, the fifth pillar of Islam. God says, "Pilgrimage to the House is a duty people owe to God, those who can afford the journey."[22] "And proclaim the pilgrimage among people. They will come to thee on foot and on every kind of camel; lean on account of journey through deep and distant mountain highways, that they may witness the benefit (provided) for them and celebrate the name of God on appointed days."[23]

These are kinds of travelling and touring in the land that Islam calls for or encourages, in order to realize its objectives on earth and affirm its teachings among people. Admittedly, there are other reasons for travelling, yet a religion that encourages the above listed kinds of travelling must provide care for travellers, especially those who get cut off from families and wealth. Helping travellers reaffirms the solidarity of the Muslim community, regardless of geographic location or place of origin.

Care for the wayfarer builds social solidarity

This form of social insurance is unique to Islam. In its social program , Islam not only guarantees the provision of residence, but provides security from unforeseen conditions that affect people who are on the road. To get the complete picture of this insurance, one must remember that it came at a time when there were no hotels, restaurants, or rest areas for travellers. Motivated by this idea of taking care of wayfarers, 'Umar bin al Khattab established stations on the road between Makkah and Madinah to help travellers and provide transportation for those who need it between oases. He also established a food storage area for those who need food on the road, and in the city.[24]

'Umar bin 'Abd al Aziz asked al Zuhri to write him a detailed outline of how to spend *zakah*, based on his knowledge of the tradition of the Prophet and the Four Successors. Among other things, al Zuhri wrote, "The share of the wayfarer must be divided in proportion to the density of traffic on the road so that roads with high number of people passing through are assigned bigger portions of *zakah* proceeds. Each traveller who has no means to continue, or go back, must be provided food until he or she achieves the purpose of his or her journey or reaches home. Places of shelter must be established, and trustworthy people assigned to manage them, so that any passing wayfarer can be provided food, shelter, and feed for his animal, until all the *zakah* funds you assign are depleted."[25] Has humanity ever witnessed such a level of caring for needy men and women wherever they may be?

Is one who wants to begin a journey a wayfarer?

Jurists differ on whether the wayfarer is only the person on the road or also the person who is at home but desires to begin a journey. The majority believes he who wants to start travelling is not a wayfarer, for the following reasons:

1. The term '*ibn al sabil*" means the person on the road ad does not include one who is at home.

2. The wayfarer is a person who is cut off from his financial means at home. A person who has not yet started travelling is not cut off from his means. Wayfarers must be helped until they reach home, regardless of their financial status at home, while a person who is home and needs financial help for travelling or other purposes, may be given as a poor person, but not as a wayfarer.[26]

Al Shafi'i believes that "wayfarers "include persons who want to start a journey but do not have sufficient means, on the grounds that such need help to travel just like the person on the road.[27]

In my opinion, the view of the majority is sounder. *Zakah* funds must not be spent on those who desire to initiate a journey. However, al Shafi'i's view may be applicable if the intended travel is for service to the Muslim community, such as travelling to call for Islam or on a scientific mission. Helping such potential travellers may also be included in the category "in the way of God". This is supported by the fact that the wayfarer is listed after, and is added to, the term "in the way of God" in the verse we are studying.

Keeping in mind that the wording of the verse allows payment for the wayfarer to be done to a third party, such as transportation company or airline company since the verse indicates that *zakah* is spent on the wayfarer and not given to him. Hanbalites believe traveller must be provided with what he or she needs to reach his or her destination, fulfill the objective of the journey, and return home. This applies when travelling is either in obedience to God, such as pilgrimage or visiting parents, or merely permissible, such as business. Hanbalites differ on travelling for the purpose of amusement only. Some argue that this travelling is not essential or needed, consequently *zakah* funds should not be spent on it,[28] while others take it at face value as travelling, i.e. a wayfarer on a pleasure journey is helped from *zakah*.

Conditions for payment

The first condition is that the wayfarer must be in need when on the road, since the purpose of the *zakah* is to help the wayfarer reach home. If he or she has means of reaching home, no payment can be made, if not, the wayfarer is given regardless of his or her richness at home and without any need to return what is given as *zakah*.

Secondly, the journey must not be in disobedience to God. This exclusion means that those who journey for sinful purposes or traders whose commodities are forbidden must not be given *zakah*, except if the traveller's life is at stake. Saving his or her life then becomes a must in *Shari'ah*.[29] The purpose of this condition is obviously to abstain from helping wrongdoers. Travelling which is not disobedience to God is of three kinds: travelling to do good deeds or worship God, such as pilgrimage, *jihad*, and seeking knowledge; travelling for lawful earthly reasons, such as on business or in search of a job; and travelling for amusement and tourism. Only giving to wayfarers on amusement journies is disputed among jurists,[30] while giving to wayfarers on other travels is unanimously lawful.

Some Malikites and Shafi'ites add a third condition, that the wayfarer must not be able to borrow to satisfy his or her needs.[31] This applies only if the wayfarer is rich at home. This condition is not accepted by the other two schools. Ibn al 'Arabi in *Ahkam al Qur'an* and al Qurtubi in his *Tafsir* reject this condition, since the wayfarer need not be obliged to anyone if he or she can only be obliged to God, by taking *zakah*.[32] Al Nawawi adds that even if the wayfarer can borrow money, he or she is not required to take loans, and may take *zakah*.[33] Hanafites recommend making loans if possible, but do not obligate it, on the grounds that making a loan exposes the borrower to the possibility of becoming unable to pay the loan back, and he or she need not take that chance.[34]

How much should the wayfarer be given?

A. Wayfarers must be given their sufficiency of food and clothing, until they reach home or a place where they have funds of their own. If the wayfarer has less than what is needed, *zakah* should be given to supplement the existing funds until they are sufficient.

B. For long journeys, a means of transportation must also be provided. Long journeys are those in which prayer is reduced, i.e. approximately eighty kilometers [fifty miles]. Rides may be purchased or rented for the wayfarer, depending on the need and the availability of *zakah* funds.

C. All needed expenses are to be given, and not only expenses caused by travelling.

D. Payment is made to the wayfarer regardless of ability to work and earn.

E. Aid is provided to the wayfarer until his or her destination is reached, if he or she is to stay there or has accessible funds there. If the wayfarer intends to finish some business and return home quickly, he or she must be given what is needed until reaching home.

F. As for the expenses at the place of destination, Shafi'ites decide they must be paid if the stay there is less than four days the same number of days as in the case of reducing prayer because of travelling. This restriction does not apply to fighters in the way of God, who are given for the whole period they stay at frontier posts, no matter how long it may be. Some scholars believe wayfarers must be given funds for the whole period they stay in the place of destination regardless of the length of the period.[35]

G. If the wayfarer returns home with leftover *zakah* money, this residual must be returned to the *zakah* fund, according to Shafi'ites.[36] Hanafites argue that wayfarers are not obligated to give back *zakah* left over from the trip.[37]

Are there wayfarers today?

Some contemporary scholars assert that today there are no more wayfarers in the original sense of the word, because of the transportation, accommodation, and banking facilities that make one's travelling easy and one's wealth accessible anywhere in the world. This is argued by the late Ahmad Mustafa al Maraghi in his explanation of the Qur'an.[38] I beg to differ with him, since there are as many wayfarers today as there were in the past:

1. Some people may be rich, but do not do business with banks, so that when they are away from their towns they are actually detached from their wealth. They may be crossing some desert far from urban centers.

2. There are refugees who are driven out of their homes and lands by aggressors or who flee from dictatorial governments. They may live for an undetermined period of time outside their countries, unable to reach their wealth which is often confiscated by the government. Like those are political refugees who seek asylum in countries other than their own.

3. Some Hanafite jurists consider individuals who, although they live in their own towns, have no access to their wealth, either because of political reasons or because of economic reasons such as businessmen whose wealth is in the form of unremittable loans to others.[39] These jurists assert that such individuals must be treated as wayfarers and given *zakah*.[40]

4. There are those who intend to initiate journeys for public service or for individual affairs that are beneficial to the public, such as students receiving training abroad.

5. Some Hanbalites include under the definition of wayfarers tramps or street beggars who have no homes.[41] Such persons are literally *ibn al sabil*, or children of the street. They may be given from the share of the wayfarers if not from the share of the poor.

6. And lastly, foundling infants may be included in this category, according to Rashid Rida, who says the term *ibn al sabil* perfectly describes foundlings since they are in fact children of the street. Islam takes good care of orphans, and foundlings are even more in need of care than orphans with known relatives.[42]

Footnotes

1. *Tafsir al Tabari*, Vol. 13, p. 320.

2. *Ibid.*

3. *Sura al Isra'*, 17:26.

4. *Sura al Rum*, 30:38.

5. *Sura al Baqarah*, 2:215.

6. *Sura al Nisa'*, 4:36.

7. *Sura al Anfal*, 8:41.

8. *Sura al Hashr*, 59:7.

9. *Sura al Baqarah*, 2:177.

10. *Sura al Mulk*, 67:15.

11. *Sura al Muzzammil*, 73:20.

12. Mentioned by al Mundhiri in al *Targhib wa al Tarhib*, Vol.2, chapter on fasting. He adds, "Reported by al Tabarani in *al Awsat* via a trustworthy chain."

13. *Sura al Ankabut*, 29:20.

14. *Sura al Imran*, 3:137.

15. *Sura al Hajj*, 22:46.

16. In *al Targhib*, al Mundhiri says, "Reported by Muslim and others." See chapter on knowledge.

17. *Ibid*, reported by al Tirmidhi, who grades it good.

18. *Sura al Tawbah*, 9:41.

19. *Ibid*, 9:42.

20. *Ibid* 9:121.

21. Reported in al Bukhari, chapter on *jihad*.

22. *Sura al Imran*, 3:97.

23. *Sura al Hajj*, 22:27-38.

24. Ibn Sa'd, *al Tabaqat*, Vol. 3, p.283.

25. *Al Amwal*, p.580.

26. *Al Sharh al Kabir*, with *al Mughni*, Vol. 2, p.702.

27. *Al Majmu'*, Vol. 6, p. 214 and *Nihayat al Muhtaj*, Vol. 6, p. 156.

28. *Al Sharh al Kabir*, Vol. 2, pp.702-703.

29. *Hashiat al Dusuqi*, Vol. 1, p. 498. Some Malikites believe he must not be given anything, even if his life is threatened, since he always has the means to safety by repentance, See *Hashiyat al Sawi*, Vol. 1, p.233.

30. *Al Majjmu'*, Vol. 6, pp.214-215, and *al Sharh al Kabir*, Vol. 2 pp. 701-702.

31. *Sharh al Khirshi on the text of Khalil*, Vol. 2, p. 219, and *Nihayat al Muhtaj*, Vol. 6, p. 156.

32. *Ahkam al Qur'an*, Vol. 2, p. 958, and *Tafsir al Qurtubi*, Vol. 8 , p. 187.

33. *Al Majmu'* Vol. 6, p. 216.

34. *Fath al Qadir,* Vol. 2, p. 18, and *Radd al Muhtar*, Vol. 2, p.64.

35. *Al Majmu'*, Vol. 6, p. 215-216, and *al Sharh al Kabir*, Vol. 2, pp.701-702.

36. *Al Majmu'*, Vol. 6, p. 216.

37. *Fath al Qadir,* Vol. 2, p.18, and *Radd al Muhtar*, Vol. 2, p.64.

38. *Tafsir al Maraghi*, Vol. 28, explanation of verse six of *sura al Hashr*.

39. *Al Bahr al Ra'iq*, Vol. 2, p.260.

40. *Radd al Muhtar, op cit.,* and *al Bahr al Ra'iq, ibid.*

41. *Al Insaf,* Vol. 3, p. 237.

42. *Tafsir al Manar*, Vol.5, p. 94.

CHAPTER EIGHT

ISSUES RELATED TO THE DESERVING CATEGORIES

Must *zakah* be divided equally between the eight categories?

God mentions in the Qur'an eight categories who deserve *zakah*. Should *zakah* be distributed each year to all eight categories? Should the proceeds be equally divided between them?

Some jurists understand the verse in this meaning, like al Shafi'i, in his *al Umm*. In *al Majmu'*, al Nawawi says, " Al Shafi'i and his disciples believe that when *zakah* is distributed by the payer or the payer's representative, the share of *zakah* workers is dropped, and the amount due must be distributed to the other seven categories, if they exist. It is not permissible to abandon an existing category. If an existing category is abandoned, its share is guaranteed by the owner. This is also the view of 'Ikrimah,'Umar bin 'Abd al Aziz, al Zuhri, and Daud."[1] Ahmad in one of several reports agrees with al Shafi'i on the equal distribution between all categories, and on the rule that at least three persons in each category except *zakah* workers be given *zakah* , because the verse is in the plural form, and three is the least number for which a plural form is used. This is the view selected by Abu Bakr, a Hanbalite.[2] The Malikite Asbagh also prefers the Shafi'ite opinion.[3]

Ibn al 'Arabi says, "It is agreed upon that it is not permissible to give all proceeds to *zakah* workers, since this does not fulfil the objective of *zakah*, which is satisfying the poor and the needs of Islam. Shafi'ites argue that the *zakah* distribution verse uses the preposition "to" [*li*] which means that proceeds must be given so that each recipient becomes owner of what he or she is given. This implies giving all of them.[4] Shafi'ites also present as evidence the saying reported by Abu Daud from Ziad bin al Harith al Sada'i: "I came to the Messenger of God (p) and gave him my covenant, A man came and said, 'Give me from the *Sadaqah*. The Messenger of God (p) said, 'God does not leave the distribution of *sadaqat* to a prophet or anyone else, so He gave the ruling and divided the proceeds into eight parts. If you are in any of these parts, I will give you your right."

Malik, Abu Hanafiah, and their disciples disagree with al Shafi'i. They do not require that distribution cover all categories, asserting that the preposition to [*li*] in the verse does not mean one must make the recipient own what is given, but means "for whom". These scholars present the "If ye disclose (acts of) charity, it is well, but if ye conceal them and make them reach the poor, that is best for you." which only mentions the poor and no reference is made to other categories, and the saying "I am ordained to take *sadaqah* from the rich among you and render it to the poor among you." Not mentioning other categories in these two texts is an indication that giving the poor alone is satisfactory.[5] Abu 'Ubaid reports that Ibn Abbas says, "If you spend *zakah* on one of these categories, it is all right, since God says 'The *sadaqat* are but for the poor and needy, ... ' which means *zakah* must not be given outside these categories." The same is reported from Hudhaifah. Ibn Shihab says, "The category which deserves *zakah* more is the one that is bigger in number and more severe in need." Sufyan and jurists from Iraq (Abu Hanifah and his disciples) believe spending *zakah* on one of the eight categories is satisfactory. Al Nakha'i suggests that when funds are plenty, it is better to distribute to all categories, but when funds are limited, one category is sufficient. A similar opinion is attributed to 'Ata'.[6]

Abu Thawr suggests that when the owner distributes *zakah*, it may be given to one category only, but when *zakah* is distributed by the state, all categories must be included. Malik adds that "it is left to the state's *zakah* agency to distribute to those categories whose needs are more intense. This is what I have heard scholars whom I respect expressing."In my opinion, this last view is most sound and reasonable.

The opinion of Siddiq Hasan Khan

Siddiq Hasan Khan in *al Rawdah al Nadiyah* argues that the fact that God restricts *zakah* distribution to the eight categories does not necessarily mean *zakah* proceeds must be divided equally among them.. Obligating Muslims to divide their *zakah* equally among the eight deserving categories entails great inconvenience and is not consistent with the behaviour of the early generations of Muslims. Additionally, when the amount of *zakah* is small, each portion would be negligible. If it were mandatory to distribute *zakah* into eight equal parts, it must be forbidden to use any eighth whose recipients do not exist at a certain time. This obviously contradicts common sense and *ijma'*. Even the saying from Zaid speaks only about *zakah* distributed by the state and it is silent on *zakah* distributed by payers.

If the state collects *zakah* and there are deservants of *zakah* in each category, every one of them can ask for his or her share of *zakah*. The state is not required to divide *zakah* proceeds among them equally or to give to individuals in every category. Such a decision depends on the needs of these categories and the relative severity of their needs.[8]

The opinion of Abu 'Ubaid

Abu 'Ubaid supports this view. He gives a full report of the outline of al Zuhari on *zakah* distribution written at the request of 'Umar bin 'Abd al Aziz and adds, "This is the perfect distribution of *zakah*, for he who can divide it, but I believe distributing it to all these categories is not obligatory, except for the state, if total proceeds of *sadaqat* are large, if there are deservants in all categories, and if the state has the needed manpower for distribution. A person who distributes his own *zakah* may spend all of it in some of these categories only. Basically this is in application of the Prophet's saying that *zakah* is due to the poor. The Prophet (p) mentions only one category, in this saying, but when he received more *zakah* funds, he gave toward heart reconciliation, and when he received even more funds, he gave to those who were under debt. All this implies that the state has a choice between distributing to all the categories or some of them, depending on what is just. Individuals can do the same."[9]

The opinion of Rashid Rida

In his explanation of the Qur'an, Rashid Rida says, "The fact that our leading scholars differ on this issue is an indication that there is no agreed upon report from the Prophet determining whether or not all categories must be included in each *zakah* distribution. Therefore, this issue must be determined after consideration of the Muslim community's needs and interests, and the size of *zakah* proceeds. The views that fit public interest best are those of Malik and al Nakha'i, while the opinion farthest from the texts and public interests is that of Abu Hanifah,[10] except when funds are very small. Giving *zakah* to one deservant in one category when proceeds are huge is not acceptable, because it does not fulfil the objective of *zakah*. This matter must be settled by the state decision-makers so as to do justice to the general interests of Muslims, especially since certain categories may sometimes be more important than others."[11]

Summary

After surveying all these views, one can briefly summarize them as follows:

1. When funds are plenty and there are deservants in all categories, distribution must cover all of them. It is not acceptable to deprive deservants who are in need; the duty of the state is to collect *zakah* and distribute it according to the needs of the deservant categories.

2. Distribution among the eight categories need not be equal, i.e. each group need not receive exactly one-eight of total proceeds, since the criteria is need. I believe the view of Malik and al Zuhri is most suitable in distributing to the categories on the basis of their respective need.[12]

3. *Zakah* may all be given to certain categories when this is necessary. Preference must be based on actual needs and public interest and not on personal opinions or prejudice.[13]

4. The poor and the needy are the most important category of all. Satisfying their needs is the main objective of *zakah*, as repeatedly mentioned in saying of the Prophet. It is not permissible to spend *zakah* on the army while tremendous need exists for food and shelter among the poor and needy. However, there may be exceptionally urgent

needs for diverting funds from the poor and needy in response to emergencies in other categories, such as defense.

5. The suggestion of al Shafi'i about *zakah* workers should be applied so that their share does not exceed one-eighth of total proceeds, in order to preserve the major part of *zakah* for fulfilling its objectives.

6. When *zakah* proceeds are small, as when an individual payer distributes his small amount of *zakah*, all of it may be spent on one deservant, since dividing such a small amount diminishes its usefulness, and would not enrich *zakah* recipients, as urged by the Shafi'i school.

Footnotes

1. *Al Majmu'*, Vol. 6, p. 185.

2. *Al Kafi by Ibn Qudamah,* Vol. 1, p. 146.

3. As quoted from al Khirshi by al Sawi in his *Hashiyah,* Vol. 1, p. 334.

4. *Ahkam al Qur'an*, Vol. 2, p. 947.

5. *Ibid.*

6. *Al Amwal*, pp. 576-578.

7. *Ahkam al Qur'an*, Vol. 2, p. 948.

8. *Al Rawdah al Nadiyah,* Vol. 1, pp. 207-209.

9. *Al Amwal*, pp. 578-581.

10. As mentioned earlier, Abu 'Ubaid reports from Ibn 'Abbas and Huadaifah that this is permissible. Also, the opinion of Abu Hanifah that *zakah* may be given to one category does not prevent distribution according to needs and public interests of Muslims.

11. *Tafsir al Manar*, Vol. 10, p. 593.

12. In *al Sharh al Saghir,* Vol. 1, p. 234. Al Dardir says, "It is encouraged to give preference to those in more need, such as giving them more or giving the needy only.

13. In *Sharh al Azhar*, Vol. 1, p. 518, it is noted, "The state can make such preference, provided no injustice is done to the other categories. Injustice exists when one poor person is given more than his needs, while another is given less than what he needs."

CHAPTER NINE

CATEGORIES TO WHOM *ZAKAH* MUST NOT BE PAID

Since *zakah* is a special tax that aims at achieving particular objectives in the lives of individuals as well as society as a whole, it is obvious that there are certain categories to whom *zakah* must not be given. These categories are:

1. The rich.

2. Those capable of earning.

3. Disbelievers and apostates who fight against Islam, and, according to the majority of jurists, People of the Pledge.

4. Children, parents, and wives of *zakah* payers.

5. Descendents of the Prophet (p) .

These will be studied in the following sections.

SECTION ONE

THE RICH

Based on the saying of the Prophet (p) "The *sadaqah* is not lawful to the rich", and his address to Mu'adh that *zakah* is ". . . to be taken from their rich and rendered to their poor", Muslim jurists unanimously believe *zakah* must not be given to the rich. Giving the rich *zakah* violates the very purpose of *zakah*, which is to enrich the poor. Yet, when it comes to defining richness that prevents receiving *zakah*, jurists do not have a unified opinion, as was shown earlier when we discussed the definition of the poor ad needy.

There is also disagreement about giving *zakah* to the rich under the title of 'in the way of God' or of those under debt. Hanafites do not allow this on the basis of the above sayings. They make an exception for *zakah* workers, since what is paid to workers is merely the price of their labour. Other leading jurists contend that the saying from Mu'adh mentions only the poor because enriching this category is the major goal of *zakah*. They point out that if *zakah* could only be given to the poor and needy, there would be no meaning to the other six categories mentioned in the *zakah* distribution verse. By the same argument through which Hanafites exempt workers, those scholars permit paying *zakah* to the rich if they are fighters in the way of God or under debt for mediating disputes.

The fact is, the verse on *zakah* dispersement includes two kinds of deservants. The first group encompasses those who are in need: the poor, the needy, slaves needing liberation, individuals under personal debts, and wayfarers. These all are given *zakah* because they need help and relief. The second group comprises those whom the Muslim community needs: workers for the *zakah* agency, individuals whose hearts are being reconciled, persons under debts caused by public service, and fighters in the way of God. These people are given regardless of their poverty or wealth. The Prophet (p) himself specifies, that "sadaqah is not lawful to the rich, except in five cases: the fighter in the way of God, the *zakah* worker, the debtor, a person who buys from a *zakah* recipient an item given as *zakah*, and a person whose poor neighbor receives *zakah* and gives him a gift from it." Al Nawawi comments, "This is a correct or good saying, reported by Abu Daud through two chains, one *mursal* and the other linked to the Messenger (p)."[2]

Children are rich if their father is rich

Whether a child is male or female. If the father is rich, the child is considered rich. However, if the son or daughter is adult, the wealth of his or her father is not considered in the determination of the richness or poverty of the child.[3] Wives are also considered according to the prosperity of their husbands. A poor woman is not a *zakah* deservant if her husband is rich.

Hanafites consider giving the wife of a rich husband from *zakah* permissible, but Abu Yusuf disagrees.[4] Most Hanafites argue that the nature of the husband's obligation to spend on his wife is contractual, while the father is obligated to spend on his young child by virtue of parenthood.[5] Some Shafi'ites go along with the Hanafites and allow payment of *zakah* to the wife of a rich man. Some even allow giving a rich man's child *zakah*.[6] As for Malikites, they believe it is not permissible to give *zakah* to any poor person whose subsistence ad expenses are the responsibility of a rich person, except if the rich person responsible for the expenses of the poor can not be reached at all.

In my opinion, *zakah* must not be given to any person whose living expenses are on the shoulders of a rich person, such as the wife or young child of a rich man. This does not apply to other relatives whose living expenses are not the duty of the rich person.

SECTION TWO

THOSE CAPABLE OF EARNING

Several sayings prohibit payment of *zakah* to the rich and to men who have no physical or mental defects or handicaps. *Zakah* is not given to the strong because they are required to work and earn, instead of depending on charity. If a capable person can not find job, he may be given *zakah*, since the issue is the availability of jobs in the market at which he can earn his living, as well as ability of the person.[9]

Hanafites believe *zakah* may be given to an income earner, if all he owns is less than *nisab*, on the grounds that such a person is, in fact, poor. Ibn al Humam points out that several scholars do not allow income earners to take *zakah*, in accordance with the saying, "The *sadaqa* is not permissible to the rich or to the strong who is safe from defects" and the Prophet's answer to two strong and capable men who asked for *zakah*: "Indeed you have no right to it, but if you wish I would give you." The last sentence indicates that asking for *zakah* is not permissible, while receiving it without asking is allowed.[10]

One may argue that the Prophct (p) gave them the option of receiving *zakah* because he was not sure about their true situation, although they looked capable of earning. This is the essence of Abu 'Ubaid's comment. He adds that strength and ability to work must be associated with the availability of suitable job yielding sufficient income. A person who is able to work but does not find a job may be given *zakah*, as indicated by the verse. "And in their wealth their is the right of he who asks and he who is deprived". Ibn 'Abbas is reported to have explained "he who is deprived" as a craftsman who does not earn sufficiently.[11]

SECTION THREE

CAN *ZAKAH* BE PAID TO NON-MUSLIMS?

Apostates and hostile unbelievers cannot be given *zakah*

Muslims unanimously agree that *zakah* cannot be paid to unbelievers who fight Muslims.[12] This *ijma'* is based on the verse "God only forbids you, with regard to those who fight you for your faith, drive you out of your homes, and support others in driving you out, from turning to them for friendship and protection. It is such as turn to them in these circumstances that do wrong."[13] Financial help to such enemies would be used against Muslims in one way or another. Unbelievers who deny the existence of God, the principle of Prophethood, or faith in the Hereafter likewise cannot be given *zakah*, and neither can apostates who turn their backs on Islam and the Muslim community after having tasted faith.

Giving *zakah* to People of the Pledge

As for People of the Pledge, i.e. the people of the Book, and all who like them, live within the Muslim society, pledging their sincerity to the state, and obeying its laws, their are differences among Muslim scholars regarding giving them *zakah* and charity.

Giving People of Pledge voluntary charity

There is nothing to prevent Muslim from giving People of the Pledge voluntary charity, out of humanitarianism as well as in consideration of their pledged mutual commitment with Muslims. Being non-Muslims does not prevent them from being given charity of Muslims, as long as they are not fighting against the cause of Islam, for "God forbids you not, with regard to those who fight you not for your faith nor drive you out of your homes, from dealing kindly and justly with them. For God loves those who are just."[14] This verse was sent particularly for those Muslims who were hesitant to give charity to their unbelieving relatives. Ibn 'Abbas says "They (the Companions) used to dislike giving charity to their kin and relatives who were unbelievers; they asked, and were permitted, to do so by this verse: 'It is not required of thee, O Apostle, to set them on the right path. God sets on the right path whom He pleases: whatever of good ye spend benefits your own souls, and ye shall only do so seeking the face of God. Whatever good ye give shall be rendered back to you, and you shall not be dealt with unjustly.'[15,16] According to Ibn Kathir, the verse means that if the giver of charity aims to please God, he or she is rewarded by God regardless of whether the recipient of the charity is righteous or not, or deserving or not. The giver is rewarded for his or her intention.[17] In another verse, God praises those who "... feed for the love of God the indigent, the orphan, and the captive."[18] Captives in Muslim society were obviously disbelievers, as reported by al Hasan and others.[19]

Giving *zakah* of *al fitr*

Zakah of *al fitr*, recompenses, and other voluntary pledges, are like voluntary charity as far as giving to the People of the Pledge is concerned. Abu Hanifah, Muhammad, and some other jurists permit paying these charities to People of the Pledge, on the grounds that texts about these charities are general, such as the verses "If ye disclose acts of charity, even so it is well, but if ye conceal them, and make them reach those really in need, that is best for you. It will remove from you some of your stains of evil"[20], "For expiation, feed ten indigent persons on an overage scale of the food of your families"[21] and "but if any is unable to do so, he should feed sixty indigent ones."[22] These verses make no distinction between indigent believers and unbelievers which is an expression of the generally required good treatment of People of the Pledge. Obviously, those scholars believe giving Muslim indigents is undoubtedly better, since it helps a person who obeys God. Abu Hanifah establishes the condition that the disbeliever must not be fighting against Muslims in order to be given *zakah* of *al fitr*.[23] Lastly, Abu 'Ubaid and Ibn Abi Shaibah report that some Followers gave monks *zakah* of *al fitr*.[24]

The view of the majority

The majority of scholars believe *zakah* must not be given to any non-Muslims. Ibn al Mundhir claims this is unanimous.[25] This view is founded on the saying reported from Mu'adh, "God prescribes *zakah* on their wealth, to be taken from the rich among them and rendered to the poor among them". "The pronoun" them refers to Muslims.

The claimed *ijma* is disputed. Ibn Sirin and al Zuhri reportedly allowed paying *zakah* to unbelievers.[26] In *al Mabsut* al Sarakhsi notes that Zufar, a disciple of Abu Hanifah, allows giving *zakah* to the People of the Pledge. Al Sarakhsi adds, "This is implied by analogy, since the objective of *zakah* enriching the poor - is fulfilled by giving any poor persons regardless of their faith." This is refuted by virtue of the above saying from Mu'adh.[27]

Ibn Abi Shaibah reports that when Jabir bin Zaid was asked to whom *sadaqah* was to be distributed, he replied, "To people in your area, Muslims and People of the Pledge," and continued "The Messenger of God (p) gave the People of the Pledge from *sadaqah* and the one-fifth.'" The question is obviously about *zakah*, but it may mean voluntary *sadaqah* as well although only *zakah* was collected and distributed at the time of the Prophet (p). At any rate, the saying is only *mursal* . Ibn Abi Shaibah also reports Umar's comment that the verse "The *sadaqat* are only for the poor..."[29] includes People of the Pledge who are chronically ill.[30] Abu Yusuf reports that 'Umar assigned a regular subsidy for an elderly Jewish man from the treasury of the Muslim state, on the grounds that the old man was covered by the above verse.[31] The author of *al Rawd al Nadir* comments that these stories indicate 'Umar believed it was permissible to give *zakah* to the People of the Book.[32] A similar opinion is quoted from Zaidis by the author of *al Manar*. The author of *al Bahr* quotes al Zuhri and Ibn Sirin as saying the same; the latter adds "this action is done because of the generality of the term" the poor "in the verse."[33]

Al Tabari reports that 'Ikrimah believes the word "needy" in the verse refers to poor people of the Book.[34] 'Ikrimah says, "Do not call poor Muslims needy. The needy means poor people of the Pledge."[35] Some jurists argue giving *zakah* to people of the Pledge is only permissible if no deservant Muslims are found, as reported by al Jassas, from 'Ubaid Allah bin al Hasan.[36] Some Abadis believe the same.[37]

Analysis and weighing

The argument of the majority depends mainly on the saying from Mu'adh, which is agreed upon as correct. However, this saying does not clearly exclude non-Muslim poor, since it may simply mean *zakah* should be collected and distributed in the same area.

This saying is often quoted to support the policy of non-transportation of *zakah* from one land to another.

On the other hand, the generality argument forwarded by Hanafites with regard to the *sadaqa* of *al fitr* is very strong. It is supported by 'Umar, al Zuhri, Ibn Sirin, 'Ikrimah, Jabir bin Zaid, and Zufar. It is further supported by the verse "God forbids you not, with regard to those who fight you not for your faith nor drive you out of your homes, from dealing kindly and justly with them."[38] After comparing these arguments, one may conclude that *zakah* must first be given to poor Muslims, since it is taken from Muslim rich alone. But there is nothing to forbid giving *zakah* to the poor people of the Pledge, as long as such action does not harm the privileges of the Muslim poor.

Obviously, the above discussion refers to giving *zakah* to poor non-Muslims because of their poverty. As for giving *zakah* to people of the Pledge for reasons other than poverty, such as reconciling their hearts and bringing them closer to Islam, the Muslim community, and the Islamic state, the matter is different. Earlier in this book, I argue that it is permissible to give non-Muslims for heart reconciliation, such an action must be done at the discretion of the Islamic government, and not of individuals.

It should be added that scholars who do not allow giving *zakah* to people of the Pledge do not mean that the poor people of the Pledge must not be helped. Rather they believe such subsidies must come out of sources other than *zakah*, such as war booty, *fai*, and *kharaj*. Abu 'Ubaid quotes 'Umar bin 'Abd al Aziz's letter to his governor in al Basrah [an area in the south of Iraq], ". . . and look after the people of the Pledge. Find those of them who are elderly, weak, and those who do not earn, then give them regular salaries from the treasury in amounts sufficient for them."[39] This shows that the Muslim ruler must feel responsibility toward the people of Pledge.

Can wrongdoers be given *zakah*?

Scholars generally permit giving *zakah* to wrongdoers, as long as they maintain the faith of Islam, on humanitarian grounds and to reconcile their hearts. *Zakah* is collected from wrongdoers so they must be covered in the general terms of the saying " ... to be taken out of the rich among them and rendered to the poor among them."[40] The only exception is that wrongdoers may not be given *zakah* in a form that helps them do what is condemned, such as buying alcoholic beverages. Some Malikites go as far as stating that if there is suspicion that wrongdoers may use *zakah* paid them for evil purposes, it must not be given to them.[41] According to Zaidis, it is not permissible to give *zakah* to wrongdoers, unless they are workers in the *zakah* agency, or for the purpose of reconciliation.

I think wrongdoers who do not harm Muslims or challenge the tenets and rites of Islam may be helped with *zakah*. There is no doubt at all that giving the righteous poor is much better. As for transgressors who openly challenge Islamic values, *zakah* must not be given to them, because Muslims are ordained to establish righteousness and prevent evil, and giving such persons in no way helps prevent evil, for God says, "The believers, men and women, are protectors one of another, they enjoin what is just and forbid what is evil."[43] This requires that the Muslim community must withhold its help to those who oppose its values, try to destroy its rites and openly challenge its laws. As for families of such transgressors, *zakah* must be given to them, if they are in need, in accordance with the verse, "No bearer of burdens can bear the burden of another."[44] Ibn Taimiyah supports this view, saying, "One must search for poor and needy righteous men and women who follow the steps of *Shari'ah*. How can a Muslim help those who challenge Islamic values and rites by their wrongdoing or transgression?"[45] He continues, "The person who does not fulfill the obligation of prayers must be advised to pray before being given *zakah*; if he accepts, *zakah* may be given to him, and if not, it may not be given."[46]

Giving *zakah* to deviant sects

There are two kinds of deviant sects. The first kind are those sects which deny essential principles of Islam. Those are outside the limits of this religion and are considered disbelievers. The second kind are those sects which differ with mainstream Sunnites on certain basic issues, without exceeding the general boundaries of Islam. Sunnites, out of their forgiving spirit toward other sects, only exclude from the benefits of *zakah* sects classified as disbelievers, and allow giving *zakah* to all Muslims regardless of any sectarian classification.[47] Obviously, the more righteous in deed and creed is preferred.

In contrast, other sects are generally strict about distributing *zakah* only inside their own sects, Ja'fari Shi'ites quote their Imam as saying, "Do not give *sadaqah* and *zakah* but to your peers." The only exception of this rule they make is giving for reconciliation of hearts. In his *Fiqh al Imam Ja'far*, Mughniyah states that "*zakah* must only be given to individuals within the sect, while voluntary charities may be given to any person who is in need."[48] In *al Hada'iq*, al Bahrani says a man came to Muhammad al Baqir and said, "May the mercy of God be upon you, take from me these five hundred *dirhams* and spend it where it belongs. It is the *zakah* of my wealth." Al Baqir answered, "You take it and give it to your needy and orphaned neighbors and your Muslim brethren."[49] This indicates that al Baqir does not preach any discrimination and believes brotherhood in Islam is above all other considerations.

Abadis do not totally agree as to whether *zakah* may be given to Muslims who do not subscribe to their school of thought. Some of their jurists permit giving *zakah* to any poor person, as long as he is not known to differ with their view. Some even allow giving *zakah* to people who belong to opposing schools of thought.[50] As for Zaidis, they forbid giving their *zakah* to certain deviating sects.

Some of our predecessors believed *zakah* must be given on the sole criteria of need and poverty, with no other questions asked. Ibn Abi Shaibah reports that Fudail asked Ibrahim about giving *zakah* to deviating people. He said, "Our ancestors asked nothing except about poverty." This is the opinion of al Mu'ayad Yahya, and al Shafi'i are reported to forbid helping individuals whose wrongdoing harms Muslims or the Islamic state, such as those who fight Muslims.[51]

SECTION FOUR

CLOSE RELATIVES OF *ZAKAH* PAYER

Relatives whose relation to the *zakah* payer is so distant that the *zakah* payer is not legally responsible for providing their living expenses, may be given *zakah* by either the *zakah* payer or the government. Scholars differ on giving *zakah* to close relatives, such as parents, brothers, sisters, uncles and aunts of *zakah* payers. *Zakah* may be given to close relatives of *zakah* payers on the basis of working in the *zakah* agency or fighting in the way of God, because the *zakah* payer is not responsible for such compensations. *Zakah* may also be given if the close relative is a wayfarer. Reconciliation of relatives' hearts is out of question, because such distribution can only be made by the government or public organizations, and not by individuals.

As for giving on the grounds of need and poverty, one must distinguish between distribution by government and by individual *zakah* payers. If the government distributes *zakah*, it may give close relatives of *zakah* payers, including their children, parents, and wives,[52] since payers fulfill their obligation by delivering *zakah* to the state. When payers distribute their *zakah* directly, they can not give it to relatives for whose provisions the *zakah* payers are responsible, such as parents, wives and children.

Ibn al Mundhir claims an *ijma'* of scholars that *zakah* must not be given to the parents in cases where the *zakah* payer is obligated to provide for their living expenses, since by giving them *zakah* he is saved the obligation of providing their living expenses.[53] Moreover, the Messenger of God is quoted as saying, "You and your wealth belong to your father."[54] and the Qur'an considers the houses of parents and their children one and the same: "It is no fault on yourselves that ye should eat in your own houses."[55] The last phrase refers to houses of one's sons, since it is obvious that there is no fault in eating in one's own house."[56] The Prophet (p) says, "The best food a man eats is that which is out of the man's own earning. That of his son is from his own earning too."[57] Based on this Hanafites argue that ownership of property is continuous between parents and their children. Thus, paying *zakah* to a parent or a child is like giving it to oneself.[58] Children and parents are treated as one unit in *zakah* distribution. There is a saying reported by al Bukhari and Ahmad from Ma'n bin Yasid that "My father gave a man in the mosque a few *dinars* to distribute as charity. Not knowing, I came and took them. My father said, "By God, I did not intend to give you." I complained to the Messenger of God (p), who said "O Yazid, you get the reward for your intention, and O Ma'n, you get what you obtained." This saying, according to al Shawkani, applies to voluntary charity and not to obligated *zakah*.[58]

Only Muhammad, and a report from Abu al 'Abbas (a Shi'ite) approve of giving *zakah* to one's parents. This is supported by a group of later Zaidis. This opinion is based on the general terms of pertinent texts and lack of authentic support for parents' exclusion.[60] Additionally, Malik reportedly approves of giving *zakah* to grandchildren as well as to great grandparents.[61] It seems that Ibn al Mundhir and the author of *al Bahr*, who both report *ijma'*[62] do not believe in the authenticity of narrations from these scholars.

However, Ibn al Mundhir quotes *ijma'* that *zakah* must not be given to parents or children who are responsible for each others' living expenses. Al Nawawi argues that there are cases in which the *zakah* payer is not responsible for the living expenses of his parents or children.[63] Ibn Taimiyah gives as an example a poor mother whose young children are rich. Her living expenses need not be charged to the children under her custody; thus, she may be given *zakah* from them.[64]

Giving *zakah* to the wife is not permissible

Ibn al Mundhir continues, "Scholars unanimously agree that a man must not give his wife *zakah*, since he is obliged to provide all her living expenses."[65] A wife is so intimate to the husband as to be like himself God says "... and among His signs is this: that He created for you mates from among yourselves"[66] God referes to the husband"s house as the wife's house in the verse "and turn them not out of their houses.[67]

Can the wife give her poor husband *zakah*?

Abu Hanifah and some other jurists do not approve of this, on the grounds that wife to husband is like husband to wife. But this analogy is incorrect when applied to *zakah* especially since we have reports to the contrary. The reasoning behind this analogy is invalid with regard to financial support, as stated by Abu 'Ubaid, since though the husband is responsible for living expenses of his wife, rich wives are not obliged to support their poor husbands.[68] Ibn Qudamah notes that since wives are not responsible for the living expenses of their husbands, they can give their *zakah* to their husbands, keeping in mind that giving *zakah* to one's wife is only prohibited to prevent the abuse of *zakah* by the husband, who is responsible for his wife's living expenses in addition to *zakah*.[69]

Ahmad, al Bukhari, and Muslim report from Zainab, the wife of 'Abd Allah bin Mas'ud, that "The Messenger of God (p) said, "O women, give charity, even out of your jewelry." She continues, "I went back to Abd Allah and said, 'You are an empty-handed person, and the Messenger of God (p) just ordered us to give charity. Go to him and ask him if it is acceptable for me to give you charity; otherwise I will give to someone else' 'Abd Allah said, 'You go to the Prophet'. Zainab continues, "I went, and found at the door of the Messenger of God (p) a woman from the Ansar who had a question like mine. The Messenger of God was so greatly esteemed by us that we did not like to knock at the door and disturb him . Then Bilal came out and we told him 'Tell the Messenger of God (p) there are two women at the door asking whether it is acceptable to give their *sadaqah* to their husbands or to spend it on orphans under their custody. And do not mention who we are.' Bilal went in and asked the Prophet, who said, ' Who are they'? Bilal answered 'A lady from the Ansar, and Zainab. The Prophet asked 'which

Zainab?' Bilal replied, 'The wife of 'Abd Allah.' Then the Prophet said 'Indeed they have two rewards. One for kindness to the kin, and one for giving charity.' "The sentence in al Bukhari"s report reads, "Is it acceptable for me to spend it on my husband and on orphans under my custody?"[70]

Al Shawkani says "this saying indicates it is permissible for a wife to give her *zakah* to her husband. This is also the opinion of al Thawri, al Shafi'i, the two disciples of Abu Hanifah, a report from Malik, and a report from Ahmad, also al Hadi, al Nasir, and al Mu'ayad bi Allah. The above saying can be a good argument if it makes a clear reference to obligatory *zakah*. Al Maziri claims it refers to *zakah* because of the words used in the saying itself, "is it acceptable". Others argue that the saying refers only to voluntary charity, especially since it uses the words "out of your jewelry." Al Shawkani remarks, "It appears that giving the wife's *zakah* to her husband is permissible, first because there is nothing to prohibit it, and second because in the above saying, the Prophet makes no distinction between voluntary and obligatory *sadaqah*.[71]

Giving *zakah* to other relatives

Giving *zakah* to one's brothers, sisters, uncles, aunts, and other relatives is disputed by Muslim scholars. Those who do not allow it do so on different grounds. Abu 'Ubaid reports from Ibrahim bin Abi Hafsah, "I asked Sa'id bin Jubair whether I could give my aunt *zakah*. He said, 'Yes, as long as she does not live with you as part of your family.'"[72] Abu 'Ubaid further reports that al Hasan says. "It is all right for a person to give *zakah* to his relatives who are not part of his household."[73] He reports 'Ata as saying that relatives who are not part of the household supported by the *zakah* payer have priority in receiving his *zakah*, if they are poor. Ibn 'Abbas says "as long as you do not give any person whom you support financially, there is no harm in giving relatives *zakah*". These scholars consider whether or not the recipient is part of the *zakah* payer's household to be the criterion for permissibility of giving *zakah* to relatives.[74]

Abu 'Ubaid reports a different view from 'Abd Allah bin Daud, whose criterion is the legal responsibility of the *zakah* payer to provide for relatives. If the state does not obligate the *zakah* payer to support a relative, *zakah* may be given to that relative.[75]

The third, most common opinion uses the criterion of the legal responsibility for financial support as set forth in *Shari'ah*. *Zakah* must not be given to anyone whose living expenses are the obligation of the payer. This is based on two points: firstly, that such a relative is in fact rich by the provision given (or that should be given) by the payer, and secondly, that the payer, by giving *zakah* to this relative, saves himself the additional cost of supporting that relative.[76] This is the view of Malik, al Shafi'i, a report from Ahmad, Zaid bin 'Ali, al Hadi, al Qasim, al Nasir, and al Mu'ayad bi Allah although some of these scholars do not agree on the specification of those relatives whose provisions for living is the responsibility of the payer.

Zaid and Ahmad believe the criteria for financial responsibility is the same as that used in the inheritance system. A person who may inherit from a certain relative is financially responsible for that relative.[77] Al Shafi'i restricts financial responsibility to parents, grandparents, children, and grandchildren only, while Malik further restricts it to children -- sons until puberty,[78] and daughters until marriage-- and the father and mother; i.e. Malik excludes grandchildren and grandparents. Obviously, both Malik and al Shafi'i exclude brothers, sisters, aunts and uncles.[79]

Another group of scholars is more permissive about giving *zakah* to relatives. Some of them argue that *zakah* may be paid to relatives (other than parents and children) for whose living expenses the *zakah* payer may be responsible. These include Abu Hanifah, his disciples, and Yahya. It is the predominant report from Ahmad, according to Ibn Qudamah. Abu 'Ubaid argues that this is the most acceptable opinion, because the Prophet (p) said, "The *sadaqah* to the needy is merely a sadaqah, but it is both a sadaqah and a kindness to kin when it is given to relatives."[80] This saying makes no distinction between obligatory and voluntary sadaqah or between relatives for whose living expenses the payer is responsible and other relatives.[81] Ibn Abi Shaibah and Abu 'Ubaid say this is also the opinion of a handful of Companions and Followers.

They quote Ibn 'Abbas as saying, "A person should give his relatives *zakah* if they are in need," and Ibrahim as reporting, Ibn Mas'ud's wife asked him about giving the *zakah* of her jewelry to her orphaned nephews who were under her custody. Ibn Mas'ud answered 'yes'." Al Hasan was asked if it was permissible to give *zakah* to one's brother, and replied "yes indeed." Ibrahim was asked whether a woman can give her sister *zakah*, and replied affirmatively. Al Dahhak remarks "If you have poor relatives, they have priority over your *zakah* compared to other people." Mujahid adds, "One's *zakah* is not accepted if it is given to others while one has needy relatives."[82]

Comparison and analysis

After surveying all these opinions, I feel that the one which allows giving *zakah* to all relatives except parents and children is most appropriate. This is also the opinion of Abu 'Ubaid and the majority of scholars since the era of the Companions and Followers. This opinion is supported by:

1. The generality of texts about the poor, which make no distinction between poor relatives and non-relatives, like "The *sadaqat* are only for the poor and the needy and the saying ". . to be taken from the rich among them and rendered to the poor among them." These texts include relatives, and any attempt to remove relatives from the categories of *zakah* deservants requires an appropriate text. This is not the case with the wife, parents, and children, who are unanimously excluded from zakah.

2. Texts that encourage helping one's relatives, such as "The *sadaqah* given to the needy is merely a *sadaqah*, but that given to one's relatives has two merits: It is a *sadaqah* and a kindness to kin,"[83] "Indeed, the best *sadaqah* is that given to a relative, even one who hides hatred,"[84] and the saying from Ibn Mas'ud wife mentioned earlier.

The argument that in giving *zakah* to these relatives, the payer benefits himself, is not absolute. It indeed applies to the *zakah* payer's wife, children, and parents, but not to other relatives, since supporting relatives other than the wife, children, and parents, is the responsibility of the Islamic state from *zakah, fai* and other sources. Relatives are responsible only when the state does not fulfill its obligation . A *zakah* payer may support relatives other than his wife, parents and children out of his own *zakah*.

We should notice that Hanafite scholars make no connection between permissibility of giving *zakah* to relatives and financial responsibility for supporting them as determined in *Shari'ah*. They hold that charging the payer with the responsibility of supporting his relatives does not prevent allowing him to give them *zakah*, as long as what is given to them is made their own property, since there is no continuity of property between relatives other than parent and children.[85] The Zaidi author of *al Rawd al Nadir* argues that giving the relatives *zakah* does not imply saving an otherwise obligatory financial support, since the obligation of support is only temporary.[86]

Al Shawkani adds that, in principle, giving one's *zakah* to relatives is permissible, since no text prevents it and the burden of proof is on anyone who claims otherwise.[87]

SECTION FIVE

THE DESCENDENTS OF PROPHET MUHAMMAD (P)

Sayings prohibiting *sadaqah* to (p) Muhammad's family

Ahmad and Muslim report that al Muttalib bin Rabi'ah (first cousin of the Prophet) "went with al Fadl bin al Abbas to the Messenger of God (p). One of them said, 'O Messenger of God, we come to ask you to appoint us on *sadaqat*, so we can earn from it like other people (who are employed) and bring you what we collect like other people do.' The Prophet said, 'Indeed, the *sadaqah* must not be taken by Muhammad or the family of Muhammad; it is merely the impurities cleansed from peoples wealth.' "In a version mentioned in *al Muntaqa*, the Prophet says, ". . . is not lawful to Muhammad, nor to the family of Muhammad."[88] Abu Daud and al Tirmidhi report that Abu Rafi' says, "The Messenger of God (p) appointed a man from the clan of bani Makhzum on *sadaqah*. The man said to me 'Come with me (to help me), and you will get some of it.' I said, 'Not until I ask the Messenger of God (p).' When I asked him, he told me 'The ex-slave of a clan is one of them, and we are a family to whom sadaqah is not lawful'." Abu Rafi' was an ex-slave of the Prophet (p). Al Bukhari reports from Abu Hurairah, "Al Hasan bin 'Ali took one date from the dates of the *sadaqah* and put it in his mouth. (he was then a child). The Prophet (p) said, 'Yech, Yech!' to get him to take it out of his mouth, and continued, 'Don't you know we do not eat from the sadaqah? "Muslim's version (as stated by al Hafiz) reads "We are those to whom the *sadaqah* is not lawful," and in a version from Ma'mar, "Indeed the *sadaqah* is not lawful to the family of Muhammad." Ahmad and al Tahawi report from al Hasan bin Ali "I was with the Prophet (p). We passed by a crate of dates collected as sadaqah. I took one and put it in my mouth. The Prophet grabbed it with the saliva on it and said, "We, the family of Muhammad, the *sadaqah* is not lawful for us." Its chain is strong.[90]

These sayings indicate that *zakah* is not permissible to the Prophet (p) and his family and descendents . It is important to determine who consists the family of the Prophet, and whether both *zakah* and voluntary charity are not permissible to them.

Whom does the family of Muhammad include?

Al Hafiz in *al Fath* and al Shawkani in *al Nail* state that there are differences among Muslim scholars on specification of the Prophet's family.[91] Al Shafi'i and a group of scholars believe the family of the Prophet includes the children of Hashem and the children of al Muttalib. Hashem is the great-grandfather of the Prophet and al Muttalib is Hashem's brother. Al Shafi'i argues that the Prophet (p) included the children of al Muttalib as well as the children of Hashem in the share assigned to the Prophet kindred, and did not include any other clan. Al Shafi'i continues that this share is given in compensation for preventing them from taking *sadaqah*. Al Bukhari reports from Jubair bin Mut'im, "I went with 'Uthman bin 'Affan to the Prophet, and said, 'O Messenger of God, you have given the children of al Muttalib out of the one-fifth from Khaibar and did not give us. We and they are at the same level.' The Messenger of God said, 'The children of al Muttalib and the children of Hashem are one thing.'"

This argument is challenged on the grounds that the children of al Muttalib were given from the share of the kindred only because of their alliance with and support of the family of the Prophet, and not as recompense for preventing them from taking *sadaqah*. Consequently, Abd Hanifah, Malik, and the Hadawis believe the family of the Prophet includes the children of Hashem alone. There are two reports about the view of Ahmad. One goes along with Abu Hanifah, and the other agrees with al Shafi'i.

The children of Hashem include the families of 'Ali, 'Aqil, Ja'far, al Abbas, and al Harith. Notice that the family of Abu Lahab is not included, because it is said that none of them embraced Islam during the life of the Prophet (although the author of *Jami al Usul* reports that his two sons, 'Utbah and Ma'tab, became Muslim the year of opening Makkah, and that the Prophet was pleased by their conversion and prayed on their behalf,) Ibn Qudamah says "We know of no dispute that to the children of Hashem, *zakah* is not permissible." Ibn Rislan and Abu Talib claim there is *ijma* on this.

According to al Tahawi, al Tabari quotes that Abu Hanifah allows paying *zakah* to the family of the Prophet, if they are denied the share of the kindred. A similar opinion is attributed to al Abhari , a Malikite and to some Safi'ites, as stated by the author of *al Fath*.

Abu Yusuf is claimed to have permitted members of the Prophet's family to receive *zakah* paid by other members of the same family. A similar opinion is attributed in *al bahr* to Zaid bin Ali, al Murtada, Abu al Abbas, and the Imamis. The same is mentioned in *al Shifa'* as attributed to the two children of al Hadi as well as to al Qasim. Al Shawkani contends that the saying which indicates this prohibition seems to cover all cases. Some scholars even claim that these sayings may reach the grade of *al mutawatir.* This is supported by a few verses: "Say: No reward do I ask you for this except the love of those near of kin,"[92] "Say: No reward do I ask of you for this, nor am I a pretender,"[93] and "Of their goods take *sadaqah* so thou might purify and sanctify them,"[94] and the saying, "The *sadaqah* is only the impurities of people's wealth," reported by Muslim.[95]

As for permitting members of the Prophet's family to take *zakah* from other members of the same Family, it is founded on a report that al 'Abbas said, "I told the Messenger of God, 'You have prohibited us from taking the *sadaqah* of people. Are the *sadaqah* of some of us lawful to others among us?' He replied, 'Yes: "The authenticity of this saying is controversial.

It may be useful here to quote the different schools' positions on this issue. In *Majma' al Anhur*, Abu Hanifah is reported to have permitted giving *zakah* to the children of Hashem. Muhammad, in *al Athar*, is quoted as saying "There are two narrations from Abu Hanifah. We hold to the one that allows giving them *zakah* since the prohibition is restricted to the era of the Prophet (p). "In *Durr al Muntaqa*, Abu Hanifah is reported to have allowed paying *zakah* from one member to another of the children of Hashem. He is also reported to have approved of giving them *zakah* in general. Al Tahawi adds "This is what we support. This is approved by al Qahastani and others."[96] Ibn Taimiyah also permits giving *zakah* from one member to another of the children of Hashem,[97] in agreement with the Ja'farite opinion.

The most restrictive opinion is that of Zaidis, who consider the prohibition of paying *zakah* to a member of the 'Prophet's family absolute and final, to the extent that they consider eating the flesh of a dead animal not as bad as a member of the Prophet's family taking *zakah*.[99]

What if no war booty or *fai'* is given the Prophet's family?

Can the Prophet's family be given *zakah* if their share of war booty and *fai'* is not given to them?

This question is answered affirmatively by a few scholars. These include some Malikites, who point out that members of the Prophet's family are prevented from taking *zakah* partly because a share of war booty and *fai'* is assigned to them. Therefore, if they are not given that share and are struck by poverty, they can be given *zakah*. Hanafites have a similar argument, as quoted in the preceding subsection . Among Shafi'ites, Abu Sa'id al Istakhri believes the family of the Prophet may be given *zakah* if they are not paid their share of booty and *fai'*. Al Nawawi quotes al Rafi'i that Muhammad bin Yahaya (a disciple of al Ghazali) believes the same.[100] Ibn Taimiyah and al Qadi

Ya'qub, a Hanbalite, present similar arguments.[101] This is also the view of the Ja'fari school.[102]

The majority of scholars believe that since the family and descendents of the Prophet (p) are not given *zakah* in order to honor them, their deprivation from booty is not sufficient grounds to give them *zakah*.[103]

Comparison and weighing

In our times, payment of *zakah* to descendents of the Prophet must be permissible, since they are not given a share of booty and *fai'*, either because the latter do not exist at all or because of arbitrary decision by rulers.

The share of the Prophet's kindred is referred to in the Qur'an several times: "And know that out of all the booty ye may acquire in war, a fifth share is assigned to God, and to the Apostle, and to near relatives, and to orphans and to the needy and to the wayfarer,"[104] and "What God has bestowed on His Apostle and taken away from the people of the townships belongs to God, to His Apostle, and to kindred, and orphans, and the needy, and the wayfarer, in order that it may not merely make a circuit between the wealthy among you."[105]

Claiming that the family of the Prophet (p) is prevented from receiving *zakah* to honor them is not so strong an argument. It seems more reasonable that they are so prohibited because of the share they are granted in those two verses. Thus, if the compensation assigned to them does not exist, they must be able to receive *zakah*, especially since many scholars believe the share of the kindred, after the death of the Prophet, must be diverted to supporting fighters in the way of God, thus leaving the family and descendents of the Prophet with nothing to support them in case of need.

The opinion that permits the family of the Prophet and their descendents to receive *zakah* is further supported by the fact that all the sayings presented in support of their prevention do not clearly name the reason for the prevention, a shown below:

A. The refusal of the Prophet to appoint his cousins on collecting *zakah* was based on his desire to have the members of his family set a good example in honesty by not taking anything from the income of the state.[106] The narration of al Bukhri implies this by wording, "Indeed, the *sadaqah* is not suitable to the family of Muhammad." This is so in order to prevent accusations and rumors of any abuse of state funds, which is perhaps why even ex-slaves of the family are prevented from taking *zakah*, as indicated by the saying from abu Rafi. This shows that they are not prevented from *zakah* because they are too honorable.

B. The saying from al Hasan that "The sadaqah is not lawful to us "is most likely a reference to the Prophet in his capacity as the head of state. 'Umar understood that, as a head of the state, he must not take anything out of *zakah*. Once, he drank some milk but when he realized it belonged to the *sadaqah*, he threw it up.[108] The author of *al Bahr* argues that the *sadaqah* is not lawful to the ruler and his family, since the Prophet prohibited it to his family.[109]

C. We must reconsider the texts about this issue. The term that appears in the sayings is "*al Muhammad*", which literally means the family or the people of Muhammad. By what authority can anyone claim that this word must include descendents of Muhammad and his relatives through the centuries?

The word *al* is used in several other verses, such as "God did choose Adam and Noah, al (the family) of Ibrahim , and al (the family) 'Imran above all people,"[110] "then al (the people) of Pharoah picked him up,"[111] "and drowned al (the people) of Pharoah."[112] This word has nothing to do with their descendents. All it means in these usages is the close family: wives, children, and all those closely associated by bond of family relation. There is nothing in the saying that allows us to include their descendents in all centuries to come; hence arises the opinion of Abu Hanifah that this prevention only applies to the Prophet's family during his lifetime and ceases after his death. This is also a view attributed to Malik, according to the author of *al Bahr*.[113] Two points must be kept in mind. Firstly, Islamic laws do not discriminate between the members of the Prophet's family and others. The Prophet (p) himself says "By God, if Fatima, daughter of Muhammad, stole, I would cut her hand,"[114] and "He whose deeds make him slow, [in his path towards God] his family relation does not make him progress faster."[115] Secondly, *zakah* is a basic obligation and a determined right, collected by the state and distributed to defined deservants. Why then should some people be excluded from being its deservants?

Finally, we must remember that there is no ijma' on preventing the descendents of the Prophet from receiving *zakah* since Abu Hanifah, some Malikites , and some Shafi'ites disagree. Thus, one can rightly represent that all that is indicated by the sayings is that the Prophet and members of his family are prevented from *zakah*, in order to purify them from suspicion of abuse of *zakah* proceeds at a time when the legislation of *Shari'ah* was still being formed. Al Dahlawi adds "this was a very good move on the part of the Prophet, one which nipped in the bud any attempt to accuse him of financial abuse."[116]

SECTION SIX

ERRORS IN JUDGEMENT IN *ZAKAH* DISTRIBUTION

Giving *zakah* to non-deservants by error of judgement

If a *zakah* payer gives his *zakah* to a person whom he thought was a deservant then finds that he was incorrect, does that payment fulfill the payer's obligation of *zakah*?

There are three major opinions on this matter. The first is that such distribution fulfills the obligation of *zakah*. This is the opinion of Abu Hanifah, Muhammad, al Hasan., and Abu 'Ubaid. This view implies that no other payment is required from the *zakah* payer, and is founded on a few sayings of the Prophet: Al Bukhari and Ahmad report from Ma'n bin Yazid, "My father put a few *dinars* as a *sadaqah* with a man in the mosque [to give them away]. Not knowing, I came by and took them. My father said, 'By God, I did not intend to give you.' I complained to the Prophet, who said, "O Yazid, you get the intention and O Ma'n you get what you have taken.'" This saying does not make any distinction between voluntary and obligatory *sadaqah*, Abu Hurairah narrates that the Prophet (p) said, "A man once said,[117] Surely I am going to give a charity tonight.' He went out with his *sadaqah* and put it in the hands of a thief, [not knowing). The next morning, it was rumored that a thief was given *sadaqah* the night before, The man said, 'My Lord, praise be only to you, indeed I shall give another *sadaqah*.' He went out with the *sadaqah* and put it in the hands of a prostitute. The next morning it was circulated that a prostitute was given *sadaqah*. The man said to himself "My Lord praise is due to You alone. Surely I will give *sadaqah*." He went out with the new *sadaqah* and put it in the hands of a rich man. The next morning, people were saying that a rich was given *sadaqah* the night before. The man said, 'My Lord, praise be to You. Should I be giving to a prostitute, a thief, and a rich man! While asleep, he was told, 'As for your *sadaqah* to the thief, it may help him be satisfied and cease stealing; as for the prostitute, she may take the *sadaqah* and quit prostitution, and as for the rich man, he may take the lesson and start spending out of what God has given him.'"[118]

There is also the saying in which the Prophet (p) told a man who asked him for charity, "If you are among those categories of deservats, I would give you your right," and the Prophet's answer to the two strong and capable men who asked him for *sadaqah*, if you wish, I would give you out of it, but the rich and the capable of earning have no share in it." If the condition was truly richness, he would have investigated their case and not merely accepted their claim.[119]

The second opinion inclines toward the other extreme, and considers that if an error of judgement results in giving *zakah* to a person who is not a deservant , the *zakah* obligation is not fulfilled, and another amount must be given. Al Shafi'i subscribes generally to this view,[120] while we have two reports about the view of Ahmad on mistakenly giving *zakah* to a rich man, one similar to that of al Shafi'i. As for giving *zakah* to a disbeliever or a member of the Prophet's family, Ahmad firmly believes such payment does not fulfill the requirement of *zakah*.

The third opinion covers the area between these two extremes. There are several sub-views in this area according to the conditions of distribution, as will be detailed in the following.

According to Hanafites, if the payer makes reasonable effort and research to find deservants, and then finds he paid *zakah* to non-deservants, such a payment is acceptable and the payer is not required to repeat his payment. However, when *zakah* is distributed without proper investigation, such payment is not acceptable if it is found that it was given to non-deservants. When payment is given to unbelievers, Abu Yusuf believes the *zakah* payer is required to make a second payment, even if *zakah* was distributed after proper investigation.[122]

According to Malikites, payment to non-deservants as a result of error in judgement does not relieve the *zakah* payer from his responsibility, and a second payment must be made unless what is given to non-deservants can be retrieved and redistributed to deservants.[123]

Zaidis believe giving *zakah* to persons considered unanimously non-deserving, by mistake, does not fulfill the obligation of *zakah*. Individuals who are unanimously treated as non-deservants are unbelievers, parents and offsprings of the payers, and the rich. If a person gives his *zakah* to individuals to whom he believes *zakah* can be given, another payment is not required.[124]

Finally, in my opinion, if a *zakah* payer makes sufficient efforts and research to find deservants but makes a mistake and gives his *zakah* to non-deservants by error of judgement, he is not responsible for that mistake, nor is he required to repeat the payment. God says, "On no soul does God place a burden greater than it can bear,"[125] and God would not suffer the reward of such a person to be lost, exactly like the person mentioned in the saying who gave his *sadaqah* to a thief, a prostitute, and a rich person. However, if the *zakah* payer did not make reasonable research, he must be charged for the result of his mistake in judgement. In all cases, whoever takes *zakah* knowing he is not a deservant must return it or at least give it to a deservant. Otherwise, what he takes is unlawful. If the *zakah* agency makes a mistake in giving *zakah* non-deservants, the *zakah* authority is not required to repeat the payment. Rather, the law enforcement body must be used to recover what was unjustly given, as recommended by Malikites.

Footnotes

1.   *Fath al Qadir*, Vol. 2, p. 21.

2.   Al Nawawi says, "Its chains of both narrations are good. Al Baihaqi gathers all chains of this saying. In these chains, Malik and Ibn Uyaynah report it *mursal*, while Ma'mar and al Thawri link the saying to the Prophet. If a saying is reported *mursal,* and linked up, it is considered linked, as long as the chain through which it is linked up is accepted, according to the correct rule of hadith research." *See al Majmu'*, Vol. 6, p.206.

3.   *Fath al Qadir*, Vol. 2 , p. 23.

4.   *Ibid.*

5.   *Ibid*, p.24.

6.   *Al Majmu'*, Vol. 6, p.191.

7.   *Sharh al Khirshi* on *Matn Khalil*, Vol. 2, p. 214.

8.   Chapter one of this part.

9.   The author of *al Bahr*, Vol. 2, p. 175, mentions the condition of al Shafi'i that the poor must be weak, chronically ill, and not beggars, but the above mentioned saying negates this condition. Ibn al 'Arabi considers restricting giving to the chronically ill false, as mentioned earlier.

10. *Fath al Qadir*, Vol. 2, p. 28.

11. *Al Amwal*, p. 557.

12. The author of *al Bahr al Zakhkhar*, Vol. 2, p. 185, quotes this *ijma'*.

13. *Sura al Mumtahinah*, 60:9.

14. *Ibid.* 60:8.

15. *Sura al Baqarah*, 2:272.

16. *Tafsir Ibn Kathir*, Vol. 4, p. 349.

17. *Ibn Kathir*, Vol. 1, p. 324.

18. *Sura al Dahr*, 76:8.

19. *Musannaf Ibn Abi shaibah*, Vol. 4, pp. 39-40.

20. *Sural al Baqarah*, 2:271.

21. *Sura al Ma'idah*, 5:89.

22. *Sura al Mujadalah*, 58:4.

23. *Al Bada'i,* Vol. 2, p. 49.

24. *Al Amwal*, pp. 613-614 and *Musannaf Ibn Abi Shaibah*, Vol. 4, p. 39.

25. *Al Majmu'* Vol. 6, p. 228. The above-mentioned *ijma'* does not include heart reconciliation.

26. *Ibid.*

27. *Al Mabsut*, Vol. 2, p. 202.

28. *Musannaf Ibn Abi Shaibah*, Vol. 4, p. 40.

29. *Sura al Tawbah*, 9:60.

30.　*Musannaf, op. cit.*

31.　*Al Kharaj,* by Abu Yusuf, p. 126, Salafiyah print. Similar to this is what is reported by al Baladhari in his history, p. 177: "'Umar bin al Khattab, upon his journey to al Jabiyah (close to Damascus) passed by some Christian lepers, and ordered them to be given *sadaqah* and their food be served to them." It is obvious that *sadaqat* means obligated *zakah,* since this *zakah* was under the governor's authority, from which foodstuff was usually given.

32.　*Al Rawd al Nadir,* Vol. 2, p. 426.

33.　*Al Bahr al Zakhhar,* Vol. 2, p. 185.

34.　*Tafsir al Tabari,* ed. Sakir, Vol. 14, p. 308.

35.　The late Abu Zahra, 'Abd al Rahman Hasan, and 'Aba al Wahhab Khallaf comment that the interpretation of the word "needy" in the verse to mean poor people of the book establishes two points: One that the poor and needy are two different categories, and two that it is permissible to give *zakah* to poor people of the Pledge, provided they are chronically ill or completely disabled. Able people of the Pledge are charged *jiziah,* and it is not rational for them to be charged *jiziah* and given *zakah* at the same time. See *Halqat al Dirasat al Ijtima'iyah,* p. 202.

36.　*Ahkam al Qur'an,* by al Jassas, Vol. 3, p. 315.

37.　*Sharh al Nil,* Vol. 2, p. 49.

38.　*Al Bada'i,* Vol. 2, p. 49.

39.　*Al Amwal,* p. 46.

40.　*Al Bahr al Zakhkhar,* Vol. 2, p. 186.

41.　*Al Sharh al Kabir* with *Hashiat al Dusuq*i, Vol. 1, p. 492. This is consistent with the Ja'fari view, as stated in *Fiqh al Imam Ja'far,* Vol. 2, p. 93, and that of the Abadis, as in *al Nil* Vol. 2, pp 141-142.

42.　*Sharh al Azhar,* Vol. 1, p. 520-1.

43.　*Sura al Tawbah,* 9:71.

44.　*Sura al An'am,* 6:164.

45.　*Fatawa Ibn Taimiyah,* Vol. 25, p. 87.

46.　*Ibid,* p. 89.

47.　See for example *Hashiat Ibn Abidin,* Vol. 2, p. 75.

48.　*Fiqh al Imam Ja'far,* Vol. 2, p. 93.

49. *Ibid*, p. 97.

50. *Sharh al Nil*, Vol. 2, p.133.

51. *Al Rawd al Nadir*, Vol. 2, p.43.

52. *Ahkam al Qur'an*, by Ibn al 'Arabi, p. 965.

53. *Al Mughni*, Vol. 2, p. 647.

54. *Tafsir Ibn Kathir*, Vol. 3, p. 305. The saying is reported by Ahmad in *al Musnad* via three chains, from 'Amr bin Shu'aib from his father from his grandfather. The late Ahmad Shakir grades all of them correct . See the sayings no. 6678, 6902, and 7001, is Vol. 11 and 12. It is also reported by Ibn Majah from Jabir, via a chain whose narrators are trustworthy , and al Tabarani from Samurah and Ibn Mas'ud via a weak chain. See *al Taisir*, by al Munawi, Vol. 1, p. 378.

55. *Sura al Nur* 24:61.

56. *Tafsir al Qurtubi,* Vol. 12 , p. 314.

57. Reported by al Tirmidhi, al Nasa'i, and Ibn Majah from 'A'ishah. The chain is graded good by al Tirmidhi and correct by Abu Hatim. See *al Taisir*, Vol. 1, p. 311. It is also reported by Ahmad with similar wording, via a correct chain, as a part of saying no. 6678 and 7001.

58. *Al Bada'i',* Vol. 2, p. 49.

59. *Nail al Awtar*, Vol. 4, p. 189.

60. *Al Rawd al Nadir*, Vol. 2, p. 421.

61. *Nail al Awtar, op. cit.*

62. *Al Bahr al Zakhkhar*, Vol. 2 , p. 186.

63. *Al Majmu'*, Vol. 6, p. 229.

64. *Ikhtiarat Ibn Taimiyah*, pp. 61-2.

65. *Al Mughni*, Vol. 2, p. 649 and *Nail al Awtar*, Vol. 4, p. 188.

66. *Sura al Rum*, 40:21.

67. *Sura al Talaq*, 65:1.

68. *Al Amwal*, p. 588.

69. *Al Mughni*, Vol. 2, p. 650.

70. *Nail al Awtar*, Vol. 4, pp. 187-188.

71. *Ibid.*

72. *Al Amwal*, pp. 582-583.

73. *Ibid.*

74. *Ibid.*

75. *Ibid.*

76. *Al Majmu'*, Vol. 6, p. 229, and *Ahkam al Qur'an*, by Ibn al 'Arabi, p. 960.

77. *Al Rawd al Nadir op cit*, and *al Mughni*, Vol. 2, p. 607.

78. The late shaikh 'Allaish, a Malikite, was asked whether the father of a student who is strong and capable of working can give him *zakah*. The answer was affirmative, since the father is not required to support an adult son who can earn, and a full-time student is a *zakah* deservant anyway. See *Fath al 'Aliy al Malik*, Vol. 1, p. 129.

79. *Al Mudawannah al Kubra*, Vol. 1, p. 256, al Khairiyah print 1324 H.

80. Reported by the five, except Abu Daud.

81. *Al Mughni*, Vol. 2, p. 648.

82. These statements are mentioned in *Musannaf of Ibn Abi Shaibah*, Vol. 4, pp. 47-8, and *al Amwal*, pp. 581-2.

83. Reported by Ahmad, al Nasa'i, al Tirmidhi, Ibn Habban, al Hakim, and al Daraqutni. Al Tirmidhi grades it good. See *Nail al Awtar*, Vol. 4, p. 189.

84. Reported by Ahmad and al Tabarani from Abu Ayub. They also report a similar saying from Hakim bin Hizam. The author of *Majma' al Zawa'id* comments that its chain is good. Al Tabarani in his *al Mu'jam al Kabir* reports the same from Umm Kulthum bint 'Uqbah; its chain narrators are those of the correct collections. See *al Rawd al Nadir*, Vol. 2, p. 422.

85. *Al Bada'i*, Vol. 2, p. 49-50.

86. *Al Rawd al Nadir*, Vol. 2, p. 423.

87. *Nail al Awtar*, Vol. 2, p. 423.

88. *Ibid*, p. 175.

89. *Al Majmu'*, Vol. 6, pp. 167-168.

90. *Fath al Bari*, Vol. 3, p. 228.

91. *Ibid,* p. 227, and *Nail al Awtar*, Vol. 4, pp. 182-4.

92. *Sura al Shura,* 42:23.

93. *Sura Sad,* 48:86.

94. *Sura al Tawbah,* 9:103.

95. Al Hafiz says "This indicates that it is permissible to give voluntary donations but not obligated *zakah.* This is the opinion of most Hanafites and the accepted view among Shafi'ites and Hanbalites. As for the opposite (allowing *zakah* but not voluntary donations), it is argued that there is no humiliation in taking obligated *zakah,* contrary to taking what is volunteered. "See *al Fath,* Vol. 3, p. 227.

96. *Majma' al Anhur,* printed with Dur al Muntaqa, p. 224.

97. *Matalib Uli al Nuha,* Vol. 2, p. 157.

98. *Fiqh al Imam Ja'far,* Vol. 9, pp. 94-95. It is stated "*Zakah* that is not obligated by texts, such as *zakah* on trade, can be given them, but certainly not *zakah* on wheat, barley, date, and raisin."

99. *Sharh al Azhar* and its commentaries, Vol. 1, pp. 520-523.

100. *Al Majmu',* Vol. 6, pp. 227-228.

101. *Matalib Uli al Nuha, op. cit.*

102. *Fiqh al Imam Ja'far, op. cit.*

103. *Al Majmu', op. cit.*

104. *Sura al Anfal,* 8:41.

105. *Sura al Hashr,* 59:7.

106. Abu 'Uabaid, Abu Yusuf in al Kharaj, and Ibn Jarir report from al Hasan bin Muhammad bin al Hanafiyah that he was asked about the shares of the Messenger and the kindred, and answered, "People differ, after the Prophet's death, on these two shares. Some say the share of kindred belongs to the relatives of the Prophet (p). Others hold it belongs to the kindred of the *Khalifah,* whoever he might be. Yet others say the share of the Prophet (p) belongs after his death to the *khalifah.* So they came to a unanimous agreement that they must spend these two shares on mares and equipment for the sake of God." He continues, "This practice continued through the periods of Abu Bakr and 'Umar."See *al Amwal,* p. 332, and *Bidayat al Mujtahid,* Vol. 1, pp. 390-391. In fact, when 'Ali become *Khalifah,* he continued the same practice as Abu Bakr and Umar. See *Al Amwal, ibid.*

107. The biography of the Prophet by Ibn Hisham, Vol. 4, p. 42, ed. Muhammad Muhiy al Din 'Abd al Hamid.

108. Reported by Malik in *al Muwatta',* chapter on *zakah.*

109. *Al Bahr al Zakhkhar*, Vol. 2, p. 184.

110. *Sura al 'Imran*, 3:33.

111. *Sura al Qasas*, 28:8.

112. *Sura al Baqarah*, 2:50.

113. *Al Bahr, op. cit.*

114. Agreed upon.

115. Agreed upon.

116. *Hujjat Allah al Balighah*, Vol. 2, p. 512.

117. From the Israelites.

118. Reported by Ahmad, al Bukhari, and Muslim.

119. *Al Mughni,* Vol. 2, p. 667.

120. *Al Rawdah,* Vol. 2, p.328.

121. *Al Mughni*, Vol. 2, p. 668.

122. *Radd al Muhtar*, Vol. 2, pp. 73-74.

123. *Al Sharh al Kabir* with *Hashiat al Dusuqi*, Vol. 1, pp. 501-502.

124. *Sharh al Azhar*, Vol. 1, pp. 526-526. and *al Bahr*, Vol. 2, p. 187.

125. *Sura al Baqarah*, 2:286.

FIQH AL ZAKAH

PART FIVE

METHODS OF *ZAKAH* DISTRIBUTION

1. The role of the state.

2. The place of intention with respect to *zakah*.

3. Payment of value in zakah.

4. Transporting *zakah*.

5. Pre-payment and delayed payment.

6. Questions about *zakah* fulfillment.

<h1 style="text-align:center">CHAPTER ONE</h1>

<h1 style="text-align:center">THE ROLE OF THE STATE</h1>

State responsibility with regard to *zakah*

As a confirmed obligation from God, *zakah* is not merely a charity left to individuals to implement, nor is its fulfillment dependent on the benevolence of the wealthy. *Zakah* is rather a social welfare institution supervised by the state, and an organized tax administered by an autonomous public organization.

The state's role in the collection and distribution of *zakah* is best supported by the verse that mentions "the workers on *zakah*"[1] as one of the categories to whom *zakah* is distributed. This verse is explicit evidence that there should be a specialized organization with workers who derive their incomes from the budget of this organization. Moreover, God says, "Out of their wealth take a *sadaqah* so thou might purify and sanctify them".[2] "Take" is addressed to the Prophet as head of the Islamic state, to the extent that when Abu Bakr succeeded the Prophet (p) as head of state, he continued using state authority and its law enforcement body to collect and distribute *zakah*. Scholars recognize that the verb "take" in the above verse is addressed to the Prophet (p) and to whoever runs the affairs of Muslims after him.

As for Sunnah, there are sayings that confirm that administering *zakah* is one of the responsibilities of the Islamic state. Al Bukhari, Muslim and others report from Ibn 'Abbas that the Prophet told Mu'adh when he sent him to Yemen, "Inform them that God obligates *sadaqah* on their wealth, to be taken from the rich among them and rendered to the poor among them. If they obey you in that, carefully avoid their dear wealth . . . " This saying indicates that *zakah* is taken from the rich and rendered to the poor by the state. Al Hafiz Ibn Hajar says, "This saying is evidence that the state is the authority that takes *zakah* and distributes it. Those who refuse to pay are forced to do so."[3] Al Shawkani quotes the same from Ibn Hajar in his *Nail al Awtar*.[4] Additionally, there are several sayings which instruct workers on *zakah*, who were called *al su'at* or *al musaddiqin*. Most of these sayings are mentioned in chapter two of part four. There are also many sayings that advise payers on
their conduct towards the collectors.

In addition to Qur'an and Sunnah, the assertion that the Islamic state is responsible for collection and distribution of *zakah* is supported by the actual practice of the Prophet (p) and the Wise Successors after him. Ibn Hajar in *al Talkhis* notes that the fact that the Messenger of God (p) and his Successors sent *zakah* collectors is quite famous. Al Bukhari and Muslim report from Abu Hurairah that the Prophet (p) sent 'Umar as a collector of *zakah*. They report from Abu Humaid that the "Prophet (p) employed a man from the tribe of al Azd named Ibn al Lutbiyah as *zakah* collector." They also report that 'Umar employed Ibn al Sa'di for that job." Abu Daud reports that the Prophet (p) employed Ibn Mas'ud as *zakah* collector. Ahmad reports that the Prophet sent Aba Jahm bin Hudhaifah and 'Utbah bin 'Amir as *zakah* collectors, and from Qurrah bin Da'mus that "the Prophet sent al Dahhak bin Qaid as *zakah* collector." Al Hakim reports in his *al Mustadrdk* that the Prophet sent Qais bin Sa'd and 'Ubadah bin al Samit as *zakah* collectors , and al Walid bin 'Uqbah as collector of *zakah* from the tribe of bani al Mustaliq.

Al Baihaqi reports From al Shfii'i that Abu Bakr and 'Umar used to send *zakah* collectors. In a version reported by al Shafi'i from Ibrahim bin Sa'd from al Zuhri, it is added that they did not delay its collection every year.

Al Shafi'i, in his former opinion, narrates that in the year of famine, 'Umar postponed *zakah*, then sent collectors to take twice as much in following year. Ibn Sa'd reports in *al Tabaqat* that the Prophet (p) sent collectors to Arab tribes on the crescent of al Muharram year 9 H. This saying is also cite by al Waqidi in his *Maghazi*.[5] Ibn Sa'd names *zakah* collectors and tribes to whom they were sent. The Prophet, he says, sent 'Uyainah bin Hisn to bani Tamim to collect and distribute *zakah*, Buraidah bin al Hasib to Aslam and Ghifar, 'Abbas bin Bishr al Ashhali to Sulaim and Muzainah, Rafi' bin Makith to Juhainah, 'Amr bin al 'As to Fazarah, al Dahhak bin Sufyan al Kilabi to bani Kilab, Busr bin Sufyan al Ka'bi to bani Ka'b, Ibn al Lutbiyah to bani Dhubian, and a man from Sa'd Hudhaim to his tribe. Ibn Sa'd adds, "The Messenger of God (p) told his collectors to take only from the surplus and to avoid the top-notch assets of the payers."[6]

Ibn Ishaq names yet other collectors the Prophet (p) sent to various tribes and provinces of the Arabian peninsula. For example, he sent al Muhajir bin Abi Umayyah to San'a', zaid bin Labid to Hadramawt, 'Adi bin Hatim to Tai' and bani Asad, al 'Ala' bin Hadrami to al Bahrain and Ali to Najran.[7] In *al Taratib al Idariyah*, al Kattani quotes Ibn Hazm in *Jawami' al Siyar* as saying "al Zubair was the *zakah* clerk appointed by the Messenger of God (p); in al Zubair's absence, Jahm bin al Salt and Hudhaifah bin al Yaman used to substitute for him."[8] Al Kattani also quotes Ibn Hajar in *al Isabah* as naming Companions employed for this job by the Prophet. These include al Arqam bin Abi al Arqam, Hudhaifah bin al Yaman, Kafiyah bin Sab' al Asdi, Kahl bin Malik al Hudhali, Khalid bin al Barsa', Abu Jahm bin Hudhaifah, Khalid bin Sa'id bin al 'As, Khuzaimah bin 'Asim al 'Ukali, etc..[9] Thus it is obvious that the Prophet (p) covered practically all Arabia with *zakah* officers. He (p) provided them with advice and instructions on how to treat payers of *zakah* and collect the right amount. He also instructed them to avoid the top-notch wealth of payers, and when they came back, he sometimes used to ask them for a full account of what they did.[10]

Scholars agree that "The state must appoint collectors of *zakah* because the Prophet (p) and the Successors after him sent collectors, and because there are always people who own assets but do not know how to pay their due *zakah*, and people who dislike such payment out of greed."[11]

Owners of *zakatable* assets are advised to help collectors and not hide any part of their wealth. Jarir bin 'Abd Allah says, "A group of nomadic Arab came to the Messenger of God (p) and said 'Some *zakah* collectors did us an injustice.' The Messenger of God (p) said, 'you must please your collectors'"[12] and Jabir bin 'Atik narrates that the Prophet (p) said, "People that you may not like [collectors] shall come to you. When they come, you should welcome them and let them do what they want. If they do justice, the result will be on their own souls, but if they do injustice, the punishment will also be on their own souls. It is necessary for completing your *zakah* that you please them, so they will pray for you."[13] Anas narrates that "a man asked the Messenger of God (p), If I give *zakah* to the person you send, would I be fulfilling it as far as God and His Messenger are concerned?' The Prophet answered, 'Yes, if you give it to my messenger, you are freed from that obligation as far as God and His Messenger are concerned. You deserve its reward, and if it is tampered with later, the sin is on whoever changes it."[14]

Companions' opinions on the role of the state

Sahl bin Abi Saleh narrates that his father said "I accumulated a zakatable amount of wealth. I asked Sa'd bin Abi Waqqas, Ibn 'Umar, Abu Hurairah, and Abu Sa'id al Khudri whether I should distribute *zakah* myself or give it to the government. They all ordered me to pay it to the government non of them disagreed." Another version reads, "I said, don't you see what this government does? 'It was at the time of the Umayyads. Should I still give it my *zakah*? They all answered 'yes, you must.'" This is reported by Sa'id bin Mansur in his *Musnad*.[15]

Ibn 'Umar says, "Pay your *sadaqat* to whoever runs your affairs. If he does right, it is his soul that will be rewarded, and if he does evil, it is on himself." Qaz'ah reports from Ibn 'Umar." Give them [the rulers] your *zakah* even if they drink wine. "Al Nawawi says "these two statements are reported by al Baihaqi via correct or good chains."[16] Al Mughirah bin Shu'bah once asked a slave of his, who was managing his assets in al Taif "what do you do with the *zakah* on my wealth?" The manager said, "I distribute part of it and I pay part to the government." Shu'bah said, "Why do you do that?" He answered, "They buy land and marry women with what we give them." Shu'bah said, "Give it to the Government, for the Messenger of God (p) indeed ordains us to give it to them." Reported by al Baihaqi in his *al Sunan al Kabir*.[17]

Rationalization of this evidence

The above mentioned verses, sayings and opinions of Companions indicate that in principle, *zakah* must be administered by the Islamic government. It is an important responsibility of the Islamic state and the public *zakah* organization.

One may ask, if the purpose of religions is to awaken human conscience, enlighten people with truth, and induce them to behave ideally by the drives of love of God or fear of His punishment, why should Islam interfere with the organization of society instead of leaving this to political authorities? Our answer is that this may be relevant to religions other than Islam, but Islam is both creed and system, moral values and laws, a guiding book and an organized state.

From the point of view of this religion, human beings cannot be dissected into departments, one for religion and the other for worldly life, nor can life itself be partitioned into allegiance to Caesar and separate allegiance to God. Life is one unit; so is the human being; so is the whole universe, all submitting to God, the One and Mighty. Islam brings forth comprehensive and universal guidance which gives liberty and dignity to the individual as well as betterment and happiness to society. Within this unified framework, the system of *zakah* is enacted assigning the collection and distribution to the state. Islam implants the desire to pay *zakah* in the hearts of believers while entrusting the state with *zakah* collection and distribution, for the following important reasons:

Firstly, some individuals may not have vivd consciences that force them to fulfill this obligation. In such cases, the right of the poor would be lost if *zakah* payment were left to individuals.

Secondly, when poor persons receive their right from the government and not directly from the rich, their dignity is preserved and there is no possibility of their humiliation in front of the payer.

Thirdly, if the distribution of *zakah* is left to individuals, it is bound to come out uneven, since each individual always has his or her personal grasp of the rules of distribution.

Fourthly, deservants include public interests such as softening hearts, fight for God's sake, or calling for Islam, that can only be determined by authorities who have an overall vision of the whole society and its major needs.

Fifthly, Islam is both a religion and a state, and the state needs funds to play its role. *Zakah* is one of the financial resources of the Islamic state.[18]

The treasury of *zakah*

If *zakah* is handled by the state, it must be run independently since God determines its distribution in the Qur'an. Thus, *zakah* should have a separate treasury and administrative body supervised by the Islamic state. The verse on *zakah* distribution refers implicitly to this autonomy by assigning a share to the workers on *zakah*. The historical practice of Muslims during the reign of Islam was to establish several sub-treasuries in the state. Four sub-treasuries are clearly identified and described by Hanafites:

1. *Zakah.*
2. *Jiziah* and *Kharaj.*
3. War booty and *rikaz* (*rikaz* is not *zakah*, according to Hanafites).
4. Lost and found assets.[19]

Apparent and non-apparent assets

Jurists usually divide *zakatable* assets into two groups. Apparent assets are those that are visible and can easily be counted by people other than the owner. They include agricultural crops and livestock. Non-apparent assets are those that can easily be hidden away by the owner. They include money and business assets.

As for apparent assets, jurists agree almost unanimously that the collection and distribution of their *zakah* must be undertaken by the state. Their *zakah* should not be left to individuals, especially since we have many reports that the Prophet (p) sent his collectors to take *zakah* on these assets. It is obvious that the state is responsible for enforcing this collection and must fight, if necessary, those who refuse to pay this *zakah*, as Abu Bakr did after the death of the Prophet.[20]

As for non-apparent assets, it is agreed that the state has the right to collect and distribute their *zakah*. However, jurists have several opinions about enforcing its payment to the government.

Hanafites argue that *zakah* on non-apparent assets should be left to the owners to distribute. They add that although in principle, the state has the right to administer this kind of *zakah*,[21] since the time of 'Uthman this task has been assigned to owners of wealth. This assignment does not eliminate the stats's authority to supervise payment of *zakah* on non-apparent assets. If the state is informed that owners of wealth in certains areas do not pay *zakah* on their non-apparent assets, its payment can be enforced by the public law inforcement authority.[22] *Zakah* on trade assets may be collected by the state if they are being transported from one place to another, but if trade assets are not transported, they are treated like other non-apparent assets.[23]

Malikites argue that *zakah* must be given to a just government without differentiation between apparent and non-apparent assets.[24] If the state is just only in the matter of *zakah* collection and distribution and is unjust in other affairs, some Mailikites argue that all *zakah* must still be paid to the state. These include al Dardir, as stated in his *al Sharh al Kabir.* Al Dusuqi in his commentary does not agree. Al Qurtubi says, "If the government is just with regard to *zakah* collection and distribution, owners are not justified in distributing *zakah* on money independently, although some say the distribution of *zakah* on money is the responsibility of the owners. Ibn al Majashawn adds, "Distribution to the poor and needy by *zakah* payers may be acceptable, but individuals should not be allowed to distribute on the other categories of deservants. Such distribution must only be made by the state.

Shafi'ites believe owners are allowed to distribute due *zakah* on their non-apparent assets independently. As for the apparent assets, the prominent view in the Shafi'ite school is that their *zakah* may also be distributed by the payer. The other opinion is that it must be given to the government. Some Shafi'ites argue that *zakah* on apparent assets must even be given to the in just government. It is, however, agreed upon by all Shafi'ites that when the government carries out the task of collecting *zakah* on apparent assets, this *zakah* must be paid to the government. If the government does not carry out this responsibility, owners have the right to distribute *zakah* on their apparent assets themselves. Al Mawardi argues that distribution of *zakah* on non-apparent assets must, in principle, be left to payers, who, however, have the right to surrender this authority to the government. Al Nawawi adds that the government also has the right to see that owners are actually fulfilling this obligation, and to demand payment to the state in case owners of non-apparent assets do not distribute their due *zakah*.[26]

Hanbalites believe giving *zakah* to the government is not obligatory, although the government has the right to undertake this task. They do not differentiate between apparent and non-apparent assets or between just and unjust states. On the other hand, Hanbalites agree that payers are allowed to distribute their *zakah* by themselves. Ibn Qudamah argues in *al Mughni* that it is preferred for the *zakah* payer to distribute his or her *zakah* by himself, so as to be sure it is given to true deservants, no matter whether it is on apparent or non-apparent assets. Ahmad says "I would like the payer to distribute his due *zakah* although it is permissible to give it to the government.

Makhul, al Hasan, Sa'id bin Jubair and Maimum believe the owner should distribute *zakah* himself. Al Thawri even allows the owner to cheat the government so as not to give it the due *zakah*, while 'Ata' says it is all right to surrender *zakah* to the government "if you know it is going to be distributed justly." Ibn Qudamah adds "Distribution of *zakah* by the owner guarantees that it will be given to true deservants, in addition to saving the amount paid to *zakah* workers. On the other hand, collectors and distributors of *zakah* are not necessarily above betraying the trust placed in them, and in any cases, *zakah* may not reach the neighbours and kin of the payer, who deserve the payer's grace more than anybody else."[27]

Zaidis believe the responsibility of collecting and distributing *zakah* belongs to the government alone, regardless of whether assets are apparent or not. If there exist a just government, the owner has no right to distribute *zakah* on his own. Their view is based on their understanding of the verse that addresses the Prophet "Out of their wealth take . . . " and the saying that *zakah* is "taken from the rich . . ." and by the fact that the Prophet and his Successors sent *zakah* collectors. They add that if the government collects *zakah* and a person decides to distribute his *zakah* by himself, he is required to make another payment of *zakah* to the government, even if the person was not aware that the government collects *zakah*.[28] If there is no Islamic government, or the *zakah* payer is not under its authority, the payer must distribute *zakah* independently.[29]

Abadis argue that the responsibility of collecting *zakah* is the government's. They agree with Zaidis that if a person distributes his own *zakah* while the government takes responsibility for collection, this person is required to make another payment of the due *zakah* to the government.[30]

Al Sha'bi, al Baqir, Abu Razin, and al Awza'i believe the government has the exclusive right to collect *zakah*, because it has better means of knowing deservants. They add that Ibn 'Umar used to give his due *zakah* to collectors sent by the rulers of the time; Ibn al Zubair sometimes, and Najdat al Haruri some other times, and that Suhail bin Abi Saleh asked Sa'd bin Abi Waqqas, "I have wealth and I want to give its due *zakah*, and you see these rulers, the way they are. What should I do? "Sa'd answered, "Give it to them." Suhail adds, "I went to Ibn 'Umar, Abu Hurairah, and Abu Sa'id, and they answered me the same." A similar opinion is reported from 'A'ishah.[31]

Comparison and weighing

Before I select one of these opinions, I should mention that almost all jurists agree on two points. Firstly the Islamic state has the right to collect and distribute *zakah* on any and all assets, apparent and non-apparent. This right is emphasized if there exists suspicion that people are not so eager to pay their *zakah* by themselves. Some jurists even state that all differences with regard to the role of the state arise about the case in which the government does not administer *zakah*, but when it does, those jurists claim there is *ijma'* on the obligation of giving *zakah* to the state.[32] Even those who disagree, accept the principle that once *zakah* collection is carried out by the state, *zakah* must be given to the state, because it is a disputed issue and any disputed issue can be settled by a political decision like legal disputes that are decided by court judgements.[33] The second point of agreement is, if the state neglects *zakah* collection, owners of assets must distribute their own *zakah*. This is based on the fact that *zakah* is a form of worship and a religious obligation that must be fulfilled by each individual, to the extent that if a government dares to exempt people from paying *zakah*, Muslims must distribute their own *zakah* independently.

Once these two points of unanimous agreement are understood, we can look at differences about whether the government has the authority to collect *zakah* on non-apparent wealth. It seems to me from examining texts on *zakah* collection and the authority of the Islamic state, that texts make no distinction between apparent and non-apparent wealth. It is stated that the Islamic state is required to administer both *zakah* collection and distribution, without any exceptions. This understanding is supported by the following points:

A. Al Razi in explaining the verse "*Sadaqat* are only to the poor . . . " says," This verse indicates that the government and its representatives are the authority responsible for collecting and distributing *zakah*, especially since God assigns a share to *zakah* workers. This means workers are needed to fulfill this obligation. Workers are appointed by the Islamic government. Thus, the government is the authority that collects *zakah*. This is emphasized by the verse which reads, 'Out of their wealth take a *sadaqah* . . .' Jurists who permit the owner to distribute his *zakah* on non-apparent wealth find supportive evidence elsewhere, such as in the verse 'And in their wealth there exists a right for he who asks and he who is deprived,' on the grounds that since this right belongs to the needy and the deprived, it may be given to them directly by the owner of the wealth."[34] In my opinion, this last sentence of al Razi is not acceptable, since it also applies to apparent items, and there is overwhelming evidence and agreement that the state collects and distributee *zakah* on apparent items.

B. Ibn al Humam, a Hanafite, says "It is evident that the verse 'Out of their wealth take a *sadaqah*' requires that the right of collecting all *zakah* belongs to the Islamic government. This was the fact at the time of the Messenger of God (p) and his first two successors. When 'Uthman was elected, he did not like to search for peoples non-apparent wealth, so he left the payment of *zakah* on such wealth to the owners themselves. The other Companions did not quarrel with him about this. This certainly does not eliminate the state's right to collect *zakah,* since if it becomes known that certain people do not pay their due *zakah* on non-apparent items, the state reserves the right to enforce payment of *zakah* to the state treasury."[35]

C. Abu 'Ubaid, al Tirmidhi, and al Daraqutni report that "the Prophet (p) once appointed 'Umar as *zakah* collector, 'Umar asked al 'Abbas for the amount of *zakah* due on his wealth. Al 'Abbas answered, 'I have pre-paid, to the Messenger of God (p), the *sadaqah* for two years.' 'Umar told this to the Prophet (p) who said, "My uncle tells the truth. We have taken from him the *sadaqah* of two years, in advance."[36] This is evidence about collecting *zakah* on non-apparent wealth, since al 'Abbas was a merchant and did not own agriculture or livestock.

D. A similar saying reads "The Prophet sent his collector to take *zakah*. Some malicious individuals spread a rumor that Ibn Jamil, Khalid bin al Walid and al 'Abbas bin 'Abd al Muttalib refuse to pay *zakah*. The Messenger of God (p) gave a speech in which he denied this on behalf of al 'Abbas and Khalid, and confirmed the accusation about Ibn Jamil. The Prophet said, 'They do an injustice to Khalid. Khalid devotes his shields and weapons for the sake of God.' Apparently, these constituted Khalid's wealth. He continued, 'As for al 'Abbas, the uncle of the Messenger of God (p) his *zakah* is due on me double.'"[37]

E. Abu Daud also reports that the Prophet (p) said "Bring me one-fourth of the tenth, one *dirham* out of each forty *dirhams* . . ."[38], which indicates that he collected *zakah* on money.

F. Moreover, there are several reports to the effect that Abu Bakr, 'Umar, 'Uthman, Ibn Mas'ud, Mu'awiyah, 'Umar bin 'Abd al 'Aziz, and others used to collect *zakah* out of salaries and grants given by the state. Abu Bakr used to ask the recipients whether they owned any wealth. If the answer was affirmative, he took out of the salary the due amount of *zakah* on the wealth. Ibn Mas'ud collected *zakah* on the salaries themselves, at a rate of twenty-five per thousand. (It is known that he did not require the passage of one year on earned income, as show earlier in this book).'Umar, when giving salaries counted the wealth of merchants, both current and future, and took *zakah* out of both.[39] Qudamah narrates, "'Uthman bin 'Affan used to ask me when I went to receive my salary, 'Do you have any wealth on which *zakah* is due?' If I said yes, he would collect the due *zakah* out of my salary, and if I said no, he would give me my salary."[40]

G. Lastly, the religious opinions reported from Ibn 'Umar and some other Companions indicate that *zakah* must be paid to the government, even if it were oppressive, without any distinction between apparent and non-apparent items of wealth.

The view of Abu 'Ubaid

A few scholars distinguish between apparent and non-apparent wealth on the grounds of the actual practice of the Prophet. They argue that no overwhelming or widespread evidence reaches us which shows that the Messenger (p) sent workers to collect and distribute *zakah* on money and business assets, as he did with respect to apparent wealth. Consequently, some leading scholars argue it is permissible either to give the *zakah* due on non-apparent wealth to the government or distribute it directly, provided that this is done with righteousness and without discrimination between recipients. Abu 'Ubaid says, "This is, I believe, the view of Sunnite scholars in both Hijaz and Iraq. As far as gold, silver, and trade assets are concerned, Muslims are trusted to fulfill this obligation, while *zakah* on livestock, grain, and fruits must only be administered by the Islamic government. Owners must not hide due *zakah* away from the Islamic government. If owners distribute the latter on their own, that does not satisfy the requirement, and *zakah* must again be given to the state. The texts we have from Sunnah and the Companions warrant this distinction. We see that Abu Bakr fought the apostates in order to collect *zakah* due on livestock. He did not do that for *zakah* due on gold, and silver."[41] Abu 'Ubaid goes on to give a reports in support of this position, but upon close examination of his quoted statements, we find them all speak about exceptional circumstances, such as corruption in government and its *zakah* agency and not normal situations. This is obvious from the fact that such opinions come about only after political unrest and conspiracies that led to the killing of 'Uthman. Abu 'Ubaid reports, via his own chain, that Ibn Sirin says "The *sadaqah* was paid to the Prophet (p) or his commissioners, then to Abu Bakr or his commissioners, then to 'Umar or his commissioners, then to 'Uthman or his commissioners. When 'Uthman was killed, people differed. Some continued to give *zakah* to the state, like Ibn 'Umar, and some started distributing it directly."[42] This is well-known about Ibn 'Umar, who says 'As long as they [the rulers] establish prayer, you must give *zakah* to them." It is even reported that he dropped this condition, saying "Give it to them even if they use it to buy dog meat for their own dishes." In answer to another person he said, "Pay it to them even if they use it to buy clothes and perfume for themselves."

But we have certain narrations to the effect that Ibn 'Umar withdrew this last opinion saying, "Put it [*zakah*] where it must properly be put."[43] A friend of his asked him, "What do you say about *zakah* since these rulers do not put it where it belongs?" Ibn 'Umar said, "Pay it to them." The man said, "If they delayed prayer, would you still pray with them?" He answered, "No." The man said, "Is not *zakah* like prayer? Ibn 'Umar said, "They confuse us; may God confuse them."[44] This is seen as acceptance of the man's point of view.

It is also reported that Ibrahim al Nakha'i and al Hasan al Basri say, "Distribute it properly yourselves and hide it properly yourselves and hide it from the rulers."[45] Maimun bin Mahran is reported to have said, "Put it in small bags and distribute it among the deservarnts that you know. Be keen to do away with all of it by the end of the month."[46] Abu Yahya al Kindi says, "I asked Sa'id Ibn Jubair about *zakah*. He said, 'Give it to the rulers'. When Sa'id left, I followed him and asked, 'Should I give it to the rulers although they do with it so- and- so?' Sa'id answered, 'Put it where God ordained you. You asked me in presence of a public audience, and I could not give you my personal opinion there'."[47]

All these narrations and opinions mentioned by Abu 'Ubaid were given after the beginning of political unrest, the rise of anger against some Umayyad commissioners, and the deviation of many of them from standards established during the period of the Wise Successors. Lastly, it may be noted that my authentic report that the Prophet (p) made a distinction between apparent and non apparent items of wealth, and that he did not sent commissioners to collect *zakah* on non-apparent items, is caused by either of the following two reasons:

1. People used to bring that *zakah* to the Messenger of God (p) out of their faith and awakened conscienceness.

2. Reckoning this kind of wealth was practically impossible, except by the owner, so owners were charged with that obligation.

This continued during the era of the first Successor, Abu Bakr. During the caliphate of 'Umar, the state expanded, and salaries were assigned to all people, including the new born. Even people of Pledge were covered by this social insurance. This program required huge resources, so it became indispensable to appoint commissioners to collect *zakah* on all of wealth, both apparent and non-apparent. Consequently, 'Umar established an administration for *zakah* collection called the system of "al 'Ashirin" i.e. "collectors of the tenth", since one-tenth was collected from foreign merchants (in application of the same treatment Muslim merchants were given in foreign countries), half a tenth was collected from merchants of the people of the Pledge (according to the treaties 'Umar had with them) and one-fourth of a tenth from Muslim merchants (as *zakah*).[48]

Scholars consider the system of collection established by 'Umar as a great facilitation for the whole society, for otherwise, *zakatable* people would have to cross long distances to bring their due *zakah* to Madinah. Thus, the same principle was applied by the Prophet, Abu Bakr, and 'Umar, except that 'Umar improved the method of collection. When 'Uthman came, huge amounts of proceeds from *fai, ghanimah, kharaj, jiziah* and *sadaqat* started pouring into the state treasury, so 'Uthman decided to collect *zakah* of apparent wealth only and to leave *zakah* of non-apparent wealth to owners to distribute themselves, under the supervision of the state. 'Uthman depended on the awakened consciences of Muslims at his time to stimulate scrupulous payment. Some jurists interpret this action of 'Uthman as the appointment of owners as representatives of the state regarding distributing *zakah* on non-apparent wealth.

In *al Bada'i,* al Kasani says,

The Prophet (p), Abu Bakr, and 'Umar collected it [*zakah*] on non-apparent items. But when funds became abundant at the time of 'Uthman, he found it was to the public benefit to assign distribution to owners. This was done with the approval of the Companions. Owners of such items became agents of the state, especially since 'Uthman said, 'Whoever owes any debt must first pay it back, then distribute *zakah* of the residual. This authorizes owners to distribute their *zakah*. Thus, the right of the state is not waived. Consequently, our colleagues hold that if it becomes known to the state that people in certain areas do not fulfil this requirement, the state reserves the right to collect it through its own commissioners.[49]

Finally, we reach the conclusion that in principle, it is the state's duty to collect *zakah* on all wealth, both apparent and non-apparent. Exceptionally, when the treasury's resources are great (as with 'Uthman) owners of wealth may be authorized to distribute *zakah* on non-apparent assets, on the condition that if they fail, the state can take charge of this collection and distribute again.

Who is responsible for administering *zakah* today?

This matter is discussed by the Professors Khallaf, al Hasan, and Abu Zahrah in their lecture on *zakah* in Damascus 1952. They say,

It is imperative that the government take responsibility for collecting *zakah* on all wealth, apparent and non-apparent, for two reasons. Firstly, many people now abandoned this obligation on all their wealth. They do not fulfill the terms of agency given by Uthman and scholars after him, and jurists state that if people do not fulfill the obligation of distributing *zakah* due on their non-apparent wealth, the state may take charge of this obligation again, and that if people do not in general pay their *zakah*, the state must force them to do so. Secondly, most formerly non apparent items of wealth have become apparent today, especially trade inventory and monetary assets, since merchants usually keep accounting records for their businesses. The same rules that apply to calculating taxes on income and profit must be used with regard to *zakah* obligated by God for poor and deprived. Money and monetary assets are mostly deposited in banks, and knowing their balances at the end of the year is an easy matter. We know that jurists agree that if non-apparent items of wealth become apparent, responsibility for the collection of their *zakah* reverts to the state. The fact that the institution of al Ashirin remained during and after Uthman's period supports this point, since al Ashirin used to collect *zakah* on merchandise being transported from one place to another. Thus, the ability to reach and count non-apparent items, obviously means they should be treated like apparent items.[50]

It must be noted that each Islamic state is called upon to establish an organization for collecting and distributing *zakah,* although I prefer that a fraction of the due *zakah* (one-fourth or one-third) be left for individuals to distribute to deservants whom they personally know, especially their kindred and neighbors. This is by analogy to the Prophet's practice of leaving part of the harvest uncounted during pre-estimation of *zakah* due on it.

Undoubtedly, assigning the responsibility of *zakah* collection and distribution to the state applies to a government that takes Islam as its ideology, Islamic laws as foundation for its constitution, and Islamic social, economic, cultural, and political standards as a basis for its social structure, even if such a government may deviate slightly in the minute details. Governments which reject Islam as basic ideology of the state are prohibited from collecting *zakah* because they cannot be entrusted with its proper fulfillment.

Refusal to pay and cheating

Authorizing the state to penalize those who do not fulfill the obligation of *zakah* and to take the due amount by force is itself an assertion of the state's vital role in *zakah* collection.

Hanafites believe that *zakah* officers my only accept payers' disclosures if ascertained under oath. A payer may claim payment is made to another officer, being in debt, or any other factor that reduces or eliminates *zakah* payment. Hanafites add that if it is discovered, even years later, that a statement made under oath about the payment of *zakah* is invalid or false, the due *zakah* must be collected. Zakah officers must not accept any claim that *zakah* on apparent wealth was paid directly by the individual.[51] However, the officer my accept a statement made under oath that *zakah* on non-apparent items was already distributed to deservants by the payer himself.[52]

Malikites assert that in case of refusal to pay, *zakah* must be collected by force, as long as it is known that the payer is wealthy, whether he or she owns apparent items or non-apparent items. Imprisonment may be the penalty for certain cases of denial of *zakah* payment. It is said that the Islamic government may go as far as to declare those who refuse to pay *zakah* rebels and fight them until the due *zakah* is collected.[53]

Shafi'ites argue that anyone who refuses to pay *zakah* must be forced to do so, and a penalty must be imposed. However, if such a refusal is caused by denial of the obligation itself, it is considered apostation and the penalty is death. al Shafi'i, in his older opinion, asserts that the penalty of refusing to pay *zakah* is a fine of half the person's wealth in addition to the due amount of *zakah*. This is in accordance with the saying narrated by Bahz bin Hakim from his father from his grandfather from the Messenger of God (p): "And he who refuses to pay, we surely shall take it, along with half his wealth. It is an obligation from among the obligations of our Lord, and none of it belongs to the family of Muhammad."[54] But the first mentioned view of Shafi'i is the correct view. The author of *al Muhadhdhab* adds, "The government may fight those who refuse to pay *zakah* as Abu Bakr, the Truthful, fought them."[55]

Unanimity about penalizing those who refuse to pay *zakah*

It is agreed upon that those who deny the obligation of *zakah* itself are treated like apostates, provided they have no excuse, such as being very new to Islam, and therefore not having yet grasped all its requirements. There is no disagreement also that *zakah* must be collected by force if payers refuse to give it without use of force.[56]

However, scholars do not agree about imposing a fine on those who refuse to pay *zakah*. Some, including Ishaq a report from Ahmad, al Awza'i, and the older opinion of al Shafi'i, believe a fine of half the payer's wealth must be collected along with the due amount, in accordance with the saying mentioned above. As for the majority, including the later opinion of al Shafi'i, only the due amount of *zakah* must be collected. This is based on three points:

A. The saying "Nothing is obligated on wealth except *zakah*."[57]

B. *Zakah* is a worship, and not fulfilling a worship is not a reason that incurs fines.

C. Many people refused to pay *zakah* during Abu Bakr's time. Although Abu Bakr fought those who refused to pay, no report is available from him or any of the Companions that a financial fine was imposed on those who were forced to pay *zakah*.[58]

As for the saying of Bahz, al Baihaqi quotes al Shafi'i as saying "It is not considered authentic by scholars of hadith. If it were authentic, I would have referred to its implication."[59] Al Baihaqi adds that both al Bukhari and Muslim do not use Bahz in their chains of narrators.[60] But one may reply that this is not sufficient reason for grading a saying weak, since there are many correct sayings outside the collections of al Bukhari and Muslim. Some scholars claim the saying of Bahz is annulled by a saying from al Bara bin 'Azib that eliminates all financial fines. This annulment cannot be supported, since it requires knowledge of chronological succession of the two sayings and such knowledge is not available.[61] Al Mawardi considers Bahz's saying in contradiction to the saying "Nothing is obligated on wealth except *zakah*", and concludes that the saying from Bahz is not meant for actual punishment but only to create fear of violating the obligation of *zakah*.[62] Al Nawaw'i adds that the saying of Bahz is graded weak by al Shafi'i and other hadith scholars.[63]

All the objections to the saying from Bahz can easily be shown as invalid, but as stated earlier in this book, the fine was imposed by the Prophet in his capacity as a head of state.[64] Thus, imposing such a fine or not is up to the Islamic state, as argued by al Qarafi, al Dahlawi, and others.[65]

The contrast between the saying from Bahz and the saying "Nothing is obligated on wealth except *zakah*" is invalid, firstly, because there are several financial obligations on wealth besides *zakah* confirmed by glorious verses of the Qur'an and explicit, correct saying, and secondly, the authenticity of the latter saying is disputed.[66]

The objection that Islam does not impose financial penalties is refuted. Ibn al Qayim in his *al Turuq al Hukmiyah* shows that we have at least fifteen cases reported from the Messenger of God (p) and his Wise Successors in which a financial penalty was imposed.[67]

Lastly, grading the saying from Bahz as weak is irrational, since it is not so graded because of weakness in the chain, but rather by the text itself, on the grounds of the previous two objections. Since these two objections have been shown to be incorrect, grading the saying weak on their grounds is also incorrect. It is noted that Bahz himself was graded weak because of this saying and not because of any weakness in his own trustworthiness. Ibn Habban says "If it were not for this saying, I would grade Bahz trustworthy" After narrating the opinion of several leading scholars about the trustworthiness of Bahz and the grading of his narrations as correct by Ahmad, Ishaq, Ibn al Madani in Tahdhib Sunan Abu Daud, Ibn al Qayyim adds:

> He who rejects this saying has no acceptable evidence since the claim that it is annulled is unfounded and has no truth. We have several sayings about the existence of financial penalties. As for the contradiction between this saying and that from al Bara', it is absurd, because the story in the saying from al Bara does not contain an action that deserves any penalty, but merely injury caused by an animal, without any intention on the part of its owner. Interpreting the saying as intending merely to create fear of violation is even more absurd. Words of the Prophet (p) cannot be taken to mean other than what the words say. As for Ibn Habban's statement, 'If it were not for this saying I would consider Bahz among the trustworthy', it is falling apart, it is illogical to consider Bahz weak because of this saying while this saying is rejected because Bahz is weak. Narrating this saying is by no means a reason for weakness anyway, since he does not differ from any trustworthy narrator on it.[68]

Strangely enough, many authors such as al Shirazi, and al Mawardi, and Ibn Qudamah object to this correct saying from Bahz, on the grounds that it contradicts the saying, "Nothing is obligated. . ." which has no value at all from the point of view of authenticity.

The Hanbalite opinion is similar to that of the Shafi'ites. Ibn Qudamah says "He who refuses to pay *zakah*, while he still believes in its obligation, must be forced to pay it by the government. However, nothing in excess of the due amount may be taken."On the other hand, Ishaq and Abu Bakr bin 'Abd al Aziz believe a fine of one-half the wealth of the payer must be collected, in accordance with the saying reported from Bahz bin Hakim. Those who refuse to pay *zakah* may be fought by the Islamic state until *zakah* is collected, without any additional fine. Al Maimuni reports that Ahmad says "Those who refuse to pay *zakah*, to the extent that they fight against the Islamic government in order to defend their position of refusal, should not be treated like Muslims in matters of inheritance and funeral, 'Abd Allah bin Mas'ud says "he who abandons *zakah* is not Muslim."This is based on Abu Bakr's stance toward those who refused to pay *zakah*. When they were pressured at the battle front, they told Abu Bakr they would pay the due *zakah* if he discontinued the fight, but his answer was, "No, I do not accept your due *zakah* until you testify that our martyrs are in heaven and those who were killed on your side are in the fire. None of the Companions is reported to have disagreed with Abu Bakr's statement, a statement that implies the rebels were unbelievers.

The other opinion which does not mark as disbelievers those who refuse to pay *zakah* is supported by the fact that *zakah* is one of the Islamic obligations whose abandonment does not negate the basic faith, as long as its obligation is not entirely denied.[69]

Lastly, according to Zaidis, a claim by a person that he does not owe any *zakah* may be accepted according to the discretion of the *zakah* commissioner and the trustworthiness of the person,[70] while a claim that the due amount was distributed directly by the payer must be supported by evidence. Otherwise, the collector should charge the *zakah* payer the due amount disregarding any claim of direct distribution.[71]

Payment of *zakah* to oppressive governments

Muslin scholars differ on paying *zakah* to oppressive governments. Some believe it is unconditionally permissible, and others declare it prohibited in all cases, with whole spectrum of views between these two extremes.

As for those who say it is unconditionally allowed to pay *zakah* to oppressive governments, their main argument is derived from a few sayings mentioned by the author of *al Muntaqa* as follows:[72]

A. It is reported from Anas that a man said, "O Messenger of God, if I give my *zakah* to your commissioner would I be fulfilling it as far as God and His Messenger are concerned?" The Prophet said "Yes, if you give it to my commissioner, you have completed it from the point of view of God and His Messenger; you get its reward, and the evil of tampering with it is on whoever tampers with it."[73]

B. It is reported from Ibn Mas'ud that the Messenger of God said, "There shall be sclfishness and matters you disapprove of after I am gone." People said, "O Messenger of God, what would you order us to do then?" He answered, "Fulfill the obligation that is on you and ask God for that which is yours."[74]

C. It is reported from Wa'il bin Hajar "I heard the Messenger of God (p) reply, when asked by a man 'What would you say if we happened to have rulers who prevented us our getting our rights and yet ask us for their right?', 'Listen and obey. They have the burden of what they do, and you have that of your deed."[75]

These sayings have an important implication, The Islamic state always needs funding for its social insurance programs and for public services, if people withhold making payments to the state because of the injustice of some rulers, many essential public services would be disrupted. Thus it is important that *zakah* keep flowing into the state treasury. However, making such payments to the state by no means implies abstaining from resisting oppression by all lawful means.

Muslims are required to pay financial dues obligated on them. While continuing to admonish and advise the rulers, in application of the general principle of ordaining what is good and forbidding what is evil. Additionally, the Islamic society has the right -- in fact it is obligated -- to remove rulers who expose their explicit disbelief. Moreover, a Muslim is obligated by God to disobey any order that conflicts with obedience to God or that requires him or her to do anything God forbids. This is in accordance with the correct saying, "Listening and obeying is a true obligation on any Muslim, both in matters he likes and in matters he does not like, unless ordered to disobey God. If he is ordered to disobey God, then there is no listening nor obeying."[76]

As for jurists who do not allow giving *zakah* to oppressors, their argument is based on the verse, "My covenant does not include the oppressors."[77] They say paying *zakah* to oppressors does not fulfill the "religious worship" aspect of *zakah*. Al Shafi'i, in one report, subscribes to this opinion. So do Ahl al Bait, as stated by al Mahdi in his al Bahr. Al Shawkani objects to this opinion, arguing that the general meaning of the above-mentioned verse is at least restricted by the saying mentioned at the beginning of this subsection.[78]

Between these two extreme opinions exist several views. Malikites assert that a ruler who is known to abuse *zakah* funds must not be given *zakah*. All effort must be made to avoid paying *zakah* to such a ruler, according to al Dardir in *al Shar al Kabir,* who continues, "But if a ruler is just in the collection and distribution of *zakah*, despite being oppressive in other issues, *zakah* must be given to him,"[79] Al Dusuqi in his commentary disagrees and says "it is rather undesirable to give *zakah* to such a ruler."[80] Zarruq, in *Sharh al Risalah*, says

> Zakah must not be paid to an unjust government unless it enforces payment, and the payer could not escape it. If the *zakah* payer can distribute the *zakah* directly, payment to the oppressive government does not fulfill the religious obligation. Ashhab notes that if *zakah* is taken by force, the religious obligation is fulfilled although it is preferable that an equal, additional amount be directly distributed to deservants. Ibn Rushd quotes differences among Malikites on whether, if an oppressive government collects *zakah* by force and does not distribute it justly, such collection fulfills the religious requirements of payers. He adds that the prominent view among Malikites is that *zakah* collected by force satisfies the religious requirement, provided it is collected as *zakah* and at the proper rates and conditions.[81]

Hanafites believe the collection of *zakah* by oppressive governments fulfills the religious requirement of the payers, provided that funds collected are distributed justly. If they are not distributed justly, *zakah* payers are religiously required to make another payment directly to deservants. This applies to *zakah* on apparent assets. As for non-apparent wealth, some Hanafites argue that the enforced collection of this *zakah* by oppressive governments does not fulfill the religious requirement of *zakah*.[82]

Hambalites, according to Ibn Qudamah in his *al Mughni*, believe *zakah* collected by oppressors satisfies the religious obligation of the payer, regardless of the manner in which funds are distributed or of the use of force in collection. Abu Saleh says "I asked Sa'd bin Abi Waqqas, Ibn 'Umar, Jabir, Abu Sa'id, and Abu Hurairah, 'should I pay my *zakah* to this government when you see what it does?' They all answered 'yes.' Ibn Qudamdh adds, "The statement of these Companions is not disputed according to what reaches us about their positions."[83] The author of *Matalib Uli al Nuha* says "Their is no disagreement in our school that it is permissible to pay *zakah* to the government, be it just or not, regardless of whether it is *zakah* on apparent or non-apparent wealth." He adds, "This is based on what is reported from the Companions. Ahmad says, 'The Companions used to pay *zakah* to the government, although they knew how it was expended. Why should I say something different?'"[84]

In my opinion, Muslims are not required to repeat payment if they are forced to pay *zakah* to oppressive government, as long as what is paid takes the very same name of *zakah*. Moreover, *zakah* should be paid to unjust governments as long as they collect and distribute justly to deservants assigned in *Shari'ah*, even if such governments are otherwise oppressive. Governments which do not distribute *zakah* properly yet enforce its collection, may be given due *zakah* as long as Muslims cannot avoid doing so.

Lastly, it must be noted that rulers to whom the above-named Companions permitted payment of *zakah* were still, at least, raising the banner of Islam and fighting its enemies, although they deviate in certain areas from the Islamic system. This does not apply to many contemporary Muslim governments, which have actually detached all bonds to this religion and abandoned its Qur'an, to the extent that some of them suppress any Islamic voice and crush those who call for Islam. Such governments must not be given *zakah* since commitment to Islam is the indispensable condition for allowing *zakah* to be given to any government.

Muslim jurists do not allow *zakah* to be given to a wayfarer who is travelling in disobedience to God. How then could *zakah* be given to government which stand in opposition to the way of God and against His religion on earth? The late reformer Rashid Rida, in his explanation of the Qur'an, brilliantly says,

> The Islamic state in the Muslim land is the authority to which *zakah* must be paid. It is in charge of collection and distribution. However, most Muslims nowadays do not have governments that establish the religion of Islam, protect Muslims, and fight only for the sake of God, or governments that collect the obligated *zakah* the way it should be, justly and rightfully. Most Muslim live either under the authority of occupying foreign troops or apostate governments that oppose Islam,[85] although these states may be headed by nominal Muslims. *Zakah* may be given to the remaining governments whose leaders believe in Islam and whose finances are not under the control of foreigners, even with the presence of certain aspects of oppression. As stated in *Sharh al Muhadhdhab* and other works, some deeply rooted scholars suggest that "if the government is unjust and does not distribute *zakah* according to *Shari'ah*, it is preferred that payers distribute *zakah* independently.

Footnotes

1. *Sura al Tawbah*, 9:60.

2. *Ibid*, 9:103.

3. *Fath al Bari*, Vol. 3, p.23.

4. *Nail al Awtar*, Vol. 4, p. 124.

5. *Al Talkhis*, Vol. 2, pp 159-160.

6. *Tabaqat Ibn Sa'd*, Vol. 2, p. 160.

7.   *Zad al Ma'ad*, Vol. 2, p. 472.

8.   *Al Taratib al Idariyah*, p. 398.

9.   *Ibid*, pp 396-8.

10.   *Zad al Ma'ad, op. cit.*

11.   *Al Majmu'*, Vol. 6, p. 167, and *al Rawdah*, Vol. 2, p. 210.

12.   Reported by Muslim.

13.   Reported by Abu Daud, according to *Nail al Awtar* Vol. 4, p.155. Al Munawi says in *al Faid* "There is no doubt the Prophet never appointed an unjust officer. All his officers and *zakah* collectors were top in their sense of justice. They include persons like 'Umar, 'Ali and Mu'adh. So the saying must mean that you are going to have collectors whom you may think are injust." Al Mazhari adds "This may be a reference to the future, when collectors may in fact be unjust. Yet rejection of payment to them may lead to general unrest and disturb the public order of the whole state."See *Faid al Qadir*, Vol. 1, p. 475.

14.   According to *Nail al Awtar. ibid*, the author of *al Muntaqa* attributes quoting this saying to Ahmad.

15.   As stated by al Nawawi in *Al Majmu'*.

16.   *Al Majmu'*, Vol. 6, pp. 162-4.

17.   *Ibid*.

18.   Al Qardawi, *Mushkilat al Faqr wa Kaifa 'Alajaha al Islam*, pp. 94-5.

19.   *Al Mabsut*, Vol. 3, p. 18, *al Bada'i*, Vol. 2, pp. 68-69 and *Radd al Muhtar*, Vol. 2, pp. 59-60.

20.   *Al Amwal*, p. 531.

21.   *Al Mughni*, Vol. 2, p. 643.

22.   *Radd al Muhtar*, Vol. 2, p. 5.

23.   *Ibid*, pp. 41-42.

24.   *Hashiat al Dusuqi*, Vol. 1, pp. 503-4.

25.   *Tafsir al Qurtubi*, Vol. 8, p. 177.

26.   *Al Rawdah*, Vol. 2, pp. 205-6.

27.   *Al Mughni*, Vol. 2, pp. 641-4.

28. *Sharh al Azhar*, Vol. 1, pp. 527-9.

29. *Ibid*, pp. 534-5.

30. *Sharh al Nil*, Vol. 2, pp. 137-8.

31. *Al Mughni*, Vol. 2, pp. 642-3.

32. *Sharh al Azhar*, Vol. 1, p. 529.

33. *Al Bahr*, Vol. 2, p. 190.

34. *Tafsir al Razi*, Vol. 16, p. 114.

35. *Fath al Qadir*, by Ibn al Humam, Vol. 1, p. 487.

36. *Al Amwal*, p 589. The saying is reported via several chains that are not safe from weakness, but they strengthen each other. See *Fath al Bari*, Vol. 3, p 214. Jurists use this saying as lawfulness of prepayment of *zakah*.

37. *Al Amwal*, pp. 592-3. The saying is reported by al Bukhari, Muslim and Ahmad, See *Nail al Awtar*, Vol. 4, p 149.

38. *Ma'alim al Sunnan*, Vol. 2, pp. 188-9, see also the notes on this saying by Ibn al Qayyim in his *Tahdhib Sunan Abu Daud*.

39. *Musannaf Ibn Abi Shaibah*, Vol. 4, pp. 44.

40. *Al Umm* by al Shafi'i, Vol. 2, p. 14.

41. *Al Amwal*, p. 573.

42. *Ibid*, p. 573.

43. *Ibid,*

44. *Ibid.*

45. *Ibid.*

46. *Ibid.*

47. *Ibid.*

48. *Ibid.* 531.

49. *Al Bada'i'*, Vol. 2, p. 7.

50. *Halqat al Dirasat al Ijtima'iyah*, 3rd session on *zakah*.

51.	It is noticed that many Hanafites do not consider *'Ushr* to be *zakah*, on the grounds that it is a fee on land. But Ibn al Humam, a leading Hanafite, rejects this view and asserts that *Ushr* is undoubtedly *zakah*. See this book chapter on *zakah* on agriculture.

52.	*Radd al Muhtar*, Vol. 2, pp. 42-43, and 54.

53.	*Hashiat al Dusuqi*, Vol. 1, p. 503.

54.	The saying is reported by Ahmad, Abu Daud and Al Nasa'i, see part I of this book. The saying is also reported by al Hakim in *al Mustadrak* who, followed by al Dhahabi, grades it correct. Yahya bin Ma'in says "Its chain would be correct if those below Bahz are trustworthy." Ahmad says "I do not know what to grade it. Its chain is allright." See *Nail al Awtar*, Vol. 4, p. 122 and *Tahdhib al Tadhib*, Vol. 1, pp. 498-9, autobiography No. 924 and *Mizan al I'tidal*, autobiography No. 1324.

55.	*Al Majmu'*, Vol. 5, pp 331-332.

56.	*Al Bahr al Zakhkhar,* Vol. 2 , p. 190.

57.	See footnote 7 in chapter 1, part VIII.

58.	*Al Sunan al Kubra*, Vol. 4, p. 105.

59.	*Ibid.*

60.	*Ibid.*

61.	*Ibid*, and *al Majmu'*, Vol. 5, p. 334.

62.	*Al Ahkam al Sultaniyah*, p. 121.

63.	*Al Rawdah*, Vol. 2, p. 209.

64.	See part I of this book.

65.	See part III chapter 2, of this book.

66.	*Al Bahr al Zakhkhar,* Vol. 2 , p. 190, *al Mughni*, Vol. 2, p. 573, and *al Ahkam al Sultaniyah* by al Mawardi, p. 121.

67.	*Al Turuq al Hukmiyah*, p. 287.

68.	*Tahdhib al Sunan* with the summary of al Mundhiri and *al Ma'alim*, Vol. 2, p. 194.

69.	*Al Mughni,* Vol. 2, pp. 573-5.

70.	*Sharh al Azhar* and its commentaries, Vol. 1, p. 530. and *al Bahr*, Vol. 2, pp. 190-1.

71.	*Ibid.*

72. *Nail al Awtar*, Vol. 4, pp. 164-5.

73. Reported by Ahmad. See *Nail al Awtar*, vol.4, p. 155.

74. Agreed upon; see *ibid.*

75. Reported by Muslim and al Tirmidhi, *ibid.*

76. Reported by the group from Ibn 'Umar; see *al Jami' al Saghir.*

77. *Sura al Baqarah*, 2:124.

78. *Nail al Awtar*, Vol. 4, p. 165.

79. *Al Sharh al Kabir*, Vol. 1, p. 502.

80. *Hashiat al Dusuqi*, Vol. 1, p.504.

81. *Sharh al Risalah*, Vol. 1, pp. 340-1.

82. *Radd al Muhtar*, Vol. 2, pp. 26-7.

83. *Al Mughni,* Vol. 2, pp. 644-5.

84. *Matalib Uli al Nuha*, Vol. 2, p. 120.

85. This describes the majority of governments in Muslim countries today.

86. *Tafsir al Manar*, Vol. 10, pp. 595-6.

CHAPTER TWO

THE PLACE OF INTENTION IN *ZAKAH*

Zakah, as a form of worship and at the same time a financial tax, has a dual character. It is a tax-worship or a worship-tax.

This two-sided characteristic of *zakah* lies at the start of the issue of intention.

Intention is indispensable in *zakah*

The overwhelming majority of jurists believe intention is a prerequisite for performing *zakah*, since it is a rite of worship, and all rites of worship demand intention. God says, "And they have been commanded no more than this: to worship God, offering him sincere devotion, being true (in faith), to establish regular prayer, and to practice *zakah*." The Messenger of God (p) says, "Deeds are considered by their intentions." Lack of intention makes the payment of *zakah* purposeless and spiritless. Intention for *zakah* payment must exist on the part of the payer, whether he pays his own *zakah* or that of persons under his guardianship.[1]

Al Awza'i disagrees with the majority and does not consider intention a prerequisite for performing *zakah*. He says, "Intention is not a necessary requirement because *zakah* is a form of debt and there is no such condition when debts are paid. Because *zakah* does not require intention, it is charged on the wealth of minor orphans and taken by force from those who refuse to pay.[2] He is replied that *zakah* as a worship requires intention, according to the saying, "Deeds are by their intentions." Its analogy to debts is not complete, since a debt can be waived by the creditor, while due *zakah* cannot be waived. Intention is further needed to distinguish *zakah* from general voluntary charity. Al Awza'i's view is shared by some Malikites, but the accredited opinion in the Malikite school is that intention is required. As for taking *zakah* by force, the payer is not rewarded by God.[3]

Intention need not be put in words. It is only a will in the payer's heart that accompanies the payment of *zakah*.[4] Some Malikites even consider acceptable intention inferred by the purposeful calculation of the due amount and its distribution to *zakah* deservants.[5]

Intention when *zakah* is collected by the government

If the government collects *zakah*, the *zakah* payer is required to have intention. The intention of the collector alone does not suffice if the payer gives *zakah* willingly, according to the majority of jurists; al Shafi'i in one report is not included.[6] Al Nawawi remarks, "As for the person who refuses to pay *zakah*, from whom the government extracts *zakah* by force, if such a person makes intention when *zakah* is taken, the condition is satisfied, even without the collector's intention. If the payer does not make the necessary intention, that of the collector suffices as far as the application of the law is concerned, and the payer need not be asked to make another payment."[7] Ibn Qudamah says, "If *zakah* is collected by the government with the use of force, the legal obligation of paying *zakah* is fulfilled." However, Abu al Khattab and Ibn 'Aqil, both Hanbalites, believe that from the religious point of view, the worship of *zakah* is not performed in such a case, because of the payer's lack of intention. Ibn 'Aqil adds, "When jurists consider *zakah* requirements satisfied in such cases, they mean that the legal, but not religious, obligation is satisfied."[8] Ibn al 'Arabi, a Malikite, explains that when *zakah* is collected by force, no reward is due the person from whom it is taken."[9] As for Hanafites, they believe *zakah* of non-apparent wealth cannot be fulfilled by forced payment extracted from the payer by the state, since the state is not, in principle, in charge of collecting this *zakah*.[10]

Time of intention

Hanafites require that intention accompany the actual payment of *zakah* to the deservants, or to the government, the same as with other worship.[11] According to Malikites, intention should exist at the time of actual payment or when the payer is preparing the amount to be paid as *zakah*. If the intention of paying *zakah* does not exist at either of these two times, any following intention does not suffice.[12] Shafi'ites accept intention followed by payment. According to al Nawawi, it is difficult to have intention simultaneously with payment.[13] Hanbalites agree with the Shafi'ites that intention may preceed actual payment.[14] I believe the timing of intention is a matter that should be founded on easiness and simplicity. Having, in general , the will to pay *zakah* satisfies the intention requirement, without need for going into minute details.

Footnotes

1. *Hashiat al Sawi* on *al Sharh al Saghir*, Vol. 1, p. 235, and *Al Rawdah*, by al Nawawa, Vol. 2 , p. 208.

2. *Al Mughni,* Vol. 2 , p. 638.

3. *Sharh al Risalah* by Ibn Naji, Vol. 1, pp. 317-8.

4. *Al Mughni*, Vol. 2, p.638, *Matalib Uli al Nuha*, Vol. 2, p. 121.

5.   *Al Sawi, op. cit.*, and *Hashiat al Dusuqi,* Vol. 1, p. 500.

6.   Al Nawawi says "this second view is the one approved by al Qadi Abu al Tayeb, the authors of *al Muhadhdhab* and *al Tahdhib* and most of the later generations' jurists. *Al Rawdah*, Vol. 2, p. 208.

7.   *Ibid*, pp. 208-209.

8.   *Al Mughni*, Vol. 2, pp. 640-641.

9.   *Sharh al Risalah,* Vol. 1, p. 318, and *al Sharh al Kabir*, Vol. 1, p. 503.

10.   *Radd al Muhtar*, Vol. 2, p. 14.

11.   *Ibid.* pp. 14-15.

12.   *Al Dusuqi,* Vol. 1, p. 500

13.   *Al Rawdah,* Vol. 2, p. 209.

14.   *Al Mughni*, Vol. 2, p. 533 and *Al Rawdah*, Vol. 2, p. 210.

CHAPTER THREE

PAYMENT IN VALUE

Jurists opinions on payment in value

Since *zakah* is calculated in the same *zakated* items (camels are taken out of camels, fruits from fruits, and money from money) the question arises whether it is permissible to give the value of what is due as *zakah* instead of payment in kind. On one side, we find jurists who allow payment in value without any reservations. These are led by the Hanafites. Scholars led by the Shafi'ites and Zahirites do not accept payment in value. In between, Malikites and Hanbalites accept payment in value in certain cases, and do not approve of it in other cases.

It is maintained in *Mukhtasar Khalil* that payment in value does not suffice. Ibn al Hajib and Ibn Bashir go along with this view. The author of *al Tawdih* states that this is not consistent with *al Mudawwanah*, in which it is stated that payment in value is undesired only.[1] Ibn Naji in *Sharh al Risalah* quotes Ashhab and Ibn al Qasim saying that payment in value is permissible.[2] The author of *al Mudawwanah* notes, "I would think payment in value would be accepted by God if the payer is obligated to do so by the government, since in disputed matters, the government's selected practice becomes binding on all."[3]

As for Hanbalites, the author of *al Mughni* says it appears that Ahmad believes payment in value unsatisfactory because it is a violation of Sunnah. However, there is a report that Ahmad approves of it, except with *zakah* of *al fitr*.

All these differences can be attributed to the different angles from which jurists perceive *zakah* as either a worship or a tax on wealth. Those who require payment in kind argue that since *zakah* is a worship, it can only be done the very same way detailed in the sayings, therefore payment must be made in the same *zakated* item. On the other hand, Abu Hanifah, his disciples, and others allow payment in value on the grounds that it makes no difference as far as relieving the poor is concerned.[5]

The evidence of the two parties

Those who do not approve payment in value bring forth the following arguments:

1. Al Juwaini, a Shafi'ite, argues that since *zakah* is one of the rites of worship it must be done exactly the way we are ordered, because only God knows best the way He wants to be worshiped. *Zakah* is the sister of prayers. No one can make any change in the format or sequence of prayers, and by the same token, no one may pay money when sayings state pay a female camel or a sheep.[6]

2. This is further emphasized by the judge Abu Bakr bin al 'Arabi, a Malikite, who says, "The test of paying *zakah* is not realized in mere reduction (by giving away some) of total wealth - - as Abu Hanifah thinks - - but requires reducing the quantity of each and every item of *zakatable* wealth, in order to break the payer's sentimental attachment to each and every item he or she owns. Payment in kind is obligated on its merit."[7]

3. Since *zakah* is meant to relieve the diverse needs of the poor, diversity of assets paid is an important convenience for the poor. It is also a sign of thankfulness and gratitude to God to give others from the very same assets He bestowed on the payer.[8]

4. On top of all this is the saying reported by Abu Daud and Ibn Majah that the Prophet (p) told Mu'adh when he sent him to Yemen, "Take grain out of grain goat out of goat, camels out of camels, and cows out of cows."[9] This is a text that must not be violated by payment in value.

Hanafites and other scholars who allow payment in kind present the following arguments:

A. God says, "Out of their wealth take a *sadaqah*." This is a general text which is satisfied by payment in value. The Prophet's explanation that one sheep is due for every forty sheep is made only for facilitating collection from owners of livestock and does not restrict the general ordinance of God. In the desert and countryside where livestock owners often live, it is difficult to find money in large quantities.

B. Al Baihaqi reports, as does al Bukhari (as suspended), that Taus says, when Mu'ad was in Yemen, he said, "Give me garments or cloth as payment of *sadaqah*. This is easier for you and better for the migrants in Madina." In another version, "Bring me cloth materials to take from you in place of corn and barley . . . ."[11] It was known that Yemen had flourishing textile industry at that time and it was easier for Yemenis to pay in cloth. Also, Yemen had excess *zakah* that used to be sent to Madinah. Mu'adh's declaration tells us that he himself did not understand the Prophet (p) to mean literally that grain must be collected out of grain and sheep out of sheep. Rather, the Prophet mean to make things easier for payers, so this is an order to the collector to accept what he is given out, at the convenience of the payer. This is supported by the report that in paying recompense for a killing by mistake, the Prophet (p) allowed cloth producers to make payment in cloth.[12]

C. Ahmad and al Baihaqi report that the Prophet (p) saw an adult female camel among the camels taken as *sadaqah*. He was angered because it was too good and said, "May God assail whoever took this camel." The collector said, "O Messenger of God, I exchanged it for two lesser-quality camels." The Prophet said, "Then it is all right." This saying is acceptable as far as its chain and its indication are concerned.[13] It also indicates that paying *zakah* in value is permissible as the taking of an adult female camel for two lesser quality camels could only be based on their values.

D. *Zakah* is meant to enrich the poor, satisfy their needs, and finance public services important for the Muslim community as well as Islam itself. This is done as well by payment in value as by payment in kind. It may even be more convenient to collect value than to collect goods and merchandise.

E. It is unanimously permissible to pay an item of the same kind of *zakated* asset which is not of the *zakatable* items themselves, such as paying purchased wheat instead of the produced wheat itself. Why not permit, by the same logic, paying *zakah* in the form of another product? This is in answer to the argument of Ibn al 'Arabi, mentioned in number two above.

F. Sa'id bin Mansur reports in his *Sunan* that 'Ata says 'Umar bin al Khattab used to take money as *sadaqah* on business inventory.[14]

After reflecting on the arguments of the two groups, it seems that the Hanafites succeed in their view. They are supported both by texts and practices of the Companions, as well as by rationality. In fact, the analogy between *zakah* and prayer, though valid in that both are pillar of Islam, is absolutely inadequate when it comes to mode of payment. This is supported by Hanafite's opponents themselves, because they obligate *zakah* on the wealth of minors and insane persons, although such individuals are not required to pray.

The Hanafite opinion is also more suitable to contemporary economic life. It is easier in calculation, collection, and distribution. If we imagine a governmental body collecting and distributing *zakah*, payment in value would save many storage and transportation expenses. This opinion is also attributed to 'Umar bin 'Abd al 'Aziz, Al Hasan, Sufian, and a report from Ahmad.[15] Al Nawawi says "This is apparently the view of al Bukhari, as shown in his correct collection."[16] Ibn Rushd comments, "Al Bukhari, though he very often disagreed with the Hanafites, takes their same view on this issue. He was indeed lead by the strength of evidence."[17] In his correct collection, Al Bukhari titles a section "Payment in value as permissible", under which he mentions the report about Mu'adh from Taus,[18] as well as sections of Abu Bakr's letter in which twenty *dirhams* or two sheep substitute for one year's difference in age of camels.

Ibn Hazm undergrades the report of Taus on the grounds that Taus did not meet Mu'adh, and says even if it were said by Mu'adh it is not binding on us, because it does not come from the Prophet (p), and because it may be in reference to *jiziah* and not *zakah*.[19] These objections are invalid, since Taus, though he did not meet Mu'adh, was the leading scholar of Yemen in the Followers' era, and the practices of Mu'adh in Yemen are very well known to him. Also, Ahmad Shakir comments that the version of Mu'adh's statement reported by Yahya bin Adam explicitly mentions the word *sadaqah*, so this report is not about *jiziah*.

Ibn Taimiyah takes a middle stand on this matter, very similar to that which I take. He says, "Payment in value without need or convenience is not permissible. The Prophet stipulates payment in value in case of need, for example, to make up for the difference in ages of camels. But paying in value out of necessity, convenience, justice, or for the benefit of the poor is allowed; Ahmad himself permits it. It is for these reasons that Mu'adh asked for payment in value in the above report."[20]

Footnotes

1. In *al Mudawwanah*, Malik says "One must not give food or goods if it is *zakah* of money that one is paying, and it is disliked that a person should buy back what he gives as *sadaqah*." It seems that the most approved view among the Malikites is that payment in value is only disliked, and not forbidden as stated by Ibn Rushd. See *Hashiat al Dusuqi*, Vol. 1, p. 502.

2. *Sharh al Risalah*, by Naji, Vol. 1, p. 340.

3. *Sharh al Risalah* by Zarruq, Vol. 1, p. 340.

4. *Al Mughni*, Vol. 3, p. 65.

5. *Al Bahr*, Vol. 2, pp. 144, 170-1, and *Fiqh al Imam Ja'far*, Vol. 2, pp. 70-71.

6. *Al Majmu'*, Vol. 5, p. 430.

7. *Ahkam al Qur'an*, 2nd part, p. 945.

8. *Al Mughni*, Vol. 3, p. 66.

9. Mentioned in *al Muntaqa*, Al Shawkani says "al Hakim grades it correct according to the criteria of al Bukhari and Muslim. In its chain 'Ata' reports from Mu'adh, but 'Ata' did not hear from Mu'adh." *Nail al Awtar*, Vol. 4, p. 152.

10. *Al Mubsut*, Vol. 2, p. 157.

11. *Al sunan al Kubra* by al Baihaqi, Vol. 4, p. 113.

12. *Al Jawhar al Naqi* by Ibn al Turkumani, printed with al Sunan al Kubra, Vol. 4, p.113.

13. *Ibid.*

14. *Al Mughni*, Vol. 3, p. 65.

15. *Ibid.*

16. *Al Majmu'*, Vol. 5, p. 429.

17. *Fath al Bari*, Vol. 3, p. 200.

18. Al Bukhari mentions the narration of Taus affirmatively but suspended, which indicates it is correct up to al Bukhari. Taus was the leading scholar in the Followers' epoch. He was well versed with the biography of Mu'adh. Al Bukhari's use of Taus narrations means it is strong evidence. See Ibid.

19. *Al Muhalla*, Vol. 6, p. 312.

20. *Fatawa Ibn Taimiyah*, Vol. 25, pp. 82-3.

CHAPTER FOUR

TRANSPORTING *ZAKAH*

Fourteen hundred years ago Islam introduced its unique principle that *zakah* must be distributed in the region in which it is collected, instead of being given to some ruler to spend on palaces, servants, and army, as was the common practice of the time. Muslim scholars agree that *zakah* should be distributed to deservants in the same geographical area from which it was collected.[1] This applies to *zakah* collected on livestock, grain, and fruits. *Zakah* on money is distributed in the area of the asset and not where the owner lives, if he or she lives away from the *zakated* wealth.[2]

This principle is based on the tradition of the Prophet (p) and his Wise Successors. When the Prophet sent *zakah* officers to any area or region, he instructed them to distribute to the poor in the same region. The instructions he gave Mu'adh (its authenticity is agreed upon) says "*zakah* is to be distributed to the poor among them . . ." Mu'adh implemented the instructions of the Prophet (p) to the letter. He divided Yemen into regions such that *zakah* was collected and distributed within each region autonomously. He wrote letters to the effect that *zakah* be distributed within the same clan from which it is collected.[3]

Abu Juhaifah says, "The *zakah* officer of the Messenger of God (p) came and collected *zakah* from the rich among us and distributed it to our poor. I was then a minor orphan, so he gave me a she-camel."[4] It is correctly reported that a bedouin Arab asked the Messenger of God (p) several questions. Among them was, "By God Who sent you, is it God who commanded you to take the *sadaqah* from our rich and distribute it to our poor?" The Prophet answered, "Yes."

Abu 'Ubaid reports that 'Umar wrote in his will "I ask my successor . . . to take from the peripheries of their wealth and distribute is among their poor."[5] This was the practice during the time of 'Umar himself. Sa'id bin al Musayyib says "'Umar sent Mu'adh as *zakah* officer to bani Kilab or bani Sa'd. Mu'adh went there, collected *zakah*, and distributed all of it, leaving nothing. He came back in the same own clothes that he went in."[6] 'Umar was once asked what to do with the *zakah* collected from bedouin Arabs. He answered, "By God, I shall render the *sadaqah* to themselves, until each of them becomes the owner of a hundred camels, male or female."[7]

Transporting *zakah* from the region in which it is collected while that region still contains poor people violates the reason for which it is collected. The author of *al Mughni* says "since *zakah* is meant to enrich the poor, permitting transporting it leaves the poor of that region in need."[8] Scholars and governors after the Prophet followed the same guidance. 'Imran bin Husain, a Companion, was appointed *zakah* officer at the time of the Umayyads. When he returned from his mission, he was asked "Where is the money?" 'Imran said, "Did you send me to bring you money?" I collected it the same way we used to at the time of the Messenger of God (p), and distributed it the same way we used to."[9] Taus was appointed *zakah* officer in one of the regions in Yemen. He was asked for his account by the governor and his answer was, "I took from the rich and gave to the destitute.[10] Farqad al Sabkhi says, I took *zakah* due on my wealth to distribute it in Makkah. There I met Said bin Jubair, who said, 'Take it back and distribute it in your hometown.'"[11] Sufyan narrates "*Zakah* was taken from al Riy to al Kufah, but 'Umar bin 'Abd al Aziz ordered it taken back to al Riy."[12]

Abu 'Ubaid says, "Scholars all agree that these reports mean people of every region have priority on their *zakah*, as long as they still have anyone in need, or until all the *zakah* is distributed." He goes on, "If the officer transports collected *zakah* while there still is need in the region from which it was collected, the government must return it to its region, as did 'Umar bin 'Abd al 'Aziz, and as stated by Sa'id bin Jubair."[13]

Al Nakha'i and al Basri allow a person to transport *zakah* in order to give it to his own kin who live away from him. Abu 'Ubaid says, "This is permitted in individual cases only, not on the massive level of *zakah* administered by the government." Abu 'Ubaid comments on the story that Abu al 'Aliyah, a Companion, used to take his due *zakah* to Madinah, "I believe he was taking it to his kindred and relatives."[14]

Cases in which transporting *zakah* is permissible

Scholars agree that all excess *zakah* funds may be transported to neighboring areas or to the central government. Abu 'Ubaid reports that Mu'adh stayed in Yemen until the Prophet died and during the era of Abu Bakr, then went to 'Umar, who confirmed his position. One year Mu'adh sent 'Umar one third of the *zakah* collected in that year.'Umar was annoyed and told him, "I did not send you as a collector or as a taker of *jiziah*. I assigned you to take from the rich and render to the poor." Mu'adh answered, "I have not sent you anything that I can find anyone to take from me here." The following year, Mu'adh sent 'Umar one half of the collected *zakah*. They exchanged statements similar to the previous year. In the third year, Mu'adh sent 'Umar all the collected *zakah*. 'Umar questioned him the same way he did the previous years, whereupon Mu'adh said, "I could not find anyone who would take any of it."[15]

'Umar's objection indicates that *zakah* must be distributed in the land where it is collected but his acceptance after Mu'adh's explanation shows that it is permissible to transport *zakah* when no deservants exist in its region.

Besides this agreed upon case, there are cases in which, though some need remains in the land of collection, it may be more beneficial to the total welfare of the society to transport some portion of the collected *zakah*. Shafi'ites, for example, do not approve of transportation in such cases. So do Hanbalites.[16] On the other hand, Hanafites consider such transportation disliked but not prohibited. They add that if transporting *zakah* is done to relieve poor relatives of the payer, or people or troops who are in desperate need in another land, it is not disliked. The same thing applies when *zakah* is transported for the benefit of the Muslim community, by Muslims in non-Muslim land to Muslim countries, or in order to help poor scholars or students. Malikites obligate the distribution of *zakah* in the area of collection, but allow transportation when the need is more pressing in other areas that in the area of collection.[18] Zaidis dislike transportation except to satisfy more pressing needs, needy relatives, or students.[19] Abadis approve of transportation if done by the government in order to strengthen the Islamic state.[20]

Discussion and Analysis

After this survey of the different opinions and texts on the transportation of collected *zakah*, it appears that the general principle is that *zakah* must be distributed in the same area where it is collected. The poor and needy in that land have priority over all others, since *zakah* is collected from their neighbors, kin, and friends.

However, I find no reason why this general principle should not have exceptions, especially if the exception is made by a just government in consultation with the representative council, in view of the public interests of Muslims and Islam. As Malik wonderfully puts it, "Transporting *zakah* is not permissible, except when done through the government's *ijtihad*, in view of pressing need."[21] Ibn al Qasim, Malik's disciple adds, "If this is done out of necessity, it is all right."[22] Suhnun is reported to say, "If the government knows a certain land has dire need, it can lawfully transport some of the collected *zakah* there. When catastrophe befalls, relieving its victims has priority above other uses of *zakah*, since a Muslim is a brother to a fellow Muslim; he does not let him down nor oppress him."[23]

In al Mudawwanah, Malik mentions that in the year when famine hit al Madinah, 'Umar wrote to Amr bin al 'As, who was in Egypt, "Help, help, to the Arabs. Send us a caravan whose beginning should reach me while its end is still at your place, loaded with flour wrapped in garments." 'Umar, when the relief arrived, divided food and clothes among the hungry people and appointed assignees to help slaughter the camels, saying, "Arabs love camels. I am afraid they may prefer to keep them alive. Have people slaughter the camels and eat their meat and fat, and give them the garments that are used as bags of flour, to wear."[24]

This opinion is supported by the three following points:

Firstly, the different geographical areas in the Islamic state form one body whose members must come to the help of any member that is in pain. This unity and solidarity is required by Islam and cannot be neglected. Secondly, there are deserving categories that can only be assessed and determined by the central government, such as reconciling hearts and spending in the way of God . The central government must acquire a certain portion of *zakah* for the shares of these deservants. In this regard, al Qurtubi quotes some scholars as suggesting that the total collection of *zakah* should be divided into segments, "whereby the share of the poor and needy is distributed locally, while other shares may be transported at the discretion of the government."[25] This matter is undoubtedly one that must be determined by the *ijtihad* of the Islamic government. It is reported that 'Umar bin 'Abd al 'Aziz once wrote to his commissioners "Distribute half of the collected *zakah* and send me the other half." Then he wrote in the following year "Distribute all of it".[26]

Thirdly, we have evidence that the Prophet (p) used to invite bedouin Arabs to send their *sadaqah* to Madinah in order to spend on the poor migrants and helper [muhajirin and ansar] Al Nasa'i reports from 'Abd Allah bin Hilal al Thaqafi, "A man came to the messenger of God (p) and said, 'I was about to be killed for what amounts to a rope or a sheep of sadaqah'.The Prophet (p) said, 'If it were not to be given the poor migrants, I would not have taken it.'" Similarly, the Prophet (p) told Qubaisah bin al Mukhariq, who asked for help in paying financial burden he carried in reconciling two groups, "Stay until the *sadaqah* comes, We will either help you or carry the whole burden for you." The Prophet was prepared to give him from the *sadaqah* of *Hijaz*, although he was from Najd.[27] 'Adi bin Hatim is known to have carried the *zakah* collected from his tribe to Abu Bakr after the death of the Prophet (p).[28] Also, Umar told Ibn Abi Dhubab when he sent him as collector right after the great famine," collect the *zakah* due for two years. Distribute half among them and send me the other half."[29] Mu'adh told the people of Yemen, "Bring me garments or cloth, I accept them from you in fulfillment of *zakah*. It is easier for you and more beneficial to the migrants Madinah." Abu 'Ubaid comments, "This certainly applies to the excess above their needs."[30] But Abu 'Ubaid's explanation is not necessarily true. Needs are subjective and have different levels, and the government has the right to determine where needs are more pressing and urgent. Lastly, it must be emphasized that the government must not transport all the collected *zakah* unless there is no local need at all for *zakah* funds.

It must be noted, however, that Shafi'ites, who are most restrictive in the matter of transportation, do not disapprove of transporting *zakah* by the government or its *zakah* agency. They center their objection only on the case when the payer distributes due *zakah* himself. Al Nawawi says, "It must be realized that the government or its *zakah* agency is permitted to transport *zakah*. The discussion on transportation is centered on the case when it is done by the payer." Al Rafi'i supports this position.[31] One may add that when there is no Islamic state or when the state does not collect *zakah*, individual payers can assume the same role and decide whether to transport due *zakah* to needy relatives, to people who are in dire need, for essential public interests of Muslims, or to a pivotal Islamic project in another country.

Footnotes

1.   *Mushkilat al Faqr wa Kaifa 'Alajaha al Islam,* by al Qardawi, p. 114.

2.   *Hashiat al Dusuqi,* Vol. 1, p. 500.

3.   Reported via a correct chain by Sa'id bin Mansur from Taus. Al Athram reports a similar story, as stated in *Nail al Awtar,* Vol. 2, p. 161.

4.   Reported by al Tirmidhi, who adds "It is good," *Ibid.*

5.   *Al Amwal,* p. 595.

6.   *Ibid,* p. 596.

7.   *Al Mussannaf,* Vol. 3, p. 205.

8.   *Al Mughni,* Vol. 2, p. 672.

9.   Reported by Abu Daud and Ibn Majah. See *Nail al Awtar,* vol. 2, p.161.

10.   *Al Amwal,* p. 595.

12.   *Ibid.*

13.   *Ibid.*

14.   *Ibid.*

15.   *Ibid.* p. 596 and *Mushkilat al Faqr.*

16.   *Al Ahkam al Sultaniyah,* by al Mawardi, pp. 119-120, *Sharh al Ghayah,* vol. 2, p. 228. Al Tibi is quoted by al Qari as saying, "It is agreed that if *zakah* is transported and distributed the obligation is fulfilled. Only 'Umar bin 'Abd al 'Aziz disagrees. He returned *zakah* transported from Khurasan to Syria to the place it was collected from." Al Qari adds, "His action does not really indicate that he disagrees with the *ijma,* but merely that it is better not to transport *zakah.*" See *al Mirqat,* Vol. 4, p. 118-119.

17.   *Radd al Muhtar,* Vol. 2, pp. 93-94.

18.   *Hashiat al Dusuqi,* Vol. 1, p. 501.

19.   *Sharh al Azhar,* Vol. 1, pp. 547-548.

20.   *Sharh al Nil,* Vol. 2, p. 138.

21.   The explanation of the Qur'an by al Qurtubi, Vol. 8, p. 175.

22.   *Ibid.*

23. *Ibid.*

24. *Al Mudawwanah al Kubra*, Vol. 1, p. 246. The report is mentioned also by al Hakim in his *al Mustadrak*. Al Hakim adds, "Correct by the criteria of Muslim." This is approved by al Dhahabi, Vol. 1, pp. 405-406.

25. *Al Qurtubi*, Vol. 8, p. 176.

26. *Al Amwal*, p. 594.

27. *Ibid.* p. 600.

28. *Ibid.*

29. *Ibid.*

30. *Ibid.*

31. *Al Majmu'*, Vol. 6, p. 175

CHAPTER FIVE

PRE-PAYMENT AND DELAYED PAYMENT OF *ZAKAH*

The obligation of *zakah* is immediate

The Hanafites' well-known view is that the obligation of *zakah* has an extended due time for payment, unless the state determines otherwise, since texts ordering its payment are not restricted timewise. This is the opinion of Abu Bakr al Jassas too. On the other hand, al Karkhi, a leading Hanafite, believes payment must be immediate, from his understanding of the same ordaining text. Ibn al Humam adds that the fact that *zakah* is relief to the poor implies that it should be immediate for otherwise it does not fulfill its role.[1]

This seems to be the right position. It is taken by the majority of scholars, including Malik, al Shafi'i, and Ahmad. Ibn Qudamah notes:

Ordinance of a ruling usually implies immediate execution, and delay may be a reason for punishment. For example, God expelled Iblis and disgraced him because he disobeyed the order to prostrate. If a person orders his servant to give him water, postponement of implementation is naturally a good reason for punishment. Permitting delays logically contradicts the order itself, especially when no time limit is set for the order's implementation . Even if one believes that ordinances, in general, leave some room for delay, one would make an exception for the ordinance of *zakah*, since postponement of payment may be indefinite, and assets as well as payers are subject to destruction or death which would harm the deservant poor and needy. Added to this is the fact that *zakah* is a repetitive rite of worship whose delay to the time of the following payment must be unlawful like the delay of prayer or fasting of *Ramadan*.

Certainly, if immediate payment may harm the payer, financially or otherwise, delay is permitted, since the Messenger of God (p) says, "There should be no harm or injury."[2] Postponement of payment of debts due other people is allowed in such case, and *zakah* need not have priority over other debts.[3]

However, all rites of worship and good deeds must as far as possible be done immediately. God says, "And race to do the good things,"[4] and "And hurry to forgiveness from your Lord, and to a Garden."[5] If immediacy is good in all righteous actions, it is more so in *zakah*, because of the need to quickly relieve the poor and needy. Muslim scholars always emphasize that good deeds should be done without delay, before obstacles and hindrances arise.[6] Also, The Prophet says "One's due *sadaqah* is not mixed with one's other wealth but brings destruction to it." This is reported by al Shafi'i, al Bukhari in his history, and al Humaidi, who explains, "This refers to due *sadaqah* that is not given away but left mixed with one's wealth."[7]

Pre-payment of *zakah*

For *zakated* assets that require the passage of one year such as livestock, money, and trade inventory, the majority of jurists believe pre-payment of *zakah* is permitted, provided the payer owns the necessary *nisab*. This opinion is shared by al Hasan, Sa'id bin Jubair, al Zuhri, al Awza'i, Abu Hanifah, al Shafi'i, Ahmad, Ishaq, and Abu 'Ubaid.[8] On the other hand, Rabi'ah, Malik, and Daud do not allow such pre-payment,[9] though some Malikites approve of the pre-payment within periods of no more than one month with certain assets such as money and merchants' inventory. However, such approval, they say, is accompanied by marking the pre-payment as disliked. Pre-payment is approved by Malikites without being disliked in two cases: When *zakah* proceeds need to be transported to more desperate needy in another area and they arrive there at the end of the year, and when *zakah* is collected by the *zakah* collectors a short period before the end of a full year. Pre-payment of *zakah* on fruits and grains is not approved.[10]

Those who do not allow pre-payment argue that the of a full year is a condition for obligation of *zakah* and that *zakah* like prayers, cannot be performed before the due time.[11]

Those who permit pre-payment provide as evidence the saying reported by Abu Daud and others, from 'Ali, that "Al 'Abbas asked the Messenger of God (p) to allow him to pre-pay his *sadaqah*. The Prophet permitted him to do so."[12] Although the chain of the saying is not free of criticism, it is supported by al Baihaqi's report from 'Ali that "The Prophet (p) appointed 'Umar on the *sadaqah*. It was rumored that Ibn Jamil, Khalid bin al Walid, and al 'Abbas, the uncle of the Prophet (p) refused to pay *zakah*. The Prophet (p) defended Khalid and al Abbas, saying we needed [some funds] and took the *sadaqah* from al 'Abbas for two years in advance."[13] This story is reported in the correct collection of Muslim from Abu Hurairah, where the Prophet reportedly adds, "As for al 'Abbas, his *zakah* is upon me and another equal amount too." Then the Prophet (p) continues "O 'Umar, didn't you know that the uncle of man is like his father?" Abu 'Ubaid comments "The Prophet said, 'it is upon me' because it is said he borrowed from al 'Abbas the *sadaqah* due for two years in advance."[14]

Moreover, pre-payment can be argued as acceptable by reasoning and analogy. It is like pre-payment of a debt due to another person.[15] Some object claiming that the condition of the completion of a year is a necessary condition just like having *nisab*, but this is incorrect since owning *nisab* is an indispensable reason for the obligation to exist, thus payment before having *nisab* is payment of something that is not obligated, not like payment before completion of the year which is in fulfillment of a required obligation.[16]

Additionally, whenever timing is added to facilitate matters the obligated person, al Khattabi argues, is permitted not to use this privilege, and timing in *zakah* is like timing in all debts of that kind.[17] Prayer and fasting are purely rites of worship, in which timing cannot be explained while *zakah* is both a rite of worship and a financial obligation at the same time.

Lastly, Hanafites and some others allow pre-payment with no time limitation, even for several years, as long as *nisab* is owned.[18] It must be noted that payment on time is always preferable, in order to avoid the gray area of dispute.

Delay of *zakah* payment

Delaying the payment of *zakah* without valid reason is not permitted, but *zakah* may be delayed in certain cases without blame, such as lack of liquid funds or, according to Shams al Din al Ramli, to wait and give it to needy relatives or to a person in more desperate need, or to investigate the needs of the available deservants. When payment is delayed, the payer guarantees the due amount in case of destruction or loss.[19]

Ibn Qudamah allows such delay only for a short time. He quotes Ahmad as saying "It is not permitted to pay *zakah* monthly installments that begin on or after the due time, nor is it permitted to delay some *zakah* due on certain assets in order to combine it with *zakah* due later on some other asset."[20] Some Malikites insist that keeping the due amount of *zakah* in order to distribute it in fragments throughout the year is not permitted.[21] The government or *zakah* commissioner may decide to postpone collection for valid reasons, such as drought, famine, or depression. Ahmad quotes 'Umar's action that "One year people were in need, so 'Umar did not collect *zakah* and took that due *zakah* the following year."[22] Abu 'Ubaid reported from Ibn Abi Dhubab that "'Umar deferred the *sadaqah* the year of famine. When people were relieved the following year, he sent for me and said, 'Collect twice the amount of *zakah*. Divide among them one half and bring me the other.'"[23] We have seen in the saying from Abu Hurairah that the Prophet (p) took the *zakah* due on al 'Abbas for two years. Abu 'Ubaid notes, "I think the Prophet delayed collection from al Abbas because of an incident of need that happened to al Abbas."[24]

Delay in *zakah* payment without valid reason is sinful and not permitted. The author of *al Muhadhdhab*, a Shafi'ite, says, "It is not permitted to delay *zakah* after it becomes due, since it is a right to other people."[25] Hanafites also believe delaying *zakah* payment unnecessarily is sinful. Al Tahawi quotes Abu Hanifah as saying that such delay is emphatically disliked. Hanafites say it is sinful to delay payment, even for a day or two. The author of *Al Badai* quotes from *al Muntaqa*, "If *zakah* is not paid within two years, it is grossly sinful."[26] I believe delaying *zakah* payment without reason beyond a short period is not permissible at all.

Loss of *zakah*

Ibn Rushd summarizes jurists' views in the case of loss of an item or amount designated as *zakah* payment:

If the due amount got lost on the way to being distributed, some jurists believe the requirement is fulfilled and no new payment is needed. Other jurists argue that the payer is a guarantor until *zakah* is actually distributed to recipients. Yet others distinguish between the case of neglect or mishandling on the part of the payer, in which the payer guarantees *zakah* to recipients and the case of no neglect, in which the payer is not considered responsible for the loss. Lastly, some jurists treat the lost amount and the total assets of the payer as community property of the poor (who owns a share in the proportion of lost *zakah* to the total) and the owner (who owns the rest). Accordingly, they divide the loss in proportion to their respective shares.[27]

Usually discussed by jurists is the case in which the *zakatable* asset is itself lost, after the due time of *zakah* but before actual payment. Ibn Rushd adds, "In this case, some jurists say *zakah* must be calculated on what is left after the loss, while others apply the principle of community property, as in partnerships." These differences exist because some jurists treat the amount of due *zakah* like interpersonal debts while others view it as a due right on the assets themselves.[28]

Can the requirement be relaxed after years pass?

If *zakah* payment is delayed, with or without valid reason, is it waived after the passage of a certain number of years, like taxes? The answer is negative, since *zakah* is a right of the poor and needy prescribed by God. Al Nawawi says, "If certain number of years pass without payment of any *zakah* that is due, the owner must pay the whole accumulated due *zakah* regardless of the reason of the delay and the residence of the owner." Ibn al Mundhir gives as example, a case in which a city falls in the hands of rebels or enemies for a few years, during which residents of that city do not pay due *zakah*. The Islamic state, when it liberates the town, must collect the due amount of *zakah* for all those years, according to Malik, al Shafi'i, and Abu Thawr. Jurists of Opinion (i.e. Hanafites) contend that *zakah* must not be charged for those years. The latter add that if someone embraces Islam in a non-Muslim country and unknowingly does not pay *zakah*, then migrates to a Muslim land, he or she must not be charged *zakah* for past years.[29] Ibn Hazm, notes,[30] If two *zakah* charges or more become simultaneously due, the accumulated amount must be paid instantly, without delay and without deduction of the *zakah* calculated on the amount due for each previous year."[31] *Zakah* is not similar to taxes in regard to the passage of years on unpaid amounts.

As when a person dies leaving debts, any due zakah must be paid out of the deceased person's estate, without need for instructions in the will to that effect. This opinion is adopted by 'Ata' , al Hasan, al Zuhri, Qatadah, Malik,[32] al Shafi'i[33], Ahmad, Ishaq, Abu Thawr, Ibn al Mundhir,[34] and the Zaidi school.[35] Al Awza'i and al Laith restrict such payment to one-third or less of the estate. Ibn Sirin, al Sha'bi, al Nakha'i, Hammad, al Thawri, and others believe it can be paid only if the person's will specifies this payment.

Abu Hanifa and his disciples add that without instructions in the will, *zakah* payment out of the deceased's estate does not satisfy the religious aspect of *zakah* and the heirs must not be required to make such payment, because *zakah* is a worship that requires intention.[36] This means the deceased is sinful for lack of payment.

Along with Ibn Qudamah, I believe that since in addition to being a worship, *zakah* is a financial obligation, and like other debts, its payment cannot be waived as a result of death.[37] Moreover, the Prophet is authentically reported to have said, "If a person dies while still owing some fasting, his close kin may fast in fulfillment." *Zakah* is even more worthy of such fulfillment than fasting, which is solely a worship. This allowance is a mercy from God, for it removes the sinful consequence of neglect on the part of the deceased.

The position of *zakah* compared to other debts

The author of *al Muhadhdhab* compares *zakah* with other debts left unpaid by a deceased person: "If *zakah* and debts to other individuals are due and the total estate is not sufficient to pay all of these obligations, jurists diverge into three opinions: (a) other people's debts must be given priority, (b) *zakah* has priority, since the Prophet (p) says in regard to pilgrimage, 'The debt owed to God has preference in payment'.[38] and (c), the estate must be divided between *zakah* and other debts, since both are equally in need of payment."[39]

Zahiris give priority to *zakah*. Ibn Hazm argues, "creditors, will, and heirs, all have no right on the estate except after due *zakah* is paid." Ibn Hazm was very critical of the Hanafite view. In *al Muhalla*, he writes "It is really surprising that they believe prayer must still be performed by a person who has willingly delayed it until its time ran out, while they say *zakah* is waived from a person who has willingly delayed it until death... Especially since *zakah* is a debt due to God and the right of the poor and needy." Ibn Hazm quotes the saying reported by Muslim from Ibn 'Abbas, "A man came to the Prophet (p) and said, "My mother died. She still has the fasting of one month unfulfilled. Should I fast for her?" The Prophet said, "If your mother owed some debts, would you pay them on her behalf ?" "Yes" said the man. The Prophet went on, "Then the debt to God has preference in payment." Ibn Hazm comments, "How can anyone claim that the debt of someone else must be paid out of the estate, while the debt of God can go without payment.?"[40]

In conclusion , the due amount of *zakah* must be paid out of the estate. It has priority above interpersonal debts . Only recently some governments have enacted laws giving priority to unpaid taxes on deceased persons estates.

Footnotes

1. *Fath al Qadir*, Vol. 1, p. 482-483, and *Radd al Muhtar* Vol. 2, pp. 13-14.

2. *Al Mughni*, Vol. 1, pp. 684-685.

3. Reported by Ahmad and Ibn Majah from Ibn 'Abbas, by Al Hakim, and al Daraqutni from Abu Sa'id, and by Ibn Majah again from 'Ubadah bin al Samit. Al Nawawi in *al Arba'in* grades it good, adding, "Also reported as *mursal* by Malik, via several chains that strengthen each other." Al Haithami says its chain is trustworthy. Ahmad Shakir comments on it under number 2867 of *al Musnad*, "Its chain is weak but its meaning is correct, and confirmed by a correct chain mentioned by lbn Majah from 'Ubadah."

4. *Sura al Baqarah*, 2:148, and al Ma'idah, 5:48.

5. *Sura al 'Imran*, 3:133.

6. *Nail al Awtar*, Vol. 4, p. 148.

7. *Ibid.*

8. *Al Mughni,* Vol. 2, p. 630.

9. *Ibid*, and *Bidayat al Mujtahid,* Vol. l, p.266.

10. *Hashiat al Dusuqi*, Vol. 1, p. 502.

11. *Al Mughni, op. cit.*

12. Reported by the five excluding al Nasa'i, but also reported by al Hakim, al Daraqutni, and al Baihaqi. Al Daraqutni and Abu Daud give more confidence to the *mursal* version. The saying is supported by other sayings. See *Nail al Awtar,* Vol. 4, pp. 159-160, and *al Majmu'*, Vol. 6, pp. 145-146.

13. *Al Sunan al Kubra*, Vol. 4, p. 111. Abu Daud al Tayalisi reports from Abu Rafi', "The Prophet (p) said to 'Umar, 'We pre-collected the *sadaqah* on al 'Abbas's wealth last year.'" See *Nail al Awtar, ibid.*

14. *Nail al Awtar, ibid.*

15. *Al Mughni, op. cit.*

16. *Ibid.*

17. *Ma'alim al Sunan*, Vol. 2, p. 224.

18. *Radd al Muhtar,* Vol. 2, pp. 29-30, and *al Bahr al Zakhkhar*, Vol. 2, p. 188.

19. *Nihayat al Muhtaj*, Vol. 2, p. 134.

20.	*Al Mughni,* Vol. 2, p. 685.

21.	*Hashiat al Dusuqi,* Vol. l, p.500.

22.	*Matalib Uli al Nuha,* Vol. 2, p. 116.

23.	*Al Amwal,* p. 374.

24.	*Nail al Awtar,* Vol. 4, p. 159.

25.	*Al Majmu',* Vol. 5, p. 331.

26.	*Radd al Muhtar,* Vol. 2, p. 14.

27.	*Bidayat al Mujtahid,* Vol. l, p. 240.

28.	*Ibid, al Muhalla,* Vol. 6, p. 363, and *Radd al Muhtar,* Vol. 2, pp. 79-80.

29.	*Al Majmu',* Vol. 5, p. 337.

30.	*Al Muhalla,* Vol. 6, p. 87.

31.	This is rightly based on that *zakah* is due on the wealthy as a personal liability, not designated for any specific item of the person's assets. See *al Mughni,* Vol. 2, pp. 679-680.

32.	*Hashiat al Dusuqi,* Vol. 1, p. 502, and *Bidayat al Mujtahid,* Vol. 1, p. 241.

33.	Al Nawawi says, "If *zakah* becomes due and the owner is able to pay it but dies before payment, it must be paid out of the estate." See *al Majmu',* Vol. 5, p. 335.

34.	*Al Mughni,* Vol. 2, pp. 683-684.

35.	*Sharh al Azhar,* Vol. 1, p. 453, and *al Bahr,* Vol. 2, p 144.

35.	This opinion of Abu Hanifah applies to *zakah* on money. There are two contradicting reports from him about *zakah* on agriculture and livestock. See *al Muhalla,* Vol. 6, pp. 88-89, and *al Majmu',* Vol. 5, pp. 335-336.

37.	*Al Majmu', ibid,* and *al Mughni,* Vol. 2, pp. 683-684.

38.	The saying is reported by al Bukhari and Muslim from Ibn 'Abbas in regard to fasting. See *ibid.*

39.	*Al Majmu',* Vol. 6, p. 231.

40.	*Al Muhalla,* Vol. 6, pp. 89-91.

41.	*Mabadi' al Nazariyah al 'Ammah li al Daribah,* by 'Abd al Hakim, al Rifa'i and Husain Khallaf, p. 143.

CHAPTER SIX

QUESTIONS ABOUT *ZAKAH* FULFILLMENT

Cheating and fraud in *zakah*

Fraud and use of tricks in order to avoid *zakah* or to get it back after payment are obviously not permissible. Malikites note that it is so from the point of view of religion, as well as from the legal point of view. They add, "Any action intended to escape *zakah* payment before it becomes due, like changing the nature of *zakatable* assets, distributing ownership among different persons so that each of them owns less than *nisab*, or slaughtering some of the herd to reduce its number to below nisab, all do not effect in waiving *zakah*, as long as it can be proven that such actions were taken in order to avoid the accrual of *zakah*. In cases like those, *zakah* accrues and must be collected."[1] Hanbalites agree with the Malikite view on actions meant to escape *zakah*. Ibn Qudamah says:

Exchanging an asset with a different one interrupts the year period and a new year must start for the new asset. But if this is done in order to escape the accrual of *zakah*, *zakah* is levied just as if nothing happened. By the same token, if the owner gives away or destroys some assets in order to make the remainder below *nisab*, *zakah* is not waived and still accrues at the end of the year. This opinion is also shared by Malik, al Awza'i, Ibn al Majashown, Ishaq , and Abu 'Ubaid..... This is founded on God's verses, 'Verily We have tried them as We tried the people of the garden, when they resolved to gather the fruits (of the garden) in the morning. But made no reservation ('If it be God's will). Then there came on the garden a visitation from thy Lord which swept away all around while they were asleep, so the garden became by the morning like a dark and desolate spot.'[2] The penalty from God is given because such persons embark on an action of intended escape payment of *sadaqah*. It is known that any action meant to forsake or evade the right of another person cannot be allowed to succeed in *Shari'ah*. For example, a man who divorces his wife during his death-sickness in order to evade her sharing in his estate cannot be successful in withholding her right to the wife's share.[3]

On the other hand, Ibn Taimiyah, in al Qawa'id al Nuraniyah, says Abu Hanifah permits tricks aimed at escaping *zakah*, and that Abu Hanifah's disciples differ on whether such tricks are disliked or not. He says Muhammad dislikes them, while Abu Yusuf does not.[4] However, upon looking into Abu Yusuf's al Kharaj, I find Abu Yusuf saying, "It is not lawful for anyone who believes in God and the last Day to elude *zakah*, to distribute the ownership of a *nisab*, that one owns, to several people in order to avoid the accrual of the *sadaqah*, or to escape proper accrual of *sadaqah* by any way or any means."[5] It is likely that Ibn Taimiyah is referring to what is commonly found in Hanafites' writing that use of loopholes is legally valid in waiving *zakah*, although *zakah* remains unfulfilled religiously, and that use of legal loopholes is sometimes disliked and sometimes not. Hanafites state for example, that it is disliked to give *zakah* to a poor person on the condition that the latter give it as a gift to the payer's needy parents. By the same token, any condition made on the poor person when *zakah* is given him is invalid, even though the recipient may be willing to fulfill it.[6] It must be noted that tricks like these, whether disliked or not, apply only to expending *zakah*. Hanafites books do not discuss cheating to escape *zakah* accrual in the first place.

Additionally, Ibn Taimiyah says that al Shifi'i only dislikes use of loopholes in order to escape the accrual of *zakah*.

Lastly, Zaidis do not approve of the use of tricks, whether they are used to avoid *zakah* accrual, to escape actual payment to deservants, or to get it back after payment.[7] The author of *Hawashi Sharh al Azhar* quotes al Shawkani, "There is no doubt that any fraud that ends up making lawful what is forbidden or vice versa must be completely prohibited. Permitting such tricks is not consistent with *Shari'ah* by any means."[8]

Exchange of prayers between collector, payer and recipient

The spiritual aspect of *zakah* is expressed - among other manifestations- in the prayers exchanged between the collector and the payer. The collector of *zakah* is asked to pray on behalf of the payer. God says, "out of their wealth take a *sadaqah* so thou might purify and sanctify them; and pray on their behalf. Verily your prayers are a source of security and comfort to them." 'Abd Allah bin Abu Awfa narrates, "The Messenger of God, when any person brought him *zakah*, used to say, 'O Lord, give them mercy!' When my father, Abu Awfa, brought him his *sadaqah*, the Prophet said, 'O Lord, give mercy to the family of Abu Awfa'."[9] This prayer is not restricted to any specific form. Al Shafi'i says, "I like the collector to say 'May God reward you for that which you give, make it a cause for purification for you, and give you blessings on what you have left for yourself.'"[10] Al Nasa'i reports that the Prophet (p) prayed on behalf of a man who sent a good she-camel, "O Lord, bless him and his camels."[11]

Zahiris and some Shafi'ites consider such prayers obligatory on the part of the collector, as one can derive literally from the above verse. However, the majority believe these prayers are recommended and not obligated, because the Prophet (p) did not include it in any of his instructions to collectors,[12] nor are government collectors required to make such prayers when they receive other dues from the payers.[13] However, these arguments do not seem to outweigh the indication of the verse.

In another saying, the Messenger (p) recommends that the payer supplicate God upon payment of *zakah*. Abu Hurairah narrates the Messenger of God says, "When you give *zakah* away, do not forget its reward. Say 'Our Lord, make it rewarding and not a loss.'"[14] 'Ali narrates that the Prophet (p) says, "There are fifteen things which if my nation does, it will be affected by catastrophes..." Among them he mentions "when it considers trust a means for gain and when it considers *zakah* a loss."[15] *Zakah* recipients are also recommended to pray on behalf of the payer on the basis of the saying from Abu Hurairah since one of its versions reads "when you are given..."[16]

Paying *zakah* by proxy

Zakah payer may choose to actuate payment by himself or by agents, attorneys, or representatives, as long as the latter are trustworthy and dependable. Some jurists require that such agents be Muslims, since *zakah* is a form of worship.[17] Additionally, some Malikites consider payment via representatives less open to pride and hypocrisy than direct payment by the owner.[18]

Payment in public

Al Nawawi says it is better for *zakah* to be paid in public where it is seen by others, so it serves as a reminder to other payers, the same way obligatory prayer is recommended collectively in public.[19] This is on the ground that *zakah* is one of the major rites of worship in Islam that must be very visible in the Muslim society. Since it is required from every *zakatable* person, it is not an object of pride or condescension, in contrast to voluntary charity, which is better done in privacy. Keenness to present the symbols of Islam and make them dominant is a sign of faith and an indication of righteousness. God says "Such, and who ever hold in honor the symbols of God, such should come truly from piety of heart."[20] This may be what the Prophet meant when he said, "And showing off which is loved by God is that done by a man in battle, or when giving the *sadaqah*."[21] This, in fact, is based on the verse, "If ye disclose acts of charity, it is well."[22]

Should recipients be told it is *zakah*?

When *zakah* is distributed by individuals, it is preferred that recipients not be told that it is *zakah*, especially since many deservants may hesitate to take *zakah* at the slightest doubt that they my not be truly deserving. The author of *al Mughni* says "When *zakah* is paid to those whom the payer thinks are poor, there is no need to inform recipients that it is *zakah*." Al Hasan says, "Do you want to humiliate him? Do not tell him." And Ahmad bin al Hasan says, "I asked Ahmad if a person who pays his *zakah* to another should tell him it is *zakah* or remain silent. Ahmad answered, 'Why should he humiliate the recipient by saying that? have him pay it without comment. Does he need to beat him over the head with that payment?'"[23] Some Malikites dislike mentioning that it is *zakah* since this disheartens the poor.[24]

Ja'farites also believe there is no need to tell the recipient that what is paid is *zakah*. Abu Basir says, "I asked al Baqir about a person who may shy away from taking *zakah*. Should I give him without calling it *zakah*? Al Baqir answered, 'Give him without naming it; do not humiliate believers.'"[25]

Waiving debts as payment of *zakah*

Al Nawawi says "Waiving the debt of a person who is unable to pay the debt back as payment of the creditor's *zakah* is not acceptable fulfillment of *zakah*, according to the most predominant opinion among Shafi'ites. This opinion is shared by Abu Hanifah and Ahmad, because *zakah* payment requires actually giving the deservants. Another view among Shafi'ites is to accept such waiving as fulfillment of *zakah* payment, a view shared by al Hasan and 'Ata', on the grounds that if the creditor gives the debtor *zakah* in cash, the debtor would pay it back to the creditor as payment of the debt. It is not approved that the creditor give his *zakah* to the debtor under the condition that the latter pay it back in fulfillment of the debt."[26] Abu 'Ubaid quotes that al Hasan does not have any objection to waiving the debt of one who is unable to pay it back, in fulfillment of *zakah*. On the other hand, Abu 'Ubaid himself strongly opposes such action, on the grounds that payment of *zakah* in this manner may hide an intention of collecting bad debts. Abu 'Ubaid adds, "It is inconsistent with Sunnah anyway."[27] Ibn Hazm approves of such waiving as *zakah* payment. He quotes a saying reported by Muslim from Abu Sa'id: "A man was financially strained at the time of the Messenger of God (p) as a result of fruits he purchased to sell. He became overburdened by debts. The Messenger of God (p) said, 'Give him sadaqah."[28] This is also the opinion of 'Ata', Ja'farites also subscribe to this view. A man asked Ja'far about loans he had given to some people who were not able to pay back. The debtors even deserved *zakah*, so his question was whether he may waive the debts in fulfillment of *zakah* payment. Ja'far answered "Yes".[29]

In my opinion, the view that accepts waiving debts off *zakah* deservants in fulfillment of payment has more substance than the other. In the Qur'an, God calls waiving debts off persons who are in financial difficulties *sadaqah*. The verse reads, "If the debtor is in difficulty, grant him time till it is easy for him to repay, but if you waive it by way of *sadaqah*, that is best for you, if ye only knew."[30]

Making things available to the poor as *zakah*

Some jurists discuss whether inviting poor persons to eat in the house of the *zakah* payer can be accepted in fulfillment of *zakah*. Hanafites and others argue that since making the poor own the amount given is an indispensable condition for fulfillment of *zakah*, providing them food to eat in the payer's house cannot be considered *zakah* payment, while giving them food, even cooked, fulfills the requirement of *zakah*.[31] Zaidis approve of making food available to the poor as *zakah* payment under the following conditions:
1. The intention of *zakah* payment.
2. Food must not be quickly perishable. It should be like dates or raisin.
3. The amount given should be substantial, i.e. beyond what is usually not counted by people.
4. The food should become at the disposal of the poor, and
5. The poor persons must know that this is in payment of *zakah*.[32]

Footnotes

1. *Bulhgat al Salik,* Vol. 1, p. 210.

2. *Sura al Qalam,* 68:17-20.

3. *Al Mughni,* Vol. 2, pp. 534-535.

4. *Al Qawa'id al Nuraniyah,* p. 89.

5. *Al kharaj,* by Abu Yusuf, p. 80.

6. *Radd al Muhtar,* Vol. 2, p.69.

7. *Sharh al Azhar,* Vol. 1, pp. 539-540.

8. *Ibid.*

9. Al Shawkani quotes from *al Muntaqa,* "it is agreed upon." See *Nail al Awtar,* Vol. 4, p. 153.

10. *Al Rawdah,* by al Nawawi, Vol. 2, p. 211.

11. *Sunan al Nasa'i,* Vol. 5, p. 30.

12. *Nail al Awtar,* Vol. *op cit.*

13. *Ibid.*

14. Reported by Ibn Majah, Vol. 1, no. 1797, and 'Abd al Razzaq in his *Jami',* as stated by al Suyuti in *al Jami' al Kabir.* Al Suyuti marks it weak, Al Munawi in *al Faid,* Vol. 1, p. 290, says the saying is not very weak. See *Nail al Awtar,* Vol. 4, pp. 152-153.

15. Its chain is weak as stated in *Nail al Awtar.*

16. In *al Faid,* Vol. 1 , p. 290, al Munawi says,"It indicates that prayers of this kind are recommended, although not usually specifically mentioned by Jurists. At least they falls under the general recommendation of prayers to God in all circumstances."

17. *Hashiat al Dusuqi,* Vol. 1, p. 498.

18. *Ibid.*

19. *Al Majmu',* Vol. 6, p. 233, and *Fiqh al Imam Ja'far,* Vol. 2, p. 96.

20. *Sura al Hajj,* 22:32.

21. Reported by al Nasa'i, Vol. 5, p. 79.

22. *Sura al Baqarah,* 2:271.

23.   *Al Mughni,* Vol. 2, p. 647.

24.   *Hashiat al Sawi* on *Bulghat al Salik,* Vol. 1, p. 335.

25.   *Fiqh al Imam Ja'far,* Vol. 2, p. 88.

26.   *Al Majmu',* Vol. 6, pp. 210-211.

27.   *Al Amwal,* pp. 595-596.

28.   *Al Muhalla,* Vol. 6, pp. 105-106.

29.   *Fiqh al Imam Ja'far,* Vol. 2, p. 91.

30.   *Sura al Baqarah,* 2:280.

31.   *Radd al Muatar,* Vol. 2, p.3.

32.   *Sharh al Azhar,* Vol. 1, p. 542.

FIQH AL ZAKAH

PART SIX

OBJECTIVES OF *ZAKAH*
AND
ITS EFFECTS ON THE INDIVIDUAL AND SOCIETY

1. Objectives of *zakah* and its effects on the individual

2. Objectives of *zakah* and its effects on society

INTRODUCTION

For a long time, many taxation specialists tried to widen the gap between taxes and social or humanistic issues, in order to prevent any adverse effect of such issues on the proceeds of taxes, claiming that taxes must have only one objective, bringing income to the treasury, and must otherwise be "neutral." It took deep social changes, several bloody revolutions, and great progression of ideas until financial experts came to realize that taxes can affect valuable socio-economic changes, can be used to reduce the economic differences among social classes, and can restore economic balance in society.

There has been no such upheaval in the history of *zakah*, for from the beginning, *zakah*, as one of the pillars of Islam, was an essential and sacred rite of worship. Muslims pay it with devotion and sincerity, in accordance with the saying of the Prophet (p) "Deeds are [weighed] by intention, and each person will have [reward] according to his own intention,"[1] and the verse "And they have been commanded no more than this: to worship God, offering Him sincere devotion, being true [in faith], to establish regular prayer, and to practice *zakah*, and that is the religion right and straight."[2]

Zakah is first of all a practice in obedience to God and a self-purification meant to prepare the human being for eternal happiness in the hereafter. Once a person's heart is purified and soul is sanctified by the complete commitment to God's orders and obligations, such a person becomes worthy of the joy of the afterlife as one of "Those whose lives the angels take in a state of purity, saying 'Peace be upon you, enter ye the Garden, because of [the good] which ye did."[3] It is this aspect of *zakah* that ties it to prayer in twenty-eight places of the Qur'an and tens of saying in Sunnah, in an unbreakable bond of association that makes it known as the sister of prayer. It is also this aspect of *zakah* that Abu Bakr had in mind when he declared war against those who refused to pay it, stating, "By God, I shall indeed fight those who separate prayer from *zakah*." Following this tradition, the books of fiqh place chapters on *zakah* immediately after chapters on prayer in the parts devoted to worships.

The obvious and essential objective of *zakah* as a worship is supplemented by moral, humanistic, social, and economic objectives which *zakah* is set to achieve by many verses and sayings. These objectives were fulfilled to various degrees when *zakah* was practiced in the early Muslim society; they concern the individual as wells as society, as will be studied in the following two chapters.

Footnotes

1. Reported by al Bukhari and Muslim.

2. *Sura al Bayinah*, 98:2.

3. *Sura al Nahl*, 16:32.

CHAPTER ONE

OBJECTIVES OF *ZAKAH*
AND ITS EFFECTS ON THE INDIVIDUAL

SECTION 1

EFFECTS OF *ZAKAH* ON PAYERS

The foremost objective of *zakah* is to elevate the spirit of human beings above the love of material acquisition. Consequently, Islam does not view the *zakah* payer as a mere source of funds or a financier, but as a person who always needs purification and sanctification, both spiritually and materially. The Qur'an summarizes this purpose in the verse "Out of their wealth take *sadaqah*, that by it thou might purify and sanctify them."

Zakah cleanses the soul of miserliness

Zakah, when paid out of submission to the command of God, is a means of purifying the soul of a Muslim from greed and miserliness. The vices of selfishness and greed must be tamed in order for human beings to elevate their spirits, to succeed in their social relations in this life, and to gain admittance to Heaven. God says, "For man is ever niggardly,"[1] and "Even though people's souls are swayed by greed."[2] Miserliness and greed are drives that intimidate humans into hypocrisy, cheating, and betrayal. The Prophet (p) says, "Three things are devastating: obeyed niggardliness, pursued desires, and self-admiration,"[3] and "Firmly avoid greed, since people before you were indeed destroyed because of greed. Greed swayed them to be misers, cut off from family and friends and vicious."[4] Moreover, God makes purification from these evils a condition for success prosperity: "And those saved from the covetousness of their own souls, they are the ones who achieve prosperity."[5]

Zakah is a purifier that trains Muslims to give and spend selflessly. It liberates their souls from the stinking love of wealth and slavery to material gains and acquisitions. Life and humanity become miserable if people are overwhelmed and enslaved by the drive of material acquisition. The Prophet (p) remarks, "Miserable is he who is enslaved to the *dinar*, miserable is he who is enslaved to the *dirham*, miserable is he who is enslaved to garments. He is miserable and regressive; may he not recover from any hurt inflicted on him."[6]

Zakah trains one to give

Zakah is a means of training Muslims on the virtues of generosity as such as it is a means of purification from greed. Being paid in a repetitive pattern year after year, regular *zakah* as well as *zakah* of *al fitr* train Muslims to give and spend for charitable purposes. The Qur'an describes believers as the righteous who have the virtue of spending for good causes. The very second page of the Qur'an begins, "A L M: This is the Book; in it is guidance sure without doubt to those who fear God, who believe in the unseen, are steadfast in prayer, and spend out of what We have provided for them."[7] This exhortation is reiterated many times in the Qur'an, such as "Those who (in charity) spend of their goods by night and by day, in secrect and in public,"[8] "Those who spend (in charity) both in prosperity or in adversity,"[9] and "Those who show patience, firmness, and self-control, who are true (in word and deed), who worship devoutly, who spend (in the way of God) and who pray for forgiveness in the early hours of the morning."[10]

Even Makkan verses begin this training in its general form. "Those who hearken to their Lord and establish prayer, who (conduct) their affairs by mutual consultation, who spend out of what We bestow on them for sustenance."[11] In his *Commentary*, al Qurtubi considers this a general reference to both *zakah* and voluntary charity, since the verse describes the character of the believers,[12] although it is reported from Ibn 'Abbas that the verse refers to *zakah*, since it associates prayer with spending, and the only spending associated in the Qur'an with prayer is *zakah*. One must remember, however, that other Makkan verses refer more explicitly to charitable spending as one of the characteristics of believers, "As to the righteous, they will be in the midst of Gardens and springs, taking joy in the things which their Lord gives them because, before then, they lived good lives. They were in the habit of sleeping but little by night. And in the hours of early dawn, they (were found) praying for forgiveness. And in their wealth and possessions (was remembered) the right of the (needy), he who asks, and he who is deprived,"[13] and "Truly man was created very inpatient, fretful when evil touches him, and niggardly when good reaches him. Not so those devoted to prayer, those who remain steadfast in their prayer, and those in whose wealth is a recognized right for the (needy) who asks and he who is deprived."[14]

Moreover, once a person is trained to spend an public interests and to give his brethren out of his own wealth, he is most likely to be freed from any urge to transgress on other people's wealth and possessions. Among the early verses revealed to the Prophet in Makkah are these words about the characters of those who spend and those who do not spend: "So he who gives and fears God, and (in all sincerity) testifies to the Best, We will indeed make smooth for him the path to bliss. But he who is a greedy miser and thinks himself self-sufficient, and lies to the Best, We will indeed make smooth for him the path to misery. Nor will his wealth profit him when he falls headlong (into the pit). Verily We take upon Ourself to guide, and verily unto Us (belong) the End and the Beginning. Therefore do I warn you of a fire blazing fiercely. None shall reach it but those most unfortunate ones, who lie (in the face of) Truth and turn their backs. But those most devoted to God shall be received far from it, those who spend their wealth for increase in self-purification, and have in their minds no favor from anyone for which a reward is expected in return, but only the desire to seek the Countenance of their Lord Most High. And soon will they attain (complete) satisfaction."[15] The Qur'an associates the characteristics of giving and testifying to the Truth with the result of having a smooth way to bliss, and the characteristics of withholding and greediness with having a smooth path to misery.

Zakah trains people to acquire divine characteristics

If man is purified from miserliness and greed, and becomes accustomed to the habit of giving and spending, his soul is upgraded from the low human trait of covetousness, "for man is ever niggardly,"[16] and spires to the high of divine perfection, since one of the characteristics of God is absolute and unlimited mercy. In his *Grand Commentary*,[17] al Razi writes "the human soul has two powers, theoretical and practical. Its theoretical power is the soul's endeavor to perfection in submission to the Greatness of God, and its practical power is its endeavor to perfection in mercy to the creatures of God. God obligates *zakah* in order to perfect the human soul in graciousness to other people, as the Prophet says[18] 'Train yourselves to the characteristics of God.'"

This encouragement to spend through *zakah* and voluntary charity resulted, with time, in the emergence of charitable trusts all over the Muslim world today, trusts devoted not only to helping the poor and needy, but to all good cause for human beings as well as animals.[20]

Zakah is an expression of thankfulness to God

Gratitude and thankfulness are of the good characteristics of human beings. *Zakah* is an expression of the thankfulness to God for the bounties He bestows on us. God, says al Ghazali, has bestowed on humans spiritual and material bounties. Prayers and other physical worships express gratitude for the grace of creation, while *zakah* and other financial worships express gratitude for the material grace of God. How disgraceful is he who sees the obvious needs of the poor and does not graciously give one-fourth of a tenth of his wealth, or thank God who gave him enough bounty to remove him from the misery and pressure of poverty.[21] The concept that *zakah* is thanks to God for His bounties is so widespread and deeply rooted in the conscious of Muslims that it is common to say that one must give *zakah* in thanks for the grace of sight, hearing, health, knowledge, etc. It is further reported that the Prophet (p) said "Everything has its *zakah*."[22]

Zakah is a cure for the love of earthly things

As a financial obligation, *zakah* aims at attenuating the lust for material acquisition. Overwhelming love for acquisition, according to al Razi, takes the soul away from the love of God and preparation for the hereafter.[23] Al Razi adds "accumulation of wealth increases the power and control of the owner, which increases his ability of enjoyment, and material enjoyment induces more desires and wants, which demand more wealth to fulfill, thus man enters into a vicious circle of seeking more satisfaction and more wealth. *Zakah* breaks this circle because it is spending for no physical joy or satisfaction. It is a liberation from materialistic enslavement, and reorientation of man towards exclusive submission to God alone."[24]

Zakah stimulates personality growth in payers

By helping others overcome their financial difficulties, *zakah* payers are enriched by feelings of self-worth and fulfillment. *Zakah* also helps extend the payer's self to reach others and grow through helping them, and gives the payer a noble sense of victory over his baser desires and material drives, over his own satan.

Zakah improves ties of mutual love

Zakah links the rich and the poor together with ties of brotherhood and love. The poor realize the true care of the rich and see one manifestation of this concern in the stream of *zakah* proceeds. Naturally, people love those who do good to them. It is said, "Hearts are kneaded with the love of those who do them good, and with the hate of those who do them harm."[25] The more the rich give out of love, the more the poor love and pray for them and for the protection and preservation of their wealth. Al Razi says this is what is meant by the verse "while that which is for the good of mankind remains on earth,"[26] and the saying of the Prophet (p) "Fortify your wealth by [paying] *zakah*."[27]

Zakah purifies wealth

Zakah purifies wealth. Because *zakah* is a right to the poor, not paying it means keeping something that belongs to others intermingled with one's wealth, and this brings wrath on the whole wealth. The Prophet (p) says "If you pay *zakah* on your wealth, you have taken away its evil."[28] Moreover, the fortification of wealth by *zakah* mentioned in the saying at the end of the previous sub-section is especially needed today, when destructive principles and bloody, communist revolutions are rampant. Some jurists add that due *zakah* is an immediate obligation on wealth itself and not merely a personal debt on the wealthy. The Prophet says "Due *sadaqah* is never left mixed with wealth but destroys that wealth," and in a different version, "When *sadaqah* is due on your wealth, and you do not pay it, the whole wealth, lawful and unlawful, i.e. yours and the due unpaid *zakah* would be demolished."[29] Furthermore, when *zakah* is not performed on a large scale in a society, the nation's wealth is exposed to natural catastrophes and disasters, for "No people prevent [The performance of] *zakah* but are deprived of rain from the sky, and if it were not for the animals, they would not be given rain."[30] Thus, the security of individual and national wealth from the factors of destruction and demolition can only be achieved by paying the due right of the poor obligated by God.

Zakah does not purify unlawfully earned wealth

Wealth earned through forbidden means cannot be purified by *sadaqah*. The Prophet says "God is good, and He does not accept but what is good,"[31] "He who acquires wealth by forbidden means, then gives it away as *sadaqah* gets no reward; the sin remains on him,"[32] and "God does not accept *sadaqah* out of unlawfully taken wealth, nor does he accept a prayer without ablution."[33]

The Prophet (p) adds, "[I swear] by He in Whose Hand is my soul, not a servant who earns wealth unlawfully and gives it as *sadaqah* but it is not accepted from him, or spends it but it is not blessed, or leaves it behind his back [after death] but it is his means to the Fire. God does not erase evil with evil; He rather remove evil with good. A corrupt [deed] does not clear another corrupt [deed]."[34] Al Qurtubi comments, "God does not accept *sadaqah* out of unlawfully acquired wealth, because such wealth is not truly owned by the payer. The payer's disposal of such wealth is thus illegal and accepting a *sadaqah* from such a person is contradictory."[35] Some Hanafites go as far as considering the act of knowingly giving out of unlawful wealth equal to denying Islam and becoming disbeliever, because such an act implies refusing the Islamic criteria of lawfulness.[36]

Zakah brings growth to Wealth

Although *zakah* seems to tax the principal of the wealthy, it is a cause of blessing and growth to his or her wealth, a blessing from God that brings prosperity, and an increase in demand for consumption goods caused by the distribution of *zakah* that brings vitality to business. This may in fact be the economic explanation of the verses "Say: verily my Lord enlarges and restricts the sustenance to such of His servants as He pleases, and nothing do ye spend in the least [in His cause] but He replaces it, for He is the Best of those who grant sustenance,"[37] "The evil one threatens you with poverty and bids you to conduct unseemly. God promiseth you His forgiveness and bounties and God careth for all and He knoweth all things,"[38] "That which ye lay out for increase through [the property of] other people will have no increase with God, but that which ye lay out for charity, seeking the Countenance of God [will increase]. It is these who will get a recompense multiplied,"[39] and "God will deprive usury of all blessing, but He will give increase for deeds of charity. For He loveth not creatures ungrateful and wicked."[40]

The effect of Providence is manifold in recompense and growth, since God gives His grace and sustenance to those who please God. To this, one must add the economic effect of *zakah* payment in increasing the payer's investment efforts in order to compensate for what is paid as *zakah*.

SECTION 2

EFFECTS OF *ZAKAH* ON RECIPIENTS

Zakah frees the receiver from the humiliation of need and helps satisfy the basic requirements of a decent living, since, except for laborers who are paid for collecting and distributing *zakah*, fighters for the sake of God, who are paid for military service, and those whose hearts are being reconciled, the recipients are the poor, the needy, slaves seeking freedom, persons under debts and wayfarers.

Zakah liberates its recipients from material needs

Living a good and prosperous life is one of Islam's objectives for all human beings. Thus men and women are urged to benefit from the grace of God manifest in food to eat, goods to consume, security in which to find refuge, and happiness to savor. The satisfaction of material needs of life is undoubtedly an essential ingredient of human happiness. The Prophet (p) says "Three [things] make for happiness: [having] a wife who pleases you when you look at her and gives you confidence about herself and your household when you are absent, a comfortable riding animal that carries you in pace with your company, and a spacious residence with meninfold utilities,"[41] and on another occasion, "Four [things] make for happiness: [having] a virtuous wife, a spacious house, a good neighbour, and a comfortable ride, and four make for misery: a wicked neighbor, a wicked wife, a bad ride, and a narrow house."[42]

Obviously, Islam likes people to be prosperous and hates poverty, especially when poverty is the result of unjust distribution of wealth or class oppression. The essential difference between Islam and materialistic systems is that while these systems consider the betterment of material living a goal in itself, Islam sees it as a means for spiritual uplifting and a liberation of human energy from seeking bread to worshiping and glorifying God. This position of Islam is expressed in the idea that making one rich is a grace from God. God tells the Messenger, "And He found thee in need and made thee rich,"[43] and tells Muslims in Madinah, "But He provided a safe asylum for you, strengthened you with His aid, and gave good things fir sustenance, that ye might be grateful."[44] The Prophet used to pray, "My Lord, I ask you guidance, righteousness, contentment, and richness."[45] Moreover, he prefers a grateful rich person over a patient poor person.[46] Prosperous living is considered part of the reward God gives to righteous believers, while poverty and miserable living are part of the punishment for disbelief or misconduct. God says "Whoever works righteousness, man or woman, and has faith, verily to him will We give a life that is good and pure,"[47] "If the people of the towns had but believed and feared God, We should indeed have opened out for them [all kinds of] blessings from heaven and earth,"[48] "And for him who fears God, He [ever] prepares a way out, and He provides for him from [sources] he could never imagine,"[49] and "God sets forth the parable of a city enjoying security and quiet, abundantly supplied with sustenance from every place. Yet was it ungrateful for the favours of God, so God made it taste of hunger and terror [closing in on it] like a garment because of the evil which [its people] wrought."[50] When Adam and Eve were sent down to earth, God gave them the laws of living. "He said, 'Get ye down, both of you together from the Garden, with enmity one to another. But if, as is sure, there comes to you guidance from Me, whosoever follows My guidance will not lose his way, nor fall into misery. But whosoever turns away from My message, verily for him is a life narrowed down, and We shall raise him up blind on the Day of Judgement.'"[51]

All the ideas nourished in Muslim lands by mysticism, which glorify and welcome poverty and condemn richness are alien to Islam. These ideas are infiltration from Asian religious and ancient Christianity.[52] God ordains *zakah* in order to use the surplus wealth of the society to satisfy the essential needs to those who are not lucky enough to get incomes on their own, so they can enjoy the bounties of God and contribute to the progress of society. In case there is no Islamic state or one which does not fulfill its duty of establishing an organization for collecting and distributing *zakah*, and individuals have to distribute their *zakah* personally, God strongly warns them not to humiliate the poor. Good says, "O ye who believe, cancel not your *sadaqat* by reminders of your generosity or by injury, like those who spend their substance to be seen of people but believe neither in God nor in the Last Day. They are, in parable, lie a hard rock on which there is a little soil. On it falls heavy rain, which leaves it just a bare stone."[53]

Giving the poor the proper feeling that they are not lost or forgotten and that society cares deeply about their needs is in itself an upgrading of their sentiments and sense of brotherhood. Human dignity and the honor given humans by God require that not a single person be neglected or left on the periphery of society. The martyr Sayyid Qutb explains:

Islam hates poverty and hates seeing people pressed by needs. Islam aims to have people devote their time and energy to matters that suit the big role assigned to human beings by God. To do so, they need to be freed from the pressure of material needs. God says, "We have honored the children of Adam, provided them with transport on land and sea, given them for sustenance things good and pure, and conferred on them special favors above a great part of Our creation."[54] God indeed honors humans by giving them reason, sentiments, and spiritual aspirations toward what is above and beyond bodily necessities. If they are deprived of the basic needs of life, they shall not have time to exert their reason, to amplify and upgrade their sentiments, aspirations and ideas. If such a thing happens, humans are indeed deprived of that honor and reduced to the level of animals seeking material needs. He is not a human being honored by God who is always occupied with the pursuit of food and drink without seeking the glories involved in the honor granted by God. The human being is indeed the vicegerent of God on earth, assigned by God the role of upgrading life in all its aspects on this planet, filling it with gloriess and joys so human beings can enjoy its beauty and perfection and thank God for all these bounties. Human beings shall not reach such heights unless their basic material needs are satisfied--unless they are freed from running behind the piece of bread.[55]

Zakah cleanses jealousy and hatred

For the recipient, *zakah* is also a means of purifying the soul from envy and hatred. A man, beaten by poverty and pressed by the material necessities of life, who sees others around him enjoying good material living and luxuries without helping him or extending any relief to him will doubtlessly be ravaged by the pressure of unsatisfied material needs and become full of hatred and enmity towards the whole society. Islam wants relations between people to be based on strong bonds of fraternity and solidarity. The bases of this solidarity are the common bonds of humanity and faith. As the Prophet (p) puts it, "And be, O servants of God, one brotherhood,"[56] and "A Muslim is the brother of a fellow Muslim."[57] Such fraternity cannot be established and stabilized if one brother has a full stomach while others are left to hunger, for this nourishes hatred end envy.

Envy is dangerous to everyone. It is a deviation in the behavior of human beings that crushes brotherhood. God says "Or do they envy people for what God had given them of His bounty?"[58] Envy and hatred are some of the most devastating social diseases that destroy people and societies. The Prophet (p) warns, "Here comes to you the illness of nations before you: Enmity, envy, and hatred. Hatred is the razor. I don't mean it razes hair, but it razes religion."[59] Love and brotherhood among people, poor and rich, are nourished by *zakah*, which strengthens the bonds in the society and cleanses the hearts and souls of people. The Prophet (p) says, "No one of you is a true believer until he loves for his brother what he loves for himself."[60]

Footnotes

1. *Sura al Isra*, 17:100.

2. *Sura al Nisa*, 4:128.

3. reported by al Tabarani in al *Mu'jam al Awsat* from Ibn 'Umar via a weak chain, according to *al Taisir*, Vol. 1, p. 570.

4. Reported by Abu Daud and al Nasa'i. See *Mukhtasar al Mundhiri*, Vol. 2, p. 263.

5. *Sura al Hashr*, 59:9.

6. Reported by al Bukhari in the chapter on jihad, and by Ibn Majah in his chapter on piety.

7. *Sura al Baqarah*, 2:1-3.

8. *Sura al Baqarah*, 2:27.

9. *Sura al 'Imran*, 3:134.

10. *Ibid*, 3:17.

11. *Sura al Shura*, 42:36-38.

12. *Tafsir al Qurtubi*, Vol. 1, p. 179.

13. *Sura al Dhariyat*, 51:15-19.

14. *Sura al Ma'arij*, 70:24-25.

15. *Sura al Lail*, 92:5-21.

16. *Sura al Isra*, 17:100.

17. *Al Tafsir al Kabir*, Vol. 16, p. 101.

18. I searched for this saying but never found it, nor did I find any one who refers to it.

19. The same meaning can be expressed in different words: Being rich by doing without things shows more strength of soul than being rich by owing things, since richness by having means one is dependent on what one has, while richness by not needing things means no dependence on anything. Accordingly, richness by not being dependent on anything is a characteristic of God, the Creator, while richness by acquisition is a characteristic of creatures. God gives His servants wealth in abundance, making them rich in the sense of having possessions, and ordains them to give *zakah* in order to upgrade them to do without wealth, which is a higher level than acquisition.

20. See the different examples of this kind of trust in my book, *al Iman wa al Hayat* (Faith and Life), chapter on mercy, pp. 291-293.

21. *Ihya' 'Ulum al Din*, Vol. 1, p. 193.

22. Reported by Ibn Majah from Abu Hurairah and by al Tabarani from Sahl bin Sa'd. Al Suyuti marks it weak, and al Mundhiri refers to its weakness in his *al Targhib*.

23. *Al Tafsir al Kabir, op. cit.*, p. 101.

24. *Ibid*.

25. Reported by Ibn 'Adi in al Kamil, Abu Nu'aim in *al Hilyah* and al Baihaqi in the chapter on Shu'ab al Iman, from Ibn Mas'ud, attributed to the Prophet via a weak chain. It is also described as falsified. However, al Baihaqi grades correct the chain that ends at Ibn Mas'ud, making the statement his instead of the Prophet's. Al Sakhawi says "It is false in both the versions attributed to the Prophet, as well as the one stopped at Ibn Mas'ud." See *al Taisir*, Vol. 1, p. 485.

26. *Sura al Ra'd*, 13:17.

27. Reported by Abu Daud as *mursal*, and by al Tabarani, al Baihaqi, and others from a group of Companions as linked up to the Prophet. Al Mundhiri says the *mursal* version is better.

28. Reported by Ibn Khuzaimah in his correct collection and al Hakim from Jabir. The saying is, however, criticized, as will be seen in part eight.

29. The grading of this saying is mentioned in volume one of this book, p.

30. Its grading is mentioned in volume one of this book, p.

31. Reported by Muslim and al Tirmidhi. See *al Targhib wa al Tarhib*, Vol. 3, p. 11. A similar saying is reported in *Sahih al Bukhari*, chapter on *zakah*, section on *sadaqah* from good earning.

32. Reported by Ibn Khuzaimah, Ibn Habban, and al Hakim. The Latter says its chain is correct. See *al Targhib*, Vol. 1, p. 266.

33. Reported by Abu Daud via a correct chain, and by Muslim. See *Fath al Bari*, Vol. 3, p. 178.

34. Reported by Ahmad and others via a chain that is graded good by some sayings critics. See al Targhib, Vol. 3, p. 14.

35. *Fath al Bari*, Vol. 3, p. 180.

36. *Radd al Muhtar*, Vol. 2, p. 27.

37. *Sura Saba'*, 34:39.

38. *Sura al Baqarah*, 2:268.

39. *Sura al Rum*, 30:39.

40. *Sura al Baqarah*, 2:276.

41. Reported by al Hakim. See *al Targhib*, Vol. 3, p. 68.

42. Reported by Ibn Habban, see *ibid*.

43. *Sura al Duha*, 93:8.

44. *Sura al Anfal*, 8:26.

45. Reported by Muslim, al Tirmidhi, and Ibn Majah, from Ibn Mas'ud.

46. As it appears from the saying, which is in the two correct collections, "the rich ones took all the reward . . . . "

47. *Sura al Nahl*, 16:97.

48. *Sura al A'raf*, 7:96.

49. *Sura al Talaq*, 65:2-3.

50. *Sura al Nahl*, 16:112.

51. *Sura Taha,* 20:123-4.

52. See al Qaradawi, *Mushkilat al Faqr*, chapter on how Islam views poverty.

53. *Sura al Baqarah*, 2:264.

54. *Sura al Isra'*, 17:70.

55. *Al 'Adalah al Ijtima 'iyah fi al Islam*, pp. 132-133.

56. Reported by Muslim from Abu Hurairah.

57. Agreed upon from Ibn 'Umar. Muslim also reported it from 'Utbah bin 'Amir, Abu Daud reports it from 'Amr bin al Ahwas and Qailah. See *Kashf al Khafa*, Vol. 2, p. 210.

58. *Sura al Nisa*, 4:54.

59. Reported by al Bazzar with a good chain and by al Baihaqi and others. See *al Targhib wa al Tarhib*, Vol. 4, p. 11.

60. Reported by al Bukhari, Muslim, Ahmad, al Tirmidhi, al Nasa'i, and Ibn Majah, from Anas, as stated in *al Jami' al Saghir*.

CHAPTER TWO

OBJECTIVES OF *ZAKAH* IN SOCIETY

A glance at the categories to whom *zakah* is expended immediately reveals the social aspect of *zakah*: "*Zakah* is for the poor and needy and those employed to administer the funds, for those whose hearts have been reconciled, for those in bondage and in debt, in the way of God, and for the wayfarer. It is ordained by God." Clearly, giving *zakah* to these categories serves important social objectives. Some of them relate to the state and public order, such as heart reconciliation and the sake of God. These two categories imply that the government must collect and distribute *zakah* toward spreading Islam, preserving the way of God, and defending the Muslim community.

Islam and social insurance

Zakah is the cornerstone of Islam's social insurance system. The mutual insurance that Islam ordains goes beyond the mere material aspect to include spiritual, psychological, moral, cultural, and civic aspects of a person's life and to foster solidarity and mutual cooperation among members of the Islamic society. In short, mutual social care in Islamic society extends to all branches of human life.[1] *Zakah* covers only the area called social insurance or social security. Social insurance systems usually require the users to pay premiums and contributions in order to participate in the benefits, while social security systems may be guaranteed by the state from its own budget. *Zakah* does not make it a condition for any recipient to participate or to have participated in the contributions; *zakah* simply provides relief to those in need and collects funds from whoever has excess.[2] *Zakah* is in fact the first system of social security ever enacted in the history of humanity, a system that does not depend on individual voluntary charity but on a governmental institution that collects regular contributions and distributes organized relief to all those who are in need. This system of *zakah* provides regular relief as well as for emergency needs. We read, for example, in the instructions prepared by al Zuhri for 'Umar bin 'Abd al 'Aziz, "There is a share in it for the ill, the handicapped, and each needy person who cannot provide fro himself, a share for the destitute until they can be removed from destitution, a share for those in prisons, for those who beg and those who do not, a share to whoever is burdened by debts, provided such debts did not arise from disobedience to God, a share for every traveler who finds no family to help him on the road. Such travelers should be given food and shelter as well as feed for their transporting animal, until they reach home."[3] This system does not cover only needy Muslims but extends to needy Jews and Christians who live in the Islamic state, as 'Umar indicated by including the elderly Jewish man[4] and the ill Christians persons in this social insurance.[5]

Social security that provides help without requiring contributions is relatively new to Western society. It appeared for the first time in the Atlantic Treaty between England and the United States, 1941, as a result of the war and the internal turmoil caused by poverty and destitution. It is shameful that researchers and students of social security claim that the idea of social security is a Western invention of the seventeenth century, as claimed by Daniel S. Girk, director of the study circle of the Arab States League held in Damascus, 1952.[7] The Islamic system of *zakah* came fourteen centuries ago with complete provision for the poor and needy, organized and implemented by the state and financed by a tax imposed on the rich only. It is part of this religion of Islam and its third pillar, without which the very faith of a Muslim is incomplete.

Zakah stimulates owners to invest their wealth in order to make up for what is paid out as due *zakah*. This is very apparent in the case of money, for the Qur'an threatens against hoarding gold and sliver. An imposition of a 2.5 percent charge on wealth is indeed strong stimulus to owners to invest, so that their wealth does not vanish as a result of repetitive deduction of *zakah* year after year. The Prophet (p) adds, "Invest the wealth of orphans so that it is not used up by [repetitive] *zakah*."

Zakah and spiritual integrity of the nation

Above all that, *zakah* aims at realizing the ideals of the Muslim society and nourishing the spiritual pillars on which the society is founded and by which it is distinctively characterized. As rightly stated by al Bahi al Khawli,

Nations are truly founded on spiritual and psychological elements in addition to material factors. Indeed, the spiritual factors count much more in creating unity and vitality in any community. Islam pays great attention to these factors and makes spending out of the income of the community--to nourish and support these factors--one of its major obligations.

One can distinguish three major factors to which Islam gives special attention. The first is freedom or liberty. One of the objectives of *zakah* is to liberate individuals in the bondage of slavery. For the first time in the history of humanity, the liberation of slaves was made, by Islam, a social obligation for which a certain portion of the community's wealth is spent. Secondly, encouraging individuals to carry out projects of public interest and to spend toward smoothing out differences between segments of the community and reconciling individuals and groups in order to avoid social unrest. Such actions are encouraged by assigning a share of *zakah* to support those who shoulder financial responsibility for these purposes. Thirdly, spending in the way of God and spreading the sound religion that comes from Him is urged. Fighting in the way of God includes defending the ideals and doctrines for which God sent His messengers, and up-holding the oneness of God and righteousness on earth.[8]

These three areas are essential pillars of the social life of the Muslim community. *Zakah* as a taxation institution is not detached from the principles and worship of the Islamic community, nor isolated from its values, morals, politics, and defense. In the following sections, we shall look at six major social problems and find how *zakah* contributes to solving them and eliminating their sources. However, in my book on the problem of poverty and its Islamic solution, one may find a detailed analysis of the treatment of each problem in specific.

SECTION ONE

THE PROBLEM OF SOCIO-ECONOMIC GAP

The presence of a great concentration of wealth side by side with severe poverty is a major social calamity that Islam does not tolerate in its society. The Qur'an emphasizes, "It is He Who has created for you all things that are on earth."[10] Arabic word "*jami'a*" used for "all" may mean all things created are for you, or things created are for all of you.

One of the objectives Islam aims for is reducing socio-economic differences by providing support and financial help to the have-nots to bring them closer to the haves. Islam tackles this problem with much of its legislation, social institutions, and economic directives in order to achieve Justice both in the distribution of wealth and the distribution of income. God says, "What God has bestowed on His Apostle [and taken away] from the people of the townships, belongs to God, to His Apostle, and to kindred and orphans, the needy, and the wayfarer, in order that it may not merely make a circuit between the wealthy among you."[11] In this section, we are discussing only the role of the institution of *zakah* in reducing economic differences. We must keep in mind that in a society which behaves according to, and is ruled by, Islam there must be people working and much smaller number of idle persons, because of the other means by which Islam discourages idleness and provides jobs. *Zakah*, as we have seen earlier, does not only provide relief to the poor but aims also at making the poor own means of production by giving them the tools and machinery necessary for productive work, so that persons given *zakah* are removed forever from the category of poor end needy deservants. This is in addition to necessary shelter and immediate relief that *zakah* provides. We also discussed in the previous part that what is given as *zakah* must become owned by the recipient so that recipients of *zakah* no longer remain have-nots.

SECTION TWO

THE PROBLEM OF BEGGARS AND BEGGING

Islam fights begging through education

Islam implants abhorance of begging inside each Muslim through training and education. Even asking for any kind of assistance is disliked, except in dire need. Abu Muslim al Khawlani says he was told by 'Awf bin Malik, "Seven, eight, or nine of us were with the Messenger of God (p) when he said, "Won't you give your pledge to the Messenger of God?" We had given our pledge not a long time ago, so we said, "We have given you our pledges!" He repeated that request three times. Then we extended our hands open and gave our pledge. One of us said, "O Messenger of God, we give you our pledge, but on what? The Prophet said, 'That you worship God and do not associate partners with him whatsoever, that you pray the five prayers, that you listen and obey . . . . . . ' and he whispered a word and continued, 'and that you do not ask people for anything.'" The narrator of the saying adds, "So it may happen that the whip of one of these people drops from his hand while riding and he does not ask anyone to hand it to him."[12] Thawban narrates that the Messenger of God (p) asked, "Who pledges to me that he will not ask people for anything so I can guarantee him the Garden?" Thawban said, "O Messenger of God, I do." The Prophet said, "Do not ask people for anything." Thawban did not ask anything from anyone.[13] Additionally, the Prophet (p) calls the receiving hand and the lower hand and the hand of the giver the upper hand. He taught his Companions to be self-sufficient and not to look for anything in the hands of other people. Abu Sa'id says, "Some people from the Ansar asked the Messenger of God (p) and he gave them. They asked him for more and he gave then, until what he had was exhausted. Then the Prophet said, 'Whatever I may have of good shall not be spared from you. But he who restrains himself shall be given self-sustenance from God; he who enriches himself, God shall make him rich, and he who trains himself to be patient, God shall make him patient. Nothing one can be given is better than patience.'"[14]

Teachings of the Prophet on self-support

The Messenger of God (p) taught his Companions two essential principles. Firstly, work is the source of gaining income and means of sustenance. Muslims are urged to traverse through tracts of the earth in search of the bounties of God through work. Work, manual or otherwise, is better than living on humiliating grants. The Prophet (p) says, "For anyone of you, taking some rope on your back and bringing a bunch of wood and selling it in order for God to preserve, with its value, the dignity of one's face, is better than asking people, whether one is given or prevents."[15]

The second principle is that asking people unnecessarily is prohibited, because it is indignifying. Muslims are prohibited from resorting to begging for relief except for those who are beaten by need. He who asks while having what satisfies his essential needs shall come on the Day of Resurrection with his begging a scar on his face. This is reiterated in several sayings. Al Bukhari, Muslim, and al Nasa'i report from Ibn 'Umar that the Prophet (p) said, "None shall persist in begging but will come to God with his face stripped of flesh." The authors of the four books on *Sunan* report that the Prophet (p) says, "He begs while he has satisfaction, his begging appears on the Day of Resurrection as a scar on his face." The Prophet was asked what the limit of satisfaction is. He answered, "Fifty *dirhams* or their equivalent in gold."[16] The face is the most honored part of one's body, and that is where the humiliating mark of begging appears. In another saying, "He who asks while he has one *uqiyyah* [equals forty *dirhams*] is overdoing it,"[17] and "He who asks yet has sufficiency is getting more and more of the Fire or of the burning wood of Hell." They said, "O Messenger of God, what is his sufficiency?" He said, "An amount that gives him dinner and supper."[18] Apparently, this means a person who earns the food of his days.

The late scholar al Dehlawi comments, "There is no real discrepancy in these sayings' descriptions of the quantity that provides sufficiency, because people have different needs and means of earning. A craftsman is excusable until he finds tools and machines that are needed so he can earn his daily food. A farmer needs different tools at different cost, a merchant needs inventory, and for he who earns his living from the *ghanimah* by fighting in the way of God, like most of the Companions of the Prophet (p), one *uqiyyah* is sufficient. On the other hand, a person who earns through carrying loads or selling wood brought in from mountain, his sufficiency is the requirement of his daily food."[19] Undoubtedly, there are two limits of sufficiency, one that prohibits begging, and one that makes taking *zakah* forbidden. The former limit is indeed stricter than the latter, because *Shari'ah* is stricter on disallowing begging except in case of extreme necessity.

Practical cure for the problem of begging

The cure for the problem of begging is twofold. The first step is providing suitable job to all those who can work. This is one of the responsibilities of the Islamic state towards its citizens; the state must not remain paralyzed when faced with the problem of unemployment. Nor must the state keep providing relief from *sadaqat* without rectifying the root of the problem. Throughout the discussion of *zakah* distribution early in this book, I repeatedly emphasized that "The *sadaqah* is not lawful to any rich person, nor to a strong and capable one." Indeed, any relief given to a person who is capable of earning is in a way encouragement of idleness. The most proper response to such a problem is what the Messenger of God did when a person asked him for relief. Anas bin Malik narrates that a person from Ansar came asking the Prophet (p) for financial help. The Prophet answered, "Isn't there anything in your house?" The man said, "Yes, a piece of cloth. We use some of it to wear and spread another part to sit on, and a cup in which we drink water." The Prophet said, "Bring them to me." He brought them, The Messenger of God (p) took them and announced, who will buy these?" A man said, "1 will take them for one *dirham*." The Prophet said, "Who Gives more than one *dirham*?" twice or thrice. Another man said, "I will take them for two *dirhams*." The Prophet gave them to him and took the two *dirhams* and gave them to the owner saying, "Buy with one of them food to send to your family and buy with the other an axe-head and bring it to Me." Than the Messenger of God tied with his own hands a piece of wood to the axe for a handle and told the man, "Go and get wood and sell . . . . I must not see you for fifteen days." The man got wood and sold it . . . . He later came to the Prophet with ten *dirhams* gained: . . . . He bought cloth with some and food with some . . . . The Messenger of God (p) said, "This is better for you than the begging that comes as a scar on your face on the Day of Resurrection. Begging is not permissible except to one of three. A destitute poor person, or a person under overwhelming debts, or a person who ought to pay ransom for an accidental homicide."[20] We observe in this story the practical teaching of the Prophet when he did not want that person to take *zakah* because he was able to earn, and such taking is not permissible except as a last resort. The government is responsible for helping to find suitable jobs for all its citizens. "This saying provides practical steps taken by Islam a long time before any other system known to humanity in order to wipe out poverty and unemployment. The treatment is not only to extend immediate relief, but to provide means of self-support and productive work. The Prophet taught that one must use all one's abilities, no matter how few they might be and to exhaust all means of productive wok before resorting to begging or asking. He taught that any job that provides lawful sustenance is honorable and dignified, even if it were getting wood on one's back and selling it, so that one is not humiliated by begging. Moreover, the Prophet helped provide the means and tools of work. He did not leave the person alone to find necessary tools and means. Above that, he gave the person a trial period so the person has enough time to examine his ability and the suitability of the job. This is a practical solution, an ideal example set fourth by the Messenger of God, an example that we have to follow step by step to solve the of unemployment and begging."[21]

The role *zakah* can play in this regard is obvious. It can provide the unemployed with the necessary tools, machinery, and capital for production, as was explained in the part on *zakah* distribution. *Zakah* can also fund job training or job rehabilitation programs. Above all, it can establish collective projects and industries run by the poor and formerly unemployed workers.

The second part of Islam's cure for begging is social insurance for those who have no income. Such persons are guaranteed a minimum standard of living suitable to a given Islamic society. Unemployment may be caused by either of two reasons: physical incapability caused by age, sickness, or handicap, or inability to find jobs. Persons in the former group are supported by *zakah* funds as long as they are incapable of earning. Persons who are unable to find jobs that produce lawful income in spite of their will and search, because of general economic depression or other economic and non-economic factors, must also be supported by *zakah*. Ahmad and others report the story of the two men who asked the Prophet (p) for help from *zakah*. The Messenger looked them up and down and found them strong and capable. He said, "I would give you if you like, but there is no share in it for the rich or the strong who can earn." It is the earner who has no share in *zakah* and not the capable person who does not find means of earning.

SECTION THREE

THE PROBLEM OF HATRED AND DISPUTE

Brotherhood is an essential objective of *Zakah*

Spreading brotherhood among the children of Adam in general and members of the Muslim society in specific is one of the basic objectives in Islam. Social solidarity, social security, and mutual cooperation strengthen brotherhood. No doubt, there is a continuous need for reconciling people who get themselves in disputes and feuds.

In the first Islamic society, established by the Prophet in Madinah, we are given an ideal scene of brotherhood, mutual love and care, in spite of the tribal and economic rivalry that existed before Islam and in spite of the ethnic and cultural differences between the migrants to Madinah (*Muhajirin*) who were from the 'Adnani branch of Arabs, and the Ansar, who lived in Madinah before migration and were of the Qahtani branch of Arabs. The *Ansar* themselves were composed of two major tribes that had been fighting each other in the city for decades, in addition to a few individuals from backgrounds totally alien to both *Muhajiran* and *Ansar*, such as the Ethiopian Bilal, the Persian Salam, and the Byzantine Suhaib. On top of that, Madinan society included rough bedouins like Abu Dharr side by side with luxuriously raised urbanites like Mus'ab bin 'Umair. This society was woven with brotherhood in a unique manner, whereby one loves for one's brother exactly what one loves for one's self. The Qur'an draws a picture of this ideal application of brotherhood: "The indigent migrants, those who were expelled from their homes and their prophet, while seeking grace from God, His good pleasure, and pleasing God and His Apostle, such are indeed the sincere ones. And those who, before them, had homes and had adopted the faith, they show their affection to such as came to them for refuge and entertain no desire in their hearts for things given to the latter, but give them preference over themselves, even though poverty was their own lot. And those saved from the covetousness of their own souls, they are the ones who achieve prosperity."[22]

Islam legislates for real life

Although this ideal brotherhood was realized in the actual life of the first Islamic society, Islam as a way of life legislates for human life without disregarding the fact that human beings sin, make mistakes, have feuds and disputes, which may go as far as destruction, bloodshed, and taking other people's resources.

Feuds that reach the stage of fighting are as old as humanity itself. The Qur'an tells us that the angels asked God when He created Adam, "Wilt Thou place therein one who will make mischief therein and shed blood? Whilst we celebrate Thy praises and glorify Thy holy name?"[23] The story of the two sons of Adam is told in the Qur'an: "Recite to them the truth of the story of the two sons of Adam. Behold, they each presented a sacrifice to God. It was accepted from one but not from the other. Said the latter, 'Be sure, I will slay thee.' 'Surely', said the former, 'God doth accept the sacrifice of those who are righteous. If thou dost stretch thy hand against me to slay me, it is not for me to stretch my hand against thee to slay thee, for I do fear God, the Cherisher of the worlds. For me, I intend to let thee draw on thyself my sin as well as thine, for thou wilt be among the companions of the Fire, and that is the reward of those who do wrong.' The selfish soul of the other led him to the murder of his brother. He murdered him and became one of the lost ones. Then God sent a raven who scratched the ground to show him how to hide the shame of his brother.'Woe unto me; said he. Was I not even able to be as this raven and hide the shame of my brother?' Then he became full of regrets."[24]

Since feuds, disputes, and even fights are facts of human life, the realism of Islam requires that these problems be addressed. Reconciling differences among people and removing factors that cause feuds and may lead to fighting is the collective responsibility of the community and the whole society. The Messenger (p) says, "Mischief in relations among people is indeed the razor."[25] In another version he continues, "I do not say it razes hair, but it razes religion."[26] The action of reconciling differences among individuals, including husband and wife, so that they do not grow into big feuds, is in fact the deed of the righteous. God says about breaches between husband and wife, "If ye fear a breach between them twine, appoint two arbitrators, one from his family and the other from hers. It they wish for peace, God will cause their reconciliation, for God has full knowledge and is acquainted with all things."[27] On the social level, when differences exist, God says, "If two parties among the believers fall into a quarrel, make ye peace between them, but if one of them transgresses beyond bounds against the other, then fight ye (all) against the one who transgresses, until it complies with the command of God. But if it complies, then make peace between them with justice and be fair, for God loves those who are fair (and just). The believers are but a single brotherhood, so make peace and reconciliation between your two (contending) brothers, and fear God that ye may receive mercy."[28] God encourages reconciliation and making peace among people in more than one place in the Qur'an. "So fear God and keep straight the relation between yourselves. Obey God and His Apostle if ye do believe,"[29] and "In most of their secret talks there is no good, but if one exhorts to a deed of charity or justice or conciliation between people, to him who does this seeking the good pleasure of God, We shall soon give a reward of the highest."[30] The messenger emphasizes this meaning and encourages bringing peace and reconciliation between quarrelling people. He says, "Shall I not guide you to what is higher in degree than prayer, fasting, and charity? It is reconciliation among people [who have quarrelled], since feud among people is the razor."[31]

However, such reconciliation may need financial sacrifices, since many differences arise from financial matters, and many others can be settled by paying ransoms. *Zakah* indeed offers a source for such payment under the title of the share of those in debt. Arbiters and mediators may accept such financial responsibility on their own shoulders, knowing that the *zakah* fund pays back such money. The saying of Qubaisah bin al Mukhariq al Hilali shows that he accepted certain financial charges in reconciling some disputing groups and came to the Prophet (p) seeking help. The Prophet told him to stay until the *sadaqah* comes, "so we can give you some money." Then the Prophet told him that any person who carries such a financial burden in reconciliation between others is allowed to ask until he recovers the amount that he accepted responsibility for. Then he must stop asking. (Reported by Ahmad and Muslim.) It is so to the extent that mediators and arbiters who reconcile differences between people of the Pledge, whether Christian or Jew, can also be compensated from *zakah* funds.[32]

A question arises whether the compensation may be paid directly to the feuding parties, or must the reconcilors first pay out of their own wealth, then ask for compensation? It seems from the words of jurists' texts that reconcilors must first pay out of their own wealth so as to be counted as one of those under financial burdens and be paid back from *zakah* funds.[33] However, I believe that the spirit of the Qur'anic verse and the purpose aimed at by *Shari'ah* in legislating a share for this purpose do not prevent paying the mediators or mediating committees firs, then allowing those people to pay the parties that are being reconciled.

SECTION FOUR

THE PROBLEM OF ACCIDENTS AND NATURAL CALAMITIES

Security and economic sufficiency

Islam attempts to guarantee each person in the Islamic society sufficiency of sustenance and security from fear, so that a human being can devote a good part of his or her energy to worshiping God. God, in showing the tribe of Quraish how great was His bounty to them, says, "For the covenants [of security and safeguard] enjoyed by the Quraish. Their covenants covering journeys by winters and summer. Let them adore the Lord of this House, Who provides them with food against hunger and with security against fear."[34] The worst that may happen to a person or a group of people is the loss of either of these two bounties. God says, "God sets forth a parable, a city enjoying security and quiet, abundantly supplied with sustenance from every place, yet was it ungrateful for the favors of God, so God made it taste of hunger and terror in extreme, [closing in on it] like a garment [from every side] because of the evil [which its people] wrought."[35] The Islamic laws guarantee every person in the Islamic state, Muslim or not, a suitable level of living, whereby food, clothing, and shelter are available in addition to health care and education. It was shown earlier that the system of *zakah* aims at satisfying the poor and the needy and their families for life.

But natural disasters may hit-unexpectedly-any person, rich or not, whether a farmer, a merchant, an industrialist, or a landlord. Natural disasters may be common to an area, like drought, flood, insecticide contamination, explosions, or they may be individual, such as accidents, fires, and loss of assets or sources of income.

Such incidents necessitated in the West the rise of insurance and insurance companies in the last few centuries. But Islamic society had through the public treasury of the state its own insurance system against such accidents and natural happenings. This Islamic system of insurance is not based on charity and voluntary contributions or on the benevolence or people, in spite of the fact that such benevolence is encouraged very much by Islamic teachings. The Prophet taught his Companions when a disaster struck a man, "Give him charity," so people gave him."[36]

"People under debt" include those hit by disasters

Individuals struck by natural disasters or accidents are not left to voluntary charity alone. They are given a share in the proceeds of *zakah*. The Prophet told Qubaisah, "Asking is not permissible, except in three cases." The Prophet mentioned among them a man struck by a disaster that wipes out his wealth. Early commentators on the Qur'an include in the category of persons under debt [al gharimin] "He whose house caught fire or whose wealth was wiped out by flood or who has debts that burden his family."[37]

How much are such persons given?

In the saying mentioned above, the Prophet (p) says such a person may ask "until he secures sufficiency of sustenance." This undoubtedly differs from one person to another, depending on factors such as the general standards of living, size of family, and social status. For a merchant whose inventory is burned, for example, securing sustenance of living may require purchasing a minimum amount of inventory sufficient for his type of business. Some jurists even argue that such people must be given amounts sufficient to put them back on their feet at the level they had before the accident took place.[38] I believe what determines how much persons struck by disasters should be given depends on the availability of funds in the *zakah* agency and on several other factors, namely other needs that draw on these funds. Lastly, it must be emphasized that the rural areas of today's Muslim countries desperately need such Islamic insurance against the financial aftermath of natural disasters and drought, because of predominant poverty and insufficiency of voluntary charity to take total responsibility for such insurance.

SECTION FIVE

THE PROBLEM OF INVOLUNTARY CELIBACY

Taking a vow of celibacy is prohibited

Islam, in as much as it does not allow unlimited, haphazard response to and practice of the sexual drive, does not allow the other extreme and does not entertain any tendency to voluntary celibacy. Suppression of the sexual drive or its elimination is not accepted by this system of Islam. Islam encourages marriage and forbids taking vows of celibacy and castration. A Muslim who is able to marry is not permitted to live in celibacy claiming that he is devoted to adoring and worshiping God. The Prophet (p) noticed once an inclination toward celibacy among some of his Companions. He immediately declared that this is an unacceptable deviation from Islam and his tradition. He says, "I am indeed the most knowledgeable among you about God ('s teachings) and the one who fears Him most, but I stand [in prayers] in the night and I sleep; I fast [sometimes] and I eat, and I marry women. He who desires not my way [of conduct] does not belong with me."[39] Sa'd bin Abi Waqqas narrates, "The Messenger of God (p) rejected the [attempted] celibacy vow of 'Uthman bin Maz'un. If he had allowed him, we would have castrated ourselves."[40] Furthermore, the Prophet called on the youth, "O young people, whoever can afford the requirement of marriage among you must marry, since marriage is better for lowering the gaze and protecting chastity."[41] Some scholars deduce that marriage is obligatory on each Muslim and refraining from marrying is not permissible for anyone who has the means to marry. Muslim must not avoid marriage because of tightness in their means of living or because of the burden of its responsibilities. God promises enrichment to those who look to marriage as a means of human satisfaction and protection against prohibited practice of the sexual drive. God says, "Marry those among you who are single or the virtuous ones among your slavers, male or female. If they are in poverty, God will give them means out of His grace."[42] The Prophet (p) says, "Three have the right to help from God: a man who seeks marriage in order to satisfy himself and protect his chastity, a slave who has a contract for freeing him or herself for a certain amount of money who intends to fulfill his duty, and a fighter in the way of God."[43]

The institution of *zakah* is one of the favors God gives the Islamic society. *Zakah* must be used to help provide marriage expenses for those who are in need, since marriage is encouraged as a human satisfaction that helps lower one's gaze and protect one's chastity, and above all, establish the Muslim family. God says, "And among His signs is this: That He created for you mates from yourselves, that ye may dwell in tranquility with them, and He has put love and mercy between your hearts. Verily in that are signs for those who reflect."[44]

This role of the *zakah* institution is not an innovation of mine or a view I fabricate, but has been decided by past leading scholars. They declare that getting married is included in provision of sufficiency of sustenance and argue that providing unmarried poor persons with financial help for getting married is an integral part of providing essential needs.[45]

SECTION SIX

THE PROBLEM OF THE HOMELESS

It was shown earlier that help for the wayfarer is one of the eight goals of *zakah* dispersement. In several places in the Qur'an, God encourages taking care of the wayfarer. Islam prefers every person to have a home and belong to a family, and does not like a status of homelessness for anyone. Consequently, adequate shelter for a person and his or her family is included under essential needs, for satisfaction of which *zakah* is enacted by God. Al Nawawi explains that essential needs include food, clothing, residence, and everything that is indispensable for life, at a level that suits the receiver and his or her social status without extravagance or miserliness.[46] Ibn Hazm adds "It is an obligation on the rich people of every region to provide for all the needs of the poor in that region. If they do not fullfill this, the government must force them to do so. If the proceeds of *zakah* and *fa'i* are not sufficient, still, satisfaction of the needs for food, clothing for summer and winter, and shelter that protects from the sun, the rain, and the eyes of passers-by, must be provided from the wealth of the rich."[47]

In the chapter on the wayfarer in part four of this book, we noted that foundlings are also covered in the benefits of *zakah*, since they are indeed "children of the street."

Footnotes

1.	For details on this mutual care and solidarity, see *Ishtirakiyat al Islam*, by Dr. Mustafa al Siba'i.

2.	*Fi Zilal al Qur'an*, by Syed Qutb, Vol. 10, p. 81.

3.	*Al Amwal*, pp. 578-580.

4.	*Ibid*, p. 46.

5.	*Tarikh al Baladhari*, p. 177.

6.	*Al Daman al Ijtima'i,* by Dr. Sadiq Mahdi, p. 126.

7.	*Halqat al Dirasat al Ijtima'iyah*, third session, p. 217.

8.	*Al Ishtirakiyah fi al Mujtama' al Islami,* by al Bahi al Khawli, pp. 141-144.

9.	*Mushkilat al Faqr wa Kaifa 'Alajaha al Islam*, by Yusuf al Qaradawi.

10.	*Sura al Baqarah*, 2:29.

11.	*Sura al Hashr*, 59:7.

12.	Reported by Muslim, Abu Daud, al Nasa'i, and Ibn Majah. See *al Targhib*, Vol. 2, chapter on warnings against begging.

13.	Reported by Abu Daud, (see *ibid*), and by al Baihaqi in his *Sunan al Kubra*, Vol. 4, p. 197.

14.	Reported by the five, Ibn Majah excluded. See *al Targhib, ibid.* Also reported from al Zubair by al Bukhari, Vol. 4, p. 195.

15. Reported from al Zubair by al Bukhari, at the beginning of the chapter on sales in his correct collection.

16. Reported by the four.

17. Reported by Abu Daud and al Nasa'i.

18. Reported by Abu Daud.

19. *Hujjat Allah al Balighah*, Vol. 2, p. 46. However, al Tahawi, a Hanafite, argues in his *Mushkil al Athar* that the Prophet (p) first made his warning strong with regard to the amount that makes asking prohibited, then made it less strong as time went by, until he reached the amount for prohibition that equals five *'uqiyyah*, which is the *nisab* of *zakah* on silver. But this view is not supported by any text. Therefore, al Dahlawi's interpretation seems to be sounder.

20. Reported by Abu Daud, al Tirmidhi, al Nasa'i, and Ibn Majah. Al Tirmidhi comments, "This is a good saying, which I do not know except through al Akhdar bin 'Ajlan, about whom Yahya bin Ma'in says 'He is good', and Abu Hatim says, 'He writes his narrations'." See *Mukhtasar Sunan Abu Daud*, by al Mundhiri, Vol. 2, p. 239-240.

21. *Mushkilat al Faqr wa Kaifa 'Alajaha al Islam.*

22. *Sura al Hashr,* 59:8-9.

23. *Sura al Baqarah,* 2:30.

24. *Sura al Ma'idah,* 5:30-34.

25. Reported by Abu Daud and al Tirmidhi.

26. This increment in the saying is mentioned by al Tirmidhi without a chain of narrators.

27. *Sura al Nisa,* 4:34.

28. *Sura al Hujurat,* 49:9-10.

29. *Sura al Anfal,* 8:1.

30. *Sura al Nisa,* 4:114.

31. Reported in Abu Daud's chapter on manners, al Tirmidhi's chapter on description of Resurrection. The latter comments, "It is correct."

32. *Matalib Uli al Nuha*, Vol. 2, p. 143.

33. In *Ghayat al Muntaha* and its commentary, it is stated that the sixth category is a person who borrows for reconciling others, even if he is rich, before he pays from his own wealth. See *ibid*, p. 144.

34. *Sura Quraish,* 106:1-4.

35.   *Sura al Nahl,* 16:112.

36.   Reported by Ahmad, Vol. 3, p. 36, by Muslim in the book on crop sharing, by Abu Daud and al Nasa'i in the chapter on sales, by al Tirmidhi in his chapter on *zakah,* and by Ibn Majah in his chapter on rulings.

37.   See chapter five on part four of this book.

38.   Mentioned by al Ghazali in his al *Ihya.* See chapter one of part four.

39.   Reported by al Bukhari.

40.   *Ibid.*

41.   *Ibid.*

42.   *Sura al Nur,* 24:32.

43.   Reported by Ahmad, al Nasa'i, al Tirmidhi, Ibn Majah, and al Hakim from Abu Hurairah via a correct chain, as stated in *al Taisir,* Vol. 1, p. 474.

44.   *Sura al Rum,* 30:21.

45.   See the discussion on this subject in chapter one of part four.

46.   *Ibid.*

47.   *Al Muhalla,* Vol. 6, p. 156.

FIQH AL ZAKAH

PART SEVEN

ZAKAH OF FAST-BREAKING
[*ZAKAH* OF *AL FITR*]

1. Its meaning, rulings, and justification

2. On whom is it obligated

3. Its amount and kind

4. Time of obligation and payment

5. Recipients of *zakah* of *al fitr*

CHAPTER ONE

MEANING, RULINGS, AND JUSTIFICATION OF FAST-BREAKING *ZAKAH*

The Meaning of fast-breaking *zakah* [*zakah* of *al fitr*]

This *zakah* is caused by breaking the fasting at the end of Ramadan. It is sometimes called "*sadaqat al Fitr*". It was shown earlier that the term "*sadaqah*" is used to mean *zakah* in Qur'an, Sunnah, and *Shari'ah*. It is also called *zakah* of human nature [*fitrah*] on the basis that it is derived from the nature of the human creature. The amount paid is sometimes called "*fitrah'* which is a derived term used only by some jurists.[1]

Zakah of fast-breaking was obligated in the second year of *Hijrah*, the same year fasting Ramadan was obligated,[2] in order to purify and sanctify those who fasted and to bring happiness to the poor on the day of *'Id*.

Distinct from other forms of *zakah*, *zakah* of *al fitr* is levied on persons and not on wealth or income. This means there are drastic differences in the conditions of *zakatability*, as will be seen in chapter two.

The obligation of fast-breaking *zakah*

The group reports from Ibn 'Umar, "The Messenger of God imposed *zakah* of breaking the fast of Ramadan, at one *sa'* of date, or one *sa'* of barley, on every Muslim, free or slave, male or female."[3] The majority of scholars, ancient and modern, understand the word "imposed" to indicate obligation; thus, *zakah* of *al fitr* is an obligation in *Shari'ah* included in the general obligation of the verse "and give *zakah*".[4] The Prophet (p) called it *zakah* and imposed it on every Muslim. Some other correct versions of the saying mention "The Messenger ordained . . . ." which clearly shows the obligatory nature of this *zakah*.[5] Abu al 'Aliah, 'Ata, and Ibn Sirin, along with al Bukhari, state that this *zakah* is obligatory.[6] This is also the view of Malik, al Shafi'i, and Ahmad.

Hanafites, who distinguish between the obligation [*fard* which is imposed by a clear-cut text such as Qur'an], and the requirement [*wajib*, which is imposed by texts which are not clear-cut, such as single chain sayings] consider *zakah* of *al fitr* only *wajib*. According to Hanafites, denying a fard equals disbelief, whereas denying a *wajib* does not, since *wajib* for them is a practical obligation only, while fard is an ideological obligation. The other three schools do not make such a distinction, so the matter is simply a difference in definitions.[7]

There is a Malikite report from Ashhab that *zakah* of *al fitr* is an "emphasized sunnah."[8] This is also the opinion of some Zahirites and Ibn al Labban, who is a Shafi'ite, on the grounds that the word *"farada"* [imposed] originally means "to estimate" in linguistics, but this is disproved by what is stated at the beginning of this section. Moreover, Ibn Daqiq al 'Id says, "Linguistically, *'farada'* originally meant 'to estimate', but it is now used in *Shari'ah* to mean 'to obligate,' so it is better to choose this meaning." Ibn al Humam says, "It is a must to take the meaning of the words of the Legislator that is used in *Shari'ah*, except when there is evidence to the contrary, especially in this case, in light of the other version, reported by al Bukhari and Muslim, in which the word *'amara'* i.e. ordained, is used."

The obligatory nature of *zakah* of *al fitr* is further supported by the fact that it is called *zakah*. This is so to the extent that after mentioning the view of Ibn al Labban, al Nawawi writers, "This is a rejected and deviant opinion; it is clearly erroneous." Ibn Rahawaih says the obligation of *zakah* of *al fitr* is like *ijma'*, and al Mundhiri quotes, "it is ijma'." But the statement of Ibn Rahawaih is apparently more precise, especially since Ibrahim bin 'Aliyah and Abu Bakr al Asamm believe this *zakah* was annulled when regular *zakah* was obligated. They support this view with a saying reported by Ahmad and al Nasa'i that when Qais bin sa'd bin 'Ubadah was asked about *zakah* of *al fitr*, he said, "The Messenger of God (p) ordained *zakah* of *al fitr* before *zakah* was ordained. When the *zakah* ordinance descended, he neither ordered us nor prevented us from continuing to pay *zakah* of *al fitr*, but we [still] do it." The chain of this saying is disputed, since it has an unknown narrator, according to al Hafiz.[9] Even if we assume it is correct, the saying does not indicate any annulment of fast-breaking *zakah*, since revealing an obligation does not imply abolishing a previous one.[10] The original order mentioned in the saying itself is still valid; an annulment requires a text.

Accordingly, it is established among Muslims that *zakah* of *al fitr* is obligatory, since the deviant view to the contrary of this is opposed by ijma' before and after it,[11] and Schacht's claim is nonsense.[12]

Justification of *zakah* of *al fitr*

Ibn 'Abbas says, "The Messenger of God (p) imposed *zakah* of *al fitr* as a purification of the faster from vain talk and bad doing, and as a food provision for the needy."[13] The worshiper may have incurred during Ramadan vain, ill words, or indecent feelings that require purification, since perfect fasting is not merely abstention from and drink, but abstention from ill-doing and offensive speech to others. Thus, *zakah* of *al fitr* is obligated to make up for any impurities and imperfections in fasting, just like voluntary and *sunnah* prayers make up for imperfections in obligatory prayers.[14]

In addition, *'Id* is a day of joy, happiness, and feasting, and the poor need help to bring the same happiness to their children and households. *Zakah* of *al fitr* is obligated to provide food to the poor on the day of *'Id*. In another saying, the Prophet is reported to say, "Make them [the poor] satisfied on this day."[15]

Footnotes

1. In his commentary, Ibn 'Abidin says, "The use of the word *'fitrah'* to mean *zakah* of *al fitr* is not eloquent. It is used only colloquially, and is considered a mistake by some scholars." In *al Qamus*, *al fitrah* is listed as *zakah* of *al fitr*, but this is considered one of the errors of *al Qamus* which is caused by confusing the religious with the linguistic meaning. Al Nawawi says it is a derived noun, probably from *fitrah*, which means "nature" or "creation". Al Abhari says *fitrah* is the *zakah* of natural creation. In brief, the word *fitrah* is an Arabic word that means creation; it is used for *zakah al fitr* because this is a *zakah* on creatures, or persons, themselves. It is used in *Shari'ah* to mean *zakah* of *al fitr* or the amount paid as *zakah* of *al fitr*. See *Radd al Muhtar*, Vol. 2, p. 78.

2. *Al Mirqat*, Vol. 4, p. 159.

3. Mentioned in *al Muntaqa*; see *Nail al Awtar*, Vol. 4, p. 179.

4. *Sura al Baqarah,* 2:11, and *al Nisa,* 4:77.

5. *Sharh al Nawawi on Muslim*, Vol. 7, p. 58, and *al Muhalla*, Vol. 6, p. 119.

6. He mentions it as suspended. In *al Fath*, al Hafiz says 'Abd al Razzaq connects it from Ibn Juraij from 'Ata, and Ibn Abi Shaibah from 'Asim al Ahwal from the other two. Al Bukhari only mentions these names because they clearly state it is obligated; otherwise, Ibn al Mundhir quotes *ijma'* on it.

7. Ibn al Humam says, "In the ultimate analysis, there is no difference between them on its meaning, since according to the other schools, the nature of this obligation does not imply that he who denies it becomes a disbeliever, and this is the meaning of 'requirement' in our school. Hanafites believe it is only *wajib* because of dispute on the degree of confirmation of its texts and their indication." See *al Mirqat*, Vol. 4, p. 160.

8. In *al Muhalla*, Vol. 6, p. 118, Ibn Hazm writes that Malik says it is not obligatory, but the late shaikh Shakir notes, "This is an error on the part of Ibn Hazm, since Malik clearly says in *al Muwatta* that *zakah* of *al fitr* is obligatory on bedouins as well as on urbanites, because the Messenger 'imposed *zakah* of breaking the fast of Ramadan . . . .' This is also stated by Ibn Rushd in *Bidayat al Mujtahid*, Vol. 1, p. 269.

9. Followed by al Suyuti in *Sharh al Nasa'i* and al Shawkani in *Nail al Awtar*, Vol. 4, p. 180, but shaikh is surprised by the statement of al Hafiz and those who follow him, and after mentioning the saying via two chains, says, "both chains are correct; they have no unknown person." Notes on *Al Muhalla*, Vol. 6, p. 119.

10. *Fath al Bari*, Vol. 4, pp. 110-111, *al Mirqat*, Vol. 4, pp. 159-160, *al Muhallah*, Vol. 6, pp. 118-119, *al Rawdah*, Vol. 2, p. 291, *Sharh Muslim*, Vol. 7, p. 58, *Nail al Awtar*, Vol. 4, p. 180, and *al Fath al Rabbani*, Vol. 9, pp. 134-137.

11. *Al Bahr al Zakhkhar*, Vol. 2, p. 195.

12. In the *Encyclopedia of Islam*, Vol. 10, p. 361, (Arabic translation), Schacht writes, "Jurists differ on the obligation of *zakah* of *al fitr*, but according to the prevailing view today, *zakah* of *al fitr* is considered obligatory. It is only Sunnah according to Malikites." This is grossly erroneous. Jurists are almost in total agreement that it is obligatory. Ibn al Mundhir quotes *ijma'* on this obligation, though he knew of the presence of a disregarded deviant view expressed by one or two persons. The accepted view among Malikites is obligation of this *zakah*. See for example, *Bulghat al Salik*, Vol. 1, p. 237, and *al Sharh al Kabir* with the notes of al Dusuqi, Vol. 1, p. 504. The view of Ibn al Ashhab is rejected in the Malikite school itself. Schacht is misled by the sentence of Ibn Abi Zaid in *al Risalah* that "*zakah* of *al fitr* is an obligated *sunnah* imposed by the Prophet (p)." The commentators explain that the author means an obligation that came in the Sunnah [as opposed the Qur'an]. See *Sharh al Risalah*, by Zarruq, Vol. 1, p. 341. Malik clearly states in *al Muwatta* that *zakah* of *al fitr* is obligatory.

13. Reported by Abu Daud in chapter on *zakah* of *al fitr*; he and al Mundhiri make no comment. At Hakim also reports the same saying and notes, "correct as per the conditions of al Bukhari; this is approved by al Dhahabi. It is also reported by Ibn Majah, al Baihaqi, and al Daraqutni, p. 219. The latter says, "No defective narrator exists in its chain." See *al Mirqat*, Vol. 4, p. 173, and *Nasb al Rayah*, Vol. 2, p. 108.

14. *Nihayat al Muhtaj*, Vol. 2, p. 108.

15. The author of *Nail al Awtar* says it is reported by al Baihaqi and al Daraqutni from Ibn 'Umar. Al Baihaqi's version is "Make them satisfied this day, so they do not go around begging". Ibn sa'd in al Tabaqat also reports it from 'A'ishah and Abu Sa'id, Vol. 4, p. 186. See *Nasb al Rayah*, Vol. 2, p. 432, and the notes on *al Muhalla*, Vol. 6, p. 120.

CHAPTER TWO

ON WHOM IS IT OBLIGATED?

The saying reported by the group from Ibn 'Umar reads "The Messenger of God (p) imposed *zakah* of breaking the fast of Ramadan . . . on every Muslim, free or slave, male or female" and in a version given by al Bukhari, Ibn 'Umar says "The Messenger of God (p) imposed . . . on every Muslim, slave or free, male or female, young or old." Abu Hurairah says *zakah* of *al fitr* is due "on every free or slave, male or female, young or old, poor or rich . . ."[1] Although these are Abu Hurairah's words, such a view is not a matter of personal opinion, so it must be taken from the Prophet (p).

These sayings indicate that *zakah* of breaking the fast is a general obligation on all Muslim individuals, regardless of freedom, sex, age, wealth, or urban or bedouin status. Al Zuhri, Rabi'ah, and al Laith believe it is obligated only on the urban population, i.e. nomads are exempt, but the wording of the sayings disproves their view.[2] Ibn Hazm reports a similar view from 'Ata and adds that the Messenger of God (p) did not make any exception.

Women

The phrase in the saying "male or female" implies that *zakah* of *al fitr* is obligated on all women, married or not. This is the view of Abu Hanifah and the Zahirites. They say that women must pay it from their own wealth.[4] The other three leading *imams* as well as al Laith and Ishaq believe that husbands are required to pay it on behalf of their wives, because *zakah* of *al fitr* is related to provision of sustenance. Al Hafiz argues that this view is disputed, since its proponents contradict themselves in the case of a slave wife when the husband is financially unable, claiming that the wife's *zakah* of *al fitr* must be paid by her master, while he is not obligated to spend on her sustenance. Also, when the wife is not Muslim, the husband is unanimously required to spend for her sustenance but not for *zakah* of *al fitr* on her behalf. Al Shafi'i presents a *mursal* saying via Muhammad bin 'Ali al Baqir, "Pay *sadaqah* of *al fitr* on behalf of those you provide for."[5] However, this saying is very weak and does not stand in argument.[6] The Imami school agrees with the Shafi'ites.[7] Al Laith adds that it must also be paid on behalf of a laborer whose wage is not defined,[8] while the Zaidis say the payer is only required to give *zakah* of *al fitr* on behalf of those whose sustenance he provides if they are related by kin, marriage, or ownership [of a slave].[9]

Children

The phrase "young or old" in the saying indicates that *zakah* of *al fitr* is obligatory on children, out of their own funds if they have any. The guardian is required to pay it out of the children's wealth. If the child has no funds, the guardian must pay it like provision for sustenance. This is the opinion of the majority. Muhammad bin Hasan says only the father is obliged to pay it, and if the child has no father, no *zakah* of *al fitr* is due.[10] Sa'id bin al Musayyib and al Hasan al Basri say it is not obligated on whoever did not fast, because it is obligated as a purification and the child does not need it. Ibn 'Abbas says, "The Messenger of God (p) imposed *zakah* of *al fitr* as a purification, for whoever fasts, from vain talk and impurities." This opinion is disputed on the ground that most of those obligated usually fast,[11] and that *zakah* of *al fitr* is also obligated to feed the poor, a purpose better achieved if it is obligated on young and old.

The fetus

No *zakah* is obligated on the fetus, according to the majority of jurists. Ibn Hazm disagrees, saying that if the fetus completes one hundred and twenty days before the dawn of the last day of Ramadan, *zakah* of *al fitr* must be paid on its behalf. The hundred and twenty days is taken from the saying which indicates it is at this age that the soul is blown into the fetus. Ibn Hazm argues that the fetus is included by the word of the Prophet "young" and reports that 'Uthman bin 'Affan used to pay *zakah* of *al fitr* on behalf of the young, old, and unborn babies. Abu Qulabah says, "They used to like paying *zakah* of *al fitr* on behalf of the young, the old, and the fetus in the womb." Ibn Hazm clarifies that Abu Qulabah met many Companions and narrates from them. Sulaiman bin Yasar answered "yes" to a question about *zakah* of *al fitr* on behalf of the fetus and adds, "no Companion is known to have differed with 'Uthman on this issue."[12]

The truth is that there is no evidence on the obligation of *zakah* of *al fitr* on unborn babies in what Ibn Hazm quotes, and it is gross arbitration to include the fetus in the meaning of the word "young". 'Uthman's action is not indicative of the obligation, although it may mean encouragement of this action. Al Shawkani quotes Ibn al Mundhir as reporting ijma' that it is not obligatory on unborn babies, and Ahmad considers this payment desirable and not obligatory.[13]

Conditions of *zakatability*

The phrase "a freeman or slave" in the saying is inclusive of the poor; Abu Hurairah explicitly mentions the poor in his statement. Accordingly, the three leading jurists, along with the majority, believe that there are only two conditions of *zakatability*, namely, Islam and owning the amount of *zakah* of *al fitr* above what is needed as provision for the day of *'Id* for the person and his family. Al Shawkani notes that this is correct because the texts are general and inclusive of the rich and poor. The terms of *zakatability* are not subject to human opinion in this case, since the purpose of this *zakah*--cleansing of vain talk, etc., includes the poor and the rich. On the other hand, the condition of owning food for the day of *'Id* is indispensable, because without this condition, the person deserves to receive *zakah* of *al fitr* and to be satisfied on that day.[14]

Abu Hanifah and his disciples disagree. They require the condition of *nisab* on the basis of the generality of the saying in al Bukhari and al Nasa'i, "No *sadaqah* is obligated except our of richness,"[15] and richness is defined by owning *nisab*. They also draw this by analogy to other forms of *zakah* that all require *nisab*. This is challenged on the grounds that this saying does not indicate an obligation of this condition, especially the version reported by Abu Daud: "The best *sadaqah* is that done out of richness."[16] Moreover, another saying, reported by Abu Daud and al Hakim from Abu Hurairah, stands in opposition, since it reads "The best *sadaqah* is the effort of a person who has little." The latter is supported by yet another saying, reported by al Tabarani from Abu Umamah, "The best *sadaqah* is that which is given secretly to a poor or done by a person who has little."

Additionally, there is the saying reported by al Nasa'i, Ibn Khuzaimah, al Hakim, (who grades it correct as per Muslim's conditions) and by Ibn Habban in his correct collection, from Abu Hurairah that the Prophet (p) said "One *dirham* is better than a hundred thousand *dirhams*!" A man said, "O Messenger of God, how could it be?" He answered, "A man who has plenty of wealth, gives as charity a hundred thousand *dirhams* out of its peripheries; and a man who has only two *dirhams* gives as charity one *dirhams*, which is one-half of his wealth."

The analogy with other forms of *zakah* is incomplete, since *zakah* of *al fitr* is on persons, while all other forms are on wealth.[17] The claim that the poor are exempt from *zakah* of *al fitr* is explicitly disproven by the general content of the saying obligating *zakah* of *al fitr* on every Muslim, by Abu Hurairah's statements[15] that names the poor as obligated to pay it, and by yet another saying reported by Ahmad and Abu Daud from Tha'labah bin Abi Saghir from his father, that the Messenger of God (p) said, "Pay the *sadaqah* of *al fitr*, one *sa'* of wheat, on behalf of each human being, young or old, free or owned, rich or poor, or male or female. As for the rich among you, God sanctifies him [by it] and as for the poor, God gives him back more than he gives."

In my personal opinion, *zakah* of *al fitr* must be obligated on the poor as well as the rich, because, in addition to the preceeding arguments, there is the objective of training everyone to give and spend in obedience to God, even just a little bit once every year. God describes the believers who fear God as "Those who spend in ease and in adversity."[18] For the same reason, I also prefer the view of Abu Hanifah obligating *zakah* of *al fitr* on women out of their own wealth.

Lastly, it should be noted that the necessary condition of capability to pay *zakah* of *al fitr* must not be overlooked. Capability is defined as owning the amount of *zakah* in excess to the food of the day of *'Id* and other necessities, such as shelter, clothing, furniture, and utensils. Anything in excess of essential needs and can be liquidated for payment of *zakah* of *al fitr* is considered a fulfillment of this condition. Books needed for profession, study, or research, usual and customary amount of lawful jewelry, means of transportation, etc., are all included into essential needs.[19]

Deferred debt does not obstruct *zakatability*

Debts that are not due by the day of *'Id* are disregarded in determining *zakatability* with respect to *zakah* of *al fitr*; i.e. a person who has excess above the *'Id* day's food, but this excess is required to pay a debt that is due by that day is exempt from *zakah*. Deferred debts do not obstruct *zakatability*, because *zakah* of *al fitr* is emphasized and ascertained on every Muslim including the poor, unlike *zakah* on wealth, which is obligated on the rich only.

Footnotes

1.   Reported by al Bukhari, Muslim, Ahmad, and al Nasa'i. See *al Fath al Rabbani*, Vol. 9, p. 139, saying no. 186.

2.   *Nail al Awtar*, Vol. 4, p. 181.

3.   *Al Muhalla*, Vol. 6, p. 132.

4.   *Al Fath al Rabbani*, Vol. 9, p. 140, saying no. 187.

5.   Also reported by al Baihaqi, Vol. 4, p. 161, via the same chain and he aids 'Ali. It is interrupted. Ibn Hazm says this is very surprising, since al Shafi'i, who does not accept *mursal* sayings, presents the worst *mursal*, which is via Ibn Abi Yahya. See *al Muhalla*, Vol. 6, p. 137. Al Baihaqi also reports the same from Ibn 'Umar via a not-strong chain, Vol. 4, p. 161. Al Daraqutni also reports it; see *Nail al Awtar*, Vol. 4, p. 181. Al Baihaqi reports from 'Ali "He or she on whom you are obliged to spend, you must give [*zakah* of *al fitr*] on their behalf." In this chain is Abd al a'la, who is not strong according to al Baihaqi, but this saying is supported by the previous one. See *al Bahr*, Vol. 2, p. 199, and *Nasb al Rayah*, Vol. 2, p. 413.

6.   *Al Jawhar al Naqi* with *al Sunnah al Kubra*, Vol. 4, p. 160.

7.   *Fiqh al Imam Ja'far*, Vol. 2, pp. 103-104.

8.   *Al Muhalla*, Vol. 6, p. 127.

9.   *Al Bahr*, Vol. 2, p. 199.

10.   *Ibid*, p. 135, *Nail al Awtar*, Vol. 4, p. 180, and *Al Muhalla*, Vol. 6, p. 137.

11.   *Ibid*.

12.   *Al Muhalla*, Vol. 6, p. 132.

13.   *Nail al Awtar*, Vol. 4, p. 181.

14.   *Ibid*, p. 186.

15. He reports it as suspended, in the chapter on the last will of his correct collection. His confirmed suspended reports are considered correct according to the majority of jurists, except Ibn Hazm.

16. Al Shawkani only mentions Abu Daud, but the saying is reported by al Bukhari, chapter on expenses, al Nasa'i, chapter on *zakah*, Ahmad in *al Musnad*, Vol. 2, p. 345, and Muslim in his chapter on *zakah*.

17. *Nail al Awtar*, Vol. 4, pp. 185-186, and *al Mughni*, Vol. 3, p. 74.

18. *Sura Al 'Imran*, 3:134.

19. *Al Mughni*, Vol. 3, p. 76, and *al Rawdah*, Vol. 2, pp. 299-300.

20. *Ibid.*

CHAPTER THREE

AMOUNT AND KIND OF *ZAKAH* OF *AL FITR*

Is one *sa'* obligated?

In the saying from Ibn 'Umar, "The Messenger of God (p) imposed . . . one *sa'* of dates or one *sa'* of barley . . . ." Abu Sa'id al Khudri said, "We used to pay *zakah* of breaking the fast of Ramadan, when the Messenger of God (p) was among us, with one *sa'* of food, one *sa'* of dried yogurt. We remained this way until Mu'awiyah came to us in Madinah and said, 'I think two mudd of the wheat of Syria is equivalent to one *sa'* of date.' People accepted that." Reported by the group, and the five reporters add, "Abu Sa'id says, 'but I continued paying it the same way I used to'." Thus, the indication of these two texts is that one *sa'* is obligatory for each person.

Al Dahlawi says *zakah* of *al fitr* is determined at one *sa'* because "this is sufficient for an average-size houschold; thus it provides satisfaction for the poor without burdening the payer."[1] There is ijma' that from foodstuffs like date and barley, one *sa'* is obligatory. If wheat or raisin is given, one *sa'* is obligatory according to three schools of jurists, Abu Sa'id, Abu al Aliah, Abu al Sha'tha, al Hasan al Basri, Jabir bin Zaid, Ishaq, al Hadi, al Qasim, al Nasir, and al Mu'ayyad bi Allah.[2]

Their argument is derived from the above mentioned saying from Abu Sa'id. Al Nawawi says, "This saying makes two important points: One, the word 'food' is used in Hijaz to mean wheats, especially when the word is used in additive relation to other foodstuff, and second, it mentions several items whose values are different, which means that the quantity of one *sa'* is intended regardless of the value."[3] Those who say it is one half a *sa'* have no evidence except the story of Mu'awiyah and a few other obviously weak sayings.[4]

As for the story of Mu'awiyah, the majority of scholars believe that it is at best the opinion of a Companion which is opposed by other Companions who knew the Prophet better than Mu'awiyah. However, the rule is that when the Companions disagree among themselves, additional evidence is needed, since the view of one of them does not have more weight than that of any other. The majority argues that the saying itself as well as the analogy are in support of one *sa'* of all food items mentioned, including wheat, and Mu'awiyah did say it was a personal view and not that he had heard it from the Prophet (p).[5] Although *ijtihd* is always permissible, it is not acceptable when there is a text.[6]

Those who say the amount is one half a *sa'* of wheat

Abu Hanifah and his disciples believe a half *sa'* of wheat is sufficient.[7] This is also the view of Zaid bin 'Ali and Yahya.[8] Ibn Hazm says, "it is correctly attributed to 'Umar bin 'Abd al 'Aziz, Taus, Mujahid, Sa'id bin al Musayyib, 'Urwah bin al Zubair, Abu Salamah bin 'Abd al Rahman, Sa'id bin Jubair, al Awza'i, al Laith, and Sufyan." Ibn Hazm also mentions reports from several Companions to the same effect, including Abu Bakr, 'Umar, 'Uthman, 'Ali, 'A'ishah, Asma bint Abu Bakr, Abu Hurairah, Jabir, Ibn Mas'ud, Ibn 'Abbas, Ibn al Zubair, Abu Sa'id. Ibn Hazm adds that reports from all of them are correct except those about Abu Bakr, Ibn 'Abbas, and Ibn Mas'ud.[9]

Abu Hanifah and his group provide the following to support their view:

Firstly, Abu Daud reports from 'Abd Allah bin Tha'labah that the Messenger of God (p) said, "*sadaqah* of *al fitr* is one *sa'* of wheat for each two persons."[10] Al Hakim reports from Ibn 'Abbas, attributed to the Prophet (p) "*Sadaqah* of *al fitr* is two mudd of wheat." Two mudd is half a *sa'*. Al Tirmidhi has a similar saying from 'Amr bin Shu'aib from his father from his grandfather. Abu Daud and al Nasa'i report a *mursal* saying from al Hasan that "The Messenger of God imposed this *sadaqah* one *sa'* of date or barley, or half a *sa'* of wheat."[11] And there are a few other sayings that, together, stand to restrict the general implications of the saying on the *sa'* by excluding wheat.[12]

Secondly, it is correctly reported that several Companions believed one half a *sa'* of wheat is obligated. Sufyan reports from 'Ali, "One half a *sa'* of wheat." It is also reported from the Four Successors and others.[13] Depending on such reports, Ibn al Mundhir says, "We know of no correct report from the Prophet on wheat,[14] which was not common in Madinah. When it became abundant during the era of the Companions, they made half a *sa'* of it equal to one *sa'* of barley. They are the leaders whose view must not be ignored." Ibn al Mundhir goes on to report via correct chains as described by al Hafiz, the same from 'Uthman, 'Ali, Abu Hurairah, Jabir, Ibn 'Abbas, Ibn al Zubair, and his mother Asma. Al Tahawi claims *ijma'* on this,[15] but the disagreement of Abu Sa'id mentioned in the saying above disproves this claim. Moreover, Hanafites argue that Abu Sa'id comment, "I continue to pay it the same way I used to at the time of the Prophet" does not imply that one *sa'* of wheat is obligatory, and no one says one cannot pay more than one half; in fact the excess is voluntary charity.[16]

As for the interpretation of "food" in the saying from Abu Sa'id as wheat, it is not agreed upon. Ibn al Mundhir says "Some people think that food here means wheat, but this is wrong. Abu Sa'id first gives the aggregate term 'food' then its details. Al Bukhari reports through Hafz bin Maisarah, 'Abu Sa'id said, "We used to pay at the time of the Prophet one *sa'* of food on the day of fitr. Our food was barley, raisin, dried yogurt, and date." This is also reported by al Tahawi via another chain with the addition of "We used not to pay any thing else."[17] Ibn Khuzaimah reports from Ibn 'Umar "The *sadaqah* at the time of the Messenger of God (p) was nothing but date, raisin, and barley, but not wheat." And Muslim reports from Abu Sa'id, "We used to pay out of three items: one *sa'* of date, one *sa'* of dired yogurt, or one *sa'* of barley." Al Hafiz, says, "All these narrations indicate that the word 'food' in the saying from Abu Sa'id does not mean wheat. Food may also mean corn, since it was commonly known in Hijaz too." Al Jawzaqi reports via Iad from Abu Sa'id "one *sa'* of date, one *sa'* of corn . . . ."[18]

Analysis and discussion

From all these arguments and evidence, it seems that wheat was not a common food in Hijaz at the time of the Prophet, so he did not impose one *sa'* on it. The saying reported by al Bukhari from Ibn 'Umar supports this, since it reads ". . . one *sa'* of date or one *sa'* of barley. People considered this equivalent to two *mudd* of wheat, " and in another version "People considered it equivalent to half a *sa'*."[19] Ibn al Qayyim quotes Abu Daud, "It is known that 'Umar made one half of a *sa'* of wheat equal one *sa'* of these other things."[20] It is however, mentioned in the two correct collections that Mu'awiyah was the one who did this. There are several *mursal* sayings that strengthen one another. Ibn al Qayyim then refers to the saying from Ibn Abi Saghir and adds that al Hasan al Basri says, "At the end of Ramadan, Ibn 'Abbas gave a speech from above the *minbar* [stand of the speaker] in Basrah saying, 'Pay the *sadaqah* of your fasting.' People seemed not to have understood. Then he added, 'Who here is from Madinah? Stand up and teach your brothers, since they do not know. The Messenger of God (p) imposed this *sadaqah*, one *sa'* of date or barley, or half a *sa'* of wheat, on each free person or slave, male or female, young or old . . . .' Then when 'Ali came and noticed the low prices, he said, 'God has given you prosperity; would you not make it one *sa'* of anything?'" Reported by Abu Daud and al Nasa'i.[22] Ibn al Qayyim adds, "Our teacher, Ibn Taimiyah, inclines toward this view, saying it is consistent with Ahmad's view about *kaffarat*, in which he equates half a *sa'* of wheat to one *sa'* of other things."[23]

It seems that sayings in support of the one half *sa'* of wheat when thoroughly scrutinized, are not weak to the extent of being rejected, nor are they well-known among the Companions. If these sayings were strong enough, they would be known to Ibn 'Umar, Abu Sa'id, Mu'awiyah, and those who heard them. It is also obvious from the text that Mu'awiyah equated half a *sa'* of wheat to one *sa'* of others on the basis of value. Abu Sa'id says, "That is the valuation of Mu'awiyah, which I do not accept or follow."[24]

It gives comfort of mind to remember that the *sa'* of other foodstuffs is clearly ordained in the saying, while nothing perfect is reported on wheat. The question of Mu'awiyah is based on prices which may differ from time to time, and if the principle of value is applied, it may give inconsistent results today, since, e.g., the price of one *sa'* of date today equals the price of several *sa'* of wheat.[25]

With the above in mind, it seems the only way out of this dispute is to consider the obligation as one *sa'* of the most common items of foodstuff, and if wheat is more expensive than other items, half a *sa'* may be applied on wheat. In all cases, payment of one *sa'* is always better.

Is it permissible to pay more than one *sa'* ?

Strangely enough, some Malikite writings express dislike of giving more than one *sa'*, since a *sa'* is the *Shari'ah* prescription and it should be binding just as it is disliked to increase in worships.[26] This argument is not very convincing, since though it is a worship, *zakah* is also a socio-financial obligation, so paying more than is due does not sidetrack it from its objectives; in fact, it is better. The Qur'an says "Whoever volunteers more, it is indeed better for him,[27] in regard to compensation payment for breaking the fast of a day of Ramadan (which is the food for a person in need.) Ahmad and Abu Daud report from Ubai bin Ka'b that the required amount of *zakah* due from a certain man was one one-year-old she-camel, but he wanted to give a better she-camel to the collector, saying that the required one was too young to be used for riding or to give milk, but Ubai [the collector] refused to accept it, and they went to the Prophet (p) for judgement. The Prophet said, "This is what is obligated on you, but if you want to volunteer more, God shall reward you for it, and we accept to take it." Then he ordered the bigger camel to be accepted and prayed God to bless the man's wealth.[28]

The above clear text indicates that giving more than is due is acceptable and rewardable. 'Ali says, "if God gives you prosperity, you should also give more."

The amount of a *sa'*

It was shown in volume one of this book that one *sa'* equals 2176 grams if measured in wheat. Since the *sa'* is a volume measure, if an item heavier than wheat is used (e.g. rice) more than 2176 grams should be given in order to make the volume of one *sa'*. Al Nawawi argues that the *sa'*, being a measure of volume, need not be estimated in weight, since food items have different weights; thus, a quantity equal to the volume measure of one *sa'* must be given, regardless of its weight.[29] Ibn Hazm adds that according to the residents of Madinah, a *sa'* is 5.33 ratl (in weight) but it differs from one item to another.[30]

Payment in kind

The sayings on *zakah* of *al fitr* mention a few food items, namely date, barley, raisin, and dried whole-milk yogurt. Some of their versions add wheat and corn. Are these the only kinds that can be paid? Malikites and Shafi'ites argue that these kinds are mentioned only as examples, and the requirement can be paid in the form of the most common food items in the payer's area or the most common food .the payer usually eats, according to some. Many Malikites believe that the month of Ramadan is the time during which the most common food item is determined,[31] while some Shafi'ites determine the most conmon food item on the day of *'Id al fitr*,[32] as long as it is eaten by most people. If several kinds are equally common, any of these kinds is suitable. Certainly, it is preferred to give the best among them.[33]

On the other hand, Hanbalites believe *fitrah* can only be-paid in the form of one of the five items mentioned above, as long as paying one of them is available and affordable.[34] Abu Hanifah and Ahmad are quoted as permitting payment in the form of flour.[35]

It seems that the Prophet (p) mentions these items merely as examples, since they were the foodstuffs known to the Arabs at his time. Consequently, if rice or corn are more used in certain lands today, payment of *zakah* of *al fitr* must be in their forms.

Ibn Hazm argues that only date or barley is acceptable as payment on the grounds of a report from Abu Mujliz that "I asked Ibn 'Umar, 'God gave us prosperity; is not wheat better than date in payment of fitrah?' He said 'My colleagues went their way and I like to follow it.'"[36] Ahmad Shakir comments that taking all the sayings on the matter together makes it clear that Ibn Hazm's argument is groundless. Mu'awiyah, for example, suggested wheat and no Companion objected to it. (Although Abu sa'id objected to the reduced quantity, he did not disapprove the kind.) The report from Ibn 'Umar given by Ibn Hazm is no evidence, since, in his personal action, Ibn 'Umar is known to be very particular in following literally the footsteps of the Prophet (p) without criticizing other Companions as long as what they do is permissible. *Zakah* of *al fitr* is legislated in order to make the poor happy on the day of the feast and giving an item like date or barley in a country where people are not accustomed to eating them does not solve the poor person's problem.[37]

Payment in value

The three leading scholars do not approve of payment in value. When Ahmad was asked about payment of *zakah* of *al fitr* in money, he answered, "I am afraid it is not satisfactory, since it is in opposition to the tradition of the Messenger of God." When he was told that it is said 'Umar bin 'Abd al 'Aziz used to accept money as payment of this *zakah*, Ahmad said, "Would they abandon the saying of the Messenger of God for the saying of someone else? Ibn 'Umar said 'The Messenger of God (p) imposed *zakah* of *al fitr* . . . .' and God says 'Obey God and obey the Messenger.'"[38] This is also the view of Malik and al Shafi'i.[39] Ibn Hazm shares the same view, on the grounds that money is only a substitute payment, and a substitute is not valid except by mutual agreement. Since *zakah* is due to God, one cannot negotiate a substitute.[40]

On the other hand, al Thawri, Abu Hanifah, and his disciples believe it is permissible to pay *zakah* of *al fitr* in value. This is also reported from 'Umar bin 'Abd al 'Aziz and al Basri.[41] Ibn Abi Shaibah reports from 'Awn, "I heard the letter of 'Umar bin 'Abd al 'Aziz being read to 'Adi in Basrah (where he was governor). It said that one-half a *dirham* per person must be taken from all salary earners."[42] Al Hasan is reported as saying, "It is permissible to pay *zakah* of *al fitr* in *dirhams*."[43] Abu Ishaq says, "I attended their (the predecessors) paying of the *zakah* of Ramadan is *dirhams*,"[44] and 'Ata is reported to have given *zakah* of *al fitr* in silver currency.[45]

This view is supported by the following:

A. The saying of the Prophet "Make them (the poor) rich on this day." Enriching them can be done by giving money as much as by giving food, more so since the poor and destitute need clothing and other materials in addition to food.

B. The Companions allowed giving one half a *sa'* of wheat in place of the foodstuffs mentioned in the saying. This is obviously based on the value, as explained by Mu'awiyah: "I think half a *sa'* of wheat from Syria equals one *sa'* of date."

C. It is easier, especially nowadays, to give money than foodstuffs, and most useful to the poor in most countries.

Lastly, It seems to me that the Prophet (p) mentions certain food items simply because paying them was easier during his time, since currency was scarce and its value not constant.

At the end of this chapter, three points need to be explained: First, Abu Hanifah and Abu Yusuf argue that when money is paid, its amount must equal the value of the required amount of wheat, barley, or date, while Muhammad believes only the value of wheat is considered. In my opinion, the value of the most common food item is the determinant of the required amount of money.[46] Second, when *zakah* of *al fitr* is paid in kind in the form of any of the items mentioned in the saying, the amount required is one *sa'* (or one-half a *sa'* for wheat) regardless of the relative value of the item selected as payment.[47] Third, Hanafites do not agree on which is better, payment in money or payment in kind. Their argument is based on which method is more beneficial for the poor.[48] Consequently, in cases where money is more useful to the poor, payment must by done in cash, and vice versa.

Footnotes

1.   *Hujjat Allah al Baighah*, Vol. 2, p. 509.

2.   *Nail al Awtar*, Vol. 4, p. 183, and *al Mughni*, Vol. 3, p. 57.

3.   *Sharh al Nawawi on Sahih Muslim*, Vol. 7, p. 60.

4.   *Ibid.*

5.   *Ibid*, pp. 61-62.

6.   *Fath al Bari*, Vol. 3, p. 374.

7.   His two disciples treat wheat like date. The author of *al Durr al Mukhtar* says this is the view upheld in this school. See *al Durr al Mukhtar*, Vol. 2, p. 83. As for raisin, there are conflicting reports from Abu Hanifah.

8. *Nail al Awtar, op. cit.*

9. *Al Muhalla*, Vol. 6, pp. 128-131, and *Nasb al Rayah*, Vol. 2, pp. 446-447.

10. See the versions of this saying in Abu Daud, chapter on *zakah*, *al Daraqutni*, pp. 223-224, *al Muhalla*, Vol. 6, p. 121, *al Sunan al Kubra*, Vol. 4, pp. 167-168, and *Nasb al Rayah*, Vol. 2, pp. 406-410.

11. *Nail al Awtar*, Vol. 4, p. 183, *al Muhalla*, Vol. 6, pp. 122-123, and *Nasb al Rayah*, Vol. 4, pp. 418-423.

12. *Nail al Awtar, Ibid.*

13. *Ibid.*

14. This is opposed by the sayings reported by al Hakim, Vol. 1, pp. 410-411, about wheat; al Dhahabi confirms the correctness of two of them--one from Ibn 'Umar, and one through Ibn Ishaq from Abu Sa'id. Both of them mention wheat. But al Baihaqi and Ibn Khuzaimah argue that wheat is not actually mentioned in these sayings and is mere error on the part of some narrators.

15. *Fath al Bari*, Vol. 3, p. 374, and *al Muhalla*, Vol. 6, pp. 128-131.

16. *Bada'i al Sana'i,* Vol. 2, p. 72, and *Nasb al Rayah* Vol. 2, p. 418.

17. *Nail al Awtar*, Vol. 4, pp. 192-193, and *Fath al Bari, op. cit.*

18. *Fath al Bari,* Vol. 3, p. 373.

19. *Sharh al Nawawi on Sahih Muslim*, Vol. 7, p. 60, and *Fath al Bari*, Vol. 3, pp. 271-272.

20. Ibn Hajar says, "By using the word 'people' Ibn 'Umar meant Mu'awiyah and his followers." This appears explicitly in the version from Ayub from Nafi' which is reported by al Humaidi in his *Musnad*. It is also reported by Ibn Khuzaimah. See *Fath al Bari*, Vol. 3, p. 372.

21. *Zad al Ma'ad,* Vol. 1, pp. 313-314.

22. Al Nasa'i, Ahmad, Ibn al Madini, and others say al Hasan did not hear from Ibn 'Abbas, since the former was in Basrah when the latter was in Madinah. But Ahmad Shakir argues that their having met each other cannot be ruled out, since they both lived in the era of 'Uthman and 'Ali, See *al Sunan al Kubra, al Jawhar al Naqi,* Vol. 4, pp. 167-169, and *Nasb el Rayah*, Vol. 2, pp. 418-419.

23. *Zad al Ma'ad, op. cit.*

24. Reported by Ibn Khuzaimah and al Hakim in their correct collections. See *al Fath* Vol. 3, p. 375, al Mustadrak, Vol. 1, p. 411, *Al Muhalla*, Vol. 6, p. 130, and *Nasb al Rayah*, Vol. 2, pp. 417-418.

25.   *Al Fath*, Vol. 3, p. 374.

26.   *Al Sharh al Kabir by al Dardir*, Vol. 1, p. 508.

27.   *Sura al Baqarah*, 2:184.

28.   Reported by Ahmad, Abu Daud, and al Hakim. The latter grades it correct and is followed by al Dhahabi.

29.   *Al Rawdah*, Vol. 2, pp. 301-302.

30.   *Al Muhalla*, Vol. 5, p. 245.

31.   *Hashiat al Dusuqi*, Vol. 1, p. 505.

32.   *Al Rawdah*, Vol. 2, p. 305.

33.   *Ibid.*

34.   *Al Mughni*, Vol. 3, p. 62.

35.   *Ibid.*

36.   *Al Muhalla*, Vol. 6, pp. 118-126.

37.   *Ibid*, p. 131-132.

38.   *Sura al Nisa*, 4:59.

39.   *Al Mughni*, Vol. 3, p. 65.

40.   *Al Muhalla*, Vol. 6, p. 137.

41.   *Al Mughni*, Vol. 3, p. 65, and *al Muhalla*, Vol. 6, p. 130. It is correctly reported from 'Umar bin 'Abd al 'Aziz.

42.   *Musannaf Ibn Abi Shaibah*, Vol. 4, p. 37.

43.   *Ibid*, p. 38.

44.   *Ibid.*

45.   *Ibid.*

46.   *Radd al Muhtar*, Vol. 2, p. 80.

47.   *Ibid*, p. 83, as quoted from *al Bada'i*.

48.   *Ibid.*

CHAPTER FOUR

TIME OF PAYMENT

Muslims unanimously agree that *zakah* of *al fitr* is obligated upon the end of Ramadan, in accordance with the previously mentioned saying from Ibn 'Umar that "The Messenger of God (p) imposed *zakah* of fast-breaking of Ramadan . . . " However, they differ in regard to the exact time this obligation becomes due. Al Shafi'i, Ahmad, Ishaq, al Thawri, and Malik (in one narration) believe *zakah* of *al fitr* is due at sunset on the last day of Ramadan, i.e. when the last day ends. Abu Hanifah and his disciples, al Laith, Abu Thawr, and Malik (in another narration) say it is due at dawn on the day of the feast, since it aims at bringing happiness to the poor on that day.[1] The difference has only one application: whether new born babies and persons who die during that night should be counted in calculating the amount of *zakah*.[2]

The last time for payment

Al Bukhari and Muslim report from Ibn 'Umar "The Messenger of God (p) ordered *zakah* of *al fitr* paid prior to *'Id* prayers." 'Ikrimah says "One should pay *zakah* before making the prayers. God says, 'But those will prosper who pay *zakah*, and gloriy the name of their Lord, and then pray.'"[3] Ibn Khuzaimah reports from Kathir, from his father from his grandfather, that the Messenger of God (p) was asked about this verse and answered, "It was sent down in regard to *zakah* of *al fitr*."[4] But this saying is weak because Kathir is very unreliable.[5] Moreover, the verse is Makkan, while *zakah* of *al fitr* was imposed after the fasting of Ramadan was prescribed in Madinah. On the other hand, al Bukhari and Muslim report from Abu Sa'id, "We used to pay, during the lifetime of the Messenger of God (p) on the day of breaking the fast . . . .," I implying that all the day is time for payment.

Al Shafi'i suggests that this *zakah* can be paid during the whole day of *'Id*, although the best time for payment is early morning before *'Id* prayers. Agreeing with al Shafi'i the majority of scholars believe delaying payment until the time for *'Id* prayers passes is undesirable, since *zakah* of *al fitr* is meant to enrich the poor on that day, so they must be given time to use it during the day itself.

Ibn Hazm says it is prohibited to delay payment until after the time of prayers, and that if *zakah* is not paid before prayers, it must nevertheless be paid later, because the due right to the poor must be fulfilled, despite the violation of God's right to payment before prayers.[6]   Al Shawkani argues that timing the payment before prayers is obligatory on the basis of the saying from Ibn 'Abbas, "He who pays it before prayers, for him it is acceptable as *zakah*, and for him who pays it after prayers it is a charity like other charities." Delaying *zakah* of *al fitr* until after the day of *'Id* ends is unanimously considered sinful, in spite of the fact that it must be paid anyway.[7]

The question of whether *zakah* of *al fitr* can be paid before the day of *'Id* also arises. Ibn Hazm's answer is an absolute no.[8] Ahmad argues that it is permissible to pay it one or two days before *'Id*, on the grounds of the saying reported by al Bukhari from Ibn 'Umar that "The Companions used to give it away one or two days before *'Id*." This is also the Malikite view.[9] Some Hanbalites say it can be paid as early as the middle of the month of Ramadan. Al Shafi'i allows it to be paid as early as the beginning of Ramadan, since, according to him, the reason for its obligation is either fasting or breaking the fast, and ones either of these exists, *zakah* of *al fitr* can be paid.[10] Abu Hanifah argues that, like *zakah* on wealth, *zakah* of *al fitr* can be paid as early as the beginning of the year. Lastly, Zaidis allow payment two years in advance.[11]

It is noticeable that the view of Ahmad and Malik seems closer to fulfilling the objective of *zakah* of *al fitr*, although one must confess that starting the collection and distribution process in the middle of the month is easier and more convenient, especially if the state or a social organization takes this responsibility.

Footnotes

1.   *Al Mughni*, Vol. 3, pp. 67-68.

2.   *Bidayat al Mujtahid,* Vol. 1, p. 273.

3.   *Sura al A'la*, 87:14-15.

4.   *Nail al Awtar*, Vol. 4, p. 195.

5.   Al Shafi'i and Abu Daud describe him as a "cornerstone of falsehood." See *al Mizan*, Vol. 3, pp. 406-407, *Tahdhib al Tahdhib*, Vol. 8, pp. 421-423, *al Tarikh of al Bukhar*i, Vol. 4, p. 217, *al Jarh wa al Ta'dill*, Vol. 2, p. 154, and *al Mustadrak,* Vol. 1, p. 128.

6.   *Al Muhalla*, Vol. 6, p. 143.

7.   *Nail al Awtar*, Vol. 4, p. 195.

8.   *Al Muhalla*, Vol. 6, p. 143 The view of Ibn Hazm coincides with that of the Imami school; see *Fiqh al Imam Ja'far*, Vol. 2, p. 106.

9.   *Al Sharh al Kabir with Hashiat al Dusuqi,* Vol. 1, p. 508.

10.   *Al Mughni,* Vol. 3, pp. 58-69.

11.   *Al Bahr,* Vol. 2, p. 196.

CHAPTER FIVE

RECIPIENTS OF *ZAKAH* OF *AL FITR*

Muslim poor and needy

According to Ibn Rushd, it is unanimously agreed upon that *zakah* of *al fitr* must be given to Muslim poor and needy, since the Prophet (p) referred to them when he said "Make them satisfied on the day of fitr." The majority of scholars do not accept giving this religious due to poor people of the Pledge. Abu Hanifah believes this is permissible and some others allow giving only monks of people of the Pledge.[1] Ibn Abi Shaibah reports that Abu Maisarah used to give *zakah* of *al fitr* to monks.[2] Similar reports come from 'Amr bin Maimun, 'Amr bin Shurahbil, and Murrah al Hamadani.[3] This is undoubtedly a humanistic gesture from Muslim jurists in trying to make everybody happy on the day of the feast.

Can it be given to the eight categories who receive *zakah*?

The Shafi'i school argues that, like any other *zakah*, *zakah* of *al fitr* must be distributed equally among the same eight categories, except when distributed by the payer--in which case the categories of "workers of the *zakah* fund" and "those whose hearts are being reconciled" are excluded.[4] This is also the view of Ibn Hazm.[5] Ibn al Qayyim rejects this view and argues that the practice of the Prophet (p) and his Companions was to give it only to the poor and needy. This is so, he continues, to the extent that some Hanbalites believe it is not permissible to distribute it otherwise. Ibn al Qayyim adds that this opinion carries more weight.[6] Malikites assert that this *zakah* must be paid exclusively to the poor and needy, even if it must be shipped to another country at the expense of the payer, because of lack of poor deservants in the land where it is due.[7] Al Hadi, al Qasim, and Abu Talib share the view of the Malikites.

Three opinions can be distinguished:

1. *Zakah* of *al fitr* must be distributed among the eight categories, which is al Shafi'i's view.

2. It is exclusively for the poor and needy.

3   It can be distributed to all eight groups, to some of them, or to the poor alone, since it is included under the general text "*Sadaqat* are only to the poor and needy . . ." This is the view of the majority of jurists.

It is important to notice that the argument for the exclusivity of payment to the poor based on the saying "Make them satisfied on this day" is not specific in preventing giving to other categories. It is like the saying that *zakah* is "taken from the rich to be rendered to the poor", yet *zakah* is paid to the eight categories. Thus, *zakah* of *al fitr* must be covered by the general text of the verse mentioned above, although it is conceivable that one must give priority to the poor and needy.

Categories excluded from *zakah*

As in the case of *zakah* on wealth, *zakah* of *al fitr* must not be given to disbelievers, apostates, the rich, or persons who can earn. It must also not be paid to persons for whose expenses the payer is responsible, such as the payer's father, son, or wife. The same details studied with regard to *zakah* on wealth apply here.

Lastly, the *zakah* payer may give his or her *zakah* to one or more poor persons, and by the same token, *zakah* collected from several payers may be given to one or more recipient, since there is no evidence to prevent any of these cases,[9] although some jurists dislike dividing one's *zakah* among several recipients and giving the *zakah* of several payers to one recipient on the grounds that this may not fulfill the objective of enriching all the poor on the day of *'Id*.[10]

As for transporting *zakah* of *al fitr* from one land to another, the same principle applied on other forms of *zakah* is applicable here; i.e., first the poor and needy in the area where *zakah* is due must be satisfied and the leftover may be transported, except in case of emergencies or higher priority.[11]

Footnotes

1.   *Bidayat al Mujtahid*, Vol. 1, p. 73.

2.   *Al Musannaf*, Vol. 4, p. 39.

3.   *Al Mughni*, Vol. 3, p. 78.

4.   *Al Majmu'*, Vol. 6, p. 144.

5.   *Al Muhalla*, Vol. 6, pp. 143-145.

6.   *Zad al Ma'ad*, Vol. 1, p. 315.

7.   *Al Sharh al Kabir wa Hashiat al Dusuqi*, Vol. 1, pp. 508-509.

8.   *Nail al Awtar*, Vol. 4, p. 195.

9.   *Al Bahr*, Vol. 2, p. 197.

10. *Al Durr al Mukhtar*, Vol. 2, p. 85, and *al Sharp, op. cit.*

11. *Al Bahr*, Vol. 2, p. 203.

FIQH AL ZAKAH

PART EIGHT

DUES AND TAXES OTHER THAN *ZAKAH*

1. The opinion that there must be no other financial dues besides *zakah*

2. The view that dues besides *zakah* may be imposed

3. Discussion and Analysis

CHAPTER ONE

THE OPINION THAT THERE ARE NO OTHER FINANCIAL DUES BESIDE *ZAKAH*

Many jurists argue that the only financial due approved in Islam is *zakah*.[1] Whoever fulfills the requirement of *zakah* will have his or her wealth purified, and need not pay anything else except voluntarily. This is the predominant view among the later generations of jurists.

Sayings used in support of this view

1. Al Bukhari, Muslim, and others report from Talhah, "A man from Najd came to the Messenger of God (p). His hair was uncombed, and his loud voice [was heard] from a distance. He does not even understand what he says, until he came close to the Messenger of God (p) and started asking him about Islam. The Messenger of God (p) said, 'Five prayers in the day and night' The man said 'Do I have to do more?' The Prophet said, 'No, unless you volunteer.' The Messenger of God (p) continued, 'And the fasting of Ramadan.' The man said, 'Do I have to fast other than this?' The Prophet answered, 'No, unless you volunteer . . .' and then the Prophet mentioned *zakah*. The man said, 'Do I have to pay anything else besides it? The Prophet said, 'No, unless you volunteer.' The man turned around and left saying, 'I shall not do anything more nor less than these.' The Messenger of God (p) commented, 'He will be successful if he honors this promise" or "he will enter the Garden if he honors this promise."[2]

2. Al Bukhari reports from Abu Hurairah, "A bedouin Arab came to the Prophet (p) and said, 'Guide me to something which if I do I shall enter the Garden. The Prophet said, 'Worship God and do not associate partners with Him whatsoever, and pray the obligated prayer, and fulfill the obligated *zakah*, and fast Ramadan.' The man said, 'By the name of He in Whose Hand is my soul, I shall not add anything to those.' When the man left, the Messenger of God (p) said, 'He who it pleases him to see a man who is among the dwellers of the Garden may look at this man.'"

In the first saying, the Prophet (p) says that there is nothing obligatory except *zakah*. This saying is a clear text to this effect. In both sayings, the two men declare that they will perform nothing besides the obligatory *zakah*, and the Prophet (p) accepts that declaration and states that this is sufficient for entering the Garden. If there were other financial obligations besides *zakah*, these men would not deserve to enter the Garden unless those other obligations are fulfilled.

3. Al Tirmidhi reports from Abu Hurairah, "The Prophet (p) said, 'If you pay the *zakah* due on your wealth you will have fulfilled all that is obligated on you.'"[3]

4. Al Hakim reports from Jabir that the Prophet (p) said, "If you pay the *zakah* on your wealth, you will have turned away its evil from you."[4]

5. Al Hakim reports from Umm Salamah that she used to wear some pieces of gold as ornaments. She asked the Prophet, "Is this hoarding?" He answered, "If you pay its due *zakah*, it is not like hoarding."[5] In some versions of this saying, the Prophet says, "Anything that reaches the amount that is *zakatable*, and its due *zakah* is paid, is not hoarding."[6] This saying indicates that the Qur'an's warning against hoarding does not apply to persons who pay *zakah* on their treasures, which indirectly means such individuals are not obligated to pay anything else. Some supporters of this view add another saying in which the Prophet (p) is reported to have said, "On wealth there are no dues except *zakah*."[7]

It is obvious that the first two sayings are correct. The third saying has a weak chain, and the fourth one is considered *nawquf* [a statement of a Companion not attributed to the Prophet] according to the most acceptable scrutinization. As for the fifth saying, there is criticism of its chain. The saying "On wealth there are no dues except *zakah*" is very weak, and, without the slightest hesitation unacceptable. In fact, it is incorrect and wrong.

Supporters of this opinion also argue that all texts which indicate the existence of financial obligations besides *zakah* can be interpreted as references to mere desirability and not to obligation. They also claim that before *zakah* was mandated, different financial obligations were obligatory, but when *zakah* was revealed to the Prophet as a financial obligation, all previous dues were annulled. Additionally, they reject a report by al Tirmidhi from Fatimah bint Qais that the Prophet (p) said, "There are other dues on wealth besides *zakah*"[8], on the ground, that al Tirmidhi himself grades it weak and it is decried as inauthentic by saying critics.[9]

Footnotes

1.   The author of *al Bahr* attributes this to the majority, Vol. 2, p, 138.

2.   Reported by the five -- al Tirmidhi is excluded. See *Majma'al al Zawa'id*, Vol. 1, p.

3. Reported by al Tirmidhi, Vol. 3, pp 97-99. He comments, "good and strange." Also reported by al Hakim, who comments, "correct". This is approved by al Dhahabi, Vol. 1, p. 390, But in *al Talkhis*, p. 177, Ibn Hajar says its chain is weak.

4. Reported by Ibn Khuzaimah, in his correct collection, and al Hakim, Vol. 1, p. 390, who comments, "correct according to the criteria of Muslim." This is approved by al Dhahabi, In *al Fath*, Vol. 3, p, 175. Al Hafiz says, "Abu Zar'ah, al Baihaqi, and others give more weight to it as a statement of Jabir himself, as it is reported by al Bazzar.

5. Reported by al Hakim, Vol. 1, p.390, who comments "correct according to the criteria of al Bukhari." This is approved by al Dhahabi. However, its chain is criticized. See of Vol. 1, of this book.

6. Reported by Abu Daud.

7. Some attribute this saying to the collection of *Sunan Ibn Majah*. But in *al Majmu*, al Nawawi says, "It is very weak, not known," Vol. 5, p. Al Baihaqi says, "Our colleague scholars mention this saying in their suspended reports. I do not know of a chain for it." See *al Sunan al Kubra*, Vol. 4, p.84. Al Hafiz al 'Iraqi objects, arguing that it is reported by Ibn Majah as "There is a right on wealth besides *zakah*" the same way it is reported by al Tirmidhi. See *Tarh al Tathrib* Vol. 4, p. 18. This means the word "no" [laisa] was included by a copying error. This is explained by the late Ahmad Shakir in his comment on quote no. 2530 in al Tabari's explanation. He gives the following as evidence: One, al Tabari reports the same saying under no. 2527, via the same chain of Yahya bin Adam from which Ibn Majah reports, and the text is "Indeed, there is a right on wealth besides *zakah*." Two, Ibn Kathir in his explanation attributes the saying to both Ibn Majah and al Tirmidhi together without any distinction between their two texts: the same is done by al Nabulsi in the *Dhakha'ir al Mawarith*, under no. 11699. Three, al Baihaqi says he does not know of chain for the saying, and if Ibn Majah actually reported it with the "no", al Baihaqi must have known it, and so must al Nawawi, who says that the saying as stated is not known. It seems that the explanation of the late Ahmad Shakir with those reasons is very valid and convincing.

8. Al Tirmidhi comments on this saying, "Its chain is not that good. In it, Abu Maimun al A'war is weak." Al Tabari also mentions it, Vol. 3, pp. 176-1771 under no. 2527 and 2530, so does al Darimi, Vol. 1, p. 385. Ibn Majah reports this saying via Yahya bin Adam no. 1786, and al Baihaqi in his *al Sunan al Kubra*, Vol. 4, p. 84.

9. Ibn Hajar gives the biography of Abu Hamzah, Maimun al A'war al Qassab in his *al Tahdhib*; so does al Bukhari in *al Tarikh al Kabir*, no 4-1-343 and Ibn Abi Hatim in *al Jarh wa al Ta'dil*, no. 4-1-235 and 236.

CHAPTER TWO

THE VIEW THAT OTHER DUES BESIDES
ZAKAH MAY BE IMPOSED

Other scholars, as early as the era of the Companions and Followers, believe there are other financial dues besides *zakah*. These include 'Umar, 'Ali, Abu Dharr, A'ishah, Abu Hurairah, al Hasan bin 'Ali, and Fatimah bint Qais (all Companions), as well as the Followers al Sha'bi, Mujahid, Taus, 'Ata, and several others.

The evidence

These people argue that the verse "It is not righteousness that ye turn your faces toward east or west, but it is righteousness to believe in God and the Last Day, and the angels, and the Book, and the messengers, to spend of your sustenance -- in spite of your love for it -- for your kin, for orphans, for the needy, for the wayfarer, for those who ask, and for the ransom of slaves, to be steadfast in prayers and practice *zakah* to fulfill the pledges which ye have made, and to be firm and patient in pain and adversity, and through out all periods of panic. Such are the people of truth, the God fearing" indicates there are dues besides *zakah*. Al Tirmidhi and others report from Fatimah bint Qais that she (or someone else) asked the Prophet (p) about *zakah*. He answered, "Indeed there are dues besides *zakah* on wealth." Then the Prophet recited this verse from sura al Baqarah: "It is not righteousness . . . ." Despite its weakness, al Tirmidhi says this saying is supported and strengthened by the verse. In fact, the verse alone is sufficient evidence, since it makes giving money one of the conditions of righteousness, in addition to prayers and *zakah*. Al Qurtubi comments, "Even despite the criticism addressed to the saying, its meaning remains correct, because it is implied by the verse itself, which reads' . . . to be steadfast in prayer and practice *zakah*.' It mentions *zakah* along with prayers, which means the words at the beginning of the verse '. . . to spend of your sustenance' refer to other payments, not included in the word '*zakah*'. Otherwise, this verse would have unnecessary repetition.[1]

No one can argue that the spending mentioned in the verse refers merely to voluntary contributions, since the verse was revealed as a reply to the Jewish vogue for formality and ritualism, to show the elements of true righteousness. Thus the verse lists only basic elements, as is obvious from the other elements mentioned in the verse: believing in God and the Last Day, and practicing prayer and *zakah*, fulfilling pledges and contracts, etc. etc..

Abu 'Ubaid strongly rejects al Dahhak's claim that this verse is annulled because *zakah* annuls every other *sadaqah* mentioned in the Qur'an. Abu 'Ubaid comments, "Such a very daring claim has no substance or supporting evidence. The words of God cannot be annulled by people's claims. If al Dahhak's claim were correct, a phrase in the verse, 'Practice *zakah*,' must have annulled another phrase in the very same verse, 'spend out of your sustenance.' Such a thing is not possible!"[2] Moreover the verse gives information about the character of the righteous, and verses which give information relating to creed or basic beliefs are not subject to annulment. Abu 'Ubaid reports from Ibn 'Abbas that "This verse was sent dow in Madinah at the time when obligations, penalties, and other behavioral requirements were being revealed."[3]

The second proof: dues on agriculture

After describing the bounty God produces for mankind, including gardens with trelisses, dates, grains, pomegranates, olives, etc. God says "Eat of their fruits in their season, but render the dues that are proper on the day that the harvest is gathered. But waste not by excess, for God loves not the wasters."[4] It is argued that this "proper due" is different from *zakah* on the following grounds:

A. The verse is Makkan and it was sent long time before *'ushr* was obligated during the Madinan period.

B. The verse orders giving the due that is proper on fruits on the day of harvest. This is not the time of *zakah* payment, since 'ushr is paid after cleaning and drying of the produce.

C. The concluding sentence in the verse "Waste not by excess . . ." is inapplicable to *zakah* which is an amount defined by *Shari'ah* and unsusceptible to extravagance or excess.[5]

Any claim that the proper dues mentioned in this verse were later annulled by *zakah* cannot be substantiated, because annulment cannot be supported by mere probability and claims. Ibn Hazm adds, "Any person's claim of annulment can only be substantiated by a text linked to the Messenger of God (p). Otherwise, anyone could claim the annulment of any verse or saying. To say any text is annulled is equal to saying that the obedience to this text of God is not needed. This can be done by the Legislator alone."[6] He continues, "What then is the proper due ordained by the above-mentioned verse? It is undoubtedly different from *zakah*. It requires that owners give on the date of harvesting some of their produce. The verse, however, does not require any definited amount or percentage. This is the opinion of some of the predecessors."[7]

In explaining this due, Ibn 'Umar says, "They used to give something besides *zakah*" 'Ata says "Whoever is present at the harvest must be given some of the produce. This is not *zakah*." Mujahid says, "The present poor persons must be given some of it." He adds, "At the time of planting they should be given something like a handful, and at the time of harvesting they should also be given." Ibrahim says "the poor should be given a bunch of the produce."[8] Similar statements are attributed to Abu al 'Aliyah, Sa'id bin Jubair, 'Ali bin al Husain and al Rabi' bin Anas.[9] Ibn Kathir says "God censures those who harvest and do not give charity, as in the story of the owners of the garden in *sura al Qalam*."[10]

We discussed earlier the issue of whether this proper due is *zakah* or not. What is important here is to assert that some great Companions, like Ibn 'Umar, and Followers like 'Ata, Mujahid, and al Nakha'i believe this verse speaks about a due on wealth besides *zakah*.

The third proof: dues on livestock

We have several authentic sayings that describe the prescription of dues on camels and horses. Al Bukhari reports from Abu Hurairah that the Prophet (p) said, "Camels whose proper dues are not given appear on the Day of Resurrection against their owner the strongest they have ever been, trampling him with their hooves , and sheep whose proper dues are not given appear before their owner the strongest they have ever been, trampling him with their hooves and knocking him with their horns." The Prophet (p) adds, "One of their dues is to milk them when they come to water [and to give away that milk]."[11] Apparently, the last sentence of the saying covers both camels and sheep, especially since in a version of the saying reported by Muslim and Abu Daud, the same sentence comes just after the talk about camels.[12] It is obvious that this sentence is part of the saying and is not added by the narrator. Al Bukhari reports the last sentence alone in reference to sharecropping in another chapter.[13]

Al Nasa'i reports from Jabir, "The Messenger of God (p) says, 'He who owns camels, cows, and sheep who does not give their dues, will be made to stand for them on the Day of Judgement on a flat ground, and then the animals with hard hooves will trample him, and those with horns will knock him with their horns. On that Day, none of them shall have its horns broken or cut off.' We asked, 'O Messenger of God, what are their proper dues?' He answered, 'To lend the male for breeding, to lend the bucket (drawer) for watering, and to give rides on them in the way of God. . . .,"[14] A similar saying is reported by Muslim from Jabir.[15] In another saying , the from Jabir, the Messenger of God (p) was asked, "What is the proper due of camels?" He said, "To slaughter the fat among them [for charity] to lend the male for breeding, and to milk them [for the poor] on the day of watering."[16]

Al Sharid says, "A man came to the Prophet (p) asking him about camels. The Messenger of God (p) said, 'Slaughter the fat among them [for charity], and give rides on the strong and fast among them and milk them [for the poor] on the day of watering.'"[17]

These sayings all indicate that the dues mentioned are obligatory. They are all different froms *zakah*. Ibn Hazm says, "It is obligatory on each owner of camels, cows, and sheep to milk them on the day they are watered, and to give what pleases him out of that milk for charity."[18] He continues, "whoever claims there are no rights in addition to *zakah* is wrong and has no base for his claim from either a text or *ijma'*. Everything that is prescribed by the Prophet (p) on wealth must be taken as obligatory. As for lending the bucket and the male for breeding, they are covered by the verse, '. . . but refuse to supply even neighborly needs.'"[19]

There are also correct reports about dues on horses, such as that of al Bukhari from Abu Hurairah that the Messenger of God(p) said, "Horses for one man are [a source of] reward, for another a means of sustenance, and for a third man a reason for guilt. He for whom they are a source of reward is the man who devotes them to fighting for the sake of God . . . they are a source of satisfaction for he who keeps them for personal use and as property without forgetting the right of God on them and their back-riding; for he who keeps them as a matter of pride, hypocrisy, and for fighting Muslims, they are a reason for sin."[20]

The fourth proof: the guest's right

We have correct saying that mandate a guest's right on a host from Khuwailid bin 'Amr. The Messenger of God (p) said, "He who believes in God and the Last Day must honor his guest. The guest's right is [to be hosted] one day and one night, and the kindness to the guest is [hosting him] three days. What is above that is a charity."[21] This indicates that honoring one's guest is obligatory, since it is related to the essence of faith, especially since what is above three days is considered charity.

In another saying from 'Abd Allah bin 'Amr, "Your body has a certain right on you, your eye indeed has a right on you, your guests indeed have a right on you, and your wife indeed has a right on you."[22] The right of guests is further emphasized in another saying from Abu Hurairah, "Any guest who appears among any people and remains deprived until morning has the right to take as much as his food would be, without any blame."[23] Al Miqdad bin Ma'dikarib narrates that the Messenger of God (p) said, "If a man hosts a guest, and the guest gets up in the morning still deprived, the guest's aid and support is the duty of every Muslim until the guest takes from the host's grain and wealth the equivalent of his food for the night,"[24] and "The food for night for the guest is obligatory on each Muslim host . He who has guests in his house and does not offer them food, it remains a debt on him."[25] Ibn Hazm says, Muslim reports from 'Uqbah bin 'Amir "We asked, 'O Messenger of God (p), you send us on certain missions and we stay overnight as guests of certain people, but they do not offer us food, so what do you see?' The Messenger of God replied, 'If you bed down at the houses of some people and they offer you whatever is suitable for guests, you should accept, but if they do not, then take from them the right of the guest that is obligatory on them.'" Ibn Hazm adds that al Bukhari reports from 'Abd al Rahman bin Abu Bakr "The Companions of al Suffah were poor people. The Prophet said, 'He who has food for two people must take with him a third one. He who has food for four people must take a fifth, and he who has food for five must take with him a sixth,' or whatever the Prophet said. Accordingly, Abu Bakr brought home with him three men and the Messenger of God brought ten."

These sayings indicate beyond any doubt that there is an emphasized right on the wealth of a Muslim host, to the extent that if this right is not given the whole Muslim community is called upon to help the guest obtain his right. Clearly enough, this right is not *zakah*. The guest may come anytime while *zakah* is obligated at definite times. Ibn Hazm says, "Offering food to the guest is an obligation on all Muslims, urban or bedouin, knowledgeable or ignorant; one night out of righteousness and three days out of kindness; what is beyond that is not obligatory, although it is encouraged. If a host withholds this due from the guest, the guest has the right to take it by force or through the court."[26]

Al Shawkani adds, "Scholars have several opinions on whether the right of the guest is obligatory or only encouraged. The majority believes that honoring guests is one of the good manners that are encouraged, while al Laith says it is obligatory on the host for one night only. The majority argues that the saying 'He who believes in God and the Last Day . . . ' encourages only and does not oblige."[27]

As for the majority's answer to the sayings about the right of the guest, al Shawkani notes:

Al Khattabi says "The right of the guest was obligatory at the time of the Prophet (p), when there was no state treasury that took care of guests, but guests must not have any right on individual Muslims' wealth. Some others argue that this was only at the beginning of Islam but not after it was well established..."[28] The truth is that honoring and offering food to guests must be obligatory for the following reasons: First, whoever does not offer the guest food is made punishable by these sayings, and penalty can only be inflicted for neglecting an obligation. Second, we must note the extreme emphasis in the saying on taking care of guests and the consideration of this action as related to faith. Third, the sentence in the saying "what is beyond that is charity" explicitly means that what is less than three days is not charity but obligation. Fourthly, the sentence, "The night of the guest is an obligatory due" is also an explicit prescription. Fifth, the sayings obligate other Muslims to aid and help the guest in order to secure his or her right. This gives the guest's right even more certainty . ... Once these points are granted, one realizes that the view of the majority is not substantiated. Thus the sayings that obligate caring for guests must be understood as restrictions of the general sayings that prohibit taking anything from Muslims without their consent. It is arbitrary to say the sayings about guests mandate mere sustenance of guests. By the same token, restricting the applicability of these sayings to bedouins in the desert is also baseless.[29]

The fifth proof

The Qur'an severely warns those who do not extend help to others. God says, "So woe to the worshipers who are neglectful of their prayers, those who want but to be seen by people, but refuse to extend even neighborly help."[30] Abu Daud reports from Ibn Mas'ud, "We understood extending neighborly help at the time of the Messenger of God (p) to mean lending the bucket and the cooking pot."[31]

Extending these small services is obligatory, because the Qur'an says "woe" to those who refuse to do it, equating it with neglecting prayers or loving to be seen by people. Such a severe warning cannot be given if this action were not obligatory. No doubt, extending such help is not included in *zakah,* so it must be an added obligation. Ibn Hazm reports from Ibn Mas'ud, "'Extending neighborly help' is giving what people used to borrow from each other, like the axe, the cooking pots, and similar things."[32]   He reports that Ibn 'Abbas explains "neighborly help" as "Lending household things," and in another version "Lending things."[33] Ibn Hazm also reports from 'Ali[34] and Umm 'Atiyah, "It is the help in household matters that is usually exchanged by people."[35] He also reports that Ibn 'Umar explains refusing to extend neighborly help as "The refusal to give the right due on wealth." Ibn Hazm adds, "This is consistent with what is mentioned earlier and with the views of 'Ikrimah, Ibrahim, and others. It is not known that any of the Companions disagreed on this matter."[36]

One must mention that Ibn Mas'ud's statement mentioned above has the same weight as a saying, because he gives the interpretation of the verse prevalent at the time of the Prophet (p), and if that interpretation happened to be incorrect, it would have been corrected by the Prophet or by the Revelation itself, as a mistake in understanding the Qur'an.

The sixth proof

There are several texts which overwhelmingly dictate that Muslims must cooperate in good doing, solidarity, and mutual help and support, and have mercy among themselves. There are texts that obligate feeding the indigent as a duty implied by brotherhood, faith and religion. God says, "And help ye one another in righteousness and piety, but help ye not one another in sin and rancor."[37] He describes the believers as "Compassionate amongst each other,"[38] and describes the path that one must follow to deserve reward from God: "But he hath made no haste on the path that is steep (and narrow), and what will explain to thee the path that is steep? It is freeing the bondsman, or giving food on a day of privation, to the orphan with claims of relation, or to the indigent down in the dust. Then will he be of those who believe and enjoin patience (constancy and self restraint), and enjoin deeds of kindness and compassion. Such are the companions of the right hand."[39] "And render to the kindred their due rights, and also to those in want and to the wayfarer,"[40] and "and to good to parents, kinsfolk, orphans, those in need, neighbors who are near, neighbors who are strangers, the companion by your side, the wayfarer, and what your right hands possess."[44]

Many verses exhort people to feed the destitute, considering such an act of benevolence a sign of faith and its neglect an implication of disbelief and denial of the Hereafter, such as "Seest thou one who denies the Judgement? Then such is one who repulses the orphan with harshness and encourages not the feeding of the indigent."[42] "They [unbelievers] will say 'We were not of those who prayed, nor were we of those who fed the indigent'"[43] and "This was he who would not believe in God most High, and would not encourage the feeding of the indigent."[44] The Messenger (p) describes the mutual solidarity, caring, and security of the Islamic society in several sayings: "The believer to the fellow believer is like a structure whose blocks are bound to [and streghthen] each other,"[45] "The example of Muslims in their mutual love, compassion, and mercy is like one single body. If one of its members aches, the other members respond with fever and insomnia,"[46] "He is not a believer who goes to sleep satiated while his neighbor besides him is hungry."[47] 'Ali narrates that the Prophet said, "Indeed, God prescribes on wealthy Muslims in their wealth contributions as much as satisfies the poor. The poor shall not suffer from hunger and nakedness except from repulsion by the rich. Verily God shall make the account difficult for them and punish them a severe punishment."[48]

Ibn Hazm defends this opinion

In his *al Muhalla*, Ibn Hazm strongly supports the view that besides *zakah*, there are other financial dues. He provides several arguments and quotes from the Qur'an, Sunnah, Companions, and Followers, and concludes, "God ordains the rich of each city to take complete care of the poor in that city. If *zakah* proceeds are not sufficient and there is no available fai' to be used, the government must force the wealthy to spend on the poor. There must be assignments for food, clothes for winter and summer, and shelter that protects them from rain, heat, sunshine, and the eyes of passers-by." His argument goes as follows:

A. From the Qur'an

God says, "And render to the kindred their due right, and also to those in want and to the wayfarer,"[48] and "And do good to parents, kinsfolk, orphans, those in need, neighbors who are near, neighbors who are strangers, the companion by your side, the wayfarer, and what your right hands possess."[50] Thus God imposes a due to the indigent and the wayfarer along with the right of the kindred, and prescribes good doing to parents, kinsfolk, needy, neighbors, and slaves. Good doing requires taking care of their physical needs. Refusing to take such care is undoubtedly wrong and sinful. In another verse God explains the reason for dwelling in Hell: "What led you into Hellfire? They will say, 'We were not of those who prayed, nor were we of those who fed the indigent'."[51] God, here, associates feeding the needy with obligatory prayers.

B. From the sayings

The Messenger of God is reported, through several chains all excellent in correctness, to have said, "He who has no mercy toward people shall not receive mercy from God."[52] Whoever has excess wealth and sees his Muslim brother hungry, naked, or lost, and does not extend help, is undoubtedly merciless. 'Abd al Rahman bin Abu Bakr says "The Companions or al Suffah were poor people, and the Messenger of God said, He who has food for two must take with him a third, and he who has food for four must take with him a fifth, or a sixth.'"[53] Ibn 'Umar narrates that the Messenger of God (p) said, "A Muslim is a brother of the fellow Muslim. He does not do him injustice or let him down."[54] Leaving a Muslim to hunger or cold while one has the ability to feed and clothe him is certainly letting him down! Abu Sa'id narrates from the Messenger of God (p), "He who has an extra ride must give it to him who has no ride, and he who has excess food must give to him who has no food." Abu Sa'id continues, "and the Prophet mentioned the kinds of wealth that he liked to mention, so many kinds that we saw that none of us has a right to any excess."[55] I believe there is unanimity among the Companions as stated by Abu Sa'id, about all that comes in this saying. Abu Musa narrates from the Prophet (p), "Feed the hungry and pay to release the captive."[56]

C. From Companions and Followers

'Umar says "If I still have ahead of me as much time as what is gone, I would take the excess wealth of the rich and distribute it among the poor migrants."[57] 'Ali says, "God prescribes on the wealth of the rich as much as is sufficient to satisfy the poor among them. If the latter suffer from hunger, nakedness, or exhaustion, it is because of privation by the rich. It is just that God ask them [the rich] the account on the Day of Resurrection and punish them for it." Ibn 'Umar says, "On wealth, there is a right besides *zakah*." 'A'ishah, al Hasan bin 'Ali, and Ibn 'Umar are known to have answered people who asked them for money "If you ask to pay for ransom of a heavy blood, or an overwhelming liability or depriving poverty, you have a right that is due." Abu 'Ubaidah and three hundred Companions on a journey were near the end of their provision of food, Abu 'Ubaidah ordered each individual's food be collected in two containers, and distributed equal rations to everyone. This represents an agreed-upon position of all these Companions, since none are known to have disagreed, We also have correct reports to the effect that al Sha'bi, Mujahid, Taus, and others all said, "There is a right on wealth besides *zakah*."

We know of no one who opposes this except al Dahhak's comment that "*Zakah* annuls every other right on wealth." The narration of al Dahhak is not even approved of, let alone his own opinion![58] The fact is, all those who accept al Dakkah's view are the first ones to differ with it in actual life, since they all believe there are rights on wealth other than *zakah*, which include providing for needy parents, for one's wife, and for slaves, feeding domestic animals, and paying debts and other liabilities. Furthermore, such people say he who is in such need of water that he is at the verge of death for want of it, is obligated to take water wherever it is found, and even to fight anyone who prevents him that right. What is the difference between fighting to avoid death from thirst and fighting to prevent death from hunger and nakedness? Indeed, the opponents' view is in opposition to *ijma'*, Qur'an, Sunnah, and analogy.

It is not permissible for any Muslim in need of food to eat the flesh of dead animals or the meat of the hog, while there exists lawful food that is in excess above the needs of its owner, whether the owner is Muslim or of the people of the Pledge. It is obligatory for the owner of excess food to feed the hungry; he who is in need does not have to eat from hog meat or the meat of a dead animal. In such cases, the poor person is permitted to fight until his right is secured. If he is killed, whoever killed him is sinful and must pay the ransom and be subjected to the due penalty (death), but if his repulsor is killed, he goes to the wrath of God because he is an aggressor, and God says, "But if one of them transgresses beyond bounds against the other, then fight ye all against the one party that transgresses until it complies with the command of God."[59] For reasons similar to these, Abu Bakr fought those who refused to pay *zakah*.[60]

Footnotes

1.   Al Tabari says, "If it is asked whether there are other dues obligatory on wealth besides *zakah*, the answer depends on the different interpretations of scholars. Some scholars believe there are obligatory dues in addition to *zakah*, based on this verse,

since God adds spending on kindred and others to prayers and practicing *zakah* in an additive form of expression. Thus, this spending must be different from *zakah*. Otherwise, it would be senseless repition, and God does not say senseless words. Each of these two additives must have different meaning." Al Tabari adds, "Other scholars believe the spending mentioned at the beginning of the verse is the same as *zakah* mentioned at its end." It seems that al Tabari is inclined toward the first opinion. See *Tafsir al Tabari*, Vol. 3, p. 348, and *Tafsir al Qurtubi*, Vol. 3, p. 42.

2. *Al Amwal*, pp. 357-358.

3. *Ibid.*

4. *Sura al An'am*, 6:141.

5. *Al Muhalla*, Vol. 5, pp. 216-217.

6. *Ibid.*

7. *Ibid.*

8. *Ibid.*

9. *Ibid.*

10. *Tafsir Ibn Kathir*, Vol. 2, pp. 181-182.

11. The correct collection of al Bukhari with the commentary of *Fath al Bari*, Vol. 3, pp. 172-173.

12. *Mukhtasar Sunan Abu Daud* by al Mundhiri, Vol. 2, p. 248.

13. Correct collection of al Bukhari, with commentary by al Sindi, Vol. 2, p. 34.

14. *Sunan al Nasa'i*, with *Sharh al Suyuti* and *Hashiat al Sindi*, Vol. 5, p, 27.

15. *Tarh al Tathrib*, Vol. 4, pp. 11-12.

16. The author of *Majma' al Zawa'id*, Vol. 3, p. 107, says, "Reported by al Tabarani in *al Awsat*; the people of its chain are those of the correct collections, except he from whom al Tabarani narrates. But Ibn Abi Hatim reports from the same and no one grades him weak."

17. Reported by al Tabarani in *al Kabir*; its chain is good; *ibid.*

18. *Al Muhalla*, Vol. 6, p.50.

19. *Sura al Ma'un*, 107:7.

20. Reported by al Bukhari, See *al Bukhari* with *Hashiat al Sindi*, Vol. 2, p. 33.

21. Reported by al Bukhari, Muslim, Malik, Abu Daud, and Ibn Majah. See *al Targhib*, Vol. 3, p.241.

22. Reported by al Bukhari - his version is above - Muslim, and others. *Ibid.*

23. Reported by Ahmad. The narrators of its chain are trustworthy, and al Hakim comments, "the chain is correct." See *al Targhib, Ibid.*

24. Reported by Abu Daud and al Hakim who says, "its chain is correct." *Ibid.*

25. Reported by Abu Daud and Ibn Majah, *al Targhib*, Vol. 3, p.241-242.

26. *Al Muhalla*, Vol. 9, p. 174.

27. *Nail al Awtar*, Vol. 2, pp. 162-163.

28. *Ibid.*

29. *Ibid.*

30. *Sura al Ma'un*, 107:4,5,7.

31. Abu Daud makes no comments on the saying. He is followed by al Mundhiri. See *Mukhtasar al Sunnan*, Vol. 2, p. 247. The saying is also reported by al Baihqi, Vol. 4, p.183.

32. Mentioned by Ibn Hazm via Ibn Abi Shaibah, *al Muhalla*, Vol. 9, p. 168.

33. *Ibid*, and *al Baihaqi*, Vol. 4, pp. 183-184.

34. *Al Muhalla, Ibid.*

35. *Ibid.*

36. *Ibid.*

37. *Sura al Ma'idah*, 5:2.

38. *Sura al Fath*, 48:29.

39. *Sura al Balad*, 95:11-18.

40. *Sura al Isra*, 17:26.

41. *Sura al Nisa'*, 4:36.

42. *Sura al Ma'un*, 107:1-3.

43. *Sura al Muddaththir*, 74:43-44.

44. *Sura al Haqqah*, 69:33-34.

45. Agreed upon.

46. Agreed upon.

47. Reported by al Tabarani and al Baihaqi; its chain is good.

48. In *al Targhib*, al Mundhiri says, 'reported by al Tabarani in *al Awsat* and *al Saghir*. Al Tabarani adds "Thabit bin Muhammad al Zahid is singled out in the chain." Al Mundhiri continues, "but Thabit is trustworthy and truthful, from whom al Bukhari and others report. Other narrators in the chain are all right. It is also reported as a statement of 'Ali. The letter seems to be more authentic." See *al Targhib* Vol. 1, chapter on *zakah*. Ibn Hazm mentions the same in *al Muhalla*, Vol. 6, p. 159, as a statement of 'Ali, via Sa'id bin Mansur.

49. *Sura al Isra'*, 17:26.

50 *Sura al Nisa'*, 4:36.

51. *Sura al Muddaththir,* 74:42-44.

52. Reported by al Bukhari, Muslim, Ahmad, and al Tirmidhi from Jarir bin 'Abd Allah; also by Ahmad and al Tirmidhi from Abu Sa'id. The meaning comes in several sayings via several chains, all correct. See *al Taisir* by al Munawi, Vol. 2, p 447.

53. Reported by Ahmad, Vol. 1, pp. 197-199, and al Bukhari in the chapter on times of pilgrimage, characteristic and attributes.

54. Reported by Ahmad, Vol. 2, p.91, and Vol. 4, p.104, by al Bukhari in his chapter on oppression or compulsion, in Muslim's chapter on piety, Abu Daud's chapter on manners, and al Tirmidhi's chapter on description of Resurrection, from Ibn 'Umar.

55. Reported in Muslim's chapter on marriage and chapter on foundlings, Abu Daud's chapter on *zakah*, and Ahmad, Vol. 3 p.34.

56. Reported by al Bukhari.

57. Ibn Hazm says the chain of this quote is excellent in correctness and greatness.

58. Only Yahya bin Sa'id grades al Dahhak weak. Ahmad, Ibn Ma'in, Abu Zar'ah, al 'Ujali, al Daraqutni, and Ibn Habban all grade him trustworthy. In *al Taqrib*, al Hafiz says, "he is truthful; has many mursal sayings." See *Mizan al I'tidal*, Vol. 2, pp. 325-326. *Tahdhib al Tahdhib*, Vol. 4, pp. 453-454. However, weakness in narration does not imply weakness in opinion, as claimed by Ibn Hazm. Ibn Abi Laila is graded weak by *hadith* critics but is a leading *fiqh* scholar.

59. *Sura al Hujurat* 49:9.

60. *Al Muhalla*, Vol. 6, pp. 156-1591.

The late Ahmad Shakir comments on Ibn Hazm's view, "This and similar views in Islamic *Shari'ah* show that Islamic law is top in its wisdom and justice. I wish our friends who are overtaken by imported man-made laws would look into these views, understand them, and realize that this religion brings forth the best law for mankind ever. If Muslims would only understand the teachings of their religion and go back to its clear spring and beautiful source -- the Qur'an and Sunnah, and apply what is ordained by our Lord in their private as well as the public lives, they would have been ahead of other nations. Was it not true that all destructive uprisings and revolutions were incited by the oppression inflicted by the rich on the poor and by the former's selfishness to secure all the goods in the world for themselves, leaving their brothers by their side dying from hunger and cold? If only the rich understood, they would realize that doing good to the poor is the first requirement of preserving their own wealth."

CHAPTER THREE

DISCUSSION AND ANALYSIS

Points of agreements and differences of the two views

After surveying the pros and cons of permitting financial dues in addition to *zakah*, we find that their differences are not as great as one may think. They all agree on certain points:

A. The obligation to provide for needy parents.

B. The obligation to spend on provisions for other needy relatives, although there are differences as to the degree of relation included in this obligation.

C. The obligation to provide for the deprived who are in desperate need of food, clothing, or shelter. In his *Ahkam al Qur'an*, al Jassas says, "The obligation is generally *zakah*, except when certain things happen that require other payments, such. as necessity of food for the hungry, clothes for the naked, or funerals for the deceased."[1] Similar to this is lending buckets, cooking pots, or axes to those in dire need, since prevention of harm is a collective obligation on all Muslims according to *ijma'*.

D. The obligation to pay for public necessities such as defending Muslim land, freeing Muslim captives taken by unbelievers, and curing diseases and relieving from famines. This is agreed upon unanimously by Muslim scholars. In *Sharh al Minhaj*, al Ramli says, "Among the collective obligations [*furud al kifayah*] are the requirement to prevent harm to Muslims including providing clothing to the clotheless and food to the hungry if *zakah* funds and public treasury funds are not sufficient. This requirement is obligated on those who have excess above their yearly needs. Moreover, the amount of help must equal, according to the most accepted view, the provision of sufficiency and not merely subsistence. Similar to food and clothing are necessities such as medical cars and other necessary services."[2]

It is mentioned in part four that al Nawawi, a Shafi'ite, believes providing for the regular army is the duty of the country's rich, besides *zakah* payment. Ibn al 'Arabi in his *Ahkam al Qur'an*, adds, "If *zakah* is practiced, and some further need arises, the rich must be obligated to provide for this need by unanimous agreement. Malik says, 'Muslims are all obligated to provide for freeing their prisoners of war, even if this were to take all their wealth.' Moreover, if a governor, by an act of oppression, does not distribute the already-collected *zakah*, the rich must still provide for the needs of the poor, according to the view I think most correct."[3] In his explanation of the Qur'an, al Qurtubi emphasizes the same: "Scholars are in agreement that if a need arises after the distribution of *zakah*, funds must be collected and used for that need."[4] In his *al I'tisam*, al Shatibi concludes, "If the public treasury is empty and the needs of the army for funds are still not satisfied, a just government can impose on the rich taxes sufficient to provide for these needs, until the treasury has funds again."[5]

All these are clear statements that there are agreed upon cases in which financial duties may exist in addition to *zakah*. Amazingly enough, those quotations are from scholars known to believe that there are no other financial duties besides *zakah*, which reveals that what they mean by this position is the prevention of oppressive and unneeded taxes usually imposed by rulers and used for their own pleasures and those of their supporters. However, this does not mean there are no real differences between the two parties.

The areas of real difference can be summarized as follows:

A. The due right on agriculture at the time of harvesting.
B. Dues on livestock.
C. The right of the guest.
D. The right to neighborly help.

All these are considered obligations by the believers in other financial duties besides *zakah* while they are viewed as desirable acts of benevolence by the opponents, except in the case of necessity, as stated by al Jassas: "Lending these tools (like the bucket, cooking pot, and axe) may be obligatory in case of necessity, when refusal to lend is a cause for blame and punishment. But refusal to lend in cases where there is no dire necessity is only a sign of bad manners and low morality that is not supposed to be a trait of Muslims, since the Prophet (p) says, 'I was revealed to in order to complete the good moralities.'[6]"[7]

E. The most important point of difference is the right of the poor to be taken care of out of the wealth of the rich, which is called for by scholars who believe that there exist duties besides *zakah*.

Weighing and discussion

These areas of dispute require study in order to discover the correct position.

A. The right of the poor to agricultural produce at the time of harvest was studied in part three of volume one, and it was concluded that this right, though mentioned in a Makkan verse, is in fact the *Ushr*, which is *zakah* itself. The early ordinance in the Makkan verse proclaims the general obligation, whose details come later in Madinah.

B. As for the right of the guest, it is apparent from the texts that this means the stranger guest traveling in an area where he knows nobody. This is almost the same as the wayfarer, that Ibn 'Abbas and several Followers even explain that the wayfarer is the guest.[8] The sayings explicity state that the guest's right is to be offered food and shelter. This is indeed different from *zakah*.

C. Extending neighborly help is undoubtedly obligated and its refusal is a cause for woe and severs censure. This due is also different from *zakah*.

D. As for the right of the poor to be taken care of from the wealth of the rich, it is a matter so well-known in *Shari'ah* that the verses or sayings about it need not be quoted. However, scholars usually give special attention to the verse "It is not righteousness . . ." and to the saying, "There are on wealth rights besides *zakah*" because these two texts are extremely explicit and to the point in laying down this principle. It is directly derived from the basic foundations of Islam and from the very nature of its system. Mutual solidarity, cooperation, care, and mercy are basic features of the Islamic system. They all implicate that the strong must help the weak and the rich must care for the poor. Neglecting this obligation amounts to basic deviation from this religion and its teachings.

A man from the tribe of Tamim once came to the Prophet (p) and said, "O Messenger of God, I am a man with plenty of wealth, big family, and I am well-established. Tell me, how should I spend, and what should I do?" The Prophet (p) said, "Pay your *zakah*, for it is a purifier that cleanses you. Extend aid to your kindred, and know and fulfill the right of he who asks, the neighbor, and the indigent."[9] The Messenger (p) established a right to the kindred, he who asks, the neighbor, and the indigent, over and above *zakah*, which is consistent with the verse, "And give the kindred his right: so also the indigent and the wayfarer," and the saying, "He who asks has a right, even if he happens to come riding on a mare."[10]

The Messenger of God (p) says, 'He who shows no mercy to others, God will show him no mercy,"[11] and "You shall not become believers until you have mutual mercy among yourselves." They said, "O Messenger of God, we all have mercy." He replied, "It is not the mercy of one toward his companion, but mercy to all people."[12]

The least that must be done to realize this mutual cooperation, solidarity, benevolence, and mercy is to see to it that no person in society is left out in the cold, without provision for an adequate level of living including food, clothing, shelter, medical care, and necessary education. If the proceeds of *zakah* and other government resources are sufficient to cover all these needs it is well and good, but if they are not, it is an ascertained obligation on the rich-- collectively-- to take care of the poor. If this is not done, all rich individuals in the society are considered sinful unless at least some of them fulfill this requirement on behalf of the others. The Islamic government must intervene and collect necessary dues from the rich in order to support all the poor. This was established by the religion of Islam fourteen centuries ago, long before Western Europe opened its eyes to such "progressive" ideas.

Discussing the evidence of the opponents

From all texts of Qur'an and Sunnah presented as argument by the opponents of financial dues beside *zakah*. It is clear that *zakah* is distinct from all other financial duties on wealth. *Zakah* is the only *permanent*, *regular*, and *well-defined* financial obligation due from the rich. It must always be paid, regardless of the existence or non-existence of poor and needy in the society. It is performed as a worship to God and an act of thankfulness for the graces He bestowe on the rich. It is a purification and sanctification of the *zakated* assets as well as the souls of their owners.

As for other financial obligations, such as dues collected to support the poor in case of inadequacy of *zakah* proceeds, these obligations are temporary ad measured only by the amount of need. Consequently, they differ according to circumstances. These obligations are not necessarily individual but collective, in the sense that if the needs are provided for by some of the richest payers, others may be exempted. One must not forget certain exceptional cases, in which such a collective obligation becomes individual and specific, like when there exists only one rich person available to extend help.

Ibn Taimiyah comments on the statement 'There are no other dues imposed on wealth besides *zakah*':

It means no dues except *zakah* are imposed only for the reason that wealth or assets are owned. Indeed, other dues are imposed on the rich, but not simply because of owning assets, such as provision for the living expenses of wives, slaves, owned livestock, needy parents and other relatives, paying due debts, feeding the hungry and clothing the naked. The latter is a collective and not individual obligation. These financial obligations are imposed for other reasons, such as family relation or the presence of dire necessity, but owning wealth is a necessary condition for their levy. Thus, owning wealth to these obligations is like being able to procure means of travel to pilgrimage: Pilgrimage is obligated only on each Muslim who is able to perform it. As for *zakah*, it is obligated by reason of owning wealth, and must be performed regardless of the need for its dispersement. It is a right due to God."[13]

Footnotes

1. Al Jassas, *Ahkam al Qur'an*, Vol. 3, p. 131.

2. *Nihayat al Muhtaj*, Vol. 7, p. 194.

3. Ibn al 'Arabi, *Ahkam al Qur'an*, part one, pp. 59-60.

4. *Tafsir al Qurtubi*, Vol. 2, p. 223.

5. *Al I'tisam*, Vol. 1, p. 103.

6. Reported by al Bukhari in *al Adab al Mufrad*, Ibn Sa'd in *al Tabaqat*, al Hakim in *al Mustadrak*, al Baihaqi via a correct chain. See *al Taisar*, Vol. 1, p. 362.

7. *Al Jassas, op. cit.* p. 584.

8. *Tafsir Ibn Kathir*, Vol. 1, p. 208.

9. Reported by Ahmad from Anas. Its narrators are those of the correct books. See *al Targhib*, Vol. 1, p. 263. Also reported by Abu Daud and Ibn al Mundhir. See *al Durr al Manthur*, Vol. 1, p. 49.

10. Reported by Ahmad and in Abu Daud, the chapter on *zakah*. Al Hafiz al 'Iraqi comments, "Its chain is good, and its narrators are trustworthy." as stated by al Suyuti in *al La'ali'*, Vol. 2, p. 140. The late Ahmad Shakir grades it correct in his notes on the *Musnad* of Ahmad, Vol. 3, p. 173.

11. Reported by al Bukhari, Muslim, and al Tirmidhi from Jarir bin 'Abd Allah.

12. Reported by al Tabarani from Abu Musa; its narrators are those of the correct books, as stated by al Mundhiri. See *al Tarhib*. Vol. 3, chapter on judgement.

13. *Fatawa Ibn Taimiyah*, Vol. 7, p. 316, chapter on faith.

FIQH AL ZAKAH

PART NINE

ZAKAH AND TAXES

Prologue

1. The essence of each of *zakah* and taxes.

2. Theoretical foundations for levying of *zakah* and of taxes.

3. Assets subject to *zakah* and to taxes.

4. Principles of levying taxes and *zakah*.

5. Proportionality and progressiveness of taxes and *zakah*.

6. Legal and moral support for *zakah* and for taxes.

7. Is it permissible to levy taxes beside *zakah*?

8. Can taxes substitute for *zakah*?

PROLOGUE

ZAKAH AND TAXES

This part is a comparison between *zakah* as prescribed in this religion of Islam and man-made taxes as decreed by taxation systems. This comparison is however, restricted to modern taxation systems adopted in many countries today, and does not study the old and undeveloped forms of taxation applied in the ancient Roman and Persian empires and in Medieval Europe. The following chapters of this book take up points of similarity and difference between *zakah* and contemporary taxes from the point of view of their natures, foundations, philosophies, characteristics, ratios , proceeds, etc.

CHAPTER ONE

THE ESSENCE OF EACH OF *ZAKAH* AND TAXES

A tax, as defined by taxation experts, is an obligatory due imposed on the payers and submitted to the state. Taxes are usually imposed according to the ability of the payers and regardless of the benefits the payers derive out of the services performed by the public authority with the tax proceeds. Tax proceeds are used for public expenditure to achieve economic, social, political , and other objectives of the state.[1] *Zakah,* as defined by Muslim jurists, is a determined right imposed by God on the wealth of Muslims, to the benefit of the categories mentioned in God's Book, such as the poor, the needy, etc. It is an expression of gratitude for God's graces, and is performed to seek His pleasure and to purify souls and wealth.

Similarities between *zakah* and taxes

The above definitions reveal the following similarities:

1. The elements of obligation and compulsion exist in both *zakah* and taxes.

2. Both taxes and *zakah* are paid to certain public body, be it the local or national authority[2] or an autonomous institution, or the public treasury.

3. In taxes, there is no reciprocity between the amount collected and services received by the payer. The payer is required to pay taxes as a member of society. *Zakah* is also paid, without any direct exchange, by every Muslim to the Islamic state, regardless of the benefits that the *zakah* payer may get from the state.

4. *Zakah* and, in their modern philosophy, taxes, have social, economic, and political objectives besides their financial objective.

Differences between *zakah* and taxes

Outside the above points of similarity, differences between *zakah* and modern taxes are numerous:

1. The first striking difference is the name, which has important indications. *Zakah* as a word means purity, growth, and blessing. The word is selected for this pillar of Islam in order to incorporate these meanings in *zakah*. "Tax" implies imposition, estimation, and charge. The Arabic word for tax, "*Daribah*", has the same indication of charge and imposition. God says "And they were covered [*duribat*] with humiliation and miserliness."[3] Consequently, a tax is looked upon as a charge and liability. While *zakah* inspires purity, sanctity, and growth. It is implied that hoarding wealth without cleansing it by giving the right God imposes to the poor makes wealth a source of sin and evil, and that giving *zakah* -- though it reduces the wealth -- in fact brings reasons for growth. God says "God will deprive interest of all blessing, but will give growth for deeds of *sadaqat*."[4] "And nothing do ye spend in his cause but he replaces it." and the Messenger (p) says, "Wealth never decreases as a result of *sadaqah*."[6]

Moreover, *zakah* gives the feeling of purification not only for assets *zakted* but for the payer himself as well as the recipient, for it purifies from vanity, hatred and selfishness provides a benevolent hand to the poor. God says, "Out of their wealth take *sadaqah* that so thou might purify and sanctify them."[7]

2. The difference in nature and substance

Zakah is a worship in gratitude and thankfulness to God, while taxes are a mere civil obligation. Intention is one of the conditions of *zakah*, since all acts of worship require intention. God says "And they have been commanded no more than this: to worship God, offering him sincere devotion."[8] *Zakah* is always cited in the sections on worship in books of Islamic jurisprudence, and is mentioned in more than twenty places in the Qur'an. *Zakah* is not obligated on non-Muslim citizens of the Islamic state, since Islam does not consider it fair to obligate non-Muslims to perform an Islamic rite of worship.

3. The third difference is in ratios and minimum exempt, *zakah* -- as an obligation from God -- is irrevocably defined and its main features given by the Legislator. *Shari'ah* determines the ratios applied on all assets, decreeing cases to which twenty percent, ten percent, five percent, or 2.5 percent rates apply. These ratios and their applicability cannot be altered by anyone or any law, regardless of changing circumstances.[9] The same applies to *nisabs*. On the other hand, a tax is enacted by people and is always subject to change and redeterminations.

4. The difference in constancy and permanence

Zakah is a fixed and permanent obligation which cannot be discontinued by any government. Even ii the government does not collect it, *zakah* remains an obligation on individual Muslims. Taxes can be changed, altered, or eliminated, depending on the circumstances and the decisions of legislative authorities. A tax is not permanent nor continuous or fixed.

5. The difference in dispersement of proceeds

Zakah has its own dispersement. Description of its recipients is given by God in the Qur'an and explained by the tradition of his Messenger (p). No one may add a new category of recipients or eliminate recipient who deserves *zakah*, to the extent that individual Muslims can, in case of need, distribute *zakah* by themselves. The dispersement of *zakah* has a humanistic aim, among others, and is surrounded by humanistic acts such as exchange of prayers between payer and recipient. Furthermore, the budget of *zakah* must remain autonomous from the public treasury, since it is "an obligation from God."[10]

Taxes, on the other hand, are levied for multiple objectives, changeable with time and circumstances. The state or proper authority determines usage of tax proceeds.

6. Taxes and *zakah* each have different relation to the state. Payment of a tax represents a relation between the payer and the local or national authorities of the state. If the tax collection is delayed by these authorities, the payer has no reason to pay the tax and cannot be blamed for lack of payment.

Zakah represents a relation between the payer and his Lord. It is God who gave him wealth, and the payer, out of obedience to God, performs *zakah* seeking God's acceptance and pleasure. If the Islamic state does not exist or does not collect *zakah*, individual Muslims are still required to fulfill this duty, just as prayers remain obligated even if one does not find a mosque for "*zakah* is the sister of prayer." Muslims are supposed to pay *zakah* with their souls pleased, hoping that God accepts their worship. This is not the case with taxes.

7. Difference exists in objectives

Zakah has spiritual and ethical objectives in addition to its socio-economic aims, while taxes have no such aspirations. The objectives of *zakah* were discussed in some detail in part six of this book. It is sufficient here to mention the verse "Out of their wealth take *zakah*, that so thou might purify and sanctify them, and pray on their behalf. Verily thy prayers are a source of security and comfort for them." The Prophet used to pray for the blessings of *zakah* payers and ordered his commissioners to do so, to the extent that some jurists consider it obligatory. Taxes are detached from such spiritual and ethical objectives. It was even maintained by taxation specialists for a long time that taxes must have but one target: furnishing the treasury with financial resources. Only recently have scholars begun to argue for the socio- economic objectives of taxes, so that the idea of tax neutrality has become a relic of the past. But taxation scholars have not yet thought of spiritual or moral objectives of their taxation systems, while *zakah* established such targets fourteen hundred years ago.

8. The most important difference between *zakah* and taxes is the different theoretical grounds for which each is imposed. Because of its importance, this topic will be discussed in a chapter of its own.

At last, it must be emphasized that all the above mentioned differences stem from the fact that *zakah* is not only a tax, not a mere financial duty, but a worship as well. It is the third pillar of Islam and one of its essential rites.

It is notable that Muslim scholars throughout centuries refer to this dual meaning of *zakah* as a tax and a worship.[11] Thus its humanistic, moral, social, economic and spiritual elements intermingle to form one institution. The author of *al Rawd al Nadir* quotes some scholars as saying

"God imposes *zakah* on the wealth of the rich as a gesture of care toward their brethren, the poor, in fulfillment of the glorious right of brotherhood and in practice of love and compassion. *zakah* includes elements of help, support, and mutual cooperation, in spite of the fact that it is a test of obedience for the wealthy, similar to other worships God prescribes to be performed physically. It means cherishing the kindred as well as performing a worship. Consequently, it requires intention and it can be performed through appointed representatives or agents. In as much as it is a financial obligation, the Islamic government can force owners of wealth to pay their due *zakah*. *Zakah* can be taken from the wealth of the child or the insane persons, who are otherwise not obligated to perform other worships. Because *zakah* is a cherishing of the poor and needy, their benefits are given priority. Because it is help to brothers and sisters, God imposes it only on the able -- the rich who own *nisab*. *Shari'ah* determines *nisab* and rates for each *zakatable* asset. Rates differ in accordance to cost and efforts involved in the process of production. Thus, the rate is ten percent on what is watered by the sky, and five percent on what is watered by animals carrying water supplies."[12]

Footnotes

1.   *Mabadi 'ilm al Maliyah*, by Muhammad Fu'ad Ibrahim, Vol. 1, p. 261.

2.   In Medieval Europe, there were taxes paid by vassals to the landlords.

3.   *Sura al Baqarah*, 2:61.

4.   *Ibid*, 2:276.

5.   *Sura Saba'*, 34:39.

6.   Reported by al Tirmidhi.

7.   *Sura al Tawbah*, 9:103.

8.   *Sura al Baiyinah*, 98:5.

9.   See p. 217 of Vol. 1, of this book.

10.   As in verse no. 60 of *Sura al Tawbah*, (sura no. 9).

11. *Bidayat al Mujtahid*, Vol. 1, p. 237.

12. *Al Rawd al Nadir*, Vol. 2, p. 389.

CHAPTER TWO

THEORETICAL FOUNDATION FOR
LEVYING TAXES AND *ZAKAH*

Legal foundation for tax levying

Several theories explain the legal foundation of taxes. The first is the contractual theory. This is adopted by many philosophers of the eighteenth century, who argue that the tax is based on a contractual relationship between the state and the individual, whereby taxes are paid in exchange for services provided by the state, such as security and other public services. This is founded on Jean Jacques Rousseau's theory of social contract. According to Mirabo, the tax is a price paid in advance by the individual for the community's protection, like in a sales contract. According to Adam Smith, the contract is like a rental one, whereby the state provides individuals with services and they pay rent for them, while Montesquieu and Hobbs argue that it is like an insurance contract, whereby the tax is a premium paid by the individual to insure protection of the rest of his wealth.

Critics of this theory believe it is ill-founded, since there is no way of realizing justice in any exchange between taxes and benefits received by the taxpayer, since it is impossible to estimate the exact benefit each citizen receives from the public expenditure on security, law enforcement, judiciary system, education, and national defense. Even if it were possible to measure the benefits received by each individual, this theory leads to the unjust conclusion that the poor, who usually need more of the state's services, must carry the largest burden of state finance. The "insurance" relationship is further criticized because it restricts the role of the state to security and protection only, and is an incomplete insurance since an insured normally compensates the insured for losses incurred, while the state does not give compensation for loss of property.

The second theory is that of state sovereignty. This theory explains taxes by the authority of the state as the sovereign body, which has the right to distribute the burden of taxes according to the principle of solidarity of all members of society, regardless of any benefits they receive from the state's services.[1]

The foundation of *zakah* levying

There are several theories that attempt to explain the theoretical foundation for *zakah*. Four theories are discussed in this chapter: the theory of obligation, the theory of vice-generency, the theory of mutual solidarity, and the theory of brotherhood.

The theory of obligation

Supporters of this theory explain *zakah* the same way other obligations are explained, i.e. that God, who is the Greater and Provider, has the right to charge his servants with an obligation in thankfulness to Him, and to test them so the wrongdoer can be distinguished from the doer of good. Human beings are not created in vain, nor are they left to be lost in nothingness, God says, "Did ye then think that we have created you a jest, and that ye would not be brought back to us?"[2] "Does man think that he will be left purposeless?"[3] Human beings are not left without a role and message . God sends messengers and prophets to guide, to warn, and to inform human beings of the commandments of God and the obligations He ordains, "so that He rewards those who do evil according to their deeds, and He rewards those who do good with what is best."[4] The same way God ordains the performance of payers five times every day and night, fasting one month every year and pilgrimage once in a lifetime, so that man can glorify the Creator and honor His rites, this same way God obligates the payment of *zakah* as a financial worship, whereby humans spend out of their dear assets in expression of thankfulness to God and in search of His pleasure, God says "And those saved from the covetousness of their own souls, they are the ones who achieve success."[5]

The theory of vicegerency

The basic element in this theory is that all goods belong, in fact, to God. Human beings are only vicegerents; God is the true owner of everything. "Yea, to God belongs all that is in the heavens and on earth."[6] "To Him belongs what is in the heavens and on earth and all between them and all beneath the soil."[7] No one, whatsoever has any share in this. "Say, call upon others whom ye fancy besides God. They have no power not the weight of an atom in the heavens or on earth. No sort of share have they therein, nor is any of them a helper to God."[8] "God is the Creator of all things, and He is the Guardian and Disposer of all affairs.[9] "It is He who created all things and ordered them in due proportion."[10] Those on whom beside God ye call cannot create even a fly if they all together for that purpose."[11]

God is the Bestower and the Giver of all things. What humans make and produce is in fact owned by God, along with man himself. Production, according to economists, utilizes already existing materials, changes the mixture of materials and their proportions.[12] God says, "Our Lord is He who gave to each thing its form and nature, and further gave it guidance."[13] "It is God who hath created the heavens and the earth, and sends down rain from the skies and with it bringeth out fruits wherewith to feed you. It is He who has made the ships subject to you, that they may sail through the sea by His command, and the rivers has He made subject to you. And He has made subject to you the sun and the moon, both dilegently pursuing their courses, and the night and the day hath, He also made subject to you. And He giveth you of all that ye ask for, but if ye count the favors of God, never will ye be able to number them."[14] Even in production, it is God who created the laws of mixing materials together and changing their characteristics. God made these laws to humans and He provides human beings with the ability to understand and use them for their benefit. Regarding God's grace to humans in agriculture, He says "See ye the seed that ye sow in the ground? Is it ye that cause it to grow, or are We the cause? Were it our will We could crumble it to dry powder and ye would be left in wonderment, [saying] 'We are indeed left with debts; indeed are we shut out'. See ye the water which ye drink? Do ye bring it down from the cloud or do we? Were it our will We could make it salt and unpalatable. Then why do ye not give thanks? See ye the fire which ye kindle? Is it ye who grow the tree which feeds the fire or do We grow it?"[15] "Then let man look at his food, for that we pour forth water in abundance, and we split the earth in fragments, and produce therein, corn and grains and nutritious plants."[16] God creats the raw materials used in trade and manufacturing. God says, "And we sent dow iron in which is material for mighty wars as well as many benefits for mankind."[17] "It was We who taught him the making of coats of mail for your benefit, to guard you from each others' violence. Will ye then be grateful?"[18]

In conclusion, all goods belong to God, and He makes them subject to humans out of His glorified grace. "And ye have no good thing but is from God,"[19] Therefore it is no surprise that human beings - the vicegerents - should spend out of these bestowed goods for purposes that God wants, and to make God's word the highest. This is the least expression of gratitude and thankfulness. God says "Spend out of the bounties We have provided for you"[20] "Yea, give them something out of the wealth which God has given to you."[21] "and spend out of the (goods) whereof He has made you vicegerents."[22] Humans are not in fact the owners of goods and assets, but only vicegerents.[23] Al Zamakhshari, explains the verse ' and spend out of that which God gave you control of "to mean that 'the goods and funds that are in your hands belong in the true sense to God, who created them. He gives them to us and authorizes as to enjoy using them. Thus they are not our goods; we are only vicegerents and representatives. We must spend out of these goods for payments of rights due to God. Spending must not be difficult for us, since we ore not doing it out of our own wealth."[24] Moreover, the fact that goods and all creatures are owned by God implies one more thing, that is, the representatives must spend in accordance with the will of the Owner. Muslim scholars express this idea very eloquently. Al Razi says, "The poor are dependent on God, and the rich are God's treasurers, since the wealth in their hands belongs to God. It is expected that the Owner would order His treasurers to spend some of the wealth in the treasury for the needy who are the Owner's dependents."[25] Ibn al 'Arabi says, "God, glorified be His absolute wisdom and praised be His commandments, gives wealth to some people out of grace and mercy to them. He makes the sign of gratitude for this grace to spend a portion for those who have not, in representation of God, who guarantees the poor their living when He says, 'There is no moving creature on earth but its sustenance depends on, and is guaranteed by, God,'[26] If the rich do not fulfill the will of the Owner out of miserliness and selfishness, they deserve the Owner's wrath and anger."[27] Many laymen in Muslim countries attribute to God the saying that 'Wealth is mine, the poor are My dependents, and the rich are My agents. If My agents treat with miserliness My dependents, I surely will make them taste My wrath without hesitation."[28] Although there is no authenticity to these words, the idea they express is undoubtedly correct its popularity among Muslim masses indicates that this concept of vicegerency is deep in the conscience of Muslims. Amazingly, beggars throughout Muslims lands, when asking people for donations, repeat, "Out of the wealth of God." Lastly, there is a saying that reads "Woe to the rich from the poor on the Day of Resurrection. The latter will say, 'our Lord, they oppressed us, depriving us of our right that you ordained on them for us.' God will say, 'By My might and highness, I shall indeed made you close to me and make them far away from me'"[29]

The theory of solidarity

Human beings are social creatures. This is known to sociologists as much as it is known to Muslim scholars. Even in the procuring of wealth and income by every individual, there is a great contribution of society. Consequently, private wealth must have a facet that is part of the society's wealth at the same time, God addresses the Muslim community, "To those weak of understanding make not over your property which God hath made a means of support for you."[30] This verse indicates that property and wealth belong to society as much as to individuals, to the extent that Muslim jurists deduct that abusers of their private wealth must be prevented from practicing control over their assets, since wealth belongs to the whole society as well. Notably, the verse says, "your property" and not "their" property. Moreover, in another verse, this meaning is more explicit. God says "O ye who believe, eat not your property among yourselves in vanities, but let there be amongst you profit and trade and mutual goodwill. Nor kill or despoil yourselves, for verily God hath been to you most merciful."[31] It must be noted that the verse forbids eating each others' property in vanity, although it expresses it as "your property".

The Muslim society and community is based on mutual solidarity and mutual support.This applies to wealth as well as persons. Eating up in vanities somebody's property is like eating society's wealth and transgressing against someone's right is like transgressing against the whole society, on the same principle "That if anyone slew a person -- unless it be for murder or for spreading mischief in the land - it would be as if he slew a whole people , and if anyone saved a life of a person, it would be as if he saved the life of a whole people."[32] Commenting on the verse, "Eat not up your property among yourselves in vanity," the late Rashid Rida says, "This expression establishes an essential principle of the Islamic system: the principle that the whole society shares in the property of individuals - in the right sense. Socialists today aim at a just principle of sharing, but they can not realize it and they shall never realize it as long as they continue their search outside Islam. Islam considers the private property of each individual Muslim a property that belongs to the whole society, yet without any violation of the rights of private ownership. Each individual is obligated to contribute to the public interests whether the person is rich or not. Above all these decreed rights on private assets to the benefit of the whole society, Islam urges the wealthy to continuously contribute through righteous and benevolent deeds to the welfare of fellow Muslims and the welfare of the community is a whole."[33]

In conclusion, the Muslim community has a certain right on each private property. This right does not deprive the individual of ownership, but takes a share of individual wealth for fulfilling the interests of the whole community. The society, as represented by its state, has a share in the assets of each rich person, a share which must be paid in order to preserve the social structure, promote the message of Islam, and defend fellow Muslims. Even if there are no poor and needy in a Muslim community, the rich must still contribute their *zakah* to finance such public services as promotion of faith and "the way of God," which is a continuous and permanent object of public expenditures.

The theory of brotherhood among Muslims

Brotherhood, the fourth explanation for the obligation of *zakah*, is rooted deeper in the heart then solidarity and is more influential since solidarity is a mutual exchange while brotherhood implies selfless giving and sacrifice. Brotherhood is a spiritual feeling directly derived from the common humanity of men and women. It requires extending any help within one's power to one's brother, and loving for one's brother what one loves for oneself.

There are two degrees of brotherhood, one based on the common human bond and the other on the common faith. All human beings -- regardless of color, ethnicity, language, social status, and religion -- spring from one source, one single origin as children of Adam and Eve. God in the Qur'an calls humans "O children of Adam"[34] or "O humanity."[35] Human relations like mercy and brotherhood exist among people. This is emphasized in the Qur'an in more than one place: "O mankind, reverence your guardian Lord who created you from a single person, created of like nature his mate, and from them twain scattered like seeds countless men and women; reverence God, through whom ye demand your mutual rights, and reverence the wombs that bore you, for God ever watches over you."[36] The word "wombs" is a reminder that all mankind came from one single soul and are all related in this human brotherhood. The Prophet (p) emphasizes this when he says, "And be all, O servants of God, brothers."[37] Human brotherhood is one of the principles in the creed of this faith. Islam calls upon men and women to believe in this human brotherhood and practice it in their lives. The Messenger (p) used to say after regular prayers, "My Lord, Our Lord, and the Lord and Owner of everything, I am a witness that you are the Diety, alone; You have no partner, My Lord, our God, and the God and Owner of everything, I am a witness that Muhammad is Your servant and Your messenger. My Lord, our Lord, and the Lord and Owner of everything, I am a witness that all servants of God are brothers."[38] This brotherhood of all human beings has many implications; among them is that no human being must be submerged in selfish enjoyment of the goods God created while others suffer. It implies that each must share with fellow humans the grace God bestows on all humanity.

Above this degree of brotherhood is another deeper and stronger degree, brotherhood in faith. Those who share together belief in this religion, in God as the only Lord of the worlds, have indissoluble spiritual and social bonds. Brotherhood in Islam is much stronger than any blood relation. God says, "Believers are one single brotherhood."[39] The spiritual brotherhood of all persons who share faith together also has important implications regarding support, aid, and sharing the material goods God created. Brotherhood among the faithful is further strengthened when they live in one society and one land. It is known in *Shari'ah* that the lands of all Muslims are one single country for all of them, and that all Muslims are members of one united society. The Messenger of God (p) explains the rights implicated by this brotherhood in several of his sayings: "A believer to a fellow believer is like one single structure whose parts are bonded together."[40] The parable of the faithful in their mutual love and mercy is like one single body: If one of its members aches, the other members respond with faver and insomnia."[41] and "The Muslim is a brother to the fellow Muslim, He does not do injustice to him nor does let him down."[42] He who leaves his brother hungry or naked while he is able to clothe or feed him is undoubtedly letting his brother down. The prophet (p) says, "He does not believe in me who goes to sleep with a full stomach while he knows that his neighbor, by his side, is hungry."[43]

Footnotes

1. In this I depend on *Mizaniyyat al Dawlah* [The State Budget] by Dr. Muhammad Hilmy Murad, Nahdat Misr print, 1955, chapter on the legal foundation of taxes, pp. 73-75.

2. *Sura al Mu'minun*, 23:115.

3. *Sura al Qiyamah*, 75:36.

4. *Sura al Najm*, 53:31.

5. *Sura al Hashr*, 59:9.

6. *Sura al Najm*, 53:31.

7. *Sura Taha*, 20:6.

8. *Sura Saba'*, 34:22.

9. *Sura al Zumar*, 39:62.

10. *Sura al Furqan*, 25:2.

11. *Sura al Hajj*, 22:73.

12. *Al Iqtisad al Siyasi,* by Dr. Raf'at Mahjub, Vol. 1, pp. 191-192, and *al Iqtisad al Siyasi* by Dr. 'Ali 'Abd al Wahid Wafi, pp. 74-76.

13. *Sura Taha,* 20:50.

14. *Sura Ibrahim,* 14:32-34.

15. *Sura al Waqi'ah,* 56:63-72.

16. *Sura 'Abasa,* 80:21-28.

17. *Sura al Hadid,* 57:25.

18. *Sura al Anbiya,* 21:80.

19. *Sura al Nahl,* 16:53.

20. *Sura al Baqarah,* 2:254.

21. *Sura al Nur,* 24:33.

22. *Sura al Hadid,* 57:7.

23. Ibn al Qayyim asks, "Is it correct to say that anyone is a vicegerent of God?" His answer is negative, since "A vicegerent (*Khalifah*) is a person who does things in the capacity of deputyship for he who appoints him. God has no deputy, nor a substitute, nor anyone who acts on his behalf. The Messenger (p) says in his prayers 'My Lord, You are the Companion in travel and the Vicegerent (*Khalifah*) on my family.' But there is nothing that prevents the use of the term for human beings because they are ordained to preserve what is under their authority and to nourish it." See *Madarij al Salikin,* Vol. 2, pp. 126-127.

24. *Al Kashshaf,* Vol. 3, p. 200.

25. *Al Tafsir al Kabir,* Vol. 16, p. 103.

26. *Sura Hud,* 11:5.

27. *Ahkam al Qur'an,* p. 945.

28. After research, I did not find any trace or origin of this narration.

29. Reported by al Tabarani in his *al Mu'jam al Awsat* and *al Saghir* from Anas, via a weak chain. *Jam' al Fawa'id,* Vol. 1, p. 142.

30. *Sura al Nisa,* 4:5.

31. *Ibid,* 4:29.

32. *Sura al Ma'idah,* 5:35.

33.   *Tafsir al Manar*, Vol. 5, p.39.

34.   This word appears five times in the Qur'an: four times in *Sura al A'raf* and once in *Sura Yasin*.

35.   The beginning of *Sura al Nisa* and of *Sura al Haj,* This is also more frequent in the Qur'an.

36.   *Sura al Nisa*, 4:1.

37.   Agreed upon.

38.   Reported by Ahmad and Abu Daud.

39.   *Sura al Hujurat*, 49:10.

40.   Agreed upon as reported from Abu Musa al Ash'ari.

41.   Agreed upon from al Nu'man bin Bashir.

42.   Reported by al Bukhari, Muslim, and Abu Daud. See *al Targhib*, Vol. 3, p. 389.

43.   Reported by al Tabarani and al Bazzar from Anas via a good chain. Also reported by al Tabarani and Abu Ya'la from Ibn 'Abbas and by al Hakim from A'ishah. See *al Targhib*, Vol. 3, p. 358.

CHAPTER THREE

ASSETS SUBJECT TO *ZAKAH* AND TO TAXES

Taxable materials, whether income or assets, are not necessarily the same as *zakatable* materials. Taxation specialists count four kinds of taxes from the point of view of taxable items: taxes on capital, on income, on persons, and on consumption. *Zakah* does not cover consumption, it is taken from the rich on what is left after consumption. *Zakah* is sometimes levied on assets, such as gold, silver and livestock, sometimes on income, such as agricultural produce, and on persons in the form of fast-breaking *zakah*. This chapter compares *zakah*s on capital, income, and persons with their tax counterparts.

SECTION ONE

ZAKAH ON CAPITAL

The advantages of capital tax without its disadvantages

Zakah on capital was enacted long before European socialists called for levying taxes on capital.[1] Proponents of taxes on capital usually present the following advantages:

1. Capital provides its owners with several social and economic benefits including security and opportunities to earn more wealth.

2. Taxes on capital reach all private wealth including wealth that does not yield any income, as compared to income tax, which is imposed only on earners.

3. By taking idle wealth, capital taxes encourage investment.

4. Capital tax encourages capitalists to increase their production to make up for the loss resulting from tax payment.

5. By imposing capital tax in addition to income tax, the need for raising income tax rates to provide additional resources to the state is eliminated.

6. Capital tax dose not burden the poor and the have-nots, and is therefore considered a socialist reform.[2]

Opponents of capital tax bring forth the following disadvantages:

1. Levying a tax on capital very often has a negative effect on the propensity to save and the ability to invest, which apparently has a negative effect on the economy as a whole.

2. It is generally difficult to determine taxable capital, since there are several definitions of capital: both economists and taxationists do not agree on a common definition. Leaving determination of taxable capital to individual tax payers or to collectors raises many discrepancies especially since some forms of capital can easily be hidden away, such as cash money.

3. Repetitive collection of tax on capital year after year may exhaust the capital itself, which is a major source of income. If the state continues levying and collecting taxes on capital, it may end up transferring private capital into the public treasury, which by itself reduces future proceeds of such a tax and shrinks the economic ability of the private sector.[3]

Recommended rules for levying taxes on capital

For reasons like the ones mentioned above, some tax specialists suggest that the government observe the following rules when imposing taxes on capital:

1. It is advisable that the amount of tax collected not be great. It must not take a big chunk of capital. The rate must be moderate, so that capital tax can be paid out of capital's income without touching the principal itself.

2. Capital tax must not be the only taxes in the system, but must rather be supplementary to other taxes, especially income tax.[4]

3. A certain minimum amount of capital must be exempt from taxes.

4. Liabilities on wealth must be excluded or deducted from the taxable amount.[5]

Islam observes these rules before other systems

Looking at *zakah* as a tax, we find that it fulfills all the requirements for a healthy tax on capital, by observing the necessary rules that eliminate the disadvantages of taxes on capital, while preserving the advantages.

1. Islam does not impose *zakah* on every kind of capital. It is only levied on growing capital. Growing capital is that wealth which usually has yield, (regardless of whether the owner renders the capital idle or profitable). This is in order to collect *zakah* from the proceeds of capital and not from the principal. The word "*zakah*" itself means inter alia -- "growth" in Arabic. Some jurists explain the use of the word "*zakah*" for this kind of levy in the Qur'an on the basis that *zakah* is levied only on growing assets.[6]

Accordingly, jewelry that is not used as growing asset is not taxable, whereas hoarded jewelry is *zakatable*, since hoarding implies making idle what is otherwise growing. Jurists agree that houses used as residences of the owners are not *zakatable*. Neither are clothes, furniture, riding animals, personal weapons, craftsmen's tools, and books used for study and research, because all these do not grow and are assigned for personal use to satisfy basic needs of the owners.[7] We must, however, note, that in man-made taxation systems residential houses are usually taxable even mobile forms of wealth are taxable in many countries.[8]

2. *Shari'ah* does not impose *zakah* on fixed capital itself, such as factories and real estate, but only on circulating capital, on the grounds that fixed capital is *zakted* via its yield and growth, like agricultural land which is not *zakted* by virtue of texts. Similar to agricultural land are buildings and other exploited capital. This principle is observed in order that *zakah* does not negatively affect the desire to save and does not induce savers to spend their income to avoid taxes levied on fixed capital.

3. *Shari'ah* does not impose *zakah* on all amounts of capital. *nisab* is considered a minimum level of richness below which *zakah* is not obligated. *Nisab* is estimated at the equivalent of eighty-five grams of gold, and *zakah* is imposed on that amount of capital once every year, provided it is in excess of what is needed to satisfy the basic needs of the owner; basic needs which differ from time to time.

4. Islam also determines the rate of *zakah* on capital at a moderate level, at only 2.5 percent, as determined for money and trade assets, and as approximated with regards to livestock. At this rate, *zakah* is intended to be collected from the yield of capital and not from the principal itself. It is remarkable that some jurists explicitly mention this point, such as Ibn Qudamah in *al Mughni*, who discusses the distinction between assets for which the passage of one year is required and those for which it is not: "Kinds for which the passage of one year is required are those designated for growth, such as livestock, trade assets, and money, so that *zakah* is actually paid out of the capital's income, thus making it easier and simpler, such that its repetition year after year does not deplete the capital itself."[9] The author of *al Hidayah*, a Hanafite, asserts that "The passage of a year is necessary because there ought to be a certain period of time for growth to be realized. This period is estimated at one year, which includes the four seasons, in which prices may fluctuate." Ibn al Humam comments in his *Fath al Qadir* that the rationale for the condition of one year is that "*zakah*, in addition to being a worship and a test from God, is meant to be a relief to the poor without depriving the payer himself or making him poor, i.e., by having the rich give out of the excess of their wealth, a little out of plenty. Obviously , obligating *zakah* on assets that do not grow leads to depletion of such assets

by *zakah* payments year after year, knowing that the *zakah* payer has other expenses too. Thus, the condition of the passage of a year for growing assets is meant to allow these assets to have sufficient time to grow and yield profits."[10]

Zakah on growing assets is meant to be collected out of the yield of the capital and not out of the capital itself. But why does *Shari'ah* make potential for growth the condition for *zakatability*, and not actual realization of profit? Ibn Qudamah answers this question "Actual growth alone is not considered the criterion because it is difficult to measure and to define accurately, especially since potentiality is considered a sufficient reason for a ruling in *Shari'ah* in many instances in place of actual realization."[12]

SECTION TWO

ZAKAH ON INCOME AND PROFIT

Income is the most important source of taxes in modern times. Years ago, income from real estate used to be predominant, but nowadays we have income from labor, capital, or both. With the advancement of industrialization and the increase in domestic and international trade, income from labor and capital increased manifold. Income includes profit from commercial and industrial activities, returns of stocks and bonds, profits of professionals, and wages and salaries of employees of the government as well as of private and public establishments.

Financial needs of modern states are better satisfied by direct taxes on income than by indirect taxes that prevailed in the past. Moreover income taxes are more acceptable by taxation scholars, because they are closest to fulfilling justice in contemporary economic systems by spreading the tax burden among all income earners.[13]

What is income?

Income is the flow of new wealth from a constant and permanent source. This source may or may not be physical. Physical sources include real estate, machinery and equipment, and money, while the non-physical source is labor, whether manual or non-manual. In most cases, income results from the combination of more than one source.[14]

This definition also implies that the sources of income are generally permanent and continuous. (Permanency does not mean absolute permanency but relative longevity) With application of the principle of allowances for capital amortization, capital becomes more permanent than labor.[15] Differences in the lifespan of the source of income are usually bases for differences in its taxability; i.e. the tax burden is distributed in such a way that the tax rate is higher on income that flows out of financial resources and lower on income that flows out of labour alone.

Zakah on income in Islam

The most obvious example of *zakah* on income is the agricultural *zakah*. Its rate differs from five to ten percent-- the higher rate applies when farming costs are minimum (i.e. the land is watered by rain), and the lower rate applies when water must be brought to the land. *Rikaz*, (*zakah* on buried treasures and minerals extracted from the earth) has a rate of 20 percent, while income from labor and professions has a rate of 2.5 percent. The rate on trade income is also 2.5 percent, since *zakah* on commercial income is integrated with *zakah* on commercial inventory, *zakah* is calculated at once on both trade assets and accrued income from trade.

Thus, Islam applies different rates of *zakah* on income, rates that vary in accordance with efforts expended. At high costs of producing the *zakatable* income, a low rate of *zakah* applies, and vice verse.

Other forms of *zakah* on income include *zakah* on the offspring of livestock, *zakah* on honey and other animal products, *zakah* on earnings of real estate and other fixed capital, as discussed in detail in part three of this book.

SECTION THREE

ZAKAH ON PERSONS

Taxes on persons

Taxes on persons, sometimes called tolls, were common in many western countries, and still exist in many states today, although their use is declining. The most important merit of a tax on heads is easiness in estimation and collection, but the main disadvantage is that it is not based on the ability of the taxable person to pay. Many governments discontinued this form of taxation for that reason, although it is still used in some states of the United States and in France.[16]

Zakah of *al fitr* is on persons

Zakah of fast breaking at the end of the month of Ramadan is levied on persons. It has the same advantages of simplicity of calculation and collection as the tax on persons. Above this however, *zakah* of fast breaking serves important spiritual, moral, and social objectives in addition to its transfer of funds like other forms of *zakah*. But unlike the tax on persons, individuals who cannot afford payment are exempt from *zakah* of *al fitr*. This is unanimously agreed upon by Muslim scholars.

By imposing this *zakah* once a year on each Muslim, Islam aims at training all Muslims to spend and sacrifice for the welfare of fellow Muslims, especially on the occasion of the religious feast days. Accordingly, exemptions from this *zakah* are much more strictly reduced than exemptions from other forms of *zakah*. Even the poor, except the totally destitute, are required to pay this *zakah*. The Messenger (p) says regarding payment of *zakah* of *al fitr*, "As for the rich among you (who pay it), God will sanctify them, and as for the poor among you (who pay it), God will render to them more than they give."[17] Fortunately, this *zakah* is today the most remembered and practiced throughout the Muslim land of all forms of *zakah*.

Footnotes

1. *I'lm al Maliyah,* by Dr. Rashid al Daqr, p. 352.

2. *Ibid*, p. 347, and *Mawarid al Dawlah* , by Dr. Sa'd Maher Hamzah, p. 166.

3. *Mawarid* , *Ibid*, p. 168.

4. *I'lm al Maliyah, op. cit.*, p. 355.

5. *Mawarid*, p. 176.

6. *Fath al Bari*, Vol. 3, p, 168.

7. *Fath al Qadir* with *Sharh al Inayah Ala al Hidayah*, Vol. 1, pp. 487-489.

8. *I'lm al Maliyah, op. cit.*, p. 335.

9. *Al Mughni*, Vol. 2, p. 625; see also p   of this book.

10. *Fath al Qadir*, Vol. 1, p. 482.

11. *Al Mughni*, Vol. 2, p. 625.

12. This is a reference to the fact that *Shari'ah* 's rulings are only founded on explicit and definable characteristics, called by jurists "the reasons" "al ilal" or "al asbab" and not on existence of the ruling's objective, which is, in the ultimate analysis, the true reason for having the ruling. For example, Islam allows a traveller to break fast in Ramadan and to reduce the four *rak'ah* prayers to two *rak'ah*. Clearly, the objective is to reduce the difficulty of the traveller. But since difficulty can not be accurately defined, the ruling does not depend on difficulty, but rather on a state in which difficulty is expected to exist, i.e. the state of travelling.

13. *Mawarid al Dawlah*, by Dr. Sa'd Maher Hamza. p. 117.

14. *Mabadi al Maliyah al Ammah* by Dr. Muhammad Fu'ad Ibrahim, Vol. 1, p. 322.

15. *Ibid.*

16. *Ibid*, pp. 305-307.

17. See part seven of this book.

CHAPTER FOUR

PRINCIPLES OF LEVYING TAXES AND *ZAKAH*

Taxes, as obligatory levies enforced by the state, must be based on certain principles of common sense, otherwise they cause unrest end disturbance. Scholars and taxation experts throughout the past few centuries have argued over these principles. Adam Smith in the eighteenth century sums up these principles as: the principles of justice, certainty, convenience, and economy.[1] This chapter consequently has four sections in which these principles are discussed in relation to both taxes and *zakah*.

SECTION ONE
THE PRINCIPLE OF JUSTICE

The principle of justice, according to Smith,[2] means all citizens of the stats must share in financing the government's expenditures, each according to his ability, i.e. in proportion to his income, which is protected by the state.[3] This principle is consistent with *Shari'ah* in general and with *zakah* itself, as will be explained in this section.

Justice is a general principle in Islam. It is one of the characters of God, one of His glorious names on which the heavens and earth are based, for the establishment of which God sent messengers and Books. The Qur'an declares in explicit words, "We sent aforetime Our apostles with clear signs, and sent down with them the Book and the Balance (of right and wrong) that people may stand forth in justice."[4] This principle of justice is apparent in *zakah* in the following manner:

1. Equality in obligation

Zakah is obligated on each Muslim who owns *nisab*, regardless of race, color, social status, or sex. The weak and the strong, the noble and the common, the governor and the subjects, the learned and the ignorant. All are equal in the obligation of *zakah*. This is not the case with taxes, especially in past Western applications when nobles and clergymen were exempt from taxes.[5]

Ibn Hazm says, "*zakah* is obligatory on men and women old and young, sane and insane, for God says 'Out of their wealth take *sadaqah*, so thou might purify and sanctify them'. This covers everyone, for all are in need of the purification and sanctification of God. The Messenger of God (p) told Mu'adh, 'Inform them that God imposes on them a *sadaqah*, to be taken from the rich among them and rendered to the poor among them.' This text includes every rich Muslim."[6]

2. Exemption of wealth below *nisab*

The principle of justice in Islam requires that those who own small amounts of wealth be exempted from *zakah*. *Zakah* is only imposed on the rich, i.e. those who own at least full *nisab*. This makes the burden of *zakah* easier on people. God says, "Take the excess,[7] and command what is right,"[8] and "They ask thee how much they are to spend. Say 'what is beyond your needs'."[9] Ibn 'Abbas explains "what is beyond your needs" in these verses as the excess of the rich.

3. Elimination of duplicity

In application of justice in *zakah*, the Messenger (p) says, "There must be no duplication in *sadaqah*."[10] Abu 'Ubaid explains, "This means *sadaqah* must not be collected twice in a year."[11] Ibn Qudamdh and others argue that the saying prevents collecting *zakah* more than once in a year for the same reason of *zakatability*.[12] Using the terms of public finance, this mean duality in taxes must be avoided.

The above-mentioned saying implies several points:

A. Abu Hanifah makes the point that."If an owner sells some livestock, he need not add already-*zakted* animals to the cash money he owns in calculating its *zakah* since such addition duplicates *zakah* on livestock in the same year, which is prevented by the saying."[13]

B. A person who pays *zakah* on cash money he owns, then purchases livestock with it, to add to his herd, need not add newly bought livestock, whose value was *zakted* as money, to the cattle he owns in the calculation of *zakah* during that same year, because such addition is partial duplication of *zakah*.[14]

C. A person who buys livestock in the amount of *nisab* as trade inventory must pay on this livestock only *zakah* of business inventory, according to Abu Hanifah, al Thawri, and Ahmad, while Malik and al Shafi'i believe such a person must pay *zakah* of livestock.[15] No scholar argues that on such inventory both *zakah* on livestock and *zakah* on trade must be collected, since this is duplication of *zakah*.

D. The argument given for exempting farm animals used in cultivation is based on the prevention of duplication of *zakah*. Since such animals work in the production of a *zakatable* asset (the agricultural produce), imposing *zakah* on such animals is thus duplication.[16] Abu 'Ubaid emphasizes, "If (these animals) work at watering and plowing, the grain that is *zakatable* includes the value of these animals' work . If one imposes *sadaqah* on the animals while the grain is also *zakted*, this makes duplication in the levy."[17]

E. Hanafites base their argument of exempting *kharaji* land from *'ushr* on the principle of "no duplication in *zakah*." They say *kharji* land is taxed on a yearly basis, thus *'ushr* and *kharaj* must not be combined on the same land.[18]

F. Jurists, in preventing duplication in *zakah*, argue that *nisab* must not be exhausted or burdened by debts, since assets that are due to others as debts must be deducted in the calculation of *zakah* and treated as non-existing from the point of view of *zakatability*.

Jurists argue that the deduction of loans from *zakatable* assets is based on the principle of avoiding of duality, since the creditor is required to pay *zakah* on such loans.[19]

4. Rates of *zakah* differ depending on efforts

Lower rates apply when the production process requires more human efforts. Accordingly, the rate of *zakah* is ten percent on grains and fruits watered by rain or rivers, and five percent when water must be carried mechanically, while the rate on earned income, salaries, and professional income is only 2.5 percent. The system of *zakah* is almost unique in these variations of rates according to effort spent in production.

5. Consideration of personal circumstances

Another important application of the principle of justice is giving attention to the personal circumstances of the *zakah* payer. *zakah* does not deal solely with *zakatable* items detached from the person himself. Taxation specialists distinguish between, what they call "personal taxes" and "physical taxes". Personal taxes take into consideration the following points:

1. Exemption of a minimum standard of living from taxes.
2. Consideration of the source of income in the levy of taxes.
3. Deduction of costs and expenditures related to income.
4. Consideration of family responsibilities.
5. Consideration of debts and loans.

Islam preceded all known taxation systems in providing for personal elements in the obligation, exemption, rates, and deductions in the *zakah* system. Long before public finance studies recognized any distinction between physical and personal taxes, Islam established the following:

A. The exemption of what is below *nisab* from *zakah*. This is founded on the principle that *zakah* is imposed on the rich for the benefit of the poor; *nisab* is a minimum level of richness. Only recently have other taxation systems started exempting income beneath a certain minimum from the burden of taxes.[20]

B. In addition to *nisab* the cost of a minimum level of living is exempt from *zakah*. The provision for living is considered among the basic needs of *zakah* payer. Jurists defined *nisab* as that amount (say 200 dirhams of silver) which is in excess of what is needed to satisfy the essential needs of the owner. This was discussed in chapter one of part three of this book, where it was emphasized that *zakah* is only taken out of excess. Muslim scholars define excess as what is above the provision needed for satisfying essential needs,[21] for the Prophet (p) says, "*Sadaqah* must only be given out of richness," and "Start (by providing) for those you are responsible for."

C. Debts are deducted from taxable assets according to the majority of scholars. This is supported by the texts and spirit of *Shari'ah* .[22] Hanafites say "Whoever owes debts that exhaust his assets, whether these debts belong to other people or to God (such as past due *zakah*), is not *zakatable*. Such a parson needs to pay liabilities due to other people as well as to God, in order to avoid people's demand and the punishment of the hereafter. Not paying due debts hinders him from entering heaven, what need is there more than this? Thus, ridding himself of these responsibilities is to him like water for the thirsty person or clothing for the naked. Such a person must indeed be exempt from *zakah*."[23]

D. Production costs and provisions for the payer's living are deducted from *zakatable* income. 'Ata says regarding *zakah* on agriculture, "Deduct your expenditures, then pay *zakah* on the residual. "This is also the view of Ibn 'Umar and Ibn 'Abbas. A similar opinion is reported from Ahmad. In trade, expenditures are also deducted before the calculation of *zakah*.[24]

E. Consideration of sources of income in *zakah* is obvious from the application of different rates according to the different sources of *zakatable* items. so that 2.5 percent applies on trade income, salaries and professional income; five or ten percent on agriculture, and 20 percent on minerals and buried treasure.

6. Justice in procedures

In addition to justice in the levy of *zakah* itself, collection procedures are also based on justice. The system emphasizes that *zakah* officers must be selected out of the best, most knowledgeable persons, who must be clearly instructed to be fair in their estimations and calculations of *zakah*. Abu Yusuf wrote to the *khalifah* Harun al Rashid "O Prince of Believers, order your ministers to select a person who is honest, trustworthy, wise; whom you can trust and whom people can also trust. Then appoint him to collect the *sadaqat*. Instruct him to assign only officers who can be trusted, after inspecting their opinions, behavior, and honesty, for the collection of *sadaqat* in different areas. I have come to know that some of the *kharaj* commissioners send men to collect *zakah* who do injustice and arbitrarily oppress people. They take what is not lawful to them. For *zakah*, you must only appoint the righteous and trustworthy people."[25]

The Prophet ordered his *zakah* commissioners to he just and moderate and to observe, to the letter, the rules and instructions of this obligation . He (p) says, "A just worker on *sadaqah* is like a fighter in the way of God."[26] He advised one of his *zakah* commissioners, "O Abu al Walid, fear God, and do not appear on the Day of Resurrection carrying a camel that shout or a cow that moos or a sheep that bleats out of embezzlement."[27]

SECTION TWO

THE PRINCIPLE OF CERTAINTY

Certainty in taxation means the tax must be well defined in an exclusive manner without ambiguity that leaves room for arbitrary application. Certainty refers to time and procedure of payment in addition to the calculation and definition of the amount that must be paid. Adam Smith believes the principle of certainty is very important, since the taxpayer must know with certainty all his obligations. Certainty, according to Smith, may even be more important than justice itself.

There is no doubt that certainty has much to do with the stability of any tax system. If the taxpayers become accustomed to the taxes, their rates, and payment procedures, tax payments become easier for them and for the government as well. Because of this, some taxation specialists, like Canard, believe that every old tax is good and every new tax is dubious. Stability of the taxation system, like stability of business law, helps build confidence in the system and its future, and thus in the prosperity of economic activities.[28]

Undoubtedly , the system of *zakah* provides a high degree of certainty. *Zakah* is imposed by God in His eternal Book; no one can add or delete any thing in it. God determines its rates which have been reported to us by God's Messenger, and we have an enormous heritage of jurisprudence that provides explanations and details. All the basic rulings of *zakah* are fixed and unchangeable by any human effort. Knowing these basic rulings is obligatory for each Muslim as part of the religion of Islam. *Zakah* is the most stable financial institution humanity has ever known.

SECTION THREE

THE PRINCIPLE OF CONVENIENCE

Convenience, the third principle of taxation given by Adam Smith, means that the tax and its collection procedures must be made most convenient to taxpayers, so they give the tax with pleasures and satisfaction, or at least without doubt or inconvenience. A quick glance at Islamic laws and instructions about *zakah* reveals how much this principle is observed. This is apparent in many occasions:

1. Ahmad reports from 'Abd Allah bin 'Umar that the Messenger (p) said "*Sadaqat* of Muslims' livestock must be collected at their watering places." in another version reported by Ahmad and Abu Daud, the Prophet (p) said, "There should be no bringing or taking away of *zakatable* assets. Their due *sadaqat* must not be collected except in their own locales."[29] According to al Khattabi, "No bringing and no taking away" means *zakah* payers must not be asked to bring their assets to the collector, nor should the payers take their assets away from the collector with the intention of making it difficult for him to pursue the *zakatable* items. *Zakatable* items must be counted and *zakah* estimated in the localities of these assets."[30] Al Shawkani adds, "This saying means the collector is the one who travels for *zakah* collection, since this is easier for payers."[31]

2. The prophet's instructions ordain taking due *zakah* out of the average quality of *zakatable* items and not the best of them. In his instructions to Mu'adh, the Prophet (p) says, "Avoid the best (quality) of their wealth," since payers usually do not like to give away the best they own. On another occasion, the Messenger (p) was displeased because a collector had taken a high quality she-camel, until the collector explained that he took this she-camel in exchange for two camels of lower quality. The Prophet (p) says "But it (*zakah* payment) must be of the average of your wealth. God does not ask you for the best, nor does he accept the worst."[32]

3. The Prophet (p) instructs estimators of *zakah* on agriculture to be moderate and to estimate on the lower side. He even orders then to make allowances for errors and for fruits used for family and charity. Abu Daud, al Tirmidhi, and al Nasa'i report that the Prophet (p) says, "When you estimate, do not count one-third, if not, do not count one fourth," and "Take it easy in estimation, since orchards may have trees assigned for eating (by family and passers-by) or charity."[33] Al Khattabi comments that one-third or one-fourth of the estimated amount of *zakatable* agricultural product is deducted to make things easier for the *zakah* payer, especially since a certain proportion is always consumed or lost before the time of harvest. 'Umar bin al Khattab used to instruct his estimators to make such deductions.

4. *Zakah* payment may be deffered if necessary, whether for individual or general reasons, like 'Umar's delay of *zakah* in the year of general famine.

SECTION FOUR

THE ECONOMICAL PRINCIPLE

The economical principle means collection cots must be minimum. These cots includes what the state pays, such as collectors' salaries and administrative and transportation costs, in addition to what the payers expend to prepare reports and accounts or to process their complaints or objections to the estimated amounts . Obviously, the purpose of a tax is to bring net income to the state to finance public expenditures. When the principle of economy is not observed, a large portion of proceeds is used to sustain the collection process itself.[34]

Islam prohibits extravagance and ordains moderation and sometimes thrift. This applies as much to public funds as to individual spending. Rather Islamic law is much keener to economize when using public funds.

It was show earlier how strict the Messenger (p) was about gifts to *zakah* officers, and economizing collection costs. He was angered by collectors who accepted gifts from payers, and asked them to give these gifts to the public treasury.

Zakah, in principle, must be spent in the same locale it is collected, it economizes transportation coats. We saw earlier how *zakah* officers went for collection and came back with no residual funds, since they distributed all proceeds in the same area. Moreover, al Shafi'i requires that no more than one-eighth of *zakah* proceeds be spent on workers in the *zakah* administration, in order to restrict administrative costs.

Footnotes

1. *Mabadi' 'Ilm al Maliyah al 'Ammah* by Dr. Muhammad Fu'ad Ibrahim, Vol. 1, pp. 262-263.

2. He was a British economist and philosopher of the eighteenth century. His book, *The Wealth of Nations* is considered the bible of the free economic system.

3. "Islam Lays Down the Foundation of Taxation," an article by Dr. Ahmad Thabit 'Awaidah.

4. *Sura al Hadid*, 57:25.

5. Ahmad Thabit 'Awaidah, *op. cit.*

6. *Al Muhalla*, Vol. 5, pp. 199-200.

7.　Excess is interpreted by some scholars as *zakah*, since *zakah* is a little taken out of plenty.

8.　*Sura al A'raf,* 7:199.

9.　*Sura al Baqarah,* 2:219.

10.　Reported by Abu 'Ubaid, *al Amwal,* p.. 375, and by Ibn Abi Shaibah.

11.　*Al Amwal, Ibid.*

12.　*Al Mughni,* Vol. 3, pp. 34-35.

13.　*Al Bahr al Ra'iq,* Vol. 2, pp. 239-240.

14.　*Ibid,* and *Rad al Muhtar,* Vol. 2, p. 21.

15.　*Al Mughni, op. cit.*

16.　*Al Amwal,* p. 381.

17.　*Ibid.*

18.　*Al Bada'i,* Vol. 2, p. 57.

19.　*Al Majmu',* Vol. 5, p. 436.

20.　See chapter one of part three of this book. pp.

21.　*Ibid.*

22.　*Ibid.*

23.　*Sharh al 'Inayah 'Ala al Hidayah,* and *Fath al Qadir,* Vol. 1, p. 486.

24.　See section seven of the chapter on *zakah* on agriculture of this book. Lately I came to know that the Ja'farite opinion is like that of 'Ata, as stated in *Fiqh al Imam Ja'far,* Vol. 2, pp. 80-81.

25.　*Al Kharaj,* by Abu Yusuf, p. 80.

26.　Reported by Ahmad, Abu Daud, al Tirmidhi, Ibn Majah, and Ibn Khuzaimah. Al Tirmidhi grades it good. See *al Targhib wa al Tarhib,* Vol. 1, p. 559. Also reported by al Hakim, Vol. 1, p. 406, who grades it correct according to Muslim's criteria. This is confirmed by al Dhahabi.

27.　Reported by al Tabarani in *al Mu'jam al Kabir.* Its chain is correct. *Ibid,* p. 563.

28.　*Mabadi'ilm, op. cit.,* p. 267.

29. Al Shawkani says, "On this saying, Abu Daud, al Mundhiri, and al Hafiz in *al Talkhis* do not comment, in its chain is Muhammad bin Ishaq, who says "from "(instead of explicitly stating that he "heard from" the next link in the chain). But on the same subject, Ahmad, Abu Daud, al Nisa'i, al Tirmidhi, Ibn Habban, and 'Abd al Razzaq have a report via 'Imran bin Husain. The saying is also reported a little differently by al Nasa'i. See *Nail al Awtar*, Vol. 4, p. 156. There is also a report by al Tabarani in his *al Mu'jam al Awsat* from 'A'ishah that "The *sadaqah* of the people of the desert must be collected at their waters and canals." Its chain is good, as stated in *Majma'al Zawa'id*, Vol. 3, p. 79.

30. *Ma'alim al Sunan*, Vol. 2, p. 205.

31. *Nail al Awtar*, Vol. 4, pp. 156-157.

32. See pp   of this book.

33. See the chapter on *zakah* on agriculture of this book.

34. *Mabadi 'ilm al Maliyah, op. cit.*, p. 266.

CHAPTER FIVE

PROPORTIONALITY AND PROGRESSIVENESS OF TAXES AND *ZAKAH*

Proportional and progressive taxes

Proportional taxes are those whose rates are constant regardless of the quantity of taxable items. If, for example, the tax rate is ten percent, and this rate applies on all income regardless of its size, then the tax is proportional. Progressive taxes are those whose rates increase with an increase in the amount of the taxable item. Progressive taxes are usually applied on the basis of income stratas. For example, the rate may be ten percent for the first one thousand units of income, twelve percent for the second one thousand, and fifteen percent for the third one thousand.[1] Progressive taxes are supported by many people nowadays, who argue that this kind of tax is more just because it distributes the burden of government expenditures according to the ability of the taxpayers. The following arguments are usually forwarded in support of progressive taxes:

1. Wealthy persons benefit from the economic law of increasing returns, so that the more they accumulate, the more they can obtain higher returns and more accumulation. This ability to accumulate and to earn increases more than proportionally, so the tax applied on such persons must also be more than proportional.

2. Progressive taxes are the most accessible means to eliminate great differences in income and wealth in a society. Whenever we are confronted with a situation of badly distributed wealth, progressive taxes rectify the situation and shrink the economic gap between rich and poor.

Zakah is proportional

It is clear that *zakah* is proportional, i.e., it does not take the principle of increasing the rate with increases in the quantity of the *zakatable* item. The applicable rate on an item is constant. This applies to all *zakatable* assets: agricultural products, livestock, trade assets, or cash.

Some contemporary researchers think *zakah* on livestock has a regressive rate, i.e., the rate declines as the amount of livestock increases. They consider such regression as an attempt to encourage cattle raising in the harsh desert environment of the Arabian peninsula.

This interpretation is incorrect, in fact, the rate of *zakah* on cattle is generally 2.5 percent, with slight differences that relate only to segmental increases in the number of animals subject to *zakah*. The rate of 2.5 percent (generally speaking) is very obvious in the case of cows and camels, while in the case of sheep there is a misunderstanding that arises from the inclusion of lambs and baby sheep. In estimating the *nisab* of forty sheep, baby sheep are not counted, and the rate is one sheep for forty sheep (2.5 percent). As the number of sheep increases above forty, baby animals are included in the total count of *zakatable* heads, but these babies are not acceptable in *zakah* payment. The rate is thus reduced to one sheep for each additional hundred sheep to make up for this inclusion of baby sheep.[2] There is an opinion reported from Ibrahim and Abu Hanifah that *zakah* on steeds has a rate of 2.5 percent, based on evaluation of their prices. This supports the general understanding that the rate on livestock is 2.5 percent.

Why is *zakah* not progressive?

Firstly, *zakah* as an eternal religious obligation, does not change because of changing circumstances. It is a worship required from every Muslim in all ages and environments, while progressive taxes are imposed to achieve rectify the transitory problem of skewed distribution of wealth and income. They are malleable tools whose rates may be altered in order to achieve their target.

Islam does not prevent the imposition of additional taxes when need arises. These taxes may have progressive rates if this is needed to achieve justice and to close the gap in distribution between rich and poor, provided such taxes are inacted by legitimate authority that represents the people and rules righteously in the light of the holy Book sent by God.

Secondly, *zakah* itself redistributes income and wealth from the rich to the poor. Consequently, it fulfills the same objective of progressive taxes by specifically raising the level of living of poor classes and levying the whole burden on the rich while taxes, even progressive ones, are usually rendered, in the form of public services, to all members of the society, including the rich themselves.

Thirdly, Islam resolves the problem of concentration of wealth and income through several means. *zakah* is but one of them. These means include the inheritance system, confiscation of wealth and income that arises from unlawful sources, prohibition of interest, usury, and monopoly. Thus the objectives of progressive taxes are fulfilled through all these means together.

Fourthly, the principle of progressiveness in taxation itself criticized by many thinkers, economists, and experts of public finance, who point to the Following weaknesses:

1. The determination of income stratas for progressiveness is very arbitrary. It has no agreed upon or rationally accepted formulation. This leads sometimes to arbitrariness in the determination of the tax itself. Equality in sacrifice, which is the dominant foundation for progressiveness, has no steady and stable rules for its application. What rate applies such equality at each additional strata of income? Is it an increment of one percent or two percent? How wide should each range of income be? And should taxpayers be divided into classes according to their incomes? All these pose real obstacles in the practical application of any progressive tax.[3]

2. Continuous progressiveness is mathematically impossible, since an increase of one percent at each additional one thousand units of income makes the rate percent an income of two million units. This means the tax is at this level more than the taxed item, which is physically impossible to carry out.[4]

3. Progressiveness in taxes may crush the rich and liquidate all accumulated capital, especially in socialist countries that are dominated by class struggle.[5]

4. Progressive taxes usually take away the amount assigned for saving and investment and do not reduce the consumption of taxpayers. They usually discourage the wealthy from investment and reduce their motivation to produce more income, and thus have negative effects on production.[6]

Footnotes

1. *Mabadi' al Nazariyah al 'Ammah li al Daribah,* by Husain Khallaf and 'Abd al Karim al Rifa'i, p. 151.

2. See *zakah* on sheep, pp.   of this book.

3. *'Ilm al Maliyah,* by Rashid al Daqr, p. 379.

4. *Ibid.*

5. *Ibid.*

6. *Mabadi 'Ilm al Maliyah,* by Muhammad Fu'ad Ibrahim, Vol. 1, p. 279.

CHAPTER SIX

ENFORCEMENT OF TAXES AND *ZAKAH*

Attempts to escape taxes

Taxes are always susceptible to evasion, even by individuals who are just and honest in their transactions with other people. Several reasons account for tax evasion: selfishness and love of wealth, the belief that a certain tax is not just, or that tax proceeds are unjustly utilized, etc. The heavier the tax, the more people will attempt to escape paying it. Escaping tax payment takes two forms. The most common is to take utmost advantage of loopholes in the taxation system itself. This form of evasion is undoubtedly within the law. The other way of escaping payment is to present incorrect information which leads to total or partial elimination of the tax. This is commonly known as tax evasion.

Certainly, cheating on taxes hurts from several aspects:

A. It reduces the proceeds of the tax .

B. It disturbes the just distribution of the tax aimed for originally by its enactment.

C. It may lead sometimes to an increase in tax rates in order to make up for funds lost because of tax cheating.

D. It may reduce some useful government activities because of limited resources.

E. It spreads dishonesty society because people tend to imitate methods of tax escape.

Consequently, all tax legislations attempt to provide legal and administrative procedures to prevent tax escape, in the following ways

1. Authorizing tax officers to inspect the documents and books of the taxpayer.

2. Requiring the payer to submit a tax return given under oath or at the risk of legal penalties for incorrect information.

3. Rewarding anyone who informs the government of cases of tax evasion.

4. Deducting certain taxes at the source, such as deducting income tax from salaries before they are paid to income earners.

5. Imposing heavy financial fines and other penalties for tax evasion.

6. Giving the tax department a legal lein on all the assets of the tax payer with priority over other creditors.[1]

Despite these preventive measures, tax evasion cases fill the courts in all countries, and the use of tax loopholes is so widespread, it has spawned a network of experts in all nations.

Endorsement of *zakah* in *Shari'ah*

Zakah is different from taxes on several bases. Its enforcement is supported by religious, moral, legal, and administrative sanctions.

The religious and moral endorsement of *zakah*

Muslims treat *zakah* as a relation between them and God before any other thing. This is the meaning of a worship. Muslim jurists emphasize this nature of *zakah* very often. Ibn al 'Arabi says, "*Zakah* is, in fact, a right to God, but He transfers His right to those for whom he guarantees sustenance when He says 'There is no moving creature on earth but its sustenance is on God'."[2] Al Kasani, a Hanafite, says, "The core of *zakah* is giving part of the owned *nisab* to God. This is done by making it the property of the poor through actual delivery to them ... God says 'Know they not that God doth accept repentance from His votaries and receivers their *sadaqah*?'[3] and the Messenger (p) says 'The *sadaqah* falls in the hands of the Most Merciful before it falls into the hands of the poor.'[4] Moreover, *zakah* is a worship, and worship is the devotion of an action completely to God."[5]

When performing *zakah*, the payer has not the slightest resentment or feeling of injustice, since *zakah* is legislated by God, Who oppresses none. God is the most just Legislator and the Nourisher and Sustainer of His servants. Why would a believer try to escape *zakah*, knowing that God, for whom it is given, knows what is secret and even what is more hidden than a secret, and that God is going to inspect everyone's account on the Day of Judgment.

Consequently, Islamic values and ethics inculcated by faith, education, and upbringing, are the strongest guarantee that payers pay their dues properly. Muslims are educated and trained to look toward the hereafter and to be moderate in their love of worldly benefits. They seek reward from God, and they spend for God's sake. They prefer what pleases God and His Messenger above all other things. A believer does not hesitate in a choice between what pleases God and His Messenger on one side and all earthly benefits and enjoyments on the other. In the Qur'an God makes it clear, "Say: If it be that your fathers, your sons, your brothers, your maids, or your kindred, the wealth that ye have gained, the commerce in which ye fear a decline, or the dwellings in which ye delight, are dearer to you than God or His apostle or the striving in His cause, than wait until God brings about His decision, and God guides not the rebelious."[6]

This kind of Faith is not consistent with escaping *zakah* payment. Rather, believers are eager to pay, as evident on many occasions in Qur'an and Sunnah. Twice in the Qur'an it is reported that believers asked the Messenger of God (p) about spending. God answers them once regarding what to spend and once regarding to whom one should give: "They ask thee how much they are to spend. Say 'what is beyond your needs,'"[7] and "They ask thee what they should spend. Say, 'whatever ye spend that is good is for parents, and the kindred, and orphans, and those in want, and for wayfarers. And whatever ye do that is good, God know it well."[8]

Willingness of Muslims to volunteer their wealth is a recurring theme in the tradition of the Prophet. Anas says, "A man from (the tribe of) bani Tamim came to the Messenger of God (p) and said, 'O Messenger of God, I have plenty of wealth. I have a family and a residence. Tell me what to do and how to spend.' The Messenger of God (p) said, 'Give the (due) *zakah* on your wealth, for it purifies you. And do good to your kindred, and recognize the right of the indigent, the neighbor, and the beggar,' The man said, 'O Messenger of God, reduce it for me.' The Prophet said, 'Give the kindred their right, and the indigent, and the wayfarer, and do not be extravagant.' He said, 'O Messenger of God, if I give my due *zakah* to your commissioner, would that be sufficient as fulfillment toward God and His Messenger?' The Messenger of God (p) said, 'Yes, if you give *zakah* to my commissioner, you have fulfilled it. You deserve its reward, and (if it is altered later) the sin of altering it is on whoever changed it.'"[9] Abu Hurairah narrates that a man said, "O Messenger of God, I have one dinar. "The Prophet said, "Give it as *sadaqah* to your own self." The man said, "I have another." The Prophet replied, "Make it a *sadaqah* to your children." The man continued, "I have a third." The Prophet said, "Make it *sadaqah* to your wife," The man then added, "I have a fourth." The Prophet said, "Make it *sadaqah* m your servant." "I still have another," the man went on. The Prophet replied, "You see for yourself."[10] Some faithful believers sometimes brang the Prophet all their wealth to be spent as charity, in spite of their need for it. The Prophet (p) disapproves of this, and usually informed such people not to give all they have. Jabir narrates , "We were with the Messenger of God (p) when a man brought a gold nugget the size of an egg and said, 'O Messenger of God, I gained this from a mine. Take it. It is a charity from me. I own nothing besides it.' The Prophet turned his face away from him . The man came from the Prophet's right side and repeated what he first said. The Prophet turned away again. Then the man came from the left side and the Prophet turned away from him again . At last the mar came from behind. The Messenger of God took the piece of gold and threw it to the man, such that if it had hit him it would have hurt, and said, 'One of you would bring all that he owns and say, this is a *sadaqah*. Then he would go begging people! The best *sadaqah* is that which comes out of richness'"[11]

The keenness of Muslims to perform *zakah* was high, as it was part of their religious requirements. Once a group of people from Syria asked 'Umar bin al Khattab to take *zakah* from them for their mares and slaves, saying "We gained some wealth in the form of mares and slaves, and we would like to pay *zakah* on them in order to be purified."[12] Another man asked 'Umar to take *zakah* on honey, saying "A property that is not *zakated* is no good."[13] Ibn Mas'ud after paying the tenth or half-tenth on his agricultural produces, used to divide the remainder into three equal parts one for his family, one to buy seeds for next year, and one for charity." Muslims believe paying *zakah* is purification and sanctification for themselves and their wealth, a source of protection and a blessing for the rest of the wealth. Abu Daud reports from Suwaid bin Ghafalah, "I went along with the Prophet's *zakah* officer or someone who went along told me . . . A man wanted to give the officer a big she-camel with a huge hump. The officer refused to accept it, so the man gave another she-camel, which he accepted. The officer said, 'I shall take this, but I am afraid the Messenger of God may be displeased by my action. He may tell me, 'you went to a man and selected the best of his camels.'"[15]

Ubai bin Ka'b says, "The Messenger of God (p) sent me as *zakah* commissioner, I went to a man, who gathered his herd for me , and I found that he owed only one she-camel, one to two years old. I told him , ' Pay one she-camel, one to two years old. This is the *sadaqah* due on you.' The man said 'This camel does not give milk, nor is it good for riding . Here is a better she-camel , stronger (but still young) with a huge hump. Please take it'. I said, 'I would not take more than what I am ordered to. The Messenger of God (p) is nearby. If you like, go to him and make him the offer you are making me. If he accepts, I will accept it. and vice versa.' The man said, 'I shall do that'. So he went with me, taking with him the she-camel which he had offered me, to the Messenger of God (p). The man said, 'O Prophet of God, your commissioner came to take the *sadaqah* of my camels. By God, no one came to me before, not the Messenger of God nor his commissioner. So I gathered my herd for him to inspect , and he said, I owe one one-to-two-year-old she-camel. Such an animal does not give milk and is not good as a ride, so I offered him a bigger she-camel that is strong, and still young , but he refused and gave it back to me. This is it. I brought it to you, O Messenger of God. Take it.' The Messenger of God (p) answered. 'That was what is due on you, but if you volunteer more, God rewards you more for it, and we accept it from you.' The man said, 'Here it is, I brought it to volunteer it, take it.' The Messenger of God (p) ordered it to be accepted, and prayed for blessings on the wealth of the man." In the version of this saying reported by Ahmad, it is stated "The man said I would not give God an animal that does not give milk and is not good for riding.'"[16] Clearly, the man feels paying *zakah* is a transaction between him and God, and therefore shies away from giving God anything less than the best.

These beliefs and sentiments are the best guarantee for proper fulfillment of *zakah*. Tax cheating is the rule and not the exception in Western countries. In France, 1936, Vincent Orion remarked, "If it were not for cheating, the rates of taxes would have been reduced." President Roosevelt said about tax evasion in the United States." Many tax cheaters suse loopholes in taxation acts; many others commit violations of the law. Either way, the spirit of the law is not observed, and 'we must fight all forms of tax evasion." The British Thames newspaper notes that a good part of Britain's budget deficit could be reduced if only the finance minister could discover practical means to prevent tax evasion."[17]

Legal and organizational endorsement of *zakah*

Shari'ah provides legal and organizational endorsement of *zakah*, in addition to the religious and moral ones. These legal and organizational guarantees include the following:

Payers ordered to cooperate with collectors

Several sayings explicitly indicate that payers are required to help *zakah* collectors. The Messenger of God (p) says, "You shall receive a group of collectors whom you may dislike. When they come, welcome them. Allow them to do what they want. If they do justice, that benefits their own selves on the Day of Judgement and if they do injustice, it is their own souls they hurt. It is part of completing *zakah* that you please them. They also should pray on your behalf."[18] Jarir bin 'Abd Allah says, "Some bedouin Arabs came to the Messenger of God (p) and said, 'Some of *zakah* collectors do injustice to us.' The Prophet (p) said, 'you must please your collectors.' They said, 'Even if they do oppression against us?' The Prophet repeated, 'you must please your collectors.'" Jarir adds, "Since I heard this from the Messenger of God (p), no *zakah* collector left me but was pleased."[19] Bashir bin al Khasasiyah says, "We asked the Messenger of God, 'Some *zakah* collectors transgress against us. Should we hide some of our wealth in amounts equal to the amount of their transgressions?' The Prophet said, 'No.'"[20]

These sayings indicate that *zakah* payers must help *zakah* collectors and are not allowed to hide any information needed for the estimation of *zakah*, even in the case when collectors do not behave rightly and do injustice to the payers. Of course, in cases of clear-out oppression on the part of the collector, *zakah* payers have the right to refuse to pay the injust part and complain to the proper authorities. In the saying reported from Anas, it is stated, 'He, among Muslims, who is asked *zakah* in its proper rate and amount, must pay it, but he who is asked more must not give more." Since the Prophet (p) determined all *zakah* rates, and these are known to all Muslims, payers and collectors.

Cheating and tricks to escape *zakah* are forbidden

Islam prohibits cheating in all its forms, especially when it is used to avoid *zakah* payment. The laws of *zakah* do not have loopholes, but some cheating, though forbidden, may take legal form, such as interrupting the passage of the year by nominal change of ownership (e.g. giving one's wealth to one's wife, and then taking it back after a few days). Prohibition of this kind of practice is clear in the general saying of the Messenger "Deeds are only by intention, and each person has only the result of his own intention." Al Bukhari argues that the saying reported from Anas on *zakah* which states, "What is combined must not be separated and what is separated must not be combined in order to avoid the *sadaqah*"[21] stands firmly against cheating and tricks. Malik explains this saying with the example that "Three people, each one owning forty sheep, each being obligated to give one sheep, cannot combine their herds together and pay only one sheep for the hundred and twenty sheep. Or, two partners, each owing 101 sheep, are obligated to give as a partnership three sheep, and must not divide their sheep so that each only pays one sheap.'[22] Abu Yusuf says, "It is not lawful to anyone who believes in God and the Last Day to withhold the *sadaqah* or to change property only to avoid the payment of *sadaqah*. It is not lawful to cheat or use any trick to avoid the *sadaqah*, by any means and for any reason."[23]

Both Hanbalites and Malikites prohibit all tricks, legal or not, that aim at escaping the payment of *zakah*. One finds in Hanbalite writing such statements as "He who purchases real estate in order to escape *zakah* must be charged the amount of *zakah* on the value of the real estate such person must be treated exactly the opposite of his intention, like one who escapes *zakah* by selling or by other actions."[24] In Malikite writings one finds similar things, as studied in chapter six of part five of this book. Purchasing exempted women's jewelry in an attempt to escape *zakah* makes *zakah* lawful and due on the amount escaped.

Imposing fines and penalties for *zakah* evasion

The saying reported by Ahmad, Abu Daud, and al Nasa'i decrees fines for rejecting payment of due *zakah*. It reads, ". . . and he who holds off payment, we shall indeed take it, along with half his wealth, an imposition decreed by our Lord none of which is lawful to the family of Muhammad." The author of *Muntaqa al Akhbar* comments, "this is evidence for collecting *zakah* from those who reject paying it, and spending it where it belongs."[25]

Fines were discussed earlier in this book and it was concluded that a fine of half the *zakatable* asset is maximum. Imposition of such fines is to be decided by the consultative and executive authorities in the Muslim society, although there are scholars who do not allow imposing any fines, on the grounds that in another saying the Prophet (p) announced, "Indeed God made unlawful to each one of you each other's blood and wealth,"[26] and that the Companions fought the rejecters of *zakah* payment, but charged them no fines above the due amount of *zakah*.[27]

Those who withhold payment of *zakah* are subject to other penalties as well. When objection to the payment of *zakah* takes a collective form, as at the time of Abu Bakr, it represents a rebellion against Islamic law. Such rebels must be fought by the Islamic state, as Abu Bakr and the Companions fought them upon the death of the Messenger of God (p).[28] Ibn Hazm says,

The ruling regarding he who does not pay *zakah* is to collect it by force, whether he likes it or not. If he continues defending himself against the law enforcement, then he is treated as a rebel . Moreover, negating the obligation is a form of apostation. But he who escapes payment through methods of cheating, without denying or holding off payment, is doing an evil act and must be subjected to legal penalties, until he submits what is due on him. If he dies during the period of the penalty, he goes to the wrath of God. This is according to the Messenger's saying "He who sees an act of evil must change it with his hand if he can." Withholding payment of *zakah* is undoubtedly an act of evil that must be changed.[29]

In part five I discussed in detail that the due amount of *zakah* is not wavered even by the passage of years, and must be collected by the law enforcement body of the Islamic state, for such a right belongs to God and is assigned to the poor and needy. No one has any authority to waive it.[30]

Footnotes

1. *Mabadi' al Nazariyah al 'Ammah li al Daribah*, by 'Abd al Karim al Rafi'i and Husain Khallaf.

2. *Sura Hud*, 11:6.

3. *Sura al Tawbah*, 9:104.

4. In his Tafsir, Ibn Jarir attributes this statement to Ibn Mas'ud. See texts 17163-17166, Vol. 14. pp. 459-451. It is reported from 'A'ishah, linked up to the Prophet (p), that "A person should give a *sadaqah* out of good earning, for God does not accept but the good. The most Merciful receives it with his hand, and He nurses it like any of you nurses a baby horse or a baby camel or a baby servant." Reported by al Bazzar via a chain of trustworthy narrators. See *Majma' al Zawa'id,* Vol. 3, p. 112.

5. *Al Bada'i,* Vol. 2 , p. 39.

6. *Sura al Tawbah,* 9:24.

7. *Sura al Baqarah,* 2:219.

8. *Ibid,* 2:215.

9. In *Majma' al Zawa'id,* Vol. 3, p. 63, al Haithami says, "It is reported by Ahmad and al Tabarani in his *al Mu'jam al Awsat.* Its narrators are those of the correct collection."

10. Reported by Abu Daud, al Nasa'i, and al Hakim. The latter grades it correct by the criteria of Muslim, and this is confirmed by al Dhahabi. See *al Mustadrak,* Vol. 1, p. 415.

11. Reported by Abu Daud and al Hakim. The latter grades it correct by the criteria of Muslim, and this is confirmed by al Dhahabi, *al Mustadrak,* Vol. 1, p. 413.

12. Reported by Ahmad and al Tabarani in *al Mu'jam al Kabir.* Its narrators are trustworthy, as stated in *Majma'al Zawa'id,* Vol. 3 m p.69. Also reported by al Hakim in his al Mustadrad, Vol. 1, pp. 400-401. He grades it correct, and this is confirmed by al Dhahabi.

13. Reported by al Bazzar and al Tabarani in his *al Mu'jam al Kabir*. In its chain is Munir bin 'Abd Allah, who is weak, as stated in *Majma' al Zawa'id*, Vol. 2, p. 77.

14. Reported by al Tabarani in *al Mu'jam al Kabir*, from Masruq. Its narrators are those of the correct collection, as in *Majma' al Zawa'id*, Vol. 3, p. 68.

15. Al Mundhiri says, "Reported by al Nasa'i and Ibn Majah. In its chain is Hilal bin Habbab, who is considered trustworthy by more than one critic, although he is criticized by others. See *Mukhtasar al Sunan*, Vol. 2, p. 196. Also reported by al Daraqutni and al Baihaqi. See *Nail al Awtar*, Vol. 4, p. 133.

16. Reported by Ahmad, Abu Daud, and al Hakim. The latter grades it correct according to Muslim's criteria, which is confirmed by al Dhahabi. See *al Mustadrak* Vol. 3, pp. 399-400. In its chain is Muhammad bin Ishaq, about whom leading critics do not agree, then he mentions in his narration the word "from" instead of, explicitly saying that he "heard from". But in this saying, he explicitly mentions his hearing. See *Mukhtasar al Sunan*, Vol. 2, pp. 198-199, and *Nail al Awtar*, Vol. 4, p. 115. In *al Majmu'*, Vol. 5, p. 427, al Nawawi' says, it is reported by Ahmad and Abu Daud via a correct or good chain." Ibn Ahmad adds in the *Musnad* of his father, "The reporter from Ubai bin Ka'b, who is Amarah bin 'Amr bin Hazm, says 'I was commissioned on *sadaqat* at the tim of Mu'awiyah. I took from the same mean thirty she-camels, four to five years old, due on 1500 camels.'" This means that the Messenger's prayer for blessing was accepted by God.

17. From the lecture, "Islam Laid down the Foundation of Modern Taxes," by Muhammad Thabit 'Awaidah.

18. Reported by Abu Daud, chapter on pleasing *zakah* commissioners. In its chain is Thabit bin Qais al Madani al Ghifari, who is disputed from the point of view of his memory. Ahmad grades him trustworthy. See *Mukhtasar al Sunan*, Vol. 2, p. 202.

19. Reported by Abu Daud, (the version mentioned above is his) Muslim, and al Nasa'i. *Ibid*.

20. Reported by Abu Daud, with no comment, and without comment also from al Mundhiri. Also reported by 'Abd al Razzaq. In its chain is Daisam al Sadusi, Ibn Habban mentions his name among the trustworthy. The author of *al Taqrib* says he is "accepted". See *Nail al Awtar*, Vol. 4, p. 156.

21. Mentioned by Ibn al Qayyim in *Ighathat al Lahfan*, Vol. 1, p, 376. In his *I'lam al Muwaqqi'in*. Ibn al Oayyim studies this subject in some detail. See Vol. 3.

22. *Al Muwatta'*, chapter on *sadaqah* of partners, Vol. 1, p. 264.

23. *Al Kharaj*, by Abu Yusuf, p. 80.

24. *Sharh Ghayat al Muntaha*, Vol. 1, p. 101, and *al Qawa'id al Nuraniyah*, p. 89.

25. *Nail al Awtar*, Vol. 4, p. 122.

26. Reported by Muslim.

27. In *al Turuq al Hukmiyah*, Ibn al Qayyim mentions fifteen cases in which a fine was actuated by the Prophet (p) and his successors. See p. 287. Refer also to chapter one of part five of this book.

28. Refer to part one of this book.

29. *Al Muhalla*, Vol. 11, pp. 313.

30. Refer to part five of this book.

CHAPTER SEVEN

IS IT PERMISSIBLE TO LEVY TAXES BESIDE *ZAKAH*?

Zakah is levied for particular purposes, decreed by God, on the wealth of Muslims, and is collected and distributed by the Islamic state. In the Islamic state permitted to impose other taxes in addition to *zakah*? Or, is *zakah* the only duty on the wealth of Muslims? A duty that must not co-exist with other taxes. We will study in the following three sections the evidence that allows imposing taxes in addition to *zakah*, the necessary conditions for levying such taxes, and the objections raised by opponents.

SECTION ONE

EVIDENCE PERMITTING LEVYING TAXES BESIDE *ZAKAH*

1. Social solidarity is a must

There is no need to repeat talking about the importance of social solidarity between members of the Muslim society, discussed in previous chapters. However, solidarity and brotherhood of Muslims, that are the foundations for *zakah* itself, also lay the grounds for imposing other taxes when the need arises.

2. Distribution of *zakah* is pre-determined

Since *zakah* can only be expended to the eight categories described in part four of this book. Muslim scholars argue that *zakah* must have an autonomous budget. Abu Yusuf, for example, says "The proceeds of *kharaj* must not be added to the proceeds of *sadaqat*, since *kharaj* is to serve all Muslims while *zakah* must only serve the categories named by God."[1] Scholars usually agree that "*Zakah* must not be spent on building bridges, highways, canals, mosques, schools, etc."[2]

No one can argue with the fact that services for which *zakah* cannot be appropriated include certain public necsseities, like schools and mosques, and these require financial resources. If the proceeds of *kharaj, ghanimah,* and *fai'* are sufficient, there is no need for imposing taxes, but if such sources do not exist or do not yield sufficient amount, other taxes need to be levied, since the rule of *usul* states, "That without which an obligation cannot be fulfilled is also obligatory."

We have seen earlier in this book that Shafi'ites do not allow payment of *zakah* to the regular army, and restrict payment to voluntary fighters. When al Nawawi was faced with the problem of insufficiency of other resources to finance the regular army, he suggested, as do many other Shafi'ites, that rich Muslims be obligated to finance the regular army.[3]

3. General rules in *Shari'ah*

The permissibility of imposing taxes besides *zakah* does not only depend on the above mentioned rule stating, "That without which an obligation cannot be fulfilled is obligatory." The general rules and principles of *Shari'ah* allow the levy of taxes when need arises. Principles which imply such possibility include the state's responsibility to care for the public interests of Muslims, the rules that "avoiding evil has priority over bringing benefits" and "small benefit can be sacrificed for the great benefit," and " individual harm may be tolerated in order to prevent common harm."[4]

Undoubtedly, application of these general rules leaves room for imposing taxes. In fact it may be deducted from these rules that texts, on certain occasions, must be imposed to secure important interests of society and state, and to prevent harm and danger. If a contemporary Islamic state, that does not have huge mineral resources, is left without taxes, it is bound to be wiped out in a very short time because of lack of internal services, let alone outside military dangers. For such reasons derived from *Shari'ah* principles, Muslim scholars opine that financing the public treasury with taxes imposed by the Islamic government is obligatory when there is need to prevent a danger or fulfill an important benefit.

Al Ghazali, a Shafi'ite known for his restrictive views, when it comes to public funds, says, "when there are no funds and the state income is not sufficient to pay for army needs, and there is danger that an enemy may transgress against the Muslim land or that evil rebels may arise, the Islamic government is allowed to impose on the rich taxes sufficient to pay for the soldiers, since we know the rule that when one must choose between two evils or two harms, the most dangerous of them must be avoided. Every sacrifice made by the rich including the sacrifice of lives and wealth, is a lesser harm than lack of means to defend the Islamic society against aggression or sinful rebellion."[5] Al Shatibi, a Malikite, says,

If we happen to have an Islamic government that needs to increase the number of its soldiers in order to defend Muslim borders and lands and the treasury is empty, the leader, provided he is just, has the right to impose on the rich what is sufficient to fulfill defense needs, until the treasury has funds again. The government has the right to make these impositions on agriculture or other products. The reason no such opinion is reported from the scholars of the early generations is the abundance of treasury funds during their times. If the Islamic government does not impose such taxes, its strength would vanish and our country would be exposed to unbelievers' aggressions. The backbone of the government and defense is the army. Those who evade the payment of levied taxes would realize that if the army were abolished, they will be hurt personally and all their wealth, not only a part of it, would be confiscated by the aggressors if such enormous harm is contrasted with the harm of tax payment, no one can argue that the latter is much lesser.[6]

4. *Jihad* and its financial requirements

Islam prescribes *jihad* on both persons and their wealth. God says, "Go ye forth (whether equiped) lightly or heavily, and strive and struggle with your wealth and your persons,"[7] "Only those true believers who have believed in God and His Apostle and have never since doubted but have striven with their wealth and their persons in the cause of God, such are the sincere ones,"[8] "That ye believe in God and His Apostle and that ye strive (your utmost) in the cause of God with your wealth and your persons,"[9] "And spend of your substance in the cause of God, and make not your own hands contribute to your destruction."[10]   All these verses ordain spending of wealth and property in the way of God. *Jihad* in wealth is an obligation in itself, like the obligation of *zakah*. The Islamic government has the right to determine the share of each person in this financial *jihad*. This is also the essence of a quotation by Ibn Taimiyah from the author of *Ghiyath al Umam*.

Armament and army expenditures today are huge. in addition to the fact that the might of a nation is not only measured by the size of its army. National strength requires superiority in several areas, including scientific research, industry, and the general economy. All these require abundant financial resources which cannot be secured except by imposing taxes. These taxes are a form of *jihad* in wealth whereby all individuals contribute to the strength and defense of their state. Such contributions pay back in the form of protection for the individual himself, his religion, and his assets.

5. Sharing the burdens as the gains are shared

Resources collected in the form of taxes are spent on public services which benefit all members of the society, such as defense and security, judicial institutions, education, health services, transportation, irrigation, etc. Each individual benefits from the presence and power of the state as well as from the services it provides. Thus each must share the financial burden that allows these services to be performed. Just as each individual benefits from the state's services and its presence, he or she is required to pay the necessary taxes, in application of the principle that gains must be comparable to sacrifices.

SECTION TWO

CONDITIONS FOR IMPOSING TAXES

There art four conditions for imposing taxes: True need, just distribution, lawful use of funds, and approval of the *shura* body of the state.

The first condition: true need for funds

There should be real need for the services to be financed by additional financial resources as well as inadequacy of treasury funds and other state resources.

In principle, private wealth is protected and should not be charged any duties above *zakah*. It is unlawful to violate this rule except in dire need. If such necessity does not exist or if the government has other financial resources, it is not lawful to impose taxes. Leading scholars have emphasized this condition for centuries. Some go as far as requiring that the treasury be completely empty, in order to deter rulers from imposing taxes without need. Islamic history reveals several instances in which Muslim scholars stood fast confronting rulers who wanted to impose taxes while they still had other resources.

When Sultan Qutuz of Egypt was preparing his troops to fight the Moguls, who by then had occupied most of Syria, he gathered all scholars, jurists and judges to consult with them on whether he could impose taxes for *jihad*. Among them were Izz al Din bin 'Abd al Salam and Badr al Din al Sinjari. After discussion, the opinion leaders agreed that Izz al Din speak for them. He said,

> If the enemy transgresses on the lands of Islam, all Muslim are obligated to fight. It is then permissible for you to collect taxes from people in the amount that helps you in this *jihad*, provided there be nothing in the public treasury and that you sell all gold ornamented clothes and all fancy tools and utensils that you and your courtiers and soldiers own, so that each person in the army has only a mare and a weapon, and all become equal to the common people. As for collecting funds from the public while your men and soldiers still have assets and luxurious things-no, it is not permissible."

A similar stand was taken later by al Nawawi before Sultan al Zaher Bibars. When the sultan wanted to fight the Tatar in Syria, he had insufficient funds in his treasury, so he asked scholars in Syria whether he could impose taxes to help the government and the army fight the enemies of Islam. All the present scholars approved and wrote their approval to the king. Al Nawawi was then absent, and the Sultan asked if there were any scholars who did not respond to his appeal. They said, "Yes, there is al Nawawi." When he came, the Sultan asked him to add his approval to those of others, but al Nawawi refused. When asked for a reason, he said, "I know that you were a slave of the previous ruler, Bandaqdar. Then you owned nothing, and God generously gave you and made you a king. I hear that you own one thousand slaves, and each of them has a gold ornamented garment, that you also own 200 female slaves, and each of them has a basket of jewelry. If you spend all that, and your slaves live with woolen garments only, and your slave women keep only their clothes, without any jewelry, after that I approve of your collecting taxes from people." The Sultan was angered and ordered al Nawawi out of the city. Al Nawawi obeyed and went out to his village, Nawa [about fifty miles south of Damascus]. When some other scholars negotiated for his return and the Sultan permitted it, al Nawawi refused and announced, "I will not go to Damascus as long as al Zaher Bibars is there," but the king died after a month.[12] al Nawawi wrote al Zaher a letter explaining, "It is not lawful to collect anything from people as long as the treasury has wealth in any form, money, property, land, or anything that can be sold. All scholars agree to this. And the treasury now, praise be to God, has much property and goods, may God always increase it."[13]

The second condition: just distribution of the burden

The burden of taxes must be distributed justly among people, so that none is ever-burdened while others are exempted without reasonable cause. Justice does not require equality among taxpayers, since treating equally what is different is as unjust as treating differently what is equal. There must be objective criteria for distributing the tax burden among the rich members of society.

Abu 'Ubaid reports from Ibn 'Umar that 'Umar used to collect from the Nabatites [foreign merchants who used to bring goods into the country] half a tenth on oil and wheat, to encourage them to bring more of these goods to Madinah, and one tenth on beans."[14] It is known that the general principle of this tax laid by 'Umar was to collect one-tenth from foreign merchants, one-half of a tenth from merchants who were people of the Pledge, and one-fourth of a tenth from Muslim merchants,[13] as reported by Anas and by al Sa'ib bin Yazid, who says, I was a commissioner to the Madinah market during 'Umar's time, and we used to collect one-tenth from the Nabatites."[17]

But with regard to oil and wheat, 'Umar apparently reduced the tax to five percent for an important economic reason, i.e. encouraging food imports that were required in the fast growing Madinah, capital of the state. This action of 'Umar indicates that tax rates may be changed according to the economic target they aim at achieving, whether in trade, import and export, industry, or agriculture.

Furthermore, since one objective of the Islamic economic system is to reduce economic differences between Muslims and decentralize wealth accumulation so that wealth and income do not circulate among the rich alone, if there are no other means except progressive taxes to achieve such a purpose, such taxes can be blessed and supported by the Islamic system. One must not forget that the personal aspects of taxes must be taken into consideration. These include the exemption of living expenses, family provisions, and debts from taxes, as mentioned earlier.

Third condition: proceeds must benefit society

Tax collection is aimed only at serving the nation. Thus tax proceeds must not be used for the whims and desires of the rulers and their inner circles, or to fulfill dictatorial purposes or individual ambitions. God establishes this principle when He details *zakah* distribution, not leaving it to be determined by any ruler, not even a Prophet. The Wise Successors, along with the great Companions, were extremely strict about the dispersement of public funds. Ibn Sa'd in his *Tabaqat* reports from Salman that 'Umar bin al Khattab once asked "Am I a king or a caliph?" Salman answered, "If you collect one single *dirham* from the Muslim land, or less, or more, and spend it on anything other than its right and proper dispersement, then you are a king and not a *khalifah*."Umar, hearing this, wept"[18] Sufyan bin Abi al 'Awja' says, "Umar bin al Khattab once asked 'By God, I am not sure, am I a *khalifah* or a king? If I am a king, this is indeed an awful thing,' A man answered, 'O Prince of Believers, there is indeed a big difference between them.' 'Umar asked, 'What?' The man said, 'The *khalifah* does not take but what is right and does not spend it except on what is right. You, praise be to God, are of that kind. Kings oppress arbitrarily. They take from this and give to that.' 'Umar remained silent."[18] Al Tabari reports, "A man who was a relative of 'Umar, asked Umar for some grant. 'Umar turned him down and asked him out. Then someone spoke to 'Umar about him, 'O Prince of Believers, so-and-so asked you but you turned him down and ordered him out.' 'Umar answered, He indeed asked me to give him from the property of God [meaning the property of the society and state]. If I do so, what would be the excuse? Then I would meet God as a betraying king!'"[19]

The fourth condition: approval of the *shura* body

Since private property is protected by Islamic law, any levy on individuals must be approved by the consultative body of the state. It is not sufficient that the ruler alone or his administrative commissioners make such a decision. *Shura* consultation is required by Qur'an and Sunnah. God commends ". . . those who hearken to their Lord and establish prayer, who conduct their affairs by mutual consultation, and who spend out of what We bestow on them for sustenance."[20] *Shura* is associated with accepting the message of God, establishing prayer, and spending for His sake. This verse establishes the essential principles of the Islamic system as early as the Makkan period. Later in Madinah, God sent down the verse, "And consult them in affairs, then when thou hast taken a decision, put thy trust in God."[21] Revealed in Madinah, in the era when details of Islamic law and life were laid down, this verse gave the general foundations for the government structure of this society. This verse was revealed just after the battle of Uhud, before which the Prophet had consulted his Companions on whether to stay in Madinah and let the enemy reach there, or to go out and fight the invaders outside the city limits. The bulk of Companions wanted to go out, while the Prophet's opinion was to stay in Madinah and fortify it, but following the majority, he went out and the result was a defeat, about 70 great Companions were killed. Even despite that, the verse reaffirmed that consultation is an essential part of the Islamic system, as if to say: You must continue to consult them and make your decisions by consultation, even after what happened as a result of following the majority's opinion.

The Prophet used to consult his Companions on all matters of substance whenever he was not given clear revelation from God about the matter. At the time of Badr, the first battle in Islam, the Prophet asked the opinion of both the *Muhajirin* and *Ansar* on whether they should seek out the Quraish caravan and where to camp in that battle. In the battle of Uhud as well, he based his decisions on consultation. At the battle of al Ahzab, the Prophet (p), wanted to accept the peace treaty offered by the unbelievers, which required that he give them one third of the produce of Madinah, but leading Companions did not accept, so he refused that offer. On the day of al Hudaibiyah, he based his decision to hold back the weapons from fighting on consultation, for he was told by Abu Bakr, "We did not come here to fight, we came only to visit the house of God." When his wife "A'ishah was accused, he also consulted Muslims, saying, "O Muslims, give me your opinion, what should I do with those who accuse my wife?" and consulted 'Ali and Usamah on how to deal with "A'ishah.[22] Ibn Kathir comments "The Prophet (p) used to consult the Companions on battles and for other decisions. Jurists dispute whether this was obligatory for him or only recommended (by God) in order to keep them happy."[23]

If this can be disputed when it comes to the Messenger (p) who is guided by God and His revelation, it cannot be disputed with respect to other leaders who are simply elected men. The verse explicitly ordains consultation, and ordinances mean obligations. Add to that the keenness of the Prophet (p) to implement this verse in all important matters. All this makes consultation obligatory for leaders especially in view of the Islamic nation's historical experience of suffering from tyrants and dictators.

Digression: Is consultative decision binding on the ruler?

The answer is certainly affirmative, on the grounds that the Prophet used to accept the opinion of the majority of his Companions after consultation. Ibn Kathir mentions that Ibn Mardawaih reports that 'Ali says, "The Messenger of God (p) was asked about the meaning of the verse, 'Then when thou hast taken a decision . . .' and he answered that it meant 'consult people of opinion and then follow them."[24] If the majority's decision based on consultation (*shura*) is not binding on the government, *shura* looses its meaning. This makes a mockery of consultation, whereby rulers consult people and then do what they want, regardless of the majority opinion.

Moreover, Muslims can make *shura* always indisputably binding by legislation, i.e. incorporating such a clause in the constitution, whereby the leader is elected on the condition that the majority's view shall be binding on the government and the head of state. The Prophet (p) says Muslims are bound by their contractual conditions."[25] Honest fulfillment of such conditions are binding on the government, without the slightest doubt, regardless of jurist opinions on whether *shura*, when unassociated with such conditions, is only informative or is binding.

The verses do not specify on what affaire *shura* is required. No doubt the words "matters" or "affairs" in the verse are general and include all affairs, yet the most important are those affairs that affect the Muslim society and its future. Certainly, taxes are of such importance as to require consultation.

SECTION THREE

ARGUMENTS AGAINST TAXES

Some scholars believe it is unlawful to impose any taxes besides *zakah*. They use three main arguments to support their views: First, the rule that nothing is obligated on wealth except *zakah* is commonly know among jurists. Second, private property is protected and any charge on it must be supported by a text. The Prophet says, "He who is killed while defending his wealth is a martyr."[26] It is, therefore, unlawful to take any part of Muslims' private property without their consent. Third, several sayings discredit levies on people and prohibit the collection of tenth [*'ushr*], such as the following:

Abu al Khair says "Maslamh bin Mukhlid, who was governor of Egypt, offered Ruwaifi' bin Thabit the position of *'ushr* commissioner. Ruwaifi' refused, saying, "I heard the Messenger of God (p) say, 'Levy collectors are in the Fire.'"[27] 'Uqbah bin 'Amir says he heard the Messenger of God (p) say, "Levy collectors do not enter Heaven."[28] Although these two sayings are criticized by *hadith* critics, they are supported by a saying reported by Muslim at the end of a story about a married woman who committed adultery and was stoned. The Prophet said, "She made such sincere repentance that if similar repentance was made by a levy collector, he certainly would be forgiven." This shows that the sin of levy collectors is in fact more severe than that of the woman who committed adultery. This is further supported by several sayings that censure *'ushr* collectors. Although none of these sayings reach the level of good or correct, they support each other: Al Tabarani in his *al Mu'jam al Kabir* reports from 'Uthman bin Abi al 'As that the Prophet (p) says, "God descends close to his creatures and forgives anyone who asks forgiveness, except a prostitute [who earns] by her body, and a *'ushr* collector."[29] Ibn al Athir in his *al Nihayah* explains that an *'ushr* collector is a tax collector.[30] Al Bighawi adds, "A tax collector is the officer who collects from merchants who pass by him a tax called *'ushr*."[31] Al Mundhiri adds, "Nowadays, they collect a tax named *'ushr*, in addition to other nameless taxes that they take unlawfully. It is like they eat fire in their stomachs. They shall have no justification when they meet their Lord, may the wrath of God be upon them, and indeed they will be severely punished."[32] Al Munawi says "the tax collector is the *'ushr* collector, he is an officer who collects taxes from people. Al Munawi quotes al Tibi as saying, "The sayings indicate that collecting such a levy is among the most dangerous sinse." Al Dhahabi considers it a great sin.[33] Al Munawi continues, "A tax collector is like a highway robber, who is worse than normal thieves, since oppressing people and imposing undue taxes on them is heavier than stealing. The tax collector, his clerk, policemen who aid him, and even those who receive salaries and grants out of such taxes, are all partners in taking unlawful property.[34]

Additionally, there are sayings that call for the lifting of *'ushr* off the shoulders of Muslim people. Sa'id bin Zaid says, "I heard the Messenger of God (p) say, 'O Arabs, thank God that He removed the *'ushr* [ten percent] off you.'"[35] A man narrates from the

Prophet (p) that "The *'ushr* are only on Jews and Christians; there should be no *'ushr* on Muslims." An other version reads, "and there are no *'ushr* on the people of Islam."[36] Al Munawi in *al Taisir* comments on this saying of Islam. "It explicitly says the ten-percent levy is on Jews and Christians, if they made their treaty of surrender on that condition, or if they enter our country to trade. There is no such levy on Muslims, except what is required as the *'ushr* of *zakah* on agriculture. This text explicitly prohibits imposing any levies on Muslims."[37]

In the remainder of this section, we shall discuss the second and third objections, since the first objection was discussed at length in part eight of this book.

Discussion of the second objection against taxes

The protection of private ownership in Islam is not contradictory to charging certain dues on this ownership. The poor, weak, and needy, have right on the wealth of the rich based on their brotherhood in humanity and in religion, as was shown when we studied the theoretical foundation of *zakah*. Society also has rights on private property, since individuals earn their wealth only in the framework of society, and one way or another, society contributes to the earning of individual property, and since without social services, life would be very inconvenient for urban people. Before all this, God has rights on private wealth. He is the Creator and true Owner of wealth. Goods are in fact God's property before anything else, and people are merely vicegerents.

If, in the Islamic society, there exist needy persons whose needs are not satisfied with all the proceeds of *zakah*, if there are public needs, military, economic, and otherwise that require resources, and if the spread and establishment of Islam requires funds, Islam approves of imposing taxes on the rich to achieve these targets, in application of the rule "that without which an obligation cannot be fulfilled is also obligatory."

Discussion of the third objection

A. The sayings about *maks*

The saying that discredit levies are mostly inauthentic, as we have seen earlier. Even those which reach the level of acceptance do not explicitly prohibit every tax, since the word used in them for tax is the Arabic *maks*, which has several meanings. In *Lisan al Arab* (the most respected Arabic dictionary), "*maks* is defined as money collected from venders in pre-Islamic markets. It is also defined as what is collected by the *'ushr* officer. Ibn al 'Arabi says that *maks* is an added *dirham* collected by the *zakah* officer above the due *zakah*, the collection of which the Prophet (p) prohibits. He mentions the saying 'A *maks* collector does not enter heaven.' *Maks* is also defined as the tax collected by the *maks* officer. Originally, the word *maks* means collection. *Maks* also means reduction; *maks* is a discount of the value of sale."[38] Al Baihaqi says, "*Maks* is reduction. If the officer reduces from the proceeds of *zakah*, he is called a *maks* collector."[39]

Accordingly, the demeaning of *maks* collectors can be understood as a warning to *zakah* officers, for a *maks* collector is the dishonest and unjust *zakah* officer, who takes from payers more than what is due or keeps part of the proceeds, that belong to the poor, for himself. This understanding is supported by some narrators' explanation of *'ushr* collectors' in the saying as officers who take *sadaqah* improperly.[40] Moreover, Abu Daud mentioned such sayings in the chapter on "collection of *sadaqah*." This understanding is also supported by sayings that threaten collectors who are not just in their calculation and collection of *sadaqah*. (Some of these sayings are mentioned earlier in chapter two of part four). Such sayings inadvertantly convinced some Companions to refuse positions as *zakah* collectors because of the great responsibility involved.

However, there is another understanding of sayings on *maks* which may be more convincing. *Maks* in these sayings is explained as unjust taxes, that were predominant all over the world at the time of Islam's rise. Taxes were collected without due right and spent only on whims of the king, taxes whose burdens were not distributed justly among those who could afford them, whose proceeds were not spent for the benefit of people, taxes that were mainly imposed on the poor, from which the rich lords were exempted. The author of al Tabyin, a Hanafite, says, texts that degrade *'ushr* collectors are references to those who "take funds from people unjustly, as done by tyrants today."[41] In *al Durr al Mukhtar* and other books, one finds similar statements.[42] These taxes are the best interpretation of the word *maks*. Also, the *'ushr* collectors threatened in the sayings are collectors used by tyrants and oppressors to collect unjust taxes.

This understanding is consistent with al Dhahabi's opinion, expressed in his *al Kaba'ir*, that "The *maks* collector is the right hand of the oppressor. Such collectors are in fact themselves oppressors, since they take what is not due and give it to those who do not deserve it."[43]

Taxes levied under the conditions listed in section two of this chapter to provide for needed services in the public interest to improve the standard of living, to educate the ignorant, to provide jobs for the jobless, to feed the hungry, to protect the frightened, and to cure the ill are not unjust. They are lawful, and the Islamic government has the right to impose them.

B. Saying about elimination of *'ushr*

The saying that *'ushr* are eliminated for Muslims, although not correct, is not explicit in indicating that all taxes are prohibited, in fact, there are several other interpretations of this saying that make it consistent with just taxation.

Abu 'Ubaid comments on this and similar sayings,

Sayings in which *'ushr* and *maks* collectors are denounced clearly refer to the predominant *Jahiliyah* [pre-lslamic) practice of both Arab and non-Arab kings, imposing taxes (ten percent) on merchants who passed through their land. This is obvious from the messages the

Prophet (p) wrote to the different regions of Arabia in which he said, "That people shall not be forced to gather in processions nor charged *'ushr*. From this we know that it was a *jihiliyah* practice which God abolished with Islam, and which was substituted by the purifying obligation of *zakah* at the rate of one-fourth of a tenth, i.e. five *dirhams* out of each two hundred *dirhams*. Commissioners who collect *zakah* the way it is obligated are not *'ushr* collectors. They do not take *'ushr*; they only take one-fourth of *'ushr*. This is explained in the saying that reads "No *'ushr* are imposed on Muslims," *'ushr* are only on Jews and Christians," and in the saying linked up to the Prophet that the *'ushr* collector" is he who collects *sadaqah* without due right." Also, this is the reason Ibn 'Umar answered the question "Do you have any information that 'Umar collected *'ushr* from Muslims.'" by replying "No, I do not." The saying of Ziyad bin Hudair that, "we used not to charge *'ushr* (ten percent) on Muslims or people of the Pledge " means that he collected from Muslims one fourth of one-tenth and from people of the Pledge one-half of one tenth.[44]

Thus, abolishing *'ushr* is the abolition of an oppressive pre-Islamic tax imposed at the rate of ten percent by kings of Arabs and non-Arabs, and substituting it by *zakah* at the rate of 2.5 percent on trade's assets. And what is meant by Jews and Christians in this saying is not people of the Pledge, but foreign Jews and Christians who came from outside the Islamic state with merchandise. They were charged ten percent, as reported by Abu 'Ubaid from 'Abd al Rahman bin Ma'qil, who says, "I asked Ziyad bin Hudair whom he used to charge ten percent? He answered, 'We did not charge ten percent on a Muslim or a person of the Pledge.' I said, 'Whom then did we used to charge ten percent?' He replied, 'Traders from non-Muslim countries, since they use to charge our merchants ten percent when they went there.'"[44] This is on the basis of equal treatment, a very common practice among nations even today. As for people of the Pledge Jews and Christians within the Muslim land - they were not charged ten percent, nor were they charged 2.5 percent like Muslims. They were charged five percent, as stated by Abu 'Ubaid, who adds "At first I did not know the reason. Then I studied a report from 'Umar and found that he made the treaty with them on that basis.[45] It seems that duplicating the rate for them as compared to the rate applied on Muslims was compensation for their exemption from any tax on livestock and money, while Muslims still had to pay *zakah* on these properties.

Al Tirmidhi gives another interpretation of the saying abolishing *'ushr*. He argues that Muslims are not charged *'ushr* because *'ushr* was the levy on persons and not on wealth, like *jiziah*. The Prophet says "*'ushr* i.e. *jiziah* is only on Jews and Christians and not on Muslims." In some versions of the saying reported by Abu Daud, the words are "There is no *kharaj* on Muslims." The word *kharaj* was used to mean *jiziah*, which used to be called "*kharaj* on heads."[47]

Strangely, in *al Taisir* al Munawii attempts to conclude that the above-mentioned sayings prohibit all taxes:

It seems that this saying did not reach 'Umar, since he imposed *maks*. Al Maqrizi and others say 'Umar was informed that when Muslim merchants went to India they were charged ten percent. He then wrote to Abu Musa al Ash'ari, then governor of Basrah, "collect from each Muslim merchant that passes by you at the rate of five *dirhams* from each 200 *dirhams*, and from people-of-the-Pledge merchants at the rate of one *dirham* out of each 20 *dirhams*." Later 'Umar bin 'Abd al 'Aziz abolished this *maks*.[48]

This is a reference to what 'Umar bin 'Abd al 'Aziz wrote to one of his governors, "Abolish the *maks*," and to another "Ride to the house in the city of rafah that is called the house of *maks*, and demolish it."[49]

In fact, this opinion of al Munawi lacks accuracy and correctness because of the following:

A. He grades the saying about *'ushr* good or correct. The saying is neither correct nor good, as he himself mentions in his comments on *Faid al Qadir*.

B. He presumes 'Umar took an action contradictory to a correct saying, and not one Companion brought that to 'Umar's attention, despite their large number and their keeness to fulfill the ordinances of the Prophet, especially in a matter that relates to masses of people.

C. He suggests that 'Umar, with full approval of all the Companions, committed a denounced action that is one of the great sins. A *maks* collector does not enter heaven. This is an obvious contradiction to the order of the Prophet that we must follow the tradition of the Wise Successors of whom Umar is one.

D. His last statement implies that 'Umarr bin 'Abd al 'Aziz abolished this oppressive ruling of 'Umar bin al Khattab. It is a historical fact that the later 'Umar was keen to follow the footsteps of 'Umar bin al Khattab, and for that reason he is considered similar to Ibn al Khattab by many historians. 'Umar bin 'Abd al 'Aziz abolished oppressive levies and practices of the Umayyads, his own folks, because his love of God and his messenger would not allow him to follow his family. It is obvious that 'Umar bin 'Abd al 'Aziz abolished unjust dues that exceeded what was right and proper, and ordered *zakah* collectors to be fair and just in their estimation and collection. For reasons like this he is called the fifth of the Wise Successors by many Muslim scholars. The position of 'Umar bin 'Abd al 'Aziz is clarified by Ibn Hazm, who reports from Zuraiq bin Hayyan al Dimashqi, a commissioner in Egypt, that 'Umar bin 'Abd al 'Aziz wrote me, 'Look after whoever passes by you of Muslims and take from what is apparent of their wealth (the trade inventory they administer) at the rate of one dinar out of each forty dinar. What is less than that is charged proportionately.'"[50]

What concerns this study is that the saying "There are no *'ushr* on Mulims" cannot be used to prohibit imposing just taxes on Muslim people when the Islamic state needs them. This saying is not accepted from the point of view of its authenticity as well as its indication.

Jurists from the four schools allow just taxes

Very seldom do jurists use the Arabic word *daribah*, which means tax. But in their writings they refer to regular levies using other names. Sometimes they call them "government charges" " duties," "*kharaj*," or "allotments."

Hanafites, both early and later generations, mention taxes and distinguish between just and proper taxes and oppressive ones. Ibn 'Abidin says "Some allotments are justified, such as fees for making water pools on rivers, for distribution of water, for irrigation, to pay night watchmen to finance the aray, or to free captive, when this is needed and the public treasury does not have funds. But some allotments are not right, such as many which are collected in our times." In *al Qunyah*, Abu Ja'far al Balkhi is quoted as saying, "What is imposed by the Islamic government on people to pay for public interests is a religiously obligated financial due similar to *kharaj*. Our teachers say, 'What is collected by the government to provide for public interests become obligatory, such as salaries for guards that protect roads and buildings and entrances of highways'. Similar to these just taxes is what is collected in khawarizm [A Muslim city in Russian-occupied Central Asia] to repair the banks of the river al Jihun, and to pay the frontier guard. Such duties are obligatory, since they are not oppressive. Every taxable person must pay them. The government must not be denounced for such levies but must not be encouraged to exceed what is necessary."[51] Ibn 'Abidin, after quoting al Balkhi's statement in his *Radd al Muhtar*, comments, "This only applies when there are no funds sufficient for these purposes in the public treasury."[52]

Al Maliqi, a Malikite says, "Imposing '*kharaj*' on Muslims is subject to the given public interests. There is no doubt in our school that it is permissible. It is obvious that we have such needs in Andalusia today, especially since we pay war booties to the enemies of Muslims, in addition to what is needed for public services and in regard to the weakness of the treasury. All this provides sufficient grounds for the lawfulness of such taxes in Andalusia today. What is important, though, is to determine the amount needed and not to impose taxes beyond that. This is left to the discretion of the Islamic government."[53]

In section one of this chapter, the views of al Ghazali and al Shatibi that it is permissible to impose taxes if need arises and there are no funds in the public treasury were cited. Ibn Taimiyah has similar view, and approves of taxes that are just and consistent with needs, while he disapproves of some others, as mentioned by the author of *Ghiyath al Umam*.[54] This means we have opinions from each of the four major schools that when needs exist and the public treasury does not have sufficient funds taxes -- within certain conditions - may be levied on rich people.

Comments on unjust taxes

Several jurisprudence rulings and opinions deal with unjust taxes, such as the following:

1. Transactions such as a guarantee agreement of unjust taxes are legal, in the sense that if a guarantor had to pay the amount of unjust taxes to the government, he has the right to collect what he paid from the guaranteed person. This does not, however, mean the government has the right to collect unjust taxes from guarantors.[55]

2. Whoever takes responsibility for just distribution of the burden of such unjust levies is rewarded by God, since leaving distribution of the burden up to the oppressive authority leads to very unjust distribution of the burden of these levies.[56]

3. It is lawful to cheat the government with regard to these levies, unless it is known that such an endeavor ends up putting more burden on other tax payers. If so, it is preferred that one not cheat in payment.[57] Ibn Taimiyah says, "When communities are charged levies by oppressive authorities, whether on heads, or on their animals, trees or wealth, or are over-charged in *zakah* or *kharaj* or other levies that are not justified in *Shari'ah* (such as sales taxes), such charges must be justly distributed among the oppressed. No one of the people unjustly charged with such taxes has any right to throw his share of the collective burden on others. They are required to distribute the burden of those unjust taxes in a fair way, as if they were lawful, since from the point of view of collection and payment, people are forced to pay unjust taxes the same way they are forced to pay just taxes, The evil of unjust taxes is carried by those who impose and collect them and not by payers. Payers in such cases are required to pay their share of the burden fairly and justly. No one has the right to escape payment if such an escape throws the burden on others."[58]

Footnotes

1. Al *kharaj* by Abu Yusuf, p. 59.

2. *Al Mughni*, Vol. 2, p. 667.

3. *Al Rawdah,* Vol. 2, p. 321, and *Tuhfat al Muhtaj*, Vol. 3, p. 96.

4. For these and similar principles and rules of *ahkam*, see *Al Ashbah wa al Naza'ir*, by Ibn Nujaim, section on general rules. See also *Usul al Tashri'* by al Khudari.

5. *Al Mustasfa*, Vol. 1, p. 303.

6. *Al I'tisam*, Vol. 2, p. 104.

7. *Sura al Tawabah,* 9:41.

8. *Sura al Hujurat*, 49:15.

9. *Sura al Saff,* 61:11.

10. *Sura al Baqarah*, 2:195.

11. *Al Nujum al Zahirah*, Vol. 7, pp. 72-73. *al Suluk li Ma'rifat Duwal al Muluk*, Vol. 1, pp. 416-417 and *Tabaqat al Shafi'iyah*, by Ibn al Subki for the biography of Izz al Din bin 'Abd al Salam.

12. *Al Islam al Muftara Alaih*, by Muhammad al Ghazali, pp. 222-223.

13. Biography of al Nawawi, by al Sakhawi, printed by Jam'iyat al Nashr wa al Ta'lif in al Azhar, 1935.

14. *Al Amwal*, p. 533.

15. *Ibid.*

16. On roads used for transporting goods from one town to another, *'ushr* collectors used to stand to collect the required tax. Ten percent was collected from foreigners, on the basis of equal treatment, since Muslim merchants abroad were also charged ten percent, according to what Abu Musa wrote 'Umar. (See al *kharaj* by Yahya bin Adam p. 172) Five percent was collected from merchants who were people of the Pledge, in accordance with the treaties signed with them. (See *al Amwal*, p. 532.) This however does not apply to the Christians of bani Taghlib, who were treated differently by special agreement. See chapter one of part two of this book.

17. *Al Amwal*, p. 533.

18. *Tabaqat Ibn Sa'd*, Vol. 3, pp. 306-307.

19. *Tarikh al Tabari*, Vol. 5, p. 19.

20. *Sura al Shura*, 42:38.

21. *Sura al 'Imran*, 3:59.

22. *Tafsir Ibn Kathir*, Vol. 1, p. 420.

23. *Ibid.*

24. *Ibid.*

25. Reported by Abu Daud in his chapter on judgements, Ibn Majah's chapter on rulings, al Hakim from Abu Hurairah. Al Hakim grades it correct according to the criteria of al Bukhari and Muslim. It is also graded correct by Ibn Habban, and by al Tirmidhi, through Kathir bin 'Abd Allah bin 'Amr bin 'Awf al Muzani from his father from his grandfather. Al Trirmidhi comments, "good correct." The version of al Tirmidhi reads, " Muslims are bound by their conditions, except a condition that makes unlawful what is lawful or makes lawful what is prohibited." It is objected that Kathir is very weak, but Ibn Hajar comments, "This saying is considered by its numerous chains." Al Hakim reports it from Anas and A'aishah via a weak chain, and al Tabarani from Rafi bin Khadij via a good chain, as stated by al Munawai in *al Taisir*, Vol. 2, p. 457. Al Shawkani comments, "It is no secret that these different sayings and chains support each other. Thus, the least that can be said about the text of these narrations is that it is good." See *Nail al Awtar*, Vol. 5, p. 254, *Kashf al Khafa*, Vol. 2, p. 209, and *Faid al Qadir*, Vol. 6, p. 272.

26. Reported by the group.

27. Reported by Ahmad via Ibn Lahi'ah, and by al Tabarani, who adds, "It means *'ushr* collector." See *al Targhib*, Vol. 1, p. 568.

28. Reported by Abu Daud, Ibn Khuzaimah, and al Hakim via Muhammad bin Ishaq. Al Hakim calls it "correct according the criteria of Muslim." Al Mundhiri adds, 'but Muslim only reports from Muhammad bin Ishaq supporting narrations." See *al Targhib*, Vol. 1, pp. 566-567.

29. In *Majma' al Zawa'id* Vol. 3, p. 88, al Haithami mentions the saying in different versions, as quoted from *al Mu'jam al Kabir* and *al Mu'jam al Awsat* both of al Tabarani and from Ahmad. He adds, "The people of the chain of Ahmad are those of the correct collections except 'Ali bin Zaid, who is criticized and who is nevertheless considered trustworthy by some."

30. *Al Nihaya*, by Ibn al Athir, Vol. 4, p. 110.

31. *Al Targhib*, Vol. 1, p. 567.

32. *Ibid.*

33. *Al Kaba'ir* by al Dhahabi, p. 119, al Bayan print, Beirut. Al Dhahabi does not define the word *maks* exactly; he only says "The *maks* collector is a real helper of oppressors. He is in fact one of the oppressors, since he takes what is not due and gives it to those who do not deserve it." Ibn Hajar al Haitami in his *al Zawajir* has a similar view.

34. *Faid al Qadir*, Vol. 6, p. 449.

35. Al Haithami in *Majma' al Zawa'id*, Vol. 3, p. 87, says, "Reported by Ahmad, Abu Ya'la, and al Bazzar. In its chain is a narrator whose name is not given but the rest of the narrators are trustworthy."

36. Reported by Ahmad, Vol. 3, p. 474, via 'Ata bin al Sa'ib, from a man of the tribe of Bakr bin Wa'il from the man's uncle, who said, "O Messenger of God, should I collect *'ushr* from my clan?" The Prophet said, "The *'ushr* are only on . . . ." The same is reported via 'Ata from Harb bin 'Ubaid Allah al Thaqafi from his uncle, and from 'Ata' from Harb bin Hilal al Thaqafi from Abu Umayyah, who is from the tribe of Taghlib, and who heard the Prophet (p) says "There are no *'ushr* on Muslims . . . ." Also reported by Abu Daud from Harb bin 'Ubaid Allah bin 'Umair from his maternal grandfather, from the latter's father linked up to the Prophet. See *Mukhtasar al Sunan*, sayings no. 2924, 2926, and 2927 Vol. 4, pp. 253-254, and the comments of al Mundhiri. 'Abd al Haqq says, "This is a saying whose chain is disputed and I know it not via an acceptable chain." Ibn al Qaffal says, "Ibn Ma'in was asked about Harb and answered, "he is know but this is not sufficient to consider him trustworthy. Many known persons are not accepted as narrators of sayings. As for Harb's grandfather, no one knows him, it is worse when it comes to the latter's father!" Al Munawi says, "Al Bukhari reports it in his *al Tarikh al Kabir*, mentioning the disturbance in its chain, and comments, 'There is no support for this narration.'" Al Tirmidhi, in the chapter on *zakah* under the title 'no *jiziah* on Muslims, mentions this saying without any chain. Ahmad in his *Musnad* reports it. Al Haithami says, "In the chain is 'Ata who was mentally disturbed, but the rest of the chain is trustworthy." See al Faid, Vol. 2, p. 561. Strangely enough, al Munawi mentions in *al Taisir*, Vol. 1, p. 358, that its chain is good or correct.

37. *Al Taisir, Ibid.*

38. *Lisan al 'Arab*, under the letters "m k s."

39. *Faid al Qadir*, Vol. 6, p. 449.

40. *Majma' al Zawa'id* Vol. 3, pp. 87-88.

41. *Al Bahr al Ra'iq*, Vol. 2, p. 249.

42. *Rada al Muhtar*, Vol. 2, p. 42.

43. *Al Kaba'ir* by al Dhahabi, p.119.

44. *Al Amwal*, pp. 707-708, Dar al Sharq print.

45. *Ibid*, pp. 709 - 710.

46. *Ahkam al Dhimiyyn wa al Musta'minin fi Dar al Islam* by 'Abd al Karim Zaidan, chapter on business taxes.

47. *Sunan al Tirmidhi,* chapter on *zakah*, title "no *jiziah* on Muslims."

48. *Al Taisir, Sharh al Jam'al Saghir,* Vol. 1, p. 368.

49. *Al Amwal, op. cit*, p. 704.

50. *Al Muhalla*, Vol. 6, p. 66.

51. *Radd al Muhtar*, Vol. 2, p. 58.

52. *Ibid*, p. 59.

53. *Tahdhib al Furuq wa al Qawa'id al Saniyah*, by Muhammad 'Ali bin Husain, printed on the margins of *al Furuq* by al Qarafi, Vol. 1, p. 141.

54. *Ghiyath al Umam,* as mentioned in *Kashf al Zunun*, Vol. 2, p.1213, chapter on government by al Juwaini, a Shafi'ite, who died the year 478 H.

55. *Rad al Muhtar*, Vol. 2, pp. 58-59.

56. *Ibid*, p. 59.

57. *Ibid*, p. 58.

58. *Matalib Uli al Nuha*, Vol. 3, pp. 569-570.

CHAPTER EIGHT

CAN TAXES SUBSTITUTE FOR *ZAKAH*?

Wealthy individuals in most contemporary societies pay several taxes, progressive and otherwise, at rates very often several times the rates of *zakah* decreed in *Shari'ah*. These taxes provide resources for the government's budget and finance the state's expenditures. No doubt, several subjects of the expenditure of contemporary states are similar to *zakah* deservants, such as funds for welfare programs that help the poor, the disable, and street beggars, or programs which provide job and training for the jobless. Most contemporary governments have one or more department for such social and welfare matters. Therefore, the question arises, will these taxes make up for the *zakah* required by *Shari'ah*? Or must Muslim taxpayers pay *zakah* individually or to organizations in addition to taxes paid to the government?

In order to answer this question, we must remember that there are three essential features of *zakah* without which. *zakah* does not exist. These are:

1. The rates as determined in *Shari'ah* (2.5 percent, five percent, or ten percent)
2. The specific intention of fulfilling a worship in obedience to God.
3. Distribution to the eight categories mentioned in the Qur'an.

Do taxes have these three characteristics? Tax rates do not follow the rates determined in *Shari'ah*, which are described in this study. Tax rates are more than *zakah* rates on certain assets and less on others. Some *zakatable* assets are not taxable at all, while some taxable assets and incomes are not *zakatable* in *Shari'ah*. Yet one may argue that when the rate of *zakah* is more than the tax rate, Muslim taxpayers should be required to distribute the difference individually, and when the tax rate is more than the *zakah* rate, *zakah* is covered. As for intention taxes do not require intention, but one can still argue that Muslim taxpayers may have the intention of paying *zakah* when they pay their taxes. As for the third characteristic of *zakah* when the state collects *zakah* it must distribute its proceeds according to Qur'an. Moreover, if the government collects *zakah*, this collection must take the name of *zakah*, since *zakah* loses its essence without its name, form, and purpose (i.e. proper distribution). For such reasons, Malikites specifically argue that if an oppressive government collects *zakah* in the name and form of *zakah*, payment to such government fulfills the *Shari'ah* requirement for individual payers. But levies and taxes collected under other names, such as *maks* and *daribah*, do not replace *zakah* and cannot be counted as *zakah* as long as they do not carry the name and the form of *zakah* especially since they may be distributed to areas which are not approved in *Shari'ah*.

Lastly, we must realize that sincere Muslims are in most countries today charged more financial dues that non-Muslims, since Muslims are required to pay taxes like everybody else, and in addition are required to pay *zakah*, either by direct distribution or through Islamic organizations.

Contradictions in Muslim societies

The above question would not have arisen if there were not gross contradictions in Muslim societies today. On one hand there are still Muslims who hold to the basics of Islam, and Islam is the official religion in most Muslim countries. Yet Islamic law has been stripped from the legislation system of most Muslim lands. Take *zakah* as an example. Although it is one of the pillars of Islam, and although many Muslims implement it individually and would like it to be part of their social system, most countries do not have a legal system for *zakah*. In all eras there are stingy persons whose love of accumulation prevents them from paying *zakah*. Such people used to be forced to pay it by the government, but now the lack of law enforcement, and the lack of *zakah* act in most Muslim countries, leaves these miserly wealthy persons *unzakated.*

In most cases, the transfer from Islamic law to imported Western laws was a result of Western colonialism that dominated Muslim lands in the nineteenth and the first half of the twentieth century. The cultural and legislative impact of colonialism was far deeper and more dangerous to Muslim society than military occupation. After the aggressive troops withdrew from most Muslim lands we found ourselves with penal codes that are not Islamic, whereby prostitution, pornography, night clubs, adultery, and drinking are legalized; with civil codes that is not Islamic, whereby interest and other unlawful transactions are made permissible in such a way that social and economic activities become dominated by foreigners and minorities. We found ourselves with social standards and financial codes whereby *zakah* is wiped out and taxes alien to the Islamic system are imposed. More painful even, is cultural colonialism that resulted from the heavy impact of military, economic, and legislative domination of the West on Muslim lands. As a result of cultural colonialism, we find "geographic" or nominal Muslims who even oppose the idea of re-establishing *zakah* and other Islamic reforms, like some so-called Muslims members of the Egyptian parliament who objected to the proposed re-installment of *zakah* law, on the grounds that they want their country secular and detached from religion like Western states in Europe.

What is required from Muslim governments regarding *zakah*?

Muslim governments today are called upon to adopt the Islamic system in all aspects of societal organization, and especially to give sufficient attention to *zakah* and establish an autonomous department to collect and distribute *zakah*, the third pilar of Islam. It is necessary to enact an accurate and detailed law of *zakah* whereby duality with other taxes is eliminated, and Muslim *zakah* payers are not disadvantaged financially as compared to non-Muslim minorities.

Muslim individuals are also called upon to pay *zakah* to the state, if the state collects it, and if not, to organizations established for such purposes, or at least individually, because this is a basic rite of Islam.

Scholars who seem to approve of taxes replacing *zakah*

We have religious opinions given at different times by renowned scholars that Muslim taxpayers may hold the intention that taxes they pay are wholly or partially in fulfillment of *zakah*. Among them is al Nawawi, who says, "Shafi'ites agree that levies collected unjustly do not stand in place of *'ushr*. But if the government takes such levies in place of *'ushr* (*zakah* on agriculture) scholars have two opinions on whether the obligation of *'ushr* is thus fulfilled or not. The correct one is that such payment fulfills the required *'ushr*. If the amount collected by the state is less than the required *'ushr* the difference must be paid by the payers."[1] Although levies referred to in this statement are not far-removed from contemporary taxes, it is important to observe that al Nawawi says "If such levies are collected in place of *zakah*," while governments today do not have in mind to collect such taxes in place of *zakah* nor to they expend their proceeds on *zakah* deservants.

Similarly, a Hanbalite writer says, "Ahmad was asked about a land in which the government takes half of one's produce. He answered, 'that is unjust. The government does not have such a right.' Then he was asked whether the payer must distribute *zakah* on the other half. He answered, what is paid the government fulfills the obligated *zakah*.' If the owner makes his intention likewise."[2] Ibn Taimiyah is quoted to have said, "levies taken by the government in the name of *maks* (taxes) can be given with the intention of paying *zakah* and obligated *zakah* is thus fulfilled, although such payments do not take the form of *zakah*."[3] This quote from Ibn Taimiyah seems to contradict his statement in *al Fatawa*, "What is collected by rulers in names other than that of *zakah* cannot be counted as *zakah* payment."[4] I wonder which of these two quotes is the correct one, or what was the final opinion of Ibn Taimiyah?

Whatever the motivation behind such opinions, they were given under presure to avoid over-burdening sincere Muslims who were already charged several oppressive taxes. The case in contemporary society is slightly different since it is presumed that existing taxes are necessitated to provide people with basic services, including defense, i.e. it is presumed that existing taxes have acceptable justifications. Therefore, these taxes cannot make up for *zakah*, even with the intention of the payer to pay *zakah*.

Scholars who do not allow considering taxes *zakah*

The majority of scholars do not approve of intending *zakah* payment when taxes are paid, and come down hard against opinions that allow it. Ibn Hajar al Haitami, a Shafi'ite, says in his *al Zawajir*,

Some corrupt merchants think the *maks* they pay can be counted as *zakah* if they make the intention of paying *zakah*. This is an unfounded notion. It is false and incorrect according to the Shafi'ite school. The government -- when it collects taxes -- does not intend to consider these taxes *zakah*, nor do they collect *zakah* according to *Shari'ah*, regarding both rates and *zakatable* assets. The government levies these taxes with the claim that their proceeds need to be spent on the army and public interests of Muslims, which I do not want to argue at this point, but given that taxes are legitimate and their proper conditions are fulfilled, these taxes are different from *zakah* and must not be considered *zakah* for they do not even carry its name. Some merchants tell me that they make intention of paying *zakah* when they give this *maks* to collectors, and if these collectors give it to non *zakah* deservants, it is their problem. This idea is also false. *maks* recipients do not usually deserve *zakah*. They are all rich or powerful and can earn. By what virtue can *zakah* be given to this kind of people? The selfishness of the merchants makes them blind so they do not see right from wrong. All they want is to save themselves the properly due *zakah*, since they are forced anyway to pay these taxes. They must realize that *zakah* obligated by God is not fulfilled by tax payments, even if accompanied by their wicked intentions. As for the oppressive taxes themselves, payers of those taxes are rewarded by God in as much as they are oppressed. Muslim scholars consider *maks* collectors thieves or armed robbers. They may, in fact, be much worse. Evidently, money collected by armed robbers cannot be considered *zakah* by the robbed. Muslim scholars warn Muslim payers repeatedly that making the intention of paying *zakah* when they pay taxes to *maks* collectors is improper and meaningless. Scholars consider those who do that ignorant.[5]

Ibn Abidin, a Hanafite, after quoting some opinions of Ibn Hajar, goes on to say,
Nowadays, *maks* collectors contract the government for certain amount they pay the government, against which they collect for themselves, very oppressively and aggressively. Payments to *maks* collectors are taken by force repeatedly, more than once a year, even when an asset is not *zakatable* at all. Such payment cannot be counted as *zakah* in the Hanafite school. The *maks* collector is not like the *zakah* collector appointed by the Islamic government to collect *zakah* from merchants passing on roads. In *al Bazzaziyah* it is stated, "If the payer makes the intention of paying *zakah* when handing over obligated *maks*, the correct opinion is that this cannot be considered *zakah*, as confirmed by al Sarakhsi."[6]

The late Shaikh Alaish, a Malikite, was asked whether a person who owns *nisab* of livestock and is forced to pay a certain amount every year to the government can count his payment as *zakah*. 'Alaish answered, "No, even with the intention of *zakah* payment, as is also the opinion of al Nasir al Laqani, and al Hattab."[7]

Rashid Rida was also asked whether taxes collected by British Christians from Indian Muslims, which sometimes reach one-fourth or one-half of the land rent, can be considered *zakah*? His answer was

The *'ushr* and half-*'ushr* obligated as *zakah* on land produce must be expended to the eight categories given in the Qur'an. If the Islamic government or its representatives collect this *zakah*, the *zakah* payer fulfills his duty by paying to the government or its representatives, who are obligated in *Shari'ah* to distribute the proceeds properly. But if the Islamic government does not collect *zakah,* owners must distribute their due *zakah* according to the ordinance of God. What is collected by Christians and others from Muslims in lands they conquered are kind of taxes whose payment does not fulfill the obligation of *zakah*. Muslims are required to pay *zakah* on the remainder after these impositions.

What concerns us of his opinion is his statement "What is collected by Christians and others," since it means taxes cannot stand for *zakah*, whether collected by Christians or non-Christians, including national governments in Muslim countries.

Mahmud Shaltut, former head of al Azhar mosque, was asked whether taxes could be counted as *zakah*. His great answer ascertained that since *zakah* is "a financial worship" it is far from being similar to taxes. Although there are certain similarities between tax and *zakah*, the differences are much greater. Taxes and *zakah* differ in their respective legislative sources, in their theoretical foundation objectives, rates, exemptions, and expenditure of proceeds, He adds,

Zakah is decreed by God, an obligation based on faith that must be performed whether there are poor and needy or not, and a permanent flow of resources for the poor and needy that exists at all times in all people, while taxes are ordained by governments when there is need. With all the differences between them, one cannot substitute for the other. Accordingly, *zakah* remains due according to the conditions know in *Shari'ah*, regardless of the payment of taxes. Taxes are obligated by law and *zakah* is obligated by the religion of God. If this sometimes makes the burden heavy for rich persons, poor must not be made to pay for this by being deprived of their right. Instead, governments must be asked to economize expenditures and reduce taxes. Governments must be questioned on the efficient use of the tax money they collect. This is one of the basic principles of the Islamic political system.

Lastly, in his *Tanzim al Islam li al Mujtama,* Muhammad Abu Zahrah answers the question as follows: "Not a substantial portion of tax proceeds is devoted to social welfare, which is the essential objective of *zakah. Zakah* is obligatory first of all. It may substitute for certain taxes, but existing taxes may not substitute for *zakah*, since they do not fulfill the needs of the poor."[10] Abu Zahrah's answer, gives only one aspect of the importance of *zakah*. Obviously, even if a sufficient proportion of taxes is devoted to the same objectives of *zakah, zakah* must still be collected because it is ordained by God and no one has any authority to freeze or abolish it. It must be collected under the same name of "*zakah*" and at the same rates and conditions prescribed by God. It must also be spent to the proper deservants mentioned in the Qur'an. Even if in certain countries the poor and needy happen to be satisfied, *zakah* must still be collected from the rich in that society and spent in the way of God or to make His word supreme.

I must add that the opinion of Shaltut and other scholars that "taxes do not make up for *zakah*" is the one with which I feel comfortable, since it is based on legitimate considerations and is safer from the point of view of practical application, since *zakah* as the third pillar of Islam must not be forgotten in actual practice. True, this means sincere Muslims must pay *zakah* in addition to taxes which they are obligated to pay by laws, but this is one way of striving for the re-establishment of this religion on earth, especially in a time like ours. Muslims are called upon to struggle to correct the abnormal situations prevailing in their countries and to erase the contradictions spawned by colonialist authority over Muslim lands. The legal and economic situation in Muslim countries must be brought back to compliance with the Islamic system. Without enormous efforts to reform Muslim societies under the guidance of the Islamic system, Muslims shall remain burdened financially, psychologically, and socially, since they live in a society whose laws and regulations are against the nature of their religion Islam. If Muslims find that in certain parts of the world governments take care of the poor and needy, this does not mean *zakah* is no longer needed, since *zakah* has several other destinations, including the call to Islam, reconciling hearts to it, preparing, training, and supporting Muslim callers and Islamic centers, in addition to actual *jihad* for making the word of God supreme. If some Muslims do not find deservants of *zakah* in their areas they can always transport their *zakah* to the nearest country where there is need for *zakah* proceeds.

As for the opinions attributed to Ibn Taimiyah, al Nawawi, and Ahmad, they deal with circumstances that are essentially different from ours in a time when governments were generally Islamic ad collected *zakah* regularly. If it were to be permitted to count as *zakah* taxes paid to governments today this would be a final abolition of this religious obligation and even the remnants that exist now would be done away with, just as it was erased from the laws and legislation of governments. This is something no one can approve, justify, or accept in any time or place.

Footnotes

1. *Al Majmu'*, Vol. 5, pp. 541-543.

2. *Sharh Ghayat al Muntaha*, Vol. 2, p. 133.

3. This is quoted by Muhammad al Manqur in *al Fawakeh al 'Adidah fi al masa'il al mufidah*, Vol. 1, p. 154.

4. *Majmu' al Fatawa,* Vol. 25, p. 93.

5. *Al Zawajir* by Ibn Hajar al Haitami, Vol. 1, p. 149.

6. *Radd al Muhthr*, Vol. 2, p. 42.

7. *Fath al 'Aliy al Malik,* Vol. 1, pp. 139-140.

8. *Tafsir al Manar*, Vol. 7, p. 576, and *Fatawa al Imam Muhammad Rashid Rida,* Vol. 1, pp. 229-230.

9. *Fatawa al Shaikh Shaltut*, pp. 116-118.

10. *Tanzim al Islam li al Mujtama'*, p. 165.

EPILOGUE

Zakah: a new and unique system

I believe the reader realizes by now that *zakah* is a unique system, unprecedented by any divine or man-made laws. It is a financial, economic, social, political, moral, and religious blend.

It is a well-defined financial tax imposed on heads sometimes, like *zakah* of *al fitr*, and other times on capital and income. Thus it represents a permanent and continuous flow of resources to the public treasury of the Islamic state, devoted to liberating men and women from the bondage of need and fulfilling their economic necessities. It fights accumulation of wealth and hoarding it away from circulation and investment

It is a social system because *zakah* secures individuals against disability, accidents, and catastrophes. It realizes humanistic aspirations of social solidarity and cooperation, in which the haves help the have-nots, the strong carry the weak, and the rich give the indigent and wayfarer. The distance shrinks between the rich and the poor, and elements of jealousy, vanity, and hatred are diminished. Moreover, the *zakah* system financially aids reformers and mediators of disputes to carry on such great missions in order to fulfill the noble social and moral objectives of *zakah*.

It is political as well, because the institution of *zakah* is part of the state. The Islamic government takes full responsibility for collecting and distributing *zakah* according to the principles of justice, and to appoint necessary personal. Additionally, some categories of distribution can only be decided by the state, such as heart reconciliation and, in general, the share spent "in the way of God."

It has a moral purpose because the very objective of *zakah* is to cleanse and purify the souls of the rich from selfishness and desire for accumulation. It aims to train the rich to sacrifice and to contribute to the welfare of other people. *Zakah* is a sword against jealousy and vanity. It aims at making brotherhood and love prevail among all people in the society.

Before all, it is a religious worship, for performing *zakah* establishes an essential pillar of Islam. It is one of the basic forms of worship through which men and women obey God and please Him. Additionally, some of its expenditures deal directly with the progress of religion: making Islam know to all people, and reconciling hearts to Islam whether they are hearts of new or prospective converts. The spending of *zakah* "in the way of God" aims at making the word of God supreme - what a glorious religious objective.

Lastly, *zakah* alone is bright evidence that this religion is from God, for Muhammad (p), an illiterate man from an illiterate and backward society, could never have thought of such a unique and just system on his own, not with all the information and resources he could muster, if it were not descending from God verse after verse, as a guidance to all human beings, if it were not taught to him by the Most Knowledgeable. Indeed, the bounties of God on Muhammad (p) and on all humanity are magnificent.

Non-Muslim writers give testimony

This unique system of *zakah*, which is misunderstood and often badly applied by many Muslims, finds admirers among non-Muslims writers who have studied it and given their opinions about it. In his book *The Preaching of Islam*, Thomas Arnold describes some of the rites of Islam, especially pilgrimage, and then goes on to speak about *zakah*: "Besides the institution of pilgrimage, we find the performance of *zakah* another basic obligation which reminds every Muslim of the verse of God, 'Believers are but one brotherhood,' which is a religious ideal realized magnificently in Islamic society in such a way that surprises all of us. It is seen in all acts of tenderness toward fellow Muslims, regardless of race, sex, color, or ancestry. A Muslim becomes a member in the bond of believers and immediately takes his place equal to other Muslims." Lloyd Rouch says, "I find in Islam the solution of the two major social problems that occupy the minds of the world. The first is in the statement of the Qur'an, 'Believers are but one single brotherhood.' This is the most beautiful principle of socialism. The second is the obligation of *zakah* on every wealthy person and allowing the poor to take it by force if the rich refuse to pay it voluntarily, and this is the cure for anarchy."[2]

Muhammad Kurd 'Ali quotes another foreign writer as saying about *zakah*, This tax, in addition to being a religious obligation required from all, is a social system and a source of income for the Muhammadan state which is used to supply and enrich the poor in a systematic, straight forward way, without any arbitrariness or enslavement. It is not a casual event in the life of the Muslim society. This marvelous system was established by Islam for the first time in the history of mankind. This tax, *zakah*, which is obligated on landlords, merchants, and the wealthy in order to be spent to the indigent, poor and disabled, brought down the barriers that divide the nation into classes, and unifies the Islamic nation into one social group based on justice. By that the Islamic system proves it is not based on hatred or selfishness."[3] Muhammad 'Ali quotes also a renown French Orientalist, Massignon, as saying "This religion of Islam has the ability to be strict in realizing the principle of equality, by imposing *zakah* on every individual, paid to the public treasury and by working against interest loans and indirect taxes that are usually imposed on necessities. At the same time, this religion stands in support of private ownership and commercial capital. Thus Islam stands once more in the middle, balanced between the theories of bourgeoisie capitalism and Bolshevik communism."[4]

The Italian writer Vagleri says in her book *In Defense of Islam* "All religions recognize to a certain degree the great moral and social importance of giving charity and encourage it as a material expression of mercy. But Islam alone achieves the glory of making such charity obligatory. Thus transforming the teachings of Christ into ordinances and then reality in the world. Each Muslim is obligated by law to devote certain fraction of his wealth to the poor and needy, wayfarers, and strangers, etc. By performing this religious obligation, believers exercise such deeper humanistic feelings; they purify their souls from selfishness and niggardliness, and hope for divine reward."[5]

Quotations from Muslim reformists

After quotations from orientalists, we give a few quotations from Muslim writers about *zakah*. Muhammad Rashid Rida, in his explanation of the Qur'an notes:

In imposing *zakah*, Islam is distinct from all religions and legislations, as confessed by most writers of many origins. If Muslims would only establish this pillar of their religion, no poor or needy or persons under pressure of debts would ever exist in their societies. Unfortunately, many Muslims neglect this obligation, and consequently cause harm to their religion and their nation. So they have become the worst of all nations in political and financial matters to the extent that they even lost control of their own countries and became dependent on other nations, even in educating their children. Muslin children today are educated in Christian missionary schools, whereby they are lost to their nations and become enslaved to foreigners. If they are questioned, "why don't you establish schools yourselves on high levels of performance, instead of sending your children to missionary schools?" they answer, 'We do not have financial resources to do so." In reality, they do not have the zeal, the mind and the will to implement their religion. And they see with their own eyes other people spending to finance schools and charitable and political organizations. Thus vow to these Muslims that have lost their religion and thus have indeed lost their worldly living. God says, "Those who forget God, He makes them forget their own souls, such are the rebellious transgressors."[6] Those who call for the reform of Muslim societies are required to start by saving the remnants of religion and dignity, by establishing organizations to collect *zakah* and distribute it according to *Shari'ah*. They must realize that the share of freeing slaves must be used to liberate people who suffer from colonialism if there is no one in the bondage of slavery, and that the share "in the way of God" must be used to re-establish the Islamic system through the glorious form of *jihad*, which preserves Islam before the aggression of disbelievers. They must spend to call for Islam and to defend its values by writing and speaking, if such defense is not viable by weapons. We must realize that if all, or the majority of Muslims perform *zakah* and spend it according to its proper designation, that would be sufficient to re-establish the glory of Islam, to regain what was stolen from Muslim land by foreigners, and to salvage Muslims from enslavement to unbelievers. This can be done only by spending one-tenth or one-quarter of a tenth from the wealth owned by the rich. We observe with our own eyes that may people who dominate over Muslim lands spend more than that for their own nations and ideologies, without even being obligated by their Lord.[7]

In his comment on the saying from Mu'adh that the Prophet (p) told him "Inform them that God imposes on them in their wealth a *sadaqah*, to be taken from the rich among them and rendered to the poor among them." Shaikh Mahmud Shaltut, former head of al Azhar mosque, says,

These Prophet's instructions indicate that *zakah* in Islam is simply a transfer of the excess wealth of the nation within itself, since it is taken from the rich and given to the poor. In other words, *zakah* only changes control of some fraction of wealth from one hand-- the hand that invests and protect -- to the other hand - the hand that works and struggle (when the yield of that work is not sufficient for all their needs), or to the hand that cannot work, which is the hand of the poor.[8]

In his book *Economic Foundations in Islam Compared to Other Contemporary Systems*, Abu al A'la al Maududi talks about the role and place of *zakah*:

What Islam in fact wants is that wealth must not be concentrated in a few hands in society, that those who acquire wealth because of good fortune or good abilities must not hoard it and must spend at least part of it to help the unfortunate that can not obtain sufficiency of sustenance. In order to achieve this objectives, Islam works through two channels. First, Islam encourages generosity, cooperation, and helping others, by all means of moral encouragement and religious stimulus, so that people, who naturally like to accumulate, would be taught to like giving some of their wealth voluntarily. Second, Islam enacts a law that requires the rich to pay a certain well-defined fraction on their wealth. This payment is *zakah*. One must not forget that *zakah* is very important element in the Islamic economic system, it is next to prayer as a pillar of Islam. The Qur'an even explicitly states that hoarding wealth is not permitted without payment of *zakah*. "Out of their wealth take *sadaqah*, so thou might purify and sanctify them."[9] The word *zakah* itself indicates that wealth accumulated by men and women is dirty and sinful if it is not purified and sanctified by paying 2.5 percent of it for the sake of God every year. Undoubtedly God is rich, nothing of this payment given to Him nor does He need it. Therefore, "the sake of God" means that one seeks to improve the lot of the poor, as well as to initiate activities that benefit the nation as a whole. God says, "*Sadaqat* are for the poor, and the needy, and those employed to administer the funds, and those whose hearts have been recently reconciled to truth, for those in bondage and in debt, in the cause of God, and for the wayfarer."[10] *Zakah* is thus an organization of mutual cooperation on the social level, among all Muslims. It is their insurance company and their reserve fund. This is the wealth that guarantees the jobless, the inable, the sick, the orphans, and the widows among them, and above all, it is the institution that helps Muslims not to worry about their material future. The simple principle established by Islam is if you are rich today, help others, for you will receive help if you become poor tomorrow. You need not to worry about what would happen to you if you become poor, or to your wife and children if you die, or how you would manage if an accident befalls you, or if you get lost on a journey without any financial means. *Zakah* is always there to enrich you, to save you, to relieve your worry about such accidents or mishaps. All you need is to pay 2.5 percent of all your wealth to this insurance institution established by God, and you feel secure about yourself and your family for all the future. You do not need this excess wealth today, so why not give it to those who need it for sustenance, and when you need help, it will be extended to you.

Thus the contrast becomes clearer between the Islamic way and the capitalist way. Capitalists urge people to accumulate wealth and to collect interest on it, so that you acquire more of other people's wealth. This is not consistent with the nature of this religion. Islam ordains that if wealth happens to accumulate in your hands, it must flow through the channels of distribution provided by Islam, so that life flourishes around you. Wealth circulation is restricted in capitalism, while it is free in the Islamic system. In capitalism, you must have some wealth to acquire anything from the common pool of wealth, while in Islam, if you have excess wealth, you must give a fraction to society, and those who need it will come and take it from the common pool. The two systems are different in both nature and approach and cannot co-exist in one place.[11]

Abu al Hasan al Nadwi, in his book *The Four Pillars*, explains that the principal feature of *zakah* is that it is based on faith and is performed for the sake of pleasing God. This does not exist in any other tax. He goes on to the second essential characteristic of *zakah*:

> The second distinguished characteristic of *zakah*, in contrast with other taxes and financial charges imposed by kings, dictators, or even republics and people's governments today, which makes *zakah* different from them from beginning to end in method, objectives, and effects, is the legislative position given it by the Prophet (p) in his statement, ". . . to be taken from the rich among them and rendered to the poor among them ". Thus, *zakah* is collected from the rich, as defined in *Shari'ah*, and distributed to categories determined by God in the Qur'an, which are not left to any man or group of people to decide. Moreover, it is always preferred that *zakah* be spent on the poor and needy in the same land it is collected from. This was the general practice of *zakah* even by governments that did not strictly follow the teachings of Islam in minute detail and did not realize the Islamic ideals in politics and government. Even under these governments, the poor and needy were not deprived of their rights, and Islamic law was not abolished.[12]

> This is very different from taxes and fees imposed by governments today. In most cases, taxes are collected from the poor and middle class and rendered to the chiefs, the rich, and the powerful. They are taken from the sweat of farmers, laborers, small craftsmen, and small businessmen, who work hard day and night, on their jobs and spent for visiting chieftains, ceremonies, and food and drink for celebrations lavish as those described in the *One Thousand and One Arabian Nights* legends. They are also spent freely by embassies of the country in other countries, and on propaganda for the government that exhausts the blood and resources of people. Proceeds are paid also to foreign journalists to write articles praising the government, something done by all kinds of governments, whether democratic, communist, capitalist or socialist. The most truthful description of these taxes is "collected from the poor among them and given to the rich." *Zakah*, which is imposed by God on the rich to help the poor, is a form of kindness and mercy to the whole nation, a bounty from God incomparable to all other taxes. It is a tax, if one must-use the term, that is least burden some and most beneficial.[13]

It is my turn to present this study to men and women of thinking, to experts of financial legislation and taxation, so they can know just how much Islam preceded modern financial and tax systems in legislating this *zakah*, based on principles of justice, that aims at the noblest objectives, and that is supported by the strongest bonds, hoping these thinkers and people of law may realize that they must observe the beliefs of this Muslim nation when they enact laws and establish *zakah* by law in all Muslim countries.

I present this study to specialists in social insurance so they may recognize that *zakah* is the first organized system of welfare in the history of mankind, that the history of governmental action in social welfare started in the seventh century with the revelation of the Qur'an, and not in Western Europe in the past few centuries. They must realize that social welfare and insurance are not contemporary inventions, but part of the original Islamic system, provided to Muslims and non-Muslims alike.

I present this study to the contemporary intelligentsia in Muslim countries who have Muslim and Arab names and faces, but European, American, Russian , or Chinese hearts and minds, so they may realize that Islam is not a religion of asceticism that lives in the corner of worship alone, but a religion and a state, a system and a faith, encompassing knowledge and action, mediation and active life, freedom and justice, rights and obligations. All these are most justly manifested in the system of *zakah*.

I present this study to all Muslim people and their contemporary governments, so they can revise their positions of the Islamic law and system, especially *zakah*, in order to remove the contradictions imposed on our lives by the empirialistic powers, and rid their societies of the effect of cultural and legislative colonialism, after they cleanse their lands from military colonialism and return to Islam as a source of law and legislation.

Lastly, I present this study to those who are concerned with Islamic jurisprudence and Islamic culture, those who call for implementing the Islamic system in their societies, hoping that they find in it a comparative study in the light of Qur'an and Sunnah which strengthens their faith that this religion can endure the onslaught of so-called "modernism" and can respond to the needs of contemporary life. Islam can again lead societies and direct their affairs toward truth, goodness, and justice under its ever rich and fertile *Shari'ah*, that is suitable to all ages and lands. And the close of our call will always be "praise be to God, the Cherisher and Sustainer of the worlds."

Footnotes

1. *The Preaching of Islam*, by Thomas Arnold, translated by Dr. Hasan Ibrahim Hasan and his colleague, p. 167.

2. *Islam and Arabic culture*, by Muhammad Kurd 'Ali.

3. *Ibid*, pp. 76-77.

4. *Ibid*.

5. *In Defense of Islam*, p. 69.

6. *Sura al Hashr*, 59:19.

7. *Tafsir al Manar*, Vol. 2.

8. *Al Islam, 'Aqidah wa Shari'ah*, by Mahmud Shaltut.

9. *Sura al Tawbah*, 9:103.

10. *Ibid*, 9:60.

11. *Usus al Iqtisad fi al Islam*, by Abu al A'la al Maududi, p. 28-131.

12. See *al kharaj*, by Abu Yusuf, especially the introduction by Burhan Sati'.

13. *Al Arkan al Arba'ah*, by Abu al Hasan al Nadwi, pp.120-122.

FIQH AL ZAKAH

INDEX

INDEX

Notes:

A. Since a great many names are mentioned in this book, this index is restricted to names appearing in the text itself and not in the footnotes.

B. This list is also restricted to names of persons who have opinions about zakah. I do not mention in this index the names of narrators.

C. I did not list the names of the leaders of the four schools of thought, because of their renown.

D. Persons are listed according to their most well-known name, whether it is the first name, last name, or title.

E. The following words are not considered in the listing of names: al, ibn, abu, umm, ibn abi, etc.

F. Each name is followed by a very brief description of the person.

INDEX OF NAMES

Al Abhari, Muhammad bin 'Abd Allah bin Saleh, Abu Bakr, the leading supporter of Malik's view in Iraq. Renowned among scholars of his age, d. 395 H.

Ahmad Thabit 'Awaidah, contemporary legislation expert in Egypt, who has a good lecture on *Islam and Taxation*.

Ahmad Shakir. See Shakir Ahmad.

Al Ajhuri, 'Ali bin Muhammad. A Malikite, d. 1066 H.

Abu al A'la al Maududi, founder of the Jama'ati Islami party in Pakistan and a great modern Islamic thinker, d. 1979 AD.

Al Amidi, Abu al Hasan 'Ali, a jurist and scholar of *usul*, author of *al Ahkam*, d. 631 H.

Anas bin Malik bin al Nadr al Ansari, who served the Prophet (p). He is one of the few Companions who narrate more sayings than anybody else.

Ashhab bin 'Abd al 'Aziz al Qaisi, jurist from Egypt, a Malikite and a great defender of the Malikite school. Abu Daud and al Nasa'i use him in their chains, d. 204. H.

Asma bint Abu Bakr al Siddiq, one of the early Muslims. The wife of al Zubair bin al 'Awwam, she mothered 'Abd Allah and 'Urwah. She is known as the "Girl with the Two Waist-bands."

Asbagh bin al Faraj, Egyptian jurist. He is Abu 'Abd Allah, trustworthy and truthful, a disciple of Ibn Wahb, the most knowledgeable of his age about Malik's opinion, d. 225 H.

Ibn al Athir, 'Ali bin Muhammad, author of *al Kamil* in history, d. 630 H.

Ibn al Athir, Majd al Din al Mubarak bin Muhammad, author of *al Nihayah*, d. 606 H.

Author of *Ghiyath al Umam*. See al Juwaini.

Author of *al Hidayah*. See al Marghinani.

Author of *al Havi*. See al Mawardi.

Author of *al 'Inayah*, a Hanafite.

Author of *al Rawd al Nadir*. See al Husain bin Ahmad.

Al Awza'i, 'Abd al Rahman bin 'Amr, well-known leading jurist, hadith critic and one of the "pillars of knowledge," d. 157 H.

Ayub al Sakhtiani, Ibn Abi Taimiyah al Basri, one of the trustworthy persons. Shu'bah used to call him the "master of jurists." Malik describes him as one of the "scholars who practice their knowledge and who fear God." D. 131 H.

Al A'zami, Dr. Muhammad Mustafa, Indian Muslim scholar, studied in al Azhar, author of a good study, in English, in which he refutes the claim of Schacht; presently professor of Islamic studies at Riyadh University.

Ibn 'Abbas. See 'Abd Allah.

Abu al 'Abbas, Ahmad bin Ibrahim al Hashimi al Hasani, a jurist from Ahl al Bait. He was Ja'fari, then became Zaidi. Some people say he remained Ja'fari, d. 353 H.

'Abd Allah bin 'Abbas bin 'Abd al Muttalib, cousin of the Prophet (p). He was the most renowned commentator on the Qur'an and a leading, most knowledgeable scholar, d. 67 H.

'Abd Allah bin 'Amr bin al 'As, a leading scholar worshiper, d. 63 or 77 H.

'Abd Allah bin Daud bin 'Amir al Hamadhani al Sha'bi, known as al Khuraibi. Trustworthy worshiper, d. 213 H.

'Abd Allah bin Mas'ud al Hudhali, one of the great early Companions, known as a reciter and a great jurist, like a mountain in knowledge, d. 32 or 33 H.

'Abd Allah bin al Mubarak bin Wadih a Hanzali. He is from Marv (now in Russian - occupied south Central Asia), known as a great scholar and one of the person most agreed-upon as trustworthy, a leading man in knowledge, righteousness, and morality, d. 181 H.

'Abd Allah bin Shaddad bin al Had al Laithi, Abu al Walid al Madani, one of the great Followers and trustworthy persons. He revolted against the Umayyads with Ibn al Ash'ath and was killed in the 81 or 82 H.

'Abd Allah bin 'Umar bin al Khattab, a leading Companion in knowledge, and piety, great scholar and jurist, taught for about sixty years and freed 1000 or more slaves, d. 73 or 74 H.

'Abd al 'Aliy al Laknawi, known as the "ocean of knowledge, the author of *Rasa'il al Arkan al Arba'ah*.

Ibn 'Abd al Barr, Abu 'Umar, Yusuf bin 'Abd Allah al Namri al Qurtubi, the scholar of the West (Andalusia) and their jurist, author of *al Tamhid, al Istidhkar, al Isti'ab* and other works, d. 463 H.

Ibn 'Abd al Hakam, Muhammad bin 'Abd Allah, Egyptian jurist, trustworthy, and a leading Malikite, d. 268 H.

'Abd al Rahman Fahmy, secretary of the Islamic Art Museum in Cairo.

'Abd al Rahman 'Isa, a graduate of al Azhar, director of Islamic teaching in al Azhar.

Ibn 'Abd al Salam, Muhammad bin 'Abd al Salam bin Yusuf. He was a judge in Tunisia, and one of the leading Malikites, d. 749 H.

'Abd al Wahhab bin 'Ali, a Malikite jurist and judge, d. 422 H.

Ibn 'Abidin, Muhammad Amin, renowned Hanafite scholar, author of *Radd al Muhtar* and other books, d. 1252 H.

'A'ishah bint Abu Bakr, the Truthful daughter of the Truthful, Mother of Believers, and the most knowledgeable woman of this Muslim nation, d. 58 H.

'Alaish, Shaikh Muhammad bin Ahmad, Egyptian, leading Malikite, d. 1299 H.

'Ali bin Abi Talib, Prince of Believers, son in-law of the Prophet (p) and his cousin, and father of the Prophet's two grandchildren, an ocean of knowledge and the Companion most famous for his judgements, d. 40 H.

Ali bin al Husain bin 'Ali bin Abi Talib, a great Follower, one of the most trustworthy and pious persons, known as the "best of worshipers," and the leading person of Ahl al Bait during his time. Ibn al Musayyib says about him, "I have not seen a more pious person than him." D. 93 H.

'Ali Mubarak Basha bin Mubarak bin Sulaiman, Egyptian historian and minister in the Egyptian government, founder of the Egyptian National Library, d. 1311 H. / 1893 AD.

Abu al 'Aliyah, Rafi bin Mahran al Riyakhi al Basri, lived in Jahiliyah and accepted Islam two years after the Prophet's death. He met Abu Bakr and prayed behind 'Umar and in unanimously known as trustworthy, d. 90 H.

'Amr bin al 'As bin Wa'il al Sahmi, well-known Companion who opened Egypt, d. 43 H.

'Amr bin al Dinar al Makki, Abu Muhammad al Athram al Jumahi, a Follower, scholar, and opinion-leader in Makkah, d. 125 or 126 H.

'Amr bin Maimun al Awdi al Hufi, He accepted Islam during the life of the Prophet (p) but did not meet him. One of the most trustworthy Followers, d. 74 H.

'Amr, bin Shurahbil al Hamdani, Abu Maisarah, trustworthy and pious worshiper, one of the best disciples of Ibn Mas'ud, a Follower and colleague of Masruq, d. 63 H.

'Amrah bint 'Abd al Rahman bin Sa'd bin Zararah. She is from the Ansar, lived in Madinah, and was raised by 'A'ishah, from whom she narrates. She was among the most knowledgeable persons in Madinah, d. 98 or 103 or 106 H.

Ibn 'Aqil, Abu al Wafa, 'Ali bin Muhammad bin 'Aqil al Baghdadi, a jurist and scholar of *usul*, leading Hanbalite of distinguished views which sometimes differ with the Hanbalite school, though he was a great admirer of Ahmad and his disciples, d. 513 H.

Ibn al 'Arabi, Muhammad bin 'Abd Allah bin Muhammad al Mu'afiri, the judge Abu Bakr, a Malikite, *mujtahid*, and leading scholar, d. 543 H.

Ibn 'Arafah, Muhammad bin Muhammad bin 'Arafah al Warghami, Abu 'Abd Allah, a Malikite. Tunisian jurist, artistic in *usul* and jurisprudence, d. 803 H.

'Ata al Khurasani bin 'Abd Allah, lived in Damascus, Muslim and the four authors of *Sunan* report his narrations, d. 135 H.

'Ata bin Abi 'Awfi bin Sa'd bin Junadah al Qaisi al Kufi. Abu al Hasan, Abu Daud, al Tirmidhi, and Ibn Majah report his narrations. So does al Bukhari in works other than his correct collection. The majority grades him weak. D. 111 H.

Umm 'Atiyyah, Nusaibah bint Ka'b (or al Harith), from the Ansar. A great Companion who went to battles with the Prophet to take care of the wounded and to fight when needed. D. 13 H.

Al Bahi al Khawli, contemporary writer and early caller for the Islamic movement in Egypt, author of *Tadhkirat al Dua'at, al Islam wa al Mar'ah al Mu'asirah*, and other books.

Al Baihaqi, Ahmad bin al Husain, a saying critic and collector and a leading scholar, author of *al Sunan al Kubra* and other books, d. 458 H.

Al Baji, Abu al Walid, Sulaiman bin Khalaf bin Sa'd, the Malikite judge, a commentator on *al Muwatta'*, d. 474 H.

Abu Bakr 'Abd al 'Aziz bin Ja'far, known as "ghulam al khallal," leading Hanbalite jurist and pious worshiper, d. 353 H.

Abu Bakr al 'Asamm, 'Abd al Rahman bin al 'Asaamm al 'Abdi. Ibn Mufti says about him, "He is trustworthy. He was one of the Qadaris". Abu Hatim says "He tells the truth and his narrations are all right; Muslim reports one saying from him, and Al Nasa'i also reports one".

Abu Bakr al Razi, See al Jassas.

Abu Bakr bin Abi Shaibah, 'Abd al Rahman bin 'Abd al Malik al Madani. His trustworthiness is disputed; some grade him weak. Al Bukhari reports only two sayings from him and al Nisa'i reports from him. D. 335 H.

Abu Bakr al Siddiq, 'Abd Allah bin Abi Quhafah, the Successor of the Messenger of God as head of state, his right-hand minister and Companion, named even in the Qur'an as the Prophet's Companion, d. 13 H.

Al Baladhari, Ahmad bin Yahya, well-known historian, author of *Futuh al Buldan*, d. 279 H.

Al Balkhi, Abu Ja'far, a Hanafite jurist.

Al Baqir, Abu Ja'far, Muhammad bin 'Ali, the best of worshipers, leading jurist of Ahl al Bait as well as a great Muslim scholar, d. 118 H.

Ibn Bashir, a Malikite jurist.

Ibn Battal.

Al Baghawi, 'Abd Allah bin Muhammad al Baghdadi, Abu al Qasim, the great trustworthy author and critic of sayings, d. 317 H.

Bilal bin Rabah, the caller for payer of the Prophet (p). One of the very early Muslims who were harshly tortured by the disbelievers, he attended all battles of the Prophet (p), d. 17, 18, or 25 H.

Schacht, Joseph, contemporary orientalist, author of the section on *zakah* in the *Encyclopedia of Islam*, known for his antagonistic views toward Islam and the *Sunnah*.

Al Dahlawi, Ahmad bin 'Abd al Rahim, known as Shah Waliy Allah, the renovator of Islam in India, d. 1176.

Deniel, S. Girk.

Ibn Daqiq al "Id, Muhammad bin 'Ali bin Wahb, Abu al Fath, Taqi al Din, leading scholar, most trustworthy, and the renovator of the seventh century, d. 702 H.

Abu al Darda, 'Uwaimer bin Zaid, a Companion from the Ansar, known as a great worshiper, d. 32 or 33 H.

Al Dardir, Ahmad bin Muhammad al 'Adawi, a Malikite professor at al Azhar in Egypt, a great scholar and worshiper, d. 1201 H.

Daud al Zahiri bin 'Ali bin Khalaf, leading jurist and scholar, founder and head of the Zahiri school, d. 270 H.

Draz, Dr. Shaikh Muhammad 'Abd Allah, one of the great Professor of al Azhar in modern times and a great writer, author of *al Naba' al 'Azim, al Din,* and other very important studies, d. 1958 AD.

Al Dahhak bin Muzahim al Hilali, known as a commentator on the Qur'an, died after the year 100 H.

Al Dhahabi, a Shafi'ite scholar who has a booklet on determination of the *dirham* and the *mithqal.*

Al Dhahabi, Muhammad bin Ahmad, Abu Abd Allah, Shams al Din, leading scholar, historian, and sayings critic, d. 748 H.

Abu Dharral Ghifari, Jundub bin Junadah, pious Companion known as "the Truth-Teller," one of the early Muslims, d. 32 H.

Fagleri, Italian Orientalist writer.

Al Fakhr al Razi, Muhammad bin 'Umar bin al Husain, Fakhr al Din, leading scholar and Qur'an commentator, a Shafi'ite, d. 606 H.

Fatimah bint Qais bin Khalid al Qurashiyah al Fihriyah, a Companion among the early migrants, d. 50 H.

Al Ghazali, Muhammad bin Muhammad, Abu Hamid, the scholar of Islam, d. 505 H.

Al Ghazali, Shaikh Muhammad, contemporary Muslim scholar from al Azhar, one of the early workers and writers of the contemporary Islamic movement, d. 1996 A.D.

Al Hadi, Abu Muhammad Yahya bin al Husain bin al Qasim, leading Ahl al Bait scholar, founder of the Hadawi school, d. 298 H.

Ibn al Humam, Kamal al Din, Muhammad bin 'Abd al Wahid al Siwasi, then al Sakandari, the great Hanafite scholar who reached the level of ijtihad, author of *al Musayarah, al Fath*, and other books, d. 861 H.

Abu Hurairah al Dawsi. His original name is disputed; he became famous as Abu Hurairah, the Companion with the sharpest memory, d. 67 or 69 H.

Ibn Habib, 'Abd al Malik, Marwan, a leading Malikite jurist, d. 238 H.

Ibn Hajar, Ahmad bin 'Ali al 'Asqalani, the shakih of Islam, famous as al Hafiz, great sayings critic, author of *al Fath, al Tahdhib*, and other works, d. 852 H.

Ibn al Hajib, 'Uthman bin 'Umar, a Malikite scholar of usul and grammar, d. 646 H, in Alexandria.

Ibn Hamid, al Hasan bin Hamid bin 'Ali, Abu 'Abd Allah al Baghdadi, Hanbalite leader of his time, d. 403 H.

Hammad bin Abi Sulaiman, Abu Isma'il al Kufi, great jurist, teacher of Abu Hanifah, and the most knowledgeable disciple of Ibrahim al Nakha'i. Al Bukhari reports from him in *al Adab al Mufrad*. Muslim and other four also report from him, d. 119 or 120 H.

Al Harbi, Ibrahim Ibn Ishaq, the saying critic and trustworthy author, d. 285 H.

Al Hasan al Basri, Ibn Abi al Hasan, Abu Sa'id, a leading scholar of Islam and one of the most famous Followers, d. 110 H.

Al Hasan bin 'Ali bin Abi Talib, grandson of the Messenger of God (p), one of the two "Masters of youth" in heaven, as said by the Prophet (p), d. 49 or 50 H.

Al Hasan bin 'Ali bin Al Hanafiyah. In *al Jawahir al Mudi'ah*, there are several persons with this name. I could not tell which one of them was this person.

Al Hasan bin Saleh bin Hai, sometimes called al Hasan bin Hai, al Hamdani, a jurist and pious worshiper who refused leadership, was honest in telling sayings and had an accurate memory. Graded correct in his narrations. Muslim and other four report from him. Al Bukhari reports from him in *al Adab al Mufrad*. Some grade him weak because he was a Shi'ite and did not use to go to Friday congregational prayers. He did not permit prayer behind deviant persons, d. 166 H.

Abu Hathamah, 'Abd Allah or Amir, al Ansari, well-known Companion, the guide of the Prophet (p) in the battle of Uhud. The Prophet (p) also sent him as estimator of fruits. Died early in the era of Mu'awiyah.

Ibn Hazm, 'Ali bin Ahmad, Abu Muhammad al Zahiri. He was a leading scholar, a *mujtahid*, and the author of *al Muhalla, al Ihkam, al Fasl*, and several others books, d. 456 H.

Al Hazimi, Abu Bakr Muhammad bin Muhammad bin Musa, a saying critic, author of *al I'tibar* and other books, d. 584 H.

Al Huqaini, 'Ali bin Ja'far bin al Hasan al Husaini al Hashimi, known as al Huqaini al Saghir in relation to a small village close to Madinah; a Zaidi jurist, d. 490 H.

Al Husain al 'Abdi bin Muhammad bin Ziad al 'Abdi al Nisaburi, a great pillar of saying criticism and an author, known as al Qabbani, d. 289 H.

Al Husain bin Ahmad al Siyaghi al Zaidi, Sharaf al Din, a moderate Zaidi scholar, author of *al Rawd al Nadir*.

Ibrahim, See al Nakha'i.

Ishaq bin Ibrahim bin Mukhlid al Hanzali, known as Ibn Rahawaih al Marwazi. He lived in Nisabur and was a leading scholar in knowledge, jurisprudence, and saying, and a teacher of al Bukhari and Muslim, d. 237 or 238 H.

Abu Ishaq, 'Amr bin 'Abd Allah al Sabi'i al Kufi, a trustworthy Follower, d. 156 or 159 H.

Al Istakhri, Abu Sa'id, al Hasan bin Ahmad, renowned Shafi'ite jurist who authored several books, d. 328 H.

'Ikrimah bin 'Abd Allah al Barbari, ex-slave of Ibn 'Abbas and his student, one of the great jurists of Makkah, and a Follower, d. 107 H.

'Imran bin Husain al Khuza'i, famous Companion, d. 52 H.

'Isa 'Abduh, modern Egyptian professor of economics and accounting.

Iyad bin Musa al Yahsubi, Abu al Fadl, the judge, a great scholar from the Islamic West, and a Malikite jurist, d. 544 H.

'Izz al Din bin 'Abd al Salam, 'Abd al 'Aziz al Sulami, Shafi'ite jurist from Damascus, known as the king of scholars, one of the most brilliant leaders of knowledge in Syria and Egypt, d. 660 H.

Jabir bin 'Abd Allah bin Haram al Ansari al Sulami, one of the Companion scholars, d. 70 H.

Jabir bin Zaid al Azdi Abu al Sha'tha al Basri, a trustworthy Follower and scholar, d. 93 H.

Ja'far al Sadiq bin Muhammad al Hashimi al Husaini, a great scholar and leading figure from Ahl al Bait, d. 148 H.

Al Jassas, Ahmad bin 'Ali, Abu Bakr al Razi, renowned Hanafite scholar and author, d. 370 H.

Ibn al Jawzi, 'Abd al Rahman bin 'Ali, Abu al Faraj, jurist, *hadith* critic, and historian, a great Hanbalite, d. 597 H.

Al Juwaini, 'Abd al Malik bin 'Abd Allah, Abu al Ma'ali, known as Imam al Haramain, author of *Ghiyath al Umam, al Irshad, al Nisamiyah,* and several other books; a leading Shafi'ite, d. 478 H.

Al Karkhi, Abu al Hasan 'Ubaid Allah bin Dallal, Hanafite jurist, great scholar and worshiper, the head of Hanafites at his time in Baghdad, d. 340 H.

Al Kasani, 'Ala al Din Abu Bakr bin Mas'ud, called "the king of scholars", a leading Hanafite, d. 587 H.

Ibn Kathir, Abu al Fida' Isma'il al Qurashi, known as a commentator on the Qur'an, saying scholar and critic, historian and jurist, d. 774 H.

Abu Khaithamah, Zuhair bin Harb, a trustworthy and accurate *hadith* scholar. Muslim reports 1281 sayings from him in his correct collection. D. 234 H.

Ibn Khaldun, 'Abd al Rahman bin Muhammad, the chairman of historians, the great renovator and scholar, founder of sociology, d. 808 H.

Khalid bin Ishaq al Jundi, Egyptian-raised Malikite scholar, author of *al Mukhtasar* in Malikite jurisprudence, d. 776 H.

Khallaf, Shaikh 'Abd al Wahhab, professor of Shari'ah in al Azhar and a great modern scholar.

Abu al Khattab, Muhfuz bin Ahmad al Kalwadhani al Baghdadi, a leading Hanbalite jurist of independent opinions, d. 510 H.

Al Khattabi, Muhammad bin Muhammad bin Ibrahim, Abu Sulaiman, well-known leading jurist, scholar of sayings and the Arabic language, d. 388 H.

Al Khiraqi, Abu al Qasim, 'Umar bin Husain bin 'Abd Allah, a Hanbalite jurist, d. 334 H.

Al Kirshi, Abu 'Abd Allah Muhammad, a Malikite, the commentator on *Mukhtasar Khalid*, d. 1101 H.

Ibn al Labban, Muhammad bin 'Abd Allah bin al Hasan, Abu al Husain, a trustworthy Shafi'ite scholar, especially in inheritance law, d. 402 H.

Ibn Abi Laila, Muhammad bin 'Abd al Rahman al Ansari al Kufi, jurist and famous judge in Kufah, lived at the same time as Abu Hanifah, honest but had a bad memory.

Al Laith bin Sa'd bin 'Abd al Rahman, leading Egyptian scholar, trustworthy, and a most generous person. Al Shafi'i says "al Laith had more knowledge than Malik but his knowledge was lost by his disciples." D. 175 H.

Al Lakhmi, 'Ali bin Muhammad, a renowned Malikite scholar, d. 748 H.

Massignon, French orientalist who lived at the turn of the century.

Maghniyah, Muhammad Jawad, contemporary Lebaness Shi'ite scholar, author of several books.

Al Mahdi, Ahmad bin Yahya bin al Murtada al Hasani al Hadawi, author of *al Bahr al Zakhkhar*, and a leading Zaidi scholar, d. 840 H.

Mahmud Abu Sa'ud, contemporary economist with special interest in Islamic economics, d. 1993.

Maimun bin Mahran al Jizri al Riqqi, one of the great trustworthy scholars, a jurist, pious worshiper, and leading Follower, who was appointed by 'Umar bin 'Abd al 'Aziz as kharaj commissioner and judge in the area of Jazirah (northeast of Syria and northwest of Iraq), d. 116 or 117 H.

Abu Maisarah. See 'Amr bin Shurahbil.

Ibn al Mjashawn, 'Abd al Malik bin 'Abd al 'Aziz, a jurist son of a jurist and opinion leader in Madinah at his time. Ibn Habib grades him as more knowledgeable than most disciples of Malik. D. 212, 213, or 214 H.

Makhluf, Shaikh Hasanain Muhammad Hasanain al 'Adawi, leading Egyptian scholar and one of the great scholars of al Azhar.

Makhluf, Shaikh Muhammad Hasaniain al 'Adawi, an Egyptian, leading Malikite scholar, famous as a Qur'an commentator and as a scholar of Arabic literature. He was deputy chairman of al Azhar, d. 1355 H. / 1936 AD.

Makhul, great Follower, one of the most trustworthy and knowledgeable scholars, he lived in Damascus, d. 112 or 113 H.

Ibn Malik.

Al Maliqi, Muhammad bin al Hasan, a Malikite jurist who has a commentary on *Mukhtasar Ibn al Hajib* in jurisprudence, d. 771 H.

Al Maqrizi, Ahmad bin 'Ali, historian of Egypt with several volumes of writings, known as *Khutat al Maqrizi*, d. 845 H.

Al Maraghi, Shaikh Ahmad Mustafa, modern Egyptian, author of a commentary on the Qur'an.

Marwan bin al Hakam bin Abi al 'As, an Umayyad, born in Madinah two years after migration of the Prophet. We have no authentic report that he heard from the Messenger of God (p). He was a clerk with 'Uthman, and governor of Madinah in Mu'awiyah's time. Became *khalifiah* after Mu'awiyah, son of Yazid, and remained so nine months. Criticism is known to be addressed to him, d. 65 H.

Masruq bin Ajda' al Hamdani, a Follower, great jurist and worshiper, a disciple of Ibn Mas'ud, d. 62 H.

Ibn Mas'ud. See 'Abd Allah.

Al Mawardi, Abu al Hasan, 'Ali bin Muhammad bin Habib al Basri al Baghdadi, renowned Shafi'ite scholar, known as the best judge, author of *al Hawi, al Ahkam al Sultaniyyah*, and other books, d. 450 H.

Al Maziri, Muhammad bin 'Ali bin 'Umar al Tamimi, a known Malikite jurist and saying critic, who wrote a commentary on Muslim's correct collection, d. 536 H.

Mu'adh bin Jabal bin 'Amr al Ansari, one of the leading Companions, d. 18 H.

Mu'awiyah bin Abi Sufyan, founder of the Umayyad *khilafah*, a Companion and one of the scribes who wrote the Qur'an for the Prophet (p) d. 60 H.

Al Mu'ayyad bi Allah, Ahmad bin al Husain bin Harun, leading scholar of Ahl al Bait, a Zaidi jurist, d. 411 H.

Ibn al Mubarak. See 'Abd Allah.

Ibn Muflih, Muhammad Abu 'Abd Allah, Shams al Din, a Hanbalite, d. 763 H.

Al Mughirah bin Shu'bah al Thaqafi, famous Companion, one of the shrewdest Arabs, d. 50 H.

Muhammad 'Abd Allah al Arabi, modern professor of finance and economics in Egyptian universities, has a good study of Islamic economics.

Muhammad 'Abduh, Shaikh, famous as one of the great reformers of modern Egypt, opinion leader in religious matters in Egypt in his time, d. 1905 AD.

Muhammad Uzair, contemporary Pakistani economist who wrote on Islamic economics.

Muhammad Baqir al Sadr, modern Shi'ite scholar from Najaf, Iraq, author of *Iqtisaduna* and *Falsafatuna*.

Muhammad Hamidullah Hyderabadi, contemporary Indian Muslim scholar, professor at the University of Paris and University of Istanbul.

Muhammad bin al Hanafiyah, (bin 'Ali bin Abi Talib), Abu al Qasim, trustworthy Follower, d. 73 or 93 H.

Muhammad bin Ka'b al Qurazi, knowledgeable on Qur'an, and a trustworthy Follower, d. 108 or 120 H.

Muhammad bin Maslamah, Hanafite scholar.

Muhammad bin al Hasan al Shaibani, disciple of Abu Hanifah, great scholar, writer of the original books in the Hanafite school, d. 189 H.

Muhammad bin Yahya, disciple of al Ghazali, head of the Shafi'ites in Nisabur, d. 548 H.

Mujahid bin Jabar al Makki, a renowned Follower, d. 135 H.

Al Munawi, Muhammad 'Abd al Ra'uf, great scholar in jurisprudence and sayings, Shafi'ite Egyptian, author of *Faid al Qadir*, and *al Taisir* as a commentary on *al Jami'al Saghir*, d. 1031 H.

Ibn al Munayyir, Ahmad bin Muhammad bin Mansur, Nasir al Din, renowned Malikite jurist. 'Izz al Din bin 'Abd ald Salam says "The land of Egypt is proud of having two persons, Ibn Daqiq al Id and Ibn al Munayyir." D. 683 H.

Ibn al Mundhir, Muhammad bin Ibrahim al Nisaburi, Abu Bakr, a great jurist. He was a *mujtahid* and leader in knowledge, authored many books, d. 319 H.

Al Mundhiri, Zaki al Din 'Abd al Salam, known leader and critic in sayings, author of *al Targhib wa al Tarhib* and *Mukhtasar Sunan Abu Daud*, d. 656 H.

Murrah al Hamdani bin Shurahil a Saksaki, Abu Isma'il al Kufi, trustworthy Follower, known as a great worshiper, used to be called "Murrah al Tayeb" or "Murrah al Khair, " d. 76 H.

Al Murtada, Muhammad bin Yahya al Wadi bin al Husain al Hashimi al Hasani, leading Zaidi jurist, inherited knowledge from his father al Hadi, d. 310 H.

Musa bin Talhah bin 'Abd Allah al Qurashi al Taimi, trustworthy Follower, a leading Muslim figure of his time, d. 103, 104, or 106 H.

Abu Musa al Ash'ari, Abd Allah bin Qais, famous Companion. The Prophet appointed him to Yemen and 'Umar appointed him as a judge, d. 44 H.

Al Muzani, Isma'il bin Yahya, a mujtahid, Egyptian disciple of al Shafi'i, and a worshiper, d. 264 H.

Al Nadwi, al Sayid Abu al Hasan 'Ali al Hasani, secretary of Nadwat al 'Ulama'in Lucknow, India, one of the greatest figures in the contemporary Islamic movement, and a famous Islamic author.

Ibn Nafi, 'Abd Allah al Sa'igh, Abu Muhammad al Madani, a disciple of Malik, the best versed in Malik's opinions. Al Shafi'i praises him, but others criticize the accuracy of his memory, d. 206 or 207 H.

Al Nahhas, Abu Ja'far, Ahmad bin Muhammad, Egyptian scholar, d. 338 H.

Ibn Haji, Qasim bin 'Isa, Malikite jurist, author of *Sharh al Risalah*, an explanation of *al Risalah*, which is by Ibn Abi Zaid, d. 837 H.

Al Nakha'i, Ibrahim bin Yazid bin Qais al Kufi, great jurist, a Follower, and one of the pillars of knowledge in al Kuraf, d. 96 H.

Al Nasir, al Hasan bin 'Ali al Husaini al Hashimi, d. 304 H.

Al Nawawi, Abu Zakariyya, Muhiy al Din Yahya bin Sharaf al Din, great jurist by unanimous opinion of scholars, a Shafi'ite scholar and critic in sayings and jurisprudence, d. 676 H.

Ibn Nujaim, al Zain, a great Hanafite scholar, called the second Abu Hanifah, author of *al Ashbah wa al Naza'ir, al Bahr al Ra'iq*, and several other volume, d. 970 H.

Al Qadi 'Abd al Wahhab. See 'Abd al Wahhab bin 'Ali.

Al Qadi Ya'qub. See Ya'qub.

Al Qaffal. He is most likely 'Abd Allah bin Ahmad bin al Qaffal al Saghir, d. 417 H.

Al Qahastani, Ahmad bin Muhammad bin 'Abd Allah, Abu al Qasim, a Hanafite jurist.

Al Qarafi, Shihab al Din Abu al 'Abbas Ahmad bin Idris bin 'Abd al Rahman, jurist and scholar of usul, great Malikite d. 684 H.

Ibn al Qasim, Abd al Rahman al 'Utaqi, Abu 'Abd Allah, Egyptian jurist, disciple of Malik, and a great defender of Malik's school, d. 191 H.

Al Qasim bin Ibrahim bin Isma'il bin al Hasan bin Ali, leading scholar from Ahl al Bait, d. 242 or 244 H.

Al Qasim bin Muhammad bin Abu Bakr the Truthful, one of the pillars of knowledge in the era of the Followers, and a great Follower, d. 108 H.

Al Qasimi, Jamal al Din Muhammad, the great scholar of Syria, who wrote a commentary on the Qur'an called *Mahasin al Ta'wil*. He was a saying scholar and critic too, d. 1332 H.

Al Rafi'i, Abu al Qasim 'Abd al Karim bin Muhammad bin 'Abd al Karim, a leading Shafi'ite figure, d. 623 H.

Al Rafi'i, Mustafa Sadiq, great modern writer in Islamic studies and Arabic literature, author of *Wahi al Qalam*, d. 1356 H. / 1937 AD.

Al Ramli, Shams al Din, author of the commentary on al Nawawi's *al Minhaj*.

Ibn Rislah.

Al Rayis, Dr. Muhammad Diya, professor of Islamic history at Egyptian universities, modern author of several useful books, including *al Kharaj fi al Dawlah al Islamiyyah*.

Abu Razin, Mas'ud bin Malik al Asadi, a trustworthy Follower who lived in Kufah d. 85 H.

Ibn Rushaid, Muhammad bin 'Amr bin Muhammad, Abu 'Abd Allah Majd al Din al Fihri al Sibti, a Malikite jurist as well as a Qur'an and sayings scholar, d. 721 H.

Ibn Rushd, Muhammad bin Ahmad, the grandfather, one of the greatest scholars in the Malikite school, d. 520 H.

Ibn Rushd, Muhammad bin Ahmad al Qurtubi al Andalusi, the judge and famous philosopher, known as Ibn Rushd the grandson, d. 595 H.

Al Qashiri, 'Abd al Rahman bin 'Abd al Karim bin Hawazin, great Shafi'ite jurist, d. 514 H.

Qatadah bin Da'amah al Sadusi, Abu al Khattab al Basri, one of the most knowledgeable Followers, d. 117 H.

Ibn al Qayyim, Abu 'Abd Allah, Shams al Din Muhammad bin Abu Bakr, a strong leading scholar, author of many beneficial volumes, d. 751 H.

Ibn Qudamah, Abu Muhammad 'Abd Allah bin Ahmad, great Hanbalite scholar and jurist, author of *al Mughni*, d. 620 H.

Ibn Qulabah, 'Abd Allah bin Zaid al Jurami al Azdi al Basri, great Follower and trustworthy jurist, d. 104 H.

Al Qurtubi, Abu 'Abd Allah Muhammad bin Ahmad al Ansari, author of a commentary on the Qur'an and a great Malikite jurist, d. 774 H.

Al Qurtubi, Ahmad bin 'Umar, commentator on the correct collection of Muslim, d. 656 H.

Al Rabi' bin Anas al Bakri al Hanafi al Basri, then al Khurasani. Al 'Ujali and Abu Hatim say "He is honest"; al Nasa'i says "He is all right." D. 139 or 140 H.

Rabi'ah bin Abi 'Abd al Rahman al Taimi, known as Rabi'ah al Ra'i, teacher of Malik, a trustworthy Follower, and renowned jurist, d. 136 H.

Sa'd bin Abi Waqqas al Zuhri, one of the early Muslims, one of the ten persons promised heaven, and one of the six persons selected by 'Umar to choose the next *khalifah*, d. 55 H.

Sahl bin Abi Hathamah al Ansari al Khazraji, the Companion son of a Companion. His year of death is not precisely know.

Sa'id bin 'Abd al 'Aziz al Tanukhi al Dimashqi, a contemporary of al Awza'i about whom al Hakim says "He is for Syria like Malik for Madinah in knowledge and leadership." D. 167 or 168 H.

Sa'id bin Jubair al Kufi, a great Follower and scholar of his time, d. 95 H.

Abu Sa'id al Khudri, Sa'd bin Malik bin Sinan al Khazraji al Ansari, one of the great Companions, one of the seven persons who narrate more than one thousand sayings from the Prophet (p) d. 74 H.

Sa'id bin al Musayyib al Qurashi al Makhzumi, known as "the master of the Followers", d. 95 H.

Salamah bin al Akwa' al Aslami, famous Companion who attended the pledge or covenant known as "Bai'at al Ridwan," d. 74 H.

Abu Salamah bin 'Abd al Rahman bin 'Awf al Zuhri al Madani, great Follower and jurist, d. 94 or 104 H.

Salim bin 'Abd Allah bin 'Umar bin al Khattab al Madani, the great jurist, one of the seven jurists of Madinah and a leading Follower, d. 107 H.

Salamn al Farisi, Abu 'Abd Allah, known as "the son of Islam," great Companion, d. 33, 36, or 37 H.

Al Sarakhsi, Muhammad bin Ahmad Abu Bakr, sun of scholars, a great Hanafite jurist who dictated his big book *al Mabsut* while in prison, d. 483 H.

Sayyid Qutb, Islamic thinker and writer, author of *Fi Zilal al Qur'an, al 'Adalah al Ijtima' iyyah, Khasa'is al Tasawwur al Islami,* and several other books, who was martyred in Egypt in 1966 AD / 1386 H.

Al Sha'bi 'Amir bin Sharahil al Kufi, leading Follower and scholar, d. 105 H.

Shahr bin Hawshab al Ash'ari, a Follower. His trustworthiness is disputed. Muslim, the four, and al Bukhari in *al Adab al Mufrad* report from him. Al Tabari says he was a jurist and a knowledgeable scholar, d. 100, 111, or 112 H.

Shakir, Shaikh Ahmad bin Muhammad, the modern Egyptian judge and scholar of sayings and Arabic language, known for his editing of many important books, such as *al Muhalla, al Risalah, Musnad Ahmad, Tafsir al Tabari,* and several others.

Shaltut, Shaikh Mahmud, former chairman of al Azhar, a modern Egyptian known for his famous religious opinions and explanations of the Qur'an. He has several useful books.

Abu al Sha'tha, Salim bin Aswad bin Hanzalah al Muharibi al Kufi, trustworthy Follower, d. 85 H.

Al Shatibi, Abu Ishaq, Ibrahim bin Musa al Lakhmi al Ghirnati al Maliki, great scholar from Andalusia, author of the two distinguished books, *al Muwafaqat* and *al I'tisam,* d. 790 H.

Al Shawkani, Muhammad bin 'Ali al Yamani al Zaidi, an independent *mujtahid,* d. 1255 H.

Ibn Shihab. See al Zuhri.

Ibn Shubrumah, 'Abd Allah bin al Tufail al Basrial Kufi, the judge, one of the trustworthy jurists, d. 144 H.

Shuraih bin al Harith bin Qais al Kindi, the great judge and one of the greatest Followers, d. 87 H.

Shuraik bin 'Abd Allah al Nakha'i al Kufi, jurist and judge, trustworthy and honest. Muslim and the four report from him, but he used to make many mistakes, d. 177 or 187 H.

Ibn Sirin, Muhammad Abu Bakr al Basri, a great Follower and jurist, d. 110 H.

Smith, Adam, founder of modern Western economics, famous for his book *The Wealth of Nations*, 1776 AD.

Al Suddi, Isma'il bin 'Abd al Rahman, al Kufi, known as al Suddi al Kabir, famous for his explanations of the Qur'an. Some people grade him trustworthy and others do not. Muslim and the four report from him. D. 127 H.

Sufyan al Thawri. See al Thawri.

Sufyan bin 'Uyainah al Hilali, a great trustworthy scholar and sayings critic, about whom al Shafi'i says, "If it were not for Malik and Sufyan, knowledge in Hijaz would have been wiped out." D. 198 H.

Suhnun, 'Abd al Salam bin Sa'id al Tanukhi, famous Malikite jurist, head of scholars in the Islamic West, d. 240 H.

Sulaiman bin Harb, Abu Ayyub al Basri, lived in Makkah and was a judge there; a trustworthy saying scholar, d. 224 H.

Sulaiman bin Musa al Dimashqi, jurist of Syria at his time, the most knowledgeable disciple of Makhul, d. 115 H.

Sulaiman bin Yasar al Hilali al Madani, former slave of Maimunah (the mother of Believers and wife of the Messenger (p)), great Follower, and one of the seven renowned jurists, d. 110 H.

Al Sadiq. See Ja'far al Sadiq.

Sadr al Shari'ah Mas'ud bin Ahmad bin Burhan, Hanafite jurist and scholar.

Al Saimari, 'Abd al Wahid bin al Husain, the judge and leading Shafi'ite scholar, d. after 386 H.

Al San'ani, Muhammad bin Isma'il al Yamani al Zaidi, author of *Subul al Salam* and other books, d. 1182 H.

Al Sawi, a Malikite jurist.

Siddiq Hasan Khan, King of Bhopal, India, great independent-minded scholar, similar to al Shawkani, d. 1307 H.

Ibn Taimiyah, Ahmad bin 'Abd al Halim, leading scholar and *mujtahid*, "shaikh al Islam" and the political and knowledge leader of his time, d. 728 H.

Abu Thawr, Ibrahim bin Khalid al Kalbi, jurist and *mujtahid*, disciple of al Shafi'i, d. 240 H.

Al Thawri, Sufyan bin Sa'id, Abu 'Abd Allah al Kufi, prince of believers in sayings and knowledge, one of the famous Muslim jurists and worshipers, d. 161 H.

Thomas Arnold.

Al Tabari, Muhammad bin Jarir, Abu Ja'far, master of Qur'an commentators, and unrivaled leader of historians; a mujtahid and independent person, d. 310 H.

Al Tahawi, Ahmad bin Muhammad bin Salamah, a jurist and leading Hanafite of his time, d. 321 H.

Talhah bin 'Abd Allah bin 'Awf al Zuhri al Madani, well-known judge, trustworthy Follower and jurist, nephew of 'Abd al Rahman bin 'Awf, d. 97 H.

Abu Talib, Yahya bin al Husain bin Muhammad, brother of al Mu'ayyad bi Allah, leading scholar of Ahl al Bait, d. 424 H.

Taus, Dhakwan bin Kisan al Yamani, Abu 'Abd Allah great renowned trustworthy Follower, d. 106 H.

Al Tibi.

'Ubadah bin al Samit al Ansari al Khazraji, Abu al Walid, one of the chairmen selected by the Prophet (p) on the night of the Pledge of al 'Aqabah, one of the Companions who collected the Qur'an during the life of the Prophet, d. 34 H.

'Ubaid Allah bin al Hasan bin Husain al 'Anbari, trustworthy Egyptian jurist and judge, d. 168 H.

Abu 'Ubaid, al Qasim bin Sallam, leading scholar and *mujtahid*, author of *al Amwal*, d. 225 H.

Abu 'Ubaidh bin al Jarrah, 'Amir bin 'Abd Allah, one of the early Muslim, great Companion, one of the ten person promised heaven, the most trustworthy person of this Ummah, d. 18 H.

Ibn 'Ubaidan, Ism'il bin Ibrahim al Basri, named in relation to his mother or grandmother, one of the most trustworthy scholars and a leader in sayings studies and critism known as "the rose of jurists," d. 193 or 194 H.

'Umar bin 'Abd al Aziz bin Marwan, Prince of Believers, the fifth of the Wise Successors, renovator of the first century of Islam, d. 101 H.

Ibn 'Umar. See 'Abd Allah.

'Umar al Hafiz bin Ahmad bin Muhammad bin Musa al Nisaburi, Hanafite scholar, disciple of Abu 'Abd al Rahman al Sulami, d. 467 H.

'Umar bin al Khattab, Prince of Relievers, one of the ten promised heaven, the gigantic leader of the Islamic states, second Successor of the Prophet (p), about whom the Prophet says, "God made truth come on his tongue and in his heart," d. 23 H.

'Urwah bin al Zubair bin al 'Awwam al Asadi al Madani, one of the seven pillars of jurisprudence in Madinah, a great Follower and scholar, d. 91 or 101 H.

"Uthman bin 'Affan, Prince of Believers, "the man with the two lights," one of the ten promised heaven, d. 35 H.

Ibn Wahb, 'Abd Allah bin Wahb bin Muslim, master of knowledge in Egypt and its great jurist, trustworthy disciple of Malik who combined jurisprudence, saying, and piety, d. 197 H.

Al Wahidi, Abu al Hasan 'Ali bin Ahmad, top professor of his time in explanation of Qur'an and in Arabic grammar, d. 468 H.

Waki' bin al Jarrah, Abu Sufian al Kufi, one of the most famous scholars and trustworthy persons of his time, known for his knowledge of sayings and for his piety, d. 196 or 197 H.

Yahya bin Adam, Abu Zakariyya al Kufi, one of the most trustworthy persons, scholar and critic of sayings, author of *al Kharaj,* d. 203 H.

Yahya bin Hamzah bin 'Ali al Hashimi al Husaini, knowledgeable Zaidi scholar and leader, d. 749 H.

Abu Ya'la, Muhammad bin al Husain al Farra, the judge, a great Hanbalite scholar, d. 458 H.

Ya'qub bin Ibrahim bin Satura al Barzabini, Abu 'Ali, the judge and great Hanbalite jurist, d. 486 H.

Abu Yusuf, Ya'qub bin Ibrahim, the disciple of Abu Hanifah, the great judge at the time of the Abbasides, a *mujtahid*, d. 182 H.

Ibn Zaid. See Jabir bin Zaid.

Ibn Abi Zaid, 'Abd Allah bin 'Abd al Rahman Abu Muhammad al Qairawani, Malikite jurist and well-known scholar, d. 386 H.

Zaid bin 'Ali bin al Husain bin 'Ali bin Abi Talib, leader and founder of the Zaidi school. Abu Ishaq al Sabi'i says "I have not seen anyone like Zaid in knowledge or grace among all the Ahl al Bait." D. 120 or 121 H.

Zaid bin Thabit al Ansari, scribe of the Qur'an, the one who collected the Qur'an at the time of Abu Bakr and 'Uthman, a great knowledgeable Companion, d. 45 H.

Abu Zahrah, Shaik Muhammad, professor of Shari'ah in various Arab universities in Egypt and elsewhere, a great modern scholar and writer.

Al Zamakhshari, Mahmud bin 'Umar, a Mu'tazilite, good writer, author of the explanation of the Qur'an called al *Kashshaf*, also author of *al Asas, al Fa'iq*, and other volumes, d. 538 H.

Al Zarkashi, Badr al Din 'Abd Allah bin Muhammad, a great Shafi'ite scholar, d. 794 H.

Zarruq, Ahmad bin Muhammad bin 'Isa al Barnasi al Maliki, a great Malikite jurist in the Islamic West, d. 899 H.

Zinbareau, modern orientalist, one of the writers of the *Encyclopedia of Islam*.

Ibn al Zubair, 'Abd Allah bin al Zubair bin al 'Awwam al Asadi al Qurashi, a Companion, great scholar, and courageous person, who was elected *khalifah* after the death of Mu'awiyah and remained so for a few years until he was killed by a Hajjaj the year 78 H.

Al Zurhri, Muhammad bin Muslim bin . . . bin Shihab, leading scholar of his time, with one of the best memories in the history of sayings and jurisprudence, d. 124 H.

Zufar bin al Hudhail bin Qais al 'Anbari, one of the great jurists, disciple of Abu Hanifah, about whom his teacher says, "He is the most knowledgeable in analogy among my disciples." D. 158 H.

REFERENCES

Note:

Reference are classified according to subject. In each subject, sequence of authors is according to the year of their death. Books whose place of printing is not mentioned were printed in Cairo. Sometime I refer to other printing not mentioned in this references; they are referred to in the footnotes. This happens because the book was authored in several places. Names of books are translated when they give an idea about their subjects, but references whose names are just general titles are not translated.

I. The Qur'an and Qur'anic Studies

The Glorious Qur'an.

Tafsir Gharib al Qur'an (Dictionary of Difficult Words in the Qur'an), by Abu Muhammad 'Abud Allah bin Muslim bin Qutaibah, 4. 276 H, ed. Ahmad Saqr, 'Isa al Babi al Halabi print.

Jami' al Bayan An Ta'wil al Qur'an, known as *Tafsir al Tabari* (explanation of the Qur'an), by al Imam al Tabari, d. 310, Dar al Ma'arif print, ed. Mahmud Muhammad Shakir, al Halabi print.

Akham al Qur'an (Rulings of the Qur'an) by al Imam al Jassas, d. 370 H, al Matba'a al Bahiyah print, Egypt.

Asbab al Nuzul (Circumstances of Revelation of Verses), by Abu Hasan, 'Ali bin Ahmad al Wahidi al Nisaburi, d. 468 H.

Mufradat al Qur'an (Dictionary of Qur'anic Vocabulary), by al Husain bin Muhammad bin al Mufaddal, known as al Raghb al Asfahani, d. 502 H., printed in the margins of *al Nihayah*, by Ibn al Athir, al Halabi print.

Al Kashshaf An Haqa'iq al Tanzil wa Daqa'iq al Ta'wil (explanation of the Qur'an), by Mahmud bin 'Umar al Zamakhshari, d. 538 H.

Ahkam al Qur'an (Rulings of the Qur'an), by a Qadi Abu Bakr bin al 'Arabi, d. 543, al Halabi print, ed. 'Ali al Bijawi.

Majma' al Bayan fi Tafsir al Qur'an (explanation of the Qur'an) by Abu 'Ali al Fadl bin al Hasan al Tubrusi al Shi'i, d. 548 H.

Al Tafsir al Kabir, called *Mafatih al Ghaib* (explanation of the Qur'an) by al Imam Fakhr al Din al Razi, d. 606, al Misriyah print, 1938.

Al Jami' li Ahkam al Qur'an (explanation of the Qur'an) by al Imam al Qurtubi, d. 774, Dar al Kutub print.

Tafsir al Qur'an al 'Azim (explanation of the Qur'an), by al Hafiz, Abu al Fida' Isma'il bin Kathir al Qurashi, d. 774, al Halabi print.

Al Intisaf min al Kashshaf (remarks on the explanation al Kashshaf).

Al Burhan fi 'Ulum al Qur'an (Qur'anic studies), by al Imam Badr al Din 'Abd Allah bin Muhammad al Zarkashi, d. 794 H, al Halabi print, ed. Abu al Fadl Ibrahim.

Al Durr al Manthur fi al Tafsir bi al Ma'thur (explanation of the Qur'an), by al Hafiz Jalal al Din al Suyuti, d. 911, al Maimaniyah print.

Al Iklil fi Istinbat al Ta'wil (commentary on the Qur'an) by al Suyuti.

Al Itqan fi 'Ulum al Qur'an (Qur'anic studies), by al Suyuti.

Rub al Ma'ani ((explanation of the Qur'an), by Shihab al Din Mahumud al Alusi al Baghdadi, d. 1270 H.

Al Futuhat al Ilahiyah, known as *Hashiat al Jumal* (notes and comments on the Qur'an).

Mahasin al Ta'wil (explanation of the Qur'an) by Jamal al Din al Qasimi, d. 1332 H / 1924 AD, al Halabi print, ed. Muhammad Fu'ad Abd al Baqi.

Tafsir al Qur'an al Hakim, known as *Tafsir al Manar* (explanation of the Qur'an), by Muhammad Rashid Rida, d. 1354 H.

Tafsir al Qur'an al Karim: The First Ten Parts (explanation of the Qur'an) by Shaikh Mahmud Shaltut, Dar al Qalam print.

Fi Zilal al Qur'an (In the Shade of the Qur'an) by the martyr Sayyid Qutb, al Halabi print.

Al Tafsir al Hadith (explanation of the Qur'an) by Muhammad 'Izzat Darwazah.

Al Mu'jam al Mufahras li Alfaz al Qur'an al Karim (index of Qur'anic verses) by
Muhammad Fu'ad 'Abd al Baqi, Jaridat al Sha'b print.

II.   Studies of Sayings and Narrators

Al Muwatta' (collection of sayings and jurisprudence rulings) by the Imam of Madinah,
Malik bin Anas, d. 179 H, printed on the margins of its commentary, *al Muntaqa*,
by al Babi, second volume, al Sa'adah print or al Halabi print.

Al Musannaf, (sayings collection) by al Imam Abu Bakr bin Abi Shaibah, d. 335,
Multan print, Pakistan, or Hyderabad print, India.

Al Musnad (sayings collection), by al Imam Ahmad bin Hanbal, d. 241 H, Dar al Ma'arif
print, ed. Ahmad Muhammad Shakir, al Maimaniyah print.

Al Jami' al Saheeh (collection of correct sayings) by al Imam Muhammad bin Isma'il al
Bukhari, d. 256 H, printed with *Fath al Bari* and a commentary called *Hashiat al
Sindi*, or printed alone by al Sha'b print.

Al Tarikh al Kabir (The Great Book of History) by al Bukhari, Hyderabad print.

Sahih Muslim (collection of correct sayings) by al Imam Muslim bin al Hajjaj al Qashiri
al Nisaburi, d. 261 H, with commentary by al Nawawi, al Misriyah print, and al
Azhar print, first ed. 1348 H.

Sunan Abu Daud (collection of sayings) by al Imam Abu Daud, Sulaiman bin al Ash'ath
al Sajastani, d. 275 H, al Sa'adah print.

Sunan Ibn Majah (sayings collection) by al Hafiz Abu 'Abd Allah Muhammad bin
Yazid al Qazwini, known as Ibn Majah, d. 275 H, al Halabi print.

Jami' al Tirmidhi (collection of sayings) by al Imam Abu 'Isa Muhammad bin 'Isa al
Tirmidhi, d. 279 H, with its explanation by Ibn al 'Arabi, known as *'Aridat al
Ahwadhi*, or with commentary by al Mubarakfuri, known as *Tuhfat al Ahwadhi*, or
printed alone as ed. by Ahmad Shakir.

Sunan al Nasa'i (sayings collection) by al Imam Abu 'Abd al Rahman, Ahmad bin
Shu'aib al Nasa'i, printed with the explanation by al Suyuti and notes by al Sindi.

Mushkil al Athar (sayings studies and criticism) by al Imam Abu Ja'far al Tahawi, d. 321
H, Hyderabad print, 1333 H.

Al Jarh wa al Ta'dil (study of narrators) by Ibn Abu Hatim al Razi, Hyderabad print.
Ma'alim al Sunan (sayings collection and study) by al Imam Abu Sulaiman al Khattabi,
d. 338, Ansar al Sunnah print. Printed along with *Mukhtasar Sunan Abu Daud* by

al Mundhiri, and *Tahdhib Mukhtasar Sunan Abu Daud* by Ibn al Qayyim, ed. Shaikh Ahmad Shakir and Shaikh Muhammad Hamid al Faqi.

Al Mustadrak 'Ala al Sahihain (Additions to the Two Correct Collections) by Abu 'Abd Allah Muhammad bin 'Abd Allah, known as al Hakim al Nisaburi, d. 405, Hyderabad print.

Al Sunan al Kbura (The Great Book of Saying) by al Hafiz Abu Bakr Ahmad bin al Husain al Baihaqi, d. 458 H, Hyderabad print.

Al Jawhar al Naqi (sayings study and cirticism) by 'Ala'al Din 'Ali bin 'Uthman al Maridini, known as Ibn al Turkumani, d. 745 H, Hyderabad print.

Al I'tibar fi al Nasikh wa al Mansukh li al 'Athar (Study on Annulment in Sayings) by al Hazimi, d. 584, Hyderabad print.

'Umdat al Ahkam (collections of correct sayings related to rulings) by al Hafiz 'Abd al Ghani bin 'Abd al Wahid al Maqdisi, d. 600 H, printed with its explanation, called *al Ihkam*, by Ibn Daqiq al 'Id, al Sunnah al Muhammadiyah print, ed. Ahmad Shakir.

Muntaqa al Akhbar li Ahadith Sayyid al Akhyar, known as *al Muntaqa* (selection of correct sayings related to rulings) by Abu al Barakat bin Taimiyyah, the grandfather, d. 652 H.

Al Targhib wa al Tarhib (collection of sayings), by al Hafiz al Mundhiri, d. 656 H, al Halabi print.

Mukhtasar Sunan Abu Daud, by al Mundhiri, printed with *Ma'alim al Sunan*, mentioned above.

Sharh al Nawawi on *Sahih Mulim (*Explanation of the Sayings in Muslim's Correct Collection*)* by al Imam al Nawawi, d. 676 H.

Al Ihkam, Sharh 'Umdat al Ahkam (explanation of sayings in *'Umdat al Ahkam*) by al Imam Abu al Fath Muhammad bin 'Ali bin Wahb Taqi al Din, known as Ibn Daqiq al 'Id, d. 702 H, printed with *'Umdat al Ahkam*.

Mishkat al Masabih (collection of sayings) by al Hafiz Waliyyu al Din Muhammad bin 'Abd Allah al Khatib al 'Umari al Tabrizi, d. 737 H, ed. Shaikh Nasir al Din al Albani, al Maktab al Islami print, Damascus.

Talkhis al Mustadrak (Summary of al Mustadrak) by al Imam al Hafiz al Dhahabi, d. 748 H, Hyderabad print.

Mizan al I'tidal (Study of narrators' biographies) by al Dhahabi, al Halabi print.

Tahdhib Sunan Abu Daud (summary of *Sunan Abu Daud,* with comments) by al Imam Abu 'Abd Allah Shams al Din Mhuammad bin Abu Bakr, known as Ibn al Qayyim or Ibn Qayyim al Jawziyah, d. 751 H, printed with *Ma'alim al Sunan.*

Nasb al Rayah li Ahadith al Hidayah (study of sayings in the Book of jurisprudence al Hidayah), by al Hafiz Jamal al Din Abu Muhammad 'Abd Allah bin Yusuf al Zaila'i al Hanafi, d. 762 H, Dar al Ma'mun print, printed with the commentary *Bulghat al Alma'i fi Takhrij al Zaila'i.*

Takhrij Ahadith al Ihya' (study and criticism of sayings in the Book al Ihya' by al Ghazali) by al Hafiz Zain al Din Abu al Fadl 'Abd al Rahim bin Husain al 'Iraqi, d. 806 H, printed with al Ihya'.

Tarh al Tathrib Sharh al Taqrib (explanation of the book al Taqrib, which is a study of narrators' biographies), by al 'Iraqi, completed by his son Abu Zar'ah, d. 827 H.

Majma' al Zawa'id wa Manba' al Fawa'id (collection of sayings in six major books) by al Hafiz Nur al Din 'Ali bin Abu Bakr al Haithami, d. 807, Maktabat al Qudsi print.

Fath al Bari Sharh Sahih al Bukhari, (Explanation of the Correct Collection of al Bukhari) by Shaikh al Islam al Hafiz Ahmad bin Hajar al 'Asqalani, d. 852, al Khairiyah print, 1319 H; also al Halabi print.

Bulugh al Maram min Adillat al Ahkam (collection of correct sayings related to rulings) by Ibn Hajr.

Talkhis al Habir fi Takhrij Ahadith al Rafi'i al Kabir (Study and Criticism of Sayings Mentioned in al Rafi'i's book) by Ibn Hajar, printed in India.

Tahdhib al Tahdhib (study of narrators' biographies), by Ibn Hajar, ed. 'Abd al Wahhab 'Abd al Latif, Dar al Kitab al 'Arabi print.

Takhrij Ahadith al Kashshaf (Study of the Sayings Mentioned in the Explanation of the Qur'an Called al Kashshaf), by Ibn Hajar.

'Umdat al Qari Sharh Sahih al Bukhari (Explanation of the Correct Collection of al Bukhari) by Badr al Din Abu Muhammad Mahmud bin Ahmad al 'Aini, d. 855 H. printed by Idarat al Tiba'ah al Muniriyyah.

Al Jami al Saghir min Hadith al Bashir al Nadhir, known as *al Jami al Saghir,* by al Suyuti, d. 911 H., al Halabi print.

Al La'ali al Masnu'ah bi al Ahadith al Mawdu'ah (study of false sayings) by al Suyuti, second volume, al Maktabah al Idariyyah print.

Zahr al Ruba 'Ala al Mujtaba (explanation of the book *Sunan al Nasa'i*) by al Suyuti.

Tadrib al Rawi 'Ala Taqrib al Nawawi (commentary on *al Taqrib* by al Nawawi--a study of narrators' biographies), by al Suyuti, ed. 'Abd al Wahhab 'Abd al Latif.

Khulasat Tahdhib al Kamal fi Asma' al Rijal (study of biographies) by Safiyyu al Din al Khazraji, d. 923 H.

Kanz al 'Ummal fi Sunan al Aqwal wa al Af'al (collection of sayings) by Shaikh 'Ali al Muttaqi, 'Ala al Din al Hindi, d. 975 H. Hyderabad print.

Mirqat al Mafatih, (commentary on *Mishkat al Masabih*) by 'Ali al Farisi, d. 1014 H, Multan print.

Al Mubin al Mu'in li Fahm al Arba'in (explanation of the forty sayings selected by al Nawawi) by al Farisi.

Faid al Qadir Sharh al Jami' al Saghir (explanation of *al Jami' al Saghir*) by al Munawi, d. 1031 H.

Al Taisir (explanation of *al Jami' al Saghir*) by al Munawi, al Maktab al Islami print, Beirut.

Kashf al Khafa wa Muzil al Ilbas (criticism of sayings common among laymen) by Isma'il al 'Ajluni, d. 1162 H.

Subul al Salam (explanation of the collection of sayings called *Bulugh al Maram*) by al San'ani, d. 1182 H, Sabih print.

Nail al Awtar (explanation of *Muntaqa al Akhbar*) by al Imam al Shawkani, d. 1250 H, al Halabi print.

Al Fawa'id al Majmu'ah fi al Ahadith al Mawdu'ah (study of false sayings), by al Shawkani.

Al Raf' wa al Takmil fi al Jarh wa al Ta'dil (study of narrators' biographies) by Shaikh Muhammad 'Abd al Hai al Laknawi al Hindi, d. 1304 H, ed. Shaikh 'Abd al Fattah Abu Ghuddah, Dar Lubnan print.

Al Ajwibah al Fadilah (study in sayings criticism and scrutinization) by al Laknawi, with comments by Abu Ghuddah, al Matb'ah al Suriyyah print, Aleppo.

Tuhfat al Ahwadhi (explanation of the collection of sayings by al Tirmidhi) by Muhammad 'Abd al Rahman bin 'Abd al Rahim al Mubarakfuri, d. 1353 H, Dar al Ittihad al 'Arabi li al Tiba'ah print, Cairo.

Al Fath al Rabbani (a study of *Musnad Ahmad* and its commentary, *Bulugh al Amani*) by Shaikh Ahmad 'Abd al Rahman al Banna, Matba'at al Fath al Rabbani print, 1357 H.

Miftah Kunuz al Sunnah (index of sayings) by the orientalist Dr. A.I. Vinsink, translated by Muhammad Fu'ad 'Abd al Haqi.

Silsilat al Ahadith al Da'ifah wa al Mawdu'ah (Series of Weak and False Sayings) by al Albani.

Al Mu'jam al Mufahras li Alfaz al Hadith (index of words in sayings) by a group of orientalists, with the help of Muhammad Fu'ad 'Abd al Baqi, Brill print, Leiden, Holland.

Mir'at al Mafatih (explanation of *Mishkat al Masabih*) by Abu al Hasan 'Ubaid Allah bin Muhammad 'Abd al Salam al Mubarakfuri, Vol. 3, Indian print, 1382 H./1962 AD.

III. Books on Jurisprudence

A. Hanafite *fiqh*

Al Kharaj (study in public finance) by al Imam Abu Yusuf, d. 182 H, al Salafiyyah print, 1352 H.

Al Mabsut, volumatic book in Hanafite *fiqh*, by the sun of jurists, al Sarakhsi, d. 483 H, al Sa'adah print, 1324. It is an explanation of the book *al Kafi* by al Hakim al Shahid, which is a collection of the books known as *Kutub Zahir al Riwayah*, by al Imam Muhammad bin al Hasan al Shaibani, disciple of Abu Hanifah, d. 189 H.

Sharh Siyar al Kabir (explanations and comments on the book *al Siyar al Kabir* by al Imam Muhammad) by al Sarakhsi, Hyderabad print, 1335 H.

Bada'i al Sana'i (volumatic book of *fiqh*) by al Kasani, d. 587 H, printed by Sharikat al Matbu'at al 'Ilmiyyah, 1327 H.

Al Hidayah (volumatic book in jurisprudence) by Shaikh al Islam Burhan al Din 'Ali bin Abu Bakr al Marghinani, d. 593 H, Mustafa Muhammad print.

Sharh al 'Inayah 'Ala al Hidayah (comments on *al Hidayah*) by Akmal al Din Muhammad bin Mahmud al Barbarti, d. 776 H, printed on the margins of *al Hidayah*.

Majma al Anhur (explanation of the book *Multaqa al Abhur*), by Shaikh Zadah, d. 951 H, printed in Istanbul.

Al Bahr al Ra'iq (an explanation of the book *Kanz al Daqa'iq*) by al Zain bin Nujaim, d. 870 H.

Al Durr al Mukhtar (explanation of the book *Tanwir al Absar*) by al Haskafi, d. 1077 H.
Durr al muntaqa (explanation of *al Multaqa*) printed on the margins of *Majma' al Anhur*, by al Haskafi.

Radd al Muhtar (comments on *al Durr al Mukhtar*) by the great scholar Muhammad Amin bin 'Abidin, d. 1252 H, al Maimaniyah print, and Istanbul print. On its margins is printed al *Durr al Mukhtar*. This book is known as *Hashiat Ibn 'Abidin.*

B. Malikite *fiqh*

Al Mudawwanah al Kubra, by al Imam Anas bin Malik, as reported from him by al Imam Suhnun bin Sa'id al Tanukhi from al Imam 'Abd al Rahman bin al Qasim, al Khairiyyah print, 1324 H.

Al Risalah, by Ibn Abi Zaid al Qairawani, d. 386 H. This is printed with its two explanations by Zarruq and Ibn Naji.

Al Muntaqa (explanation of Malik's *al Muwatta'*) by al Qadi Abu al Walid Sulaiman al Baji, d. 494 H, Vol. 2, al Sa'adah print. On its margins is *al Muwatta'.*

Bidayal al Mujtahid, by the judge Ibn Rushd, d. 595, al Istiqamah print, 1371. It is in fact a comparative study in jurisprudence.

Mukhtasar Khalil by Abu al Diya Khalil bin Ishaq, d. 776 H, printed with its explanation by al Dardir and commentary by al Dusuqu.

Sharh al Risalah, bin Ibn Naji, d. 837 H, al Jamaliyyah print.

Sharh al Risalah, by Zarruq, d. 899 H. This and the previous listing are printed together with *al Risalah.*

Sharh al Khirshi by Abu 'Abd Allah Muhammad al Khirshi, d. 1106. It is an explanation of *Mukhtasar Khalil.*

Sharh al Zurqani (explanation of *al Muwatta'*).

Tahdhib al Furuq wa al Qawa'id al Saniyyah (commentary and notes on *al Furuq*) by Shaikh Muhammad 'Ali bin Shaikh Husain, a Malikite.

Al Sharh al Kabir by Ahmad bin Muhammad al 'Adawi al Khalwati, known as al Dardir, d. 1201. It is an explanation of *Mukhasar Khalil.*

Al Sharh al Saghir (comments on *Aqrab al Masalik*), both by al 'Adawi, al Halabi print.

Hashiat al Dusuqu, by Muhammad bin 'Arafah al Dusuqi, d. 1230 H.

Bulghat al Salik li Aqrab al Masalik, by Shaikh Ahmad bin Muhammad al Sawi, d. 1241 H.

Fath al 'Aliyy al Malik, by Shaikh Muhammad 'Alaish, d. 1299 H, Mustafa Muhammad print.

C. Shafi'ite *fiqh*

Al Umm, by al Imam Muhammad bin Idris al Shafi'i, d. 204 H, al Amiriyyah print in Bulaq, Egypt.

Al Ahkam al Sultaniyyah (political theory and ruling related to government), by al Qadi Abu al Hasan al Mawardi, d. 450 H, al Halabi print.

Al Muhadhdhab, by Abu Ishaq al Shirazi, d. 476 H, al Muniriyyah print.

Al Wajiz, by al Imam Abu Hamid Muhammad al Ghazali, d. 505 H.

Fath al 'Aziz (explanation of *al Wajiz*) by al Imam al Rafi'i, d. 623 H.

Al Majmu' (explanation of *al Muhadhdhab*) by al Nawawi, d. 676 H. The previous four books are printed by al Muniriyyah, along with *Talkhis al Qadir* by al Hafiz Ibn Hajar.

Rawdat al Talibin, by al Imam al Nawawi, second volume, printed by al Maktab al Islami.

Al Minhaj, by al Nawawi, printed with its two following explanations:

Tuhfat al Minhaj (explanation of *al Minhaj*) by Ibn Hajar al Haithami, d. 974 H.

Nihayat al Muhtaj (explanation of *al Minhaj*) by Shams al Din al Ramli, d. 1004 H, al Halabi print, along with its two commentaries, one by al Shubramallis, d. 1087 H, and the other by al Rashidi, d. 1096 H.

D. Hanbalite *fiqh*

Mukhtasar al Khiraqi, by Abu al Qasim 'Umar bin Husain bin 'Abd Allah al Khiraqi, d. 334 H, printed with *al Mughni*.

Al Ahkam al Sultaniyyah (political theory and ruling related to government) by al Qadi Abu Ya'la al Hanbali, d. 458 H, ed. Shaikh Muhammad Hamid al Faqi, al Halabi print, 1356 H.

Al Mughni, by Shaikh al Islam Ibn Qudamah al Maqdisi, d. 630 H, al Manar print. It is an explanation of *Mukhtasar al Khiraqi*.

Al Kafi, by Ibn Qudamah, printed by al Maktab al Islami, Damascus.

Al Sharh al Kabir, by Ibn Qudamah, the grandson, d. 681 H. It is an explanation of *al Muqni'* by the grandfather.

Fatawa Ibn Taimiyyah, Kurdistan print in Cairo, 1326 H.

Al Ikhtiyarat, by Ibn Taimiyyah, printed with the fourth edition of his *Fatawa*.

Al Furu' by Ibn Muflih, d. 763 H, printed with its commentary *Tashih al Furd'*.

Tashih al Furu' (commentary on *al Furu'*), by Abu al Hasan al Mawardi al Hanbali, d. 875 H, printed by Dar 'Umar li al Tiba'ah, by al Mawardi, printed by Matba'at al Sunnah al Muhammadiyyah.

Al Insaf, by al Mawardi, printed by Matba'at al Sunnan al Muhammadiyyah.

Al Rawd al Murbi', (explanation of *Zad al Mustaqni'*) by Shaikh Mansur bin Unus al Bahwati, d. 1051 H, printed with its commentary by Shaikh 'Abd al 'Aziz al 'Anqari, as edited by Shaikh 'Abd al Latif al Subki, by Matba'at al Sunnah al Muhammadiyyah, 1374 H.

Ghayat al Muntaha, by Shaikh Mir'i bin Yusuf al Karmi, d. 1033 H, printed with the following explanation.

Matalib Uli al Nuha (explanation of *Ghayat al Muntaha*) by Shaikh Mustafa al Suyuti al Rahbani, d. 1243 H, printed by al Maktab al Islami, Damascus, first printing 1380 H.

Manar al Sabil (*Sharh al Dalil*) by Shaikh Ibrahim bin Muhammad bin Salim bin Dwayyan, d. 1353 H, printed by al Maktab al Islami.

E. Zahiri *fiqh*

Al Muhalla by Imam Abu Muhammad 'Ali bin Ahmad bin Sa'id bin Hazm al Andalusi, d. 546 H, al Muniriyyah print, ed. Shaikh Ahmad Shakir.

F. Zaidi *fiqh*

Majmu al Fiqh al Kabir, by al Imam Zaid bin 'Ali, d. 132, printed with its explanation, al Rawd al Nadir.

Al Bahr al Zakhkhar, by al Imam al Mahdi, Yahya bin al Murtada, d. 840 H, al Sa'adah print. It is in fact a study in comparative *fiqh*.

Matn al Azhar, printed with its explanation.

Al Rawd al Nadir (explanation of *Majmu' al Fiqh al Kabir*) by Sharaf al Din al Husain bin Ahmad bin al Husain al Siyaghi al San'ani, d. 1221 H, al Sa'adah print. It is also a book in comparative *fiqh*.

Sharh al Azhar (*Explanation of al Azhar*), by Abu al Hasan 'Abd Allah bin Muftah, d. 877 H, printed by Sharikat al Tamaddun, 1332 H.

G. Imami Ja'fari *fiqh*

Shara'i al Islam fi Fiqh al Imamiyyah, by Shaikh Ja'far bin al Hasan al Hilli, d. 771 H.

Al Mukhtasar al Nafi' fi Fiqh al Imamiyyah (summary of *Shara'i al Islam*) by al Hilli, printed by Dar al Kitab al 'Arabi.

Jawahir al Kalam (explanation of *Shara'i al Islam*) by Shaikh Muhammad Hasan al Najafi, printed in Hijr, Iran, 1278 second volume.

Fiqh al Imam Ja'far al Sadiq, by Muhammad Jawad Mughniyyah, printed by Dar al 'Ilm li al Malayin, Beirut.

H.   Financial and Administrative Islamic *Fiqh*

Al Kharaj, by al Imam Abu Yusuf, mentioned earlier. It was written upon request of al *khalifah* Harun al Rashid.

Al Kharaj (Taxation System in Islam*)* by Yahya bin Adam, d. 203 H, Salafiyyah print, 1352 H, ed. Ahmad Shakir.

Al Amwal (Wealth--a study on the financial and economic system of the state), by al Imam Abu 'Ubaid al Qasim bin Sallam, d. 234 H, ed. Shaikh Muhammad Hamid al Faqi.

Al Ahkam al Sultaniyyah, by al Mawardi, mentioned earlier.

Al Ahkam al Sultaniyyah, by Abu Ya'la, mentioned earlier.

Al Siyasah al Shar'iyyah, by Shaikh al Islam Ibn Taimiyyah, d. 728 H, printed by Dar al Kitab al 'Arabi.

I.   General References in Jurisprudence

Al Qawa'id al Nuraniyyah al Fiqhiyyah, by Ibn Taimiyyah.

Majmu Fatawa Shaikh al Islam Ibn Taimiyyah (*Ibn Taimiyyah's Collected Religious Opinions*), collected by 'Abd al Rahman bin Muhammad bin Qasim al Asimi al Najdi al Hanbali, printed by Matabi' al Riyad.

Zad al Ma'ad fi Hady Khair al 'Ibad (a study of the personal and political conduct of the Messenger (p)) by Ibn al Qayyim, printed by Matba'at al Sunnah al Muhammadiyyah, ed. Muhammad Hamid al Faqi.

Al Turuq al Hukmiyyah, by Ibn al Qayyim, al Madani print.

Al Rawdah al Nadiyyah (explanantion of al *Durar al Bahiyyah*) by Siddiq Hasan Khan, printed by Idarat al Tiba'ah al Muniriyyah.

Al Durar al Bahiyyah, by al Imam al Shawkani, printed with al *Rawdah al Nadiyyah*.

Al Din al Khalis, by Shaikh Mahmud Khattab al Subki, d. 1352 H, eight volume, al Istiqamah print, 1370 H.

Fatawa al Imam Muhammad Rashid Rida (Rashid Rida's Religious Opinions) printed by Dar al Kitab al Jadid, Beirut.

Halqat al Dirasat al Ijtima'iyyah li Jami'at al Duwal al 'Arabiyyah, 3rd session, lecture by professor 'Abd al Rahman Hasan, Muhammad Abu Zahrah, and 'Abd al Wahhab Khallaf, on *zakah* and expenditures on relatives, pages 330 plus.

Al Tibyan fi Zakah al Athman (a study of *zakah* on money and values) by Shaikh Muhammad Hasanain Makhluf al 'Adawi.

Bahjat al Mushtaq fi Hukm Zakah al Awraq (study of *zakah* on paper currency) by Ahmad al Husaini.

Al Fiqh 'Ala al Madhahib al Arba'ah (Jurisprudence of the Four Schools) by a committee supervised by the Ministry of Awqaf in Egypt, fifth printing.

Muqaranat al Madhahib fi al Fiqh (Comparative Study of Schools of Jurisprudence) by Mahmud Shaltut and Muhammad 'Ali al Sayes, Sabih print, 1373 H.

Al Islam, 'Aqidah wa Shari'ah, by Mahmud Shaltut, Dar al Qalam print or al Azhar print.

*Al Fatawi (*Religious Opinions*)* by Mahmud Shaltut, al Azhar print.

*Fatawa Islamiyyah (*Islamic Religious Opinions*)* by Shaikh Husain Muhammad Makhluf, al Halali print.

*Ahkam al Mu'amalat al Shar'iyyah (*Religious Rulings on Transactions) by Shaikh 'Ali al Khafif.

*Al Mu'amalat al Hadithah wa Ahkamuha (*Modern Transactions and Their Rulings*)* by Shaikh 'Abd al Rahman 'Isa, Mukhaimir print.

*Ahkam al Dhimmiyyin wa al Musta'minin fi Dar al Islam (*Rulings on People of the Pledge and People Protected by the State in the Land of Islam*)* by Dr. 'Abd al Karim Zaidan.

Fiqh al Sunnah (Jurisprudence of the Sunnah) by Shaikh Sayyid Sabiq, third volume, printed by Dar al Kitab al 'Arabi.

Al Halal wa al Haram fi al Islam (Lawful and Unlawful in Islam) by al Qaradawi, printed by al Maktab al Islami.

IV. References on *Usul* and General Rules of *Fiqh*

Al Risalah, by al Imam al Shafi'i, ed. Ahmad Shakir, al Halabi print.

Al Ihkam fi Usul al Ahkam, by Ibn Hazm, al Muniriyyah print or al Imam print.

Al Mustasfa min 'Ilm al Usul, by al Imam al Ghazali, Mustafa Muhammad print.

Usul al Sarakhsi, by al Sarakhsi, Hyderabad print.
Rawdat al Nazir wa Jannat al Manazir, by Ibn Qudamah, author of al Mughni.

Al Ihkam fi Usul al Ahkam, by Abu al Hasan Ali bin Abi 'Ali al 'Amidi, d. 631 H, Sabih print.

Takhrij al Furu' 'Ala al Usul (Relations of Rulings to Principles and Rules) by al Imam al Zanjani, d. 656 H. ed. Dr. Muhammad Adib Salih, University of Damascus print.

Al Furuq, by al Imam al Qarafi, d. 684 H, al Halabi print.

Al Ihkam fi Tamyiz al Fatawa min al Ahkam, by al Qarafi, ed. Shaikh 'Abd al Fattah Abu Ghuddah, printed in Aleppo.

Al Qiyas (Analogy) by Shaikh al Islam Ibn Taimiyyah, al Salafiyyah print.

I'lam al Muwaqi'in, by al Shatibi, d. 751 H, al Sa'adah print, ed. Muhammad Muhyi al Din 'Abd al Hamid.

Al Muwafaqat, by Ibn al Qayyim, d. 790, ed. Shaikh 'Abd Allah Draz, printed by Matba'ah al Sharq al Adna fi al Muski, Cairo.

Al I'tisam, by al Shatibi, al Manar print.

Al Ashbah wa al Naza'ir, by Ibn Nujaim, d. 970 H.

V.   General Islamic Studies

Ihya' 'Ulum al Din, by al Imam al Ghazali, al Halabi print.

Talbis Iblis, by al Imam Abu al Faraj 'Abd al Rahman bin al Jawzi, d. 597 H, al Muniriyyah print.

Al Kaba'ir, by al Hafiz al Dhahabi, al Bayan print, Beirut.

Ighathat al Lahfan, by Ibn al Qayyim, al Halabi print.

Madarij al Salikin, by Ibn al Qayyim, al Sunnah al Muhammadiyyah print.

Bada'i al Fawa'id, by Ibn al Qayyim, al Muniriyyah print.

Al Zawajir, by Ibn Hajar al Haitami al Makki.

Hujjat Allah al Balighah, by the scholar of all India, Ahmad bin 'Abd al Rahim al Dahlawi, known as Shah Waliyyu Allah, d. 1176 H.

Al Taratib al Idariyyah, by 'Abd al Hai al Kattani al Fasi, al Ahliyyah print, Rahat, 1346 H.

Al Wahi al Muhammadi (The Revelation of Muhammad) by Shaikh Muhammad Rashid Rida, al Manar print.

Al Islam, Din 'Am Khalim (Islam, an Eternnal and Comprehensive Religion) by Muhammad Farid Wajdi.

Al Arkan al Arba'ha (The Four Pillars) by Abu al Hasan al Nadwi, Ma'tuq Ikhwan print, Beirut.

Usul al Iqtisad fi al Islam (Economic Principles in Islam) by Abu al A'la al Maududi, al Hashimiyyah print, Damascus.

Al Islam wa al Hadarah al Gharbiyyah (Islam and Western Civilization) by Muhammad Kurd 'Ali, printed by Lajnat al Ta'lif wa al Tarjamah wa al Nashr, second printing.

Al Islam wa al Awda'al Iqtisadiyyah (Islam and Economic Situations) by Muhammad al Ghazali, fifth print.

Al Islam al Muftara 'Alaih Baina al Shuyui'yyin wa al Ra's Naliyyin (Islam Blasphemed Between Communists and Capitalists, by al Ghazali.

Al Ishtirakiyyah fi al Mujtama' al Islami (Socialism in Islamic Society) by al Bahi al Khawli, printed by Matba'at al Istiqlal al Kubra.

Ishtirakiyyat al Islam (The Socialism of Islam) by Dr. Mustafa al Siba'i, printed by al Dar al Qawmiyyah, Cairo.

Al Iqtisad wa al Siyasah fi Daw' al Islam (Economics and Politics in the Light of Islam) authored under the supervision of the Islamic Studies Society in the College of Commerce, University of Cairo, 1951.

Tanzim al Islam li al Mujtama' (Islam's Organization of Society) by Muhammad Abu Zahrah.

Haqa'iq al Islam wa Abatil Khusumeh (Truths of Islam and the Falsehoods of its Enemies) by 'Abbas Mahmud al 'Aqqad.

Khutut Ra'isiyyah fi al Iqtisad al Islami (Outlines in Islamic Economics) by Mahmud Abu al Sa'ud.

Da'irat al Ma'arif al Islamiyyah al Awrubbiyyah (Islamic European Encyclopedia) published in Arabic by Ahmad al Shantatawi, 'Abd al Hamid Yunus, and Ibrahim Khurshid.

Al Da'wah ila al Islam (The Preaching of Islam) by Thomas Arnold, translated by Dr. Hasan Ibrahim Hasan and a colleague of his, printed by Lajnat al Bayan al 'Arabi.

Sirat al Rasuh (The biography of the Prophet) by Muhammad 'Izzat Darwazah.

Al 'Ibadah fi al Islam (Worship in Islam) by Yusuf al Qaradawi, first printing, al Nasr print.

Al 'Adalah al Ijtima'iyyah fi al Islam (Social Justice in Islam) by the martyr Sayyid Qutb, fifth printing, al Halahi print.

Falsafat al Zakah 'Ind al Muslimin (The Muslim Philosophy of Zakah) by 'Abd al 'Aziz Sayyid al Ahl, printed in Beirut.

Majmu'at al Watha'iq al Siyasiyyah fi 'Ahd al Rasul wa al Khulafa al Rashidin (Collection of Political Documents from the Era of the Prophet and the Wise Successors) by Dr. Muhammad Hamidullah al Hyderabadi, second printing, Dar al Irshad print, Beirut.

VI. Fiscal and Taxation

Mabadi' 'Ilm al Maliyyah al 'Ammah (Principles of Public Finance) by Dr. Muhammad Fu'ad Ibrahim, first volume.

'Ilm al Maliyyah (Public Finance) by Dr. Rashid al Daqr, Damascus print.

Mawarid al Dawlah (State Resources) by Dr. Sa'd Maher Hamzah, printed by al Matba'ah al Maliyyah.

Mabadi' al Nazariyyah al 'Ammah li al daribah (Principles of the General Theory of Taxation) by Dr. Husain Khallaf and 'Abd al Karim al Rifa'i.

Mizaniyat al Dawlah (State Budget) by Dr. Muhammad Hilmi Murad.

Tashri' al Dara'ib (Taxation Legislation) by Murad, first volume, Nahdat Misr Print, 1955.

Al Nuzum al Naqdiyyah wa la Masrafiyyah (Monetary and Banking System) by Dr. 'Abd al 'Aziz Mur'i.

Al Iqtisad al Siyasi (Political Economics) by Dr. 'Ali 'Abd al Wahid Wafi, al Halabi print, fifth edition.

Al Iqtisad al Siysal (Political Economics) by Dr. Rif'at al Mahjub.

VIII.   Social Studies

Al Daman al Ijtima'i (Social Insurance) by Dr. Sadiq Mahdi al Sa'id.

Halqat al Dirasat al Ijtima'iyyah, mentioned earlier.

'Ilm al Ijtima' (Sociology) by Dr. Ahmad al Khashshab.

VIII.   Biography of the Prophet, History, and Other Biographies

Sirat Ibn Hisham (Ibn Hisham's Biography of the Prophet) by Ibn Hisham, ed. Muhammad Muhyi al Din 'Abd al Hamid.

Sirat 'Umar bin 'Abd al 'Aziz (Biography of 'Umar bin 'Abd al 'Aziz), by Ibn 'Abd al Hakam, Dar al Fikr print, Damascus.

Tarikh al Umam wa al Muluk (History of Nations and Dynasties) by al Imam Abu Ja'far al Tabari, al Husainiyyah print.

Wafiyyat al A'yan (Death of Renowned Persons) by Ibn Khillakan d. 631 H.

Al Bidayah wa al Nihayah (The Beginning and the End--history) by the historian al Hafiz Abu al Fida' Isma'il bin Kathir, al Sa'adah print.

Al Jawahir al Mudiyyah fi Tabaqat al Hanafiyyah (biographies of Hanafites) by Muhyi al Din al Qurashi, d. 775, Hyderabad print.

Tabaqat al Hanabilah (biographies of Hanbalites) by Ibn Abi Ya'la, d. 527 H.

Tabaqat al Shafi'iyyah (biographies of Shafi'ites) by Taj al Din al Subki, d. 771 H.

Al Dibaj al Mudhahhab fi Ma'rifat A'yan al Madhhab (biographies of certain schools) by Ibn Firhawn, d. 799 H.

Al Fawa'id al Bahiyyah fi Tabaqat al Hanafiyyah (biographies of Hanafites) by Abu al Hasanat 'Abd al Hai al Laknawi, d. 1304 H.

Nuzhat al Khawatir, by 'Abd al Nai bin Fakhr al Din al Hasani al Laknawi, director of Nadwat al 'Ulama', Laknow, India, d. 1341 H, the father of Abu al Hasan al Nadwi.

Al A'lam (The Renowned) by Khair al Din al Zerkeli.

Al Kharaj fi al Dawlah al Islamiyyah (Taxes in the Islamic State) by Muhammad Diya' al Din al Rayyis, Nahdat Misr print.

Al Nuqud al 'Arabiyyah wa 'Ilm al Numiyyat (Arabian Currencies) by Father Anstas al Karmali.

Al Nuqud al 'Arabiyyah, Madiha wa Hadiruha (Arabian Currencies, Past and Present) by Dr. 'Abd al Rahman Fahmy.

Sanj al Sikkah fi Fajr al Islam (Minting of Currencies in the Dawn of Islam) by Dr. 'Abd al Rahman Fahmy.

IX. Language and Encyclopedia

Gharib al Hadith (Difficult Words in Hadith) by Abu al Qasim bin Sallam, d. 225 H, Hyderabad print.

Al Nihayah fi Gharib al Hadith wa al 'Athar (The Final Study of Difficult Words in Saying and Traditions) by Abu al Sa'adat Majd al Din al Mubarak bin Muhammad, known as Ibn al Athir, d. 606 H, al Khairiyyah print.

Lisan al Arab (The Arabic Tongue) by Jamal al Din Abu al Fadl Muhammad bin Mukarram bin Manzur al Ansari al Afriqi al Misri, d. 711 H, Beirut printing, 1956 AD.

Al Misbah al Munir (Arabic dictionary) by Ahmad bin Muhammad bin 'Ali al Muqri al Fayumi, d. 770 H, al 'Amiriyyah print, Egypt, 1912 AD.

Al Qamus al Muhit (dictionary) by Majd al Din al Fairuzabadi, d. 817.

Taj al 'Arus fi Sharh al Qamus (commentaries and notes on *al Qamus*) by Muhammad Murtada al Zabidi, d. 1205 H.

Al Mu'jam al Wasit (Medium-size Dictionary) collected by the Arabic Language Congress in Cairo.

X. Miscellaneous References

The Bible, Old and New Testaments.

Al Muhadarat al 'Ammah li Idarat al Thaqafah al Islamiyyah bi al Azhar (Public Lectures of the Directorate of Islamic Culture in al Azhar) first, second, and third sessions, al Azhar print.

Al Mu'tamar al Awwal li Majma' al Buhuth al Islamiyyah (The First Conference of the Congress of Islamic Research) in Cairo, by a group of researchers, al Azhar print.

Majallat al Azhar (Al Azhar Review).

Majallat Hadarat al Islam (Islamic Culture Review), Damascus.

Majallat al Muslimun (The Muslims Review), Cairo.